PRESERVING
YELLOWSTONE'S
NATURAL
CONDITIONS

James A. Pritchard

PRESERVING YELLOWSTONE'S
NATURAL CONDITIONS

*Science and
the Perception
of Nature*

University of Nebraska Press

Lincoln & London

Library of Congress Cataloging-in-Publication Data
Pritchard, James A., 1954–
    Preserving Yellowstone's natural conditions : science
and the perception of nature / James A. Pritchard.
        p.   cm.
    Based on a revised version of the author's thesis
(Ph.D.) — University of Kansas, 1996.
    Includes bibliographical references (p.   ) and index.
    ISBN 0-8032-3722-7 (cloth : alk. paper)
    1. Nature conservation—Yellowstone National Park.
2. Wildlife management—Yellowstone National Park.
I. Title.
QH76.5.Y45P75   1999
333.7'2'0978752—dc21   98-51144
                                                CIP

In Memory of my Father,
Lt. Harlow Bryan Pritchard, USN, (ret).

and in Honor of my Mother,
Elma Jean (Spitznaugle) Pritchard

CONTENTS

ILLUSTRATIONS

MAPS

ACKNOWLEDGMENTS

I have discovered what writers mean when they express gratitude to all the people who contributed ideas toward the fruition of a large project. Indeed, this book has profited immensely from notions I gathered from discussions with many folks from different perspectives over a long period of time. The original idea for the project came from a discussion with someone familiar with Yellowstone and science, writer Paul Schullery. I owe NPS historian Richard West Sellars a special thank you for his encouragement and helpful questioning. Conversations with all the following people helped me think about larger issues as well as the details of this topic in new ways: Paul Hirt, Paul Sutter, Mary Meagher, John Good, John Varley, Don Despain, Bill Barmore, Peter Gogan, Frank Singer, Tim Clark, Wayne Hamilton, Richard Keigley, Susan Rhoades Neel, Mark Boyce, Norm Bishop, Kat Anderson, Brian Black, Diane Debinski, Bill Clark, Brent Danielson, Dan Smith, and Paul Vohs. Kurt Alt of Montana Fish and Game imparted a small fraction of his extensive knowledge about wildlife and people, and Fred King also discussed his thoughts with me.

Yellowstone Park historians Lee Whittlesey and Tom Tankersley shared their wealth of knowledge about the park and helped me locate documents in the Yellowstone Branch of the National Archives. Librarians and archivists at several collections helped me find boxes and boxes of really neat old letters and documents. Vanessa Christopher, Susan Kraft, and Elsa Kortje were more than gracious as I spent hours sifting through photographs in the Yellowstone curator's office. Tom DuRant of the NPS Harpers Ferry Center also assisted me in locating several important photographs.

Thanks to all the folks who read parts of the manuscript, whether many moons ago or very recently. They include Doug Houston, Mary Meagher,

Jerry DeSanto, Thomas Offutt, Lee Whittlesey, a helpful anonymous reviewer for the press, Paul Hirt, Paul Sutter, Diane Debinski, Bill Clark, Brent Danielson, Paul Rich, Donald Worster, Ken Armitage, John Clark, and Bob Dekosky. Their comments have made this a richer and more accurate work. While I would like to credit someone else for any errors in fact or interpretation, readers should hold the above parties entirely blameless.

Lastly, thanks to my family, Diane the human tornado, and my daughter, Zoe, for their patience and infinite support.

INTRODUCTION

Researchers have already cast much darkness on the subject, and if they
continue their investigations we shall soon know nothing at all about it.
Mark Twain

Since 1920 Yellowstone's visitors have gathered by campfires eagerly await-
ing the illustrated lecture of the ranger-naturalist. Adults as well as children
are fascinated by stories and facts about wild animals. If tourists remain in
the park for a little over a week, they can attend a complete cycle of lectures
that discuss a variety of park wildlife, the great fires of 1988, and the subsequent regrowth of vegetation in the park. During the summer of 1995,
naturalists described how wildlife management in the park today differs
from Yellowstone's policies during the earlier days of the park.

The campfire lecturer related how in those times park rangers herded bison into corrals where the animals were fed hay cultivated in the park, shot
wolves and coyotes on sight, delivered edifying lectures at bear feeding platforms, fed the elk until both scientists and managers thought they became
too abundant, and then began to shoot these excess elk. Today, the buffalo
herds of Yellowstone roam entirely free (that is, until they reach the park's
border), predatory animals are protected, bears seek sustenance from natural foods, and the ungulate populations are left to nature's regulatory devices. Policies allowing natural fires to burn remained in force until the unusual fires of 1988. Finally, the reintroduction of a significant predator, the
wolf, promises to restore an important ecological force to the landscape.
It is a remarkable fact that Yellowstone's policies provide one of the few
American landscapes where nature proceeds for the most part unhindered,
largely free of the conscious (as well as unintentional) manipulation of flora
and fauna our culture practices on a vast scale. Because nature is the primary
agent at work, the Yellowstone landscape can reveal important lessons
about the natural world.

In stark contrast to the ranger's view of nature's processes working out for the best, recent critics of the National Park Service have suggested that a philosophy of letting nature take its course is causing havoc in Yellowstone and other parks. This is not just an internal scientific dispute over arcane points, but a disagreement that appears in the national popular press, prompting public concern over the management of well-known and -loved public spaces.[1] The issues are so contentious that Congress has convened hearings on Yellowstone issues several times since 1967. These recent critiques have raised important and legitimate issues for investigation and debate within the scientific and conservation communities.

At least one of these criticisms, however, has conveyed to the general public some fundamentally flawed notions about the origins of wildlife management practice and philosophy. While National Park Service administrators increasingly sought to use the legitimacy of science to bolster their arguments for particular management policies, to suggest that managers purposefully misused science distorts and oversimplifies the history of park management, as well as the history of science.[2] Other critical accounts have underplayed the complex set of influences that shaped management policies.

This dispute is ultimately between two profoundly different world-views, the first advocating human intervention as essential to the proper management of wildlife in the national parks, the second view suggesting that humans are not *required* to intervene in nature, and that we can learn something from watching nature at work. Several, if not most of the critiques and analyses of park policies assign a recent origin to the concept of managing for natural processes. But current policies that emphasize observing nature at work in Yellowstone are not a recent offshoot of environmental philosophy. We cannot understand the management of our parks or hope for enlightened park management if we fail to see our parks in a historical context.

Interest in watching natural processes and managing for them actually began with the inception of American ecology. During the early years of the twentieth century, ecologists, including Charles C. Adams and Victor Shelford, conceived a scientific purpose for Yellowstone and the other national parks. This purpose, "preserving natural conditions," endured essentially intact while all else around it changed during the ensuing eighty years. Scientists, conservationists, and managers over the years brought new interpretations and definitions to the notion of natural conditions and devised new approaches to achieve those conditions. Although at some points in time the goal became subconscious or was overlooked, the idea of Yellowstone as a place to preserve natural conditions represented a powerful and enduring theme in the park's history since 1916.

Some of the practical effects of this idea can be seen in the history of Yellowstone's wildlife populations. National parks stopped controlling predators, albeit haltingly and reluctantly, during the early 1930s. Shortly after World War II, Yellowstone dismantled its buffalo ranching facilities, intending to present wild animals in their natural setting. Park administrators closed the bear feeding platforms with the same idea of eliminating the most garish zoo-like features of the park, although garbage dumps hidden from public view remained available to the bears for quite some time. To preserve a "natural" range, Yellowstone rangers began a systematic program of transporting (and eventually slaughtering) "surplus" elk in the 1920s. Since the late 1960s, however, park biologists have questioned prevailing ideas about what a rangeland should look like in a natural condition. Today, Yellowstone no longer sponsors a fish hatchery that artificially augments sport fish populations. This book, then, is about the idea of preserving natural conditions, and about some of the people who advocated this point of view for Yellowstone.

The book's second purpose is to demonstrate how Yellowstone's wildlife management throughout the twentieth century has been embedded within a historical context of changing scientific theory, shifting cultural expectations for the parks, changes in management direction (often initiated by a change in personnel), friction between ambitious people and between agencies, participation of nongovernmental organizations of various stripes, legal mandates, and the region's economic enterprises, including tourism, ranching, and hunting. These factors interacted with one another, continually shaping wildlife policies in the park, sometimes through political pressure on Park Service officials.[3]

The bison serve as an example of the complexities and ironies of management aimed at preserving natural conditions in a park visited by millions of tourists. Recent controversy over Yellowstone's roaming bison herds represents some of the essential conflicts between the park's mission and the uses of national forest and private lands immediately adjacent to the park. After the great game slaughter of the latter part of the nineteenth century in the American West, conservationists interested in big game realized that Yellowstone Park contained the last remaining wild bison in the United States. Park officials hired a knowledgeable, if irascible, fellow named C. J. "Buffalo" Jones who interbred some of the bison with domestic herds from

Texas and Montana, building the herd up to a size deemed safe from extinction. Park officials created the "buffalo ranch," a Yellowstone institution for many years that propagated and managed the bison much the same way ranchers dealt with cattle. This bison herd became a major attraction for tourists, always a dependable wildlife spectacle. The Yellowstone herd was employed in the movie industry for filming stampeding buffalo herds, reenacting the days of the Wild West. National Park Service promoter Horace Albright delighted in showing off Yellowstone's bison to visiting dignitaries.

But in 1929 a change of administration portended changes for the management of Yellowstone's bison herd. Roger B. Toll, closely associated with the National Park Service's new Wildlife Division, assumed the duties of superintendent. Scientists of the Wildlife Division had been trained at the University of California, Berkeley, and brought with them an ecological perspective. Toll employed these new attitudes as he redefined the park's role in managing wildlife. He believed a more natural presentation of wildlife was appropriate to Yellowstone, but Horace Albright vigorously disagreed. Albright wanted to enhance the visitor experience, while Toll argued that the tourists' visit would be heightened by witnessing animals in their natural haunts and habits. In the early 1950s Superintendent Edmund Rogers dismantled the buffalo ranch as well as other structures such as a wildlife pen near Mammoth Hot Springs. From that time through the 1970s the bison grazed undisturbed within the park, rarely venturing beyond the park's artificial boundaries. In the late 1980s, however, the bison stirred up considerable dispute during winter and spring as they began to migrate more frequently out of the park.

As the bison crossed Yellowstone's boundary lines, they passed out of NPS jurisdiction onto lands that were private or administered by other agencies with quite different mandates. The bison emerged onto a landscape that had no room for the symbol of the American West. From 1988 to 1989 over five hundred bison leaving the park in search of more verdant pastures were shot by hunters and game officers in the state of Montana. Some of those ambled straight onto property owned by the Church Universal and Triumphant on Yellowstone's northern border, while on the western border bison wandered into the Targhee National Forest. In the winters of 1994–95 and 1995–96, over four hundred bison were slaughtered each year. During the winter of 1996–97, the slaughter intensified, when deep snows encouraged more bison to migrate earlier, down to lower elevation range. This time around, park officers cooperated with Montana's game officers and agents from the federal Animal and Plant Health Inspection Service (APHIS) in shipping over seven hundred bison to meat-processing facilities. Almost a third of Yellowstone's bison were slaughtered, sparking public protest.

The reason for the slaughter is that Montana livestock producers feared their cattle could have contracted brucellosis from the bison. Actually, it may be more accurate to say that Montana's livestock producers feared that APHIS would revoke Montana's brucellosis-free status. Ironically, it is very probable that the bison originally contracted the disease from domestic cattle during the late nineteenth century or the early twentieth century.[4] For its own reasons, APHIS chooses to overlook or disagree with scientific evidence suggesting that it is extremely difficult for cattle to contract brucellosis from bison. Cattle would have to come into contact with or lick a freshly deposited bison placenta to pick up the disease, an unlikely occurrence, easily preventable by excluding domestic stock from particular areas at certain times. The brucellosis organism is thought to be killed by direct sunlight, and there is still no documented case of disease transmission from wild bison to domestic stock.

Although elk are known to carry the disease and wander freely across park boundaries, APHIS and the livestock industry have never suggested that elk should be stopped at the border. The essential reason is because elk have been established deeply in modern culture as a game species monitored and harvested since the inception of game management. The elk also represent a controllable resource, unlike the bison, which have a reputation for their intractable nature and hard treatment of fences. Despite the supposed difficulty of controlling bison, today they are being raised for meat in more than a few places, and the slaughter of bison at Yellowstone's border points to a very exacting degree of human control over bison movements. There is a great irony in envisioning the bison as wild and free, and as symbols of the nobler aspects of the American West while they roam within the park, yet treating them as pariahs as they cross onto unhallowed ground. The bison seem to represent something uncontrolled and dangerous to be stopped at all costs precisely at the park's border. The greater fear is that federal and state agencies might reassign and rearrange human uses of the landscape that people have become habituated to during the twentieth century. The park border remains not an ecological border but a cultural boundary delimiting particular ways of understanding and using the landscape.[5]

Management of the bison today reflects many of the ambiguities and ironies associated with wildlife management in Yellowstone since the park's creation. First, the science associated with bison is disputed—while stock-men and APHIS biologists declare a great danger of brucellosis transmission to domestic stock, bison defenders claim that these concerns are unsubstantiated. Second, wildlife management in Yellowstone has been shaped and sometimes curtailed by public opinion, by the actions of other agencies, and by Congress. In the case of the bison, APHIS and the Montana Department of Fish and Game held jurisdiction over wildlife beyond the border. Ultimately, pressure from Congress forced Yellowstone authorities to contain the movement of bison and participate in their slaughter, actions the Park Service was very reluctant to undertake. Third, cultural expectations about nature sometimes face a rude surprise when the public discovers the limits of conservation in Yellowstone. In ways similar to attitudes at the turn of the century, the general public still assumes that the park offers a haven for wildlife. Public opinion has been sympathetic to the bison, yet a popular distaste for the slaughter has not influenced the outcome so far. In an age when ecosystem management is discussed in a growing variety of venues and when a growing regional economy is shifting away from traditional extractive industries, a public that is increasingly aware of ecological issues will question why the public lands around the park that are managed for multiple use cannot find room for the bison.

Nature and culture met in Yellowstone, a landscape that became inscribed with important cultural meanings during the twentieth century. Historian Judith Meyer wrote about a special sense of place found in Yellowstone, built by generations of tourists who discussed Yellowstone as a place of beauty, as a unique landscape, as a wilderness, as a place for education, and as a place for recreation enjoyed in a democratic atmosphere. Popular expectations for a park experience were built from published and unpublished accounts, revealing the national parks as "deeply humanized landscapes."[6] Perhaps the human landscape of rustic hotels and boardwalks that built those enduring cultural memories deserves a measure of respect and some share of our affection. Meyer suggests that Yellowstone's enduring spirit of place might be a more reliable guide to management than changing scientific conceptions of nature.[7]

When they wrote home about the wilderness of Yellowstone, many tourists celebrated the wildlife of the park, and that feeling still persists. Today, a few elk grazing near the road can hold up traffic for ten minutes. For the first time many people in Yellowstone see animals not through Marty Stouffer's *Wild America* television camera, but immediately alive and uncaged. Sighting Yellowstone's animals often evokes what Rachel Carson called "a sense of wonder." City people first learn about nature's creatures at the bird feeder or at the zoo, but in Yellowstone, here is the essence of the wild—elk, bison, even bears wandering around unrestrained, without bars or a roof over their heads. Wild animals, those entities Farley Mowat called "the Others," in a fundamental sense have symbolized nature for generations of visitors. For millions of citified tourists of the twentieth century, travel to Yellowstone has become a pilgrimage to see nature itself, a wild and primitive nature untamed by civilization.

While Yellowstone's sense of place may be its most enduring feature, it is important to note how our expectations for experiencing nature in the national parks have changed remarkably along the way, guided by increasing ecological knowledge. Tourists of the first half of the twentieth century saw no harm in feeding snacks to bears "begging" by the roadside, but the cultural understanding that painted the bears as charming bandits also created an untenable situation involving disrupted feeding patterns, numerous personal injuries to humans, and resulting control measures ending in death for many bears. While some visitors today regret the fact that the bears are much more elusive than they used to be, many tourists take extra time to search for wildlife and are rewarded with views of bison, grizzly bears, and wolves, all visible from the roadside with a pair of binoculars.

Today, scientists and land managers face long-standing dilemmas with no clear answers, and disagreement within the scientific community can make management choices problematic. Because science is not simply a set of facts, but competing notions about how the world works, decisions about land management and wildlife in Yellowstone cannot hope to be entirely "true," some sort of unshakable and final wisdom. Yellowstone's wildlife management conundrums might be best understood as the product of eighty years of cultural and scientific change, bound to evolve yet further. Remarkable changes in ecological understanding and Yellowstone's shifts in management policy are ultimately clues to our cultural understandings of nature. During the 1910s and 1920s scientists contributed the idea of "preserving natural conditions" to the park's goals and purposes, and that vision has proved to be an enduring element of what our parks are about. By examining the origins of ecological ideas and how they were used in Yellowstone, we can better understand how wildlife management evolved in the park, as well as begin to fathom our own expectations of the wild nature we hope to find in our national parks.

PRESERVING
YELLOWSTONE'S
NATURAL
CONDITIONS

A PRESERVATIONIST YELLOWSTONE

1872–1915

The territory surrounding the upper Yellowstone River has always attracted human curiosity and wonderment. The earliest written reports of the Yellowstone plateau and its unearthly geological wonders came from fur trappers anxious to add to their stock in trade. From early on, animals and what they offered people have played a part at least as great as geysers in creating an identity for the region and a place in human hearts for the institution we call Yellowstone National Park. Aboriginal hunting marked the first phase of human relationships with the area's wildlife, followed by a period of intensive market hunting when Euro-Americans came to the American West. This extensive slaughter led to a movement for the protection of wildlife at Yellowstone. Until 1916 state and federal agencies took a protective stance toward the wildlife they viewed as beneficial. The establishment and early administration of Yellowstone National Park set physical limits and precedents affecting the future of wildlife populations.

Native Americans had been present in the Yellowstone area from early on, although it is difficult to determine exactly how intensively they used the region as a resource for hunting. When Euro-American trappers arrived on the scene in the 1820s and 1830s, they encountered a group of Shoshones, the Sheepeaters, named after a major element of their diet. Until very recently, historic accounts held that in contrast to the Crow or the Shoshone, the Sheepeaters were a reclusive and traditional people who did not survive long after the fur trade era. A small population occupied the high regions around the upper Yellowstone, developing sophisticated bows for hunting game, yet never sharing some of the other cultural adaptations of their nearby plains relatives. Revisionist accounts portray the Sheepeaters as a hardy subgroup of the Shoshone that mixed rather easily with their relatives in the region. Recent scholarship suggests that hunting parties from Crow or Shoshone tribes in the region paid routine visits to the park. While it is clear that Native Americans had more influence on the landscape than previously thought, scholars and scientists continue to debate to what extent the aboriginal peoples in or near Yellowstone's high plateau affected the population levels of ungulates and other animals.[1]

The travels and exploits of trappers remain stirring tales of the adventure and hardship that accompanied the early American explorations of the Yellowstone country. At a fur-trade rendezvous in southern Wyoming, Jim Bridger described sights that seemed incredible, a place "where Hell bubbled up."[2] Although few believed his embellished tales, evidently he possessed enough credibility to stir others to investigate for themselves.

In 1869 Charles W. Cook, David E. Folsom, and William Peterson explored the forested high country up the Yellowstone River and reported their discovery of a great canyon cleft by spectacular waterfalls, a very large lake, and an area of thermal features later known as the Lower Geyser Basin. The very next summer a party led by Henry Dana Washburn, the surveyor general of Montana, carried the explorations farther to find the even stranger Upper Geyser Basin, naming features such as the Old Faithful Geyser. Traveling with the party were Montana politician Nathaniel Pitt Langford and lawyer Cornelius Hedges. Accounts of their journey shortly appeared in the *Helena Daily Herald* and the *New York Times*. The Northern Pacific Railroad underwrote lectures by Langford in East Coast cities. Among the audience in Washington DC sat Ferdinand Vandiveer Hayden, director of the U.S. Geological and Geographical Survey of the Territories. Evidently, Hayden may have already made plans to map the upper Yellowstone country before he heard Langford's lecture.[3]

Congress appropriated forty thousand dollars toward an official expedition led by Hayden to embark during the field season of 1872. The Hayden expedition to the headwaters of the Yellowstone primarily focused on accurate mapping and description of the region's geography, including the unusual thermal features. Other curiosities, such as petrified trees, were carefully noted. The expedition represented the twilight of the great surveys of the American West. The Hayden party also embodied natural history traditions of the nineteenth century—the team carefully recorded the living creatures they encountered, for example, producing the first listing of butterflies known to inhabit the area.[4]

Along with the expedition's scientist-cartographers traveled photographer William Henry Jackson and artist Thomas Moran, whose paintings portrayed a natural Yellowstone seductive in its transcendent beauty. National political leaders found Moran's images of the Yellowstone landscape compelling. When Congress appropriated ten thousand dollars to purchase Moran's seven-by-twelve-foot canvas, the *Grand Canyon of the Yellowstone*, later displayed in the Senate lobby, Yellowstone became a cultural icon of nature. The public also found something worthy of celebration in the Yellowstone landscape, yet in the popular mind Yellowstone went beyond an appreciation of the spectacular. During the twentieth century millions of tourists went to Yellowstone to see what nature looked like. The national parks came to embody cultural expectations of nature.

Legend has it that the idea of a national park originated around a campfire in Yellowstone. Late one night during the 1870 Langford expedition, one of the gentlemen suggested that the hot springs would make an attractive resort, and each member of the party should lay claim to a part of the surrounding land. Cornelius Hedges countered with the notion that the area might be made into a national park, rather than divided up for private gain, and the idea won instant enthusiasm. The story remains compelling, with tour leaders regularly retelling the episode as their bus trundles over the small concrete bridge near the junction of the Madison and Firehole Rivers on the western side of the grand loop. Historians have questioned the campfire myth, however, suggesting that the genesis of the national park idea was much more complex than a single conversation under the star-studded sky. Actually, the campfire story did not appear until Nathaniel P. Langford revised his diary for publication in 1905, thirty-five years after his explorations. As far back as the 1830s, artist George Catlin had suggested a "nation's park" on the Great Plains, an idea never realized because of the vast extent of land required to create his vision of a reserve where buffalo and Native Americans would carry on a traditional way of life he documented in paintings. The concept of a national park did not become part of general discourse until much later. In the latter part of the nineteenth century, most people thought in terms of "public" rather than "national" parks. City parks formed the best-known parkscape model, created partly to remedy the effects of a rapidly industrializing economic culture. Cornelius Hedges was probably thinking in terms of a state park, such as the federal grant of Yosemite to the state of California. The story of the campfire creation of the national park idea is a myth, but it is a story that serves a symbolic purpose and explains in simple terms how Americans created the world's first national park.[5]

Historian Aubrey Haines agreed with Louis C. Cramton, who in 1932 suggested that the establishment of Yellowstone represented the maturation of the national park idea, to which many people contributed. Historian Alfred Runte has argued that "cultural insecurity" played a primary role in the adoption of "nature as proof of national greatness." Unlike Europe, America had no great cathedrals or palaces that revealed a deep and meaningful, if not a glorious, past. From the time of Jefferson, Americans began to find that our country's landscape provided something they could take pride in. Runte suggests that congressional protection for California's Yosemite Valley and the nearby Mariposa Grove of Sierra redwoods in 1864 was stimulated by these "ideals and anxieties" of American culture. "Cultural nationalism," writes Runte, impelled lawmakers toward establishing national parks in the United States. The establishment of Yellowstone in 1872 reaffirmed monumental landscape as an object of national pride.[6]

A combination of influences persuaded Congress to establish Yellowstone Park. Moran's paintings, Jackson's photographs, and Hayden and Langford's lobbying clearly influenced Congress to consider legislation reserving the area at the headwaters of the Yellowstone to protect the unusual geological features from private exploitation. Railroad officials also influenced the creation of the first national parks, because they anticipated tourist traffic on their lines and in the swank hotels that were built at nearby locations such as Gallatin Gateway (about forty miles northwest of Yellowstone). Jay Cooke, associated with the Northern Pacific Railroad, urged Hayden to recommend a public park in his official report to Congress. Hayden subsequently argued that establishing a national park would "mark an era in the popular advancement of scientific thought, not only in this country, but in the civilized world," and grandly proclaimed that a national park would represent "a tribute from our legislators to science."[7] Historian Richard West Sellars suggests that neither business interests nor altruism dominated the decision: Yellowstone's significance "lay in the collaboration between private business and the federal government to foster a new kind of public land use in the West."[8] Writer Joseph Sax describes a coalition of two interests that facilitated the creation of the first national parks: "On one side a repugnance at the seemingly boundless materialism that infused American life, a spiritual attachment to untrammeled nature, and a self-congratulatory attitude toward preservation of nature's bounty; and on the other a commitment to economic progress wherever it could be exacted, nationalistic pride, and the practical use of nature as a commodity supportive of tourism and commercial recreation."[9] The creation of Yellowstone thus came out of an odd mixture of preservationists and tourism promoters that coalesced during the next few decades, supporting and shaping the national parks through the 1920s.

President Ulysses S. Grant signed the legislation creating Yellowstone National Park on March 1, 1872, which provided for "the preservation, from injury or spoliation, of all timber, mineral deposits, natural curiosities, or wonders within said park, and their retention in their natural condition." Congress also assigned the secretary of the interior the task of preventing the "wanton destruction of the fish and game found within said park," and of preventing the capture or killing of animals "for the purposes of merchandise or profit."[10] Yellowstone's inception thus embodied a protective stance regarding its wildlife, as well as a simple and straightforward concept of a "natural condition," a place unexploited and unspoiled by human hand.

The concept of a public park was well developed in eastern urban settings. Beginning in 1858 Frederick Law Olmstead offered plans for New York's Central Park, and later designed city parks for Buffalo and Boston. When transposed to Yellowstone's wilderness setting, however, the idea of a public park created unforeseen problems over the following eighty years. Most significant were continuing conflicts between visitors and wildlife and between the development of visitor amenities and wildlife. During the early days of park administration, engineers developed a road system in Yellowstone to accommodate increasing traffic catering to tourists. The establishment of the road system, completed in 1905, created a physical legacy that the National Park Service inherited when it took over Yellowstone's administration in 1916.

Embedded in the idea of a public park was an anthropocentric purpose. Planners created parks so that people could use them; in the late nineteenth century, reformers and city commissioners embraced the idea that in a rapidly industrializing age, a natural landscape served to refresh the moral character and invigorate the jaded nerves of city-bound people. But urbanites needed tourist facilities to visit Yellowstone. Although the first roads and tourist amenities were relatively primitive, their establishment created important precedents and a permanent pattern of human use on the landscape. Although professional landscape architects employed by the National Park Service designed park facilities to blend in with their natural surroundings, the general location of hotels and other tourist facilities was preordained by major scenic attractions, the original road system leading to them, and the hotels built early on by railroad interests. When a declining bear population met burgeoning numbers of tourists in the late twentieth century, the initial placement of roads and tourist facilities came back to haunt wildlife biologists who realized that human activities interfered with the subsistence activities of the grizzly bear population.

Park superintendent Philetus W. Norris initiated the construction of a road system in Yellowstone. By 1878, 70 miles of road connected Mammoth Hot Springs south to the road heading west to present-day West Yellowstone, and farther south to the Upper Geyser Basin. Norris secured the park's first appropriation of ten thousand dollars for the 1879 fiscal year, and by 1881 the park had 153 miles of roads and 204 miles of trails.[11] In 1882 General Philip H. Sheridan convinced Missouri Senator George Graham Vest to give the U.S. Army Corps of Engineers the responsibility for park road development.[12] Lieutenant Dan C. Kingman arrived at the park in August 1883 and soon designed an ambitious road plan that involved constructing a double wagon track connecting Mammoth Hot Springs to the thermal features at Norris Hot Springs, on to the Upper Geyser Basin where Old Faithful spouted, eastward over the mountains to Yellowstone Lake, north to the Grand Canyon of the Yellowstone, and back to the west to rejoin the road at Norris. This route became known as the grand loop road. Although it was already late in the season, Kingman began construction southward from Mammoth Hot Springs past the great blocky towers of limestone known as the Hoodoos, toward the Golden Gate, a narrow cleft in the mountainous cliffs that accessed the plateaus stretching away to the south. By 1886 Kingman built passable roads from Mammoth to the Upper Geyser Basin and from Norris to the Grand Canyon. Kingman's successors were less productive, but the pace of road construction picked up again in June of 1891 when Lieutenant Hiram M. Chittenden assumed the task. Chittenden surmised that park roads had purposes different from ordinary roads, as hauling freight was not a primary consideration. Road design for parks called for easy grades, but more importantly determined that routes should pass as many objects of interest in the vicinity as possible. In 1892 Chittenden sounded like the first tourist in a hurry when he suggested that "everything should be done to reduce to a minimum the irksomeness of the long drives that separate the principal points of interest in the park."[13] Chittenden brought the no-nonsense engineer's expertise to the art and theory of landscape architecture in Yellowstone. By 1899 the loop road through the interior of the park was virtually complete, and by 1905 the entire road system that exists today, including the east and south entrance roads, had been constructed after the expenditure of $1,830,359.

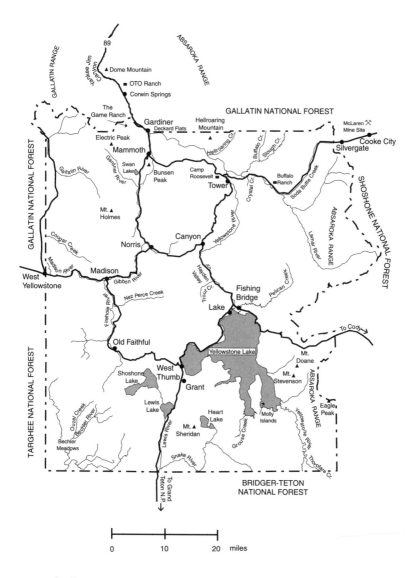

1. Map of Yellowstone with sites mentioned in the narrative. Created by Sarah Broadbent, courtesy Yellowstone Center for Resources, Yellowstone National Park, National Park Service.

At the same time this road system was constructed for the park, the Northern Pacific Railroad built hotels to cater to its customers. Railway passengers disembarked at West Yellowstone or at Gardiner, Montana, there boarding stages to continue their journey into Yellowstone. In 1883 the Yellowstone Park Improvement Company (a branch of the Northern Pacific) built the first hotel in Yellowstone at Mammoth Hot Springs, a facility that helped accommodate about ten thousand visitors each year by the late 1890s. Several times between 1886 and the turn of the century, the railroad reorganized its poorly performing business, finally expanding the duties of stockholder Harry Child to include the supervision of all its park facilities. Child in turn hired architect Robert Reamer to design the showcase Old Faithful Inn. Built in 1903–4, the inn represented an innovative effort in rustic style, featuring rough stone, a massive fireplace beneath a ceiling astounding in height, walls and supporting structures created from beautifully gnarled native logs. Visitors finally could visit Yellowstone's wilderness and enjoy the wonderland of nature, yet rest comfortably in a charming atmosphere of the outdoor life. By 1913 the Yellowstone Park Association had built additional hotels at Mammoth, on the north shore of Yellowstone Lake, and at Canyon, accommodating many of the fifty thousand annual visitors by 1915.[14]

Ultimately, the early road system determined the physical imprint of human activity on the park landscape, with long-lasting effects. Roads that connected the major geological and scenic attractions have remained in place. Although a few facilities, such as hotels and camps, were built but later removed, major visitor amenities growing up around the road system proved resistant to alteration, even in recent times when biologists realized that the roads, campgrounds, and hotels interfered with the habitat needs of wildlife at locations such as Grant Village and Fishing Bridge.

During the late nineteenth century and the early twentieth century, a few wildlife species became focal points in park management when Yellowstone Park officials participated in a greater national crusade to protect large game animals threatened with extinction in the American West. The early mechanisms of protecting wildlife in Yellowstone evolved from 1872 through 1894, alongside changing scientific and public perceptions of wildlife. Many people feared, with good reason, that several wildlife species were bound for extinction. Market hunting came close to wiping the once populous bison herds of the Great Plains off the face of the earth during the 1870s and 1880s, and the disappearance of vast flocks of passenger pigeons also demonstrated the destructive potential of market hunting. But this economic activity was not restricted to eastern birds or plains bison; market hunters also exploited the wapiti of the Rocky Mountains, sometimes utilizing the same techniques employed with the bison, stripping carcasses of hide and tongue and leaving the remainder to rot.

In 1868 Frederick, Henry, and Phillip Bottler had settled onto a ranch about thirty miles north of the present park boundary, on the Yellowstone River. They and other market hunters discovered abundant wildlife from the wide Yellowstone Valley southward up the river into the area of the present park. Although the park's establishment in 1872 clearly outlawed hunting "for the purposes of merchandise or profit," hunters took large numbers of elk and other animals in the park. In 1875 park superintendent Norris estimated that market hunters, including the Bottler brothers, had killed four thousand elk (possibly in the Lamar Valley area) plus large numbers of bighorn sheep, deer, antelope, moose, and bison, taking for the most part only tongues and hides. Other observers also noticed and lamented the slaughter during 1874 and 1875. General William E. Strong claimed that more than four thousand elk were killed by market hunters in the Mammoth Springs Basin. George Bird Grinnell also visited the park and reported that three thousand elk had been killed for their hides, ranging from the hot springs north forty miles to Trail Creek. While it is unclear exactly what geographical areas Strong and Norris referred to, it is evident that many elk grazed in the area, and that the slaughter was immense both within and outside the park. Congress and federal administrators looked to the army as an obvious choice for an organization that could handle the policing responsibilities required. The early days of army administration set important parameters for the future of the park.[15]

Superintendent Norris's concerns helped launch a national crusade to protect bison and elk in Yellowstone. Norris, in making his first annual report in 1877, had been so concerned about reports of the great slaughter of game animals in the region that he recommended a large game preserve be established in the northwest corner of the park. This game preserve would encompass a large portion of the Lamar River Valley, where two or three gamekeepers would keep watch over the herds of elk, antelope, and buffalo. Gamekeeper Harry Yount was appointed on June 21, 1880, but he gave up the impossible task in the fall of 1881, recommending that a police force be assembled to guard the park's wildlife. In 1880 Secretary of the Interior Carl Schurz urged that hunting be outlawed in the park. After General Philip H. Sheridan visited the park in the summer of 1882, he urged Congress to prevent the slaughter of game by expanding the park's boundaries.[16] In 1883 Secretary of the Interior Henry Moore Teller expanded restrictions on hunting in the park by outlawing hunting for sport or subsistence, as well as market hunting.[17]

The slaughter of the elk within and immediately north of Yellowstone slowed down in the early 1880s because of local pressures against market hunting, public indignation over the slaughter of the park wildlife reported in national magazines, a changing market in hides, and a changing climate among hunters as sportsmen's magazines such as *Forest and Stream* began to object to excessive killing.[18] Yet poachers continued to defy the law, and public concern continued. So in 1886 Congress assigned the U.S. Army to Yellowstone, to protect the wildlife as well as the natural thermal features of the park. Although a few troopers took advantage of the large numbers of elk close at hand, observers thought the protection offered by the army for game animals dramatically cut down human-caused mortality in the elk and bison populations.[19]

In 1894 Yellowstone received a more substantial congressional mandate for the protection of its wildlife. Legislation was hurried along by a flagrant violation of the game laws when army troops caught poacher Edgar Howell after he shot five buffalo near Pelican Creek. On March 12, 1894, as Scout Felix Burgess and Sergeant Troike escorted their prisoner to the guardhouse at Fort Yellowstone, the soldiers happened upon the "Yellowstone National Park Game Expedition." That party included Emerson Hough, who promptly wrote and dispatched an article decrying poaching in Yellowstone for *Forest and Stream* magazine. The publication's editor, noted conservationist George Bird Grinnell, persuaded members of Congress that the situation was very serious. On March 26, Representative John Fletcher Lacey of Iowa introduced H.R. 6442, identified as "An act to protect the birds and animals in Yellowstone National Park, and to punish crimes in said park," and President Grover Cleveland duly signed the bill into law on May 7, 1894. Over the next six years Lacey, Teller, and Senator George Frisbie Hoar led the political advocacy for national wildlife protection. Passed in 1900, the "Lacey Act" represented a comprehensive game law that limited market hunting of both mammal and bird species and effectively ended the use of rare and exotic bird plumage for millinery purposes.[20]

The 1894 wildlife protection law for Yellowstone stated that the park "shall be under the sole and exclusive jurisdiction of the United States," thus ascribing authority over wildlife in Yellowstone to the federal government.

This action settled the immediate issue of who would protect Yellowstone's wildlife, but prior to this time the states held that authority, and hence in the long run friction ensued over jurisdiction. The legislation then proscribed "the killing, wounding, or capturing at any time of any bird or wild animal," named penalties for infractions, and created judicial mechanisms for enforcement. Congress included two important exceptions—it prohibited all killing and capturing of wildlife "except dangerous animals, when it is necessary to prevent them from destroying human life or inflicting an injury," and it excepted fishing, allowing the use of hook and line, but outlawing traps and nets. A protectionist urgency dominated the legislation, as the secretary of the interior was designated to make regulations "for the protection of the animals and birds in the park from capture or destruction, or to prevent their being frightened or driven from the park." For the next thirty years conservationists pushed exactly this sort of solution to wildlife problems. They created wildlife refuges throughout North America where ducks, geese, and other animals would be protected against market or sport hunting, at that time thought to be the animals' worst enemy. Bolstered by this legislation, the military authorities stationed in Yellowstone acted vigorously to prevent poaching of bison and elk.[21]

Despite protection within the park, the bison herd continued to dwindle, and by 1894 many thought the Yellowstone bison were doomed. In 1895 the Smithsonian Institution recommended construction of an enclosure for the native park animals that "Uncle Billy" Hofer built on Alum Creek. The haystack placed inside the enclosure failed to attract the Hayden Valley buffalo, so Hofer never sprung the trap. The Lamar River Valley bison herd originated in a small nucleus estimated in 1900 to number about forty animals. In 1901 Superintendent Captain John Pitcher asked Congress for money to buy bison that would be kept in a fenced enclosure in the park, and fifteen thousand dollars was appropriated for the purpose. C. J. Jones, otherwise known as "Buffalo Jones," had developed a reputation as an expert on buffalo by capturing calves from a remnant herd in Colorado and crossbreeding his own semidomesticated buffalo herd with cattle in Garden City, Kansas. He had kept careful track of Yellowstone's situation and offered his services to the secretary of the interior, arriving at the park in 1902. By importing three bulls from the Goodnight herd of Texas and eighteen cows from Conrad Allard's herd in western Montana, Jones created a semidomesticated herd. Evidently, the wild Lamar bison mixed with the imports; in 1934 wildlife experts concluded that the Lamar herd was probably "a hybrid of *Bison*

bison bison from Texas, *Bison bison septemtrionalis* from Montana, and *Bison bison haningtoni*, possibly the mountain form."[22] Jones turned out to be "a man of puritanical morals," and soon rangers ostracized him. After he ended up at odds with Superintendent Pitcher, Buffalo Jones resigned in September 1905. The bison herd expanded and so part of the herd was moved to Rose Creek in the Lamar Valley, a place eventually known as the buffalo ranch, where a domesticated herd was held until 1952. Thus by 1910 the effort to preserve bison in Yellowstone began to achieve success.[23]

Citizens and governments of the neighboring states also strove to protect wildlife. During the late nineteenth century, states appointed game wardens to supervise hunting on state lands, in response to the nationwide slaughter of wild animals by hide hunters as well as by overly enthusiastic sportsmen. Concern over dwindling elk herds led directly to the formation of state game agencies and the regulation of sport hunting in Montana and Wyoming. When Wyoming became a state in 1890 it created the office of fish commissioner but waited until 1899 to overhaul its hunting regulations and create the position of state game warden, filled by Swedish immigrant Albert Nelson. These state wildlife agencies assumed jurisdiction over wildlife within their borders.[24] Although Yellowstone was a federal reservation where wildlife was protected under the 1894 park protection law, wildlife did not respect lines on a map, wandering from Yellowstone's jurisdiction into territory administered by state game departments. Disagreements between state and federal agencies over wildlife policy were perhaps inevitable, sometimes fueling interagency conflict over jurisdiction.

The first professional organization for wildlife managers began in Yellowstone. In July 1902 W. F. Scott, Montana's first state game warden, convened a conference at Mammoth Hot Springs. Only thirty-one states employed a game warden or had a post of game commissioner in 1902, so the eight wardens and commissioners from the northwest who went to this conference was not a bad showing. The group decided to create a permanent organization, calling it the National Association of Game and Fish Wardens and Commissioners. The group met again in 1904, and in 1906 at least twenty-three people from fourteen states attended, including Major John G. Pitcher, acting superintendent of Yellowstone, Theodore S. Palmer of the Bureau of Biological Survey, and George Oliver Shields of the League of American Sportsmen. In 1907 Palmer used the example of Yellowstone as a successful protection program, as he told the association that artificial propagation and feeding of wild animals should be used in addition to hunting regulation.[25]

The movement to rescue large ungulates in Yellowstone from extinction was the exception to a general national indifference to wildlife populations. Only very gradually did a national movement to protect wildlife emerge, beginning around the turn of the century. William T. Hornaday, by several accounts a former hunter who experienced a dramatic epiphany, led a nationwide antihunting campaign. Actually, Hornaday did not stop hunting entirely but adopted the bow and arrow as a more sporting approach, while he castigated greedy "game hogs."[26] Chief taxidermist at the U.S. National Museum from 1882 to 1890, he became the first director of the New York Zoological Park in 1896, serving until his retirement in 1926. In his 1913 book Our Vanishing Wild Life Hornaday argued that halfway measures, such as limited seasons or bag limits, would fail to save game species from extinction—only long, closed seasons would suffice. He called on scientists to participate actively in conservation, lamenting the "appalling extent to which the zoologist has abdicated in favor of the sportsman." He lambasted scientific organizations such as the California Academy of Sciences, the Chicago Academy of Sciences, the Rochester Academy, the Philadelphia Zoological Society, and the National Zoological Park, warning: "All the zoological Neros should not fiddle while Rome burns."[27]

In 1914 Hornaday raised one hundred thousand dollars from wealthy friends and protectors of wildlife to establish the Permanent Wild Life Protection Fund in New York and began to lobby Congress for the creation of federal wildlife reserves and the establishment of bag limits.[28] His efforts reached an important crux in 1917 when the U.S. Senate and House considered the Chamberlain bill (S. 4418), which established game sanctuaries in national forests. Hornaday feared that the bill would allow states that did not want federal game sanctuaries to veto the creation of such reserves. During the consideration of this bill, the Wyoming legislature passed a "memorial" or resolution that Hornaday claimed struck at the very concept of "the game sanctuary idea."[29] Hornaday argued that the Wyoming legislature's action breathed "a spirit of open rebellion" against the federal government. Some of the earliest rivalries between state and federal governments for authority and jurisdiction over wildlife began with this episode. Protection of game animals in Yellowstone created gratifying short-term effects, but the establishment of the park also created the beginnings of management difficulties only realized much later such as the imposition of a human landscape over a natural one.

Just as game conservationists and administrators protected the few buffalo left in Yellowstone, they also made efforts on behalf of the native elk herd in Yellowstone. From the 1880s through the 1920s sportsmen and conservationists, as well as most administrators and scientists, were convinced that elk were in very serious trouble in the American West. The U.S. Army, which administered Yellowstone from 1886 to 1916, protected the elk against poachers. As Horace M. Albright later wrote, the federal government "could not declare perpetual closed seasons on killing game," because game animals belonged to the states. The mechanism the park used to prevent hunting of elk was to prohibit trespass by hunters on federal land. Major Lloyd Milton Brett, the park's last military superintendent from 1910 to 1916, fed hay to the elk during his administration. His rationale was that encroaching civilization had pushed the elk up the valley into the park, where the elk found themselves short of winter range. Normally, thought Brett, the elk would have wandered down and out of the high elevation to spend their winter at lower elevations where food was more plentiful. But modernity lapped up to the edges of the park, denying elk and bison their habitual migrations. Because the elk had been chased off their traditional winter range, feeding was necessary to see them through the slim winter months.[30]

By various measures plenty of elk wandered in and about Yellowstone. By 1911, farmers in the valley of the Yellowstone, just to the north of the park, complained to Park County sheriff John Killorn that elk were feeding off private range during winter months, breaking down fences and "eating up the farmers hay which makes a very heavy loss to some of them that they are unable to stand."[31] These elk occupied the northern areas of the park, expanding their range in the summer and seeking lower elevation range in the winter. In 1911 the media reported that elk in Jackson Hole were starving, and in response several western states applied to the Department of Interior for a boxcar or two of elk to be shipped by rail. The chief of the U.S. Biological Survey (USBS) notified the U.S. Forest Service (USFS) district forester in December that his agency was attempting to raise funds from the Boone and Crockett Club of New York to transport elk off these "overstocked ranges" to restock game ranges elsewhere.[32] Lieutenant Colonel L. M. Brett, Yellowstone acting superintendent, reported in 1912 that "an approximate accurate census" of the wintering herd revealed over thirty thousand elk on the northern range.[33]

Because market hunting and agricultural settlement had extirpated elk from broad segments of their original range from Iowa through areas of the Rocky Mountains, zoo directors and the new state game agencies and com-

1. William T. Hornaday, here pictured with Yellowstone Park Ranger Sam Woodring, c. 1928. Courtesy Yellowstone Photo Archives.

missions now began to look to Yellowstone as a source of elk, as a virtual warehouse of game animals now rare or absent in other areas of the country. In the early part of the century, Yellowstone began to ship elk to zoological parks located throughout the United States and Canada. The very first request for elk was in 1907 from the Board of Park Commissioners in Vancouver, British Columbia, and the U.S. government responded by donating two Yellowstone elk for zoo exhibition. The Department of Interior granted permission to capture elk in Yellowstone, with the understanding that the animals would be protected against hunters in their new homes. States without restrictive hunting laws, such as Kentucky, were denied requests until their state legislature passed protective laws that would be operative for at least ten years to allow a firm reestablishment of an elk herd on a particular game range. Zoological parks and depleted game ranges across the country acquired elk from Yellowstone in this way. Fish and game commissions of Minnesota, Georgia, Kentucky, Ohio, Colorado, and other states requested elk to stock on game ranges. Fraternal organizations, such as the Benevolent and Protective Order of Elks (BPOE), from Vermont to Alabama requested elk for municipal zoos. Wyoming restocked game ranges just east of the park with the Yellowstone wapiti. Individual citizens sought elk but were advised that only state game commissions, zoos, and game refuges could receive elk. The number of requests for elk grew significantly in 1912, and in 1913 a veritable flood of applications requested shipments of elk from Yellowstone to zoos and game ranges across the country. From 1907 to 1913 Yellowstone shipped 777 elk, almost 500 in 1912 alone. Although trapping and shipping elk began as a means for the Department of Interior to fulfill requests from zoological parks, eventually officials started to use the shipments as an outlet for elk, which the officials believed could not be accommodated on the available winter range.[34]

A few administrators and scientists suspected that elk were becoming more plentiful than food in Yellowstone. George Bird Grinnell, at that time associated with the Boone and Crockett Club, reasoned that because the herd was protected from hunters within the park, it was increasing, but its food supply remained steady. Hence some of the elk "must either be fed at public expense or must starve to death."[35] From correspondence between Grinnell and the Department of the Interior and the Bureau of Biological Survey we see the first development of the idea that agencies might do something to limit the size of the herd. Grinnell thought that elk mortality from hunting and natural causes did not amount to six thousand per year, and "if they did, I do not believe that this is nearly enough."[36]

The Bureau of Biological Survey also became involved with the management of wildlife in the Yellowstone area. It is important to see what sort of outlook the agency brought to bear when it made recommendations. The bureau traced its origins to the work of naturalist C. Hart Merriam, appointed by the American Ornithologists' Union to chair its Committee on the Migration of Birds. Deciding that volunteers could not organize so much information, Merriam consulted with Smithsonian secretary Spencer F. Baird and chose to ask the federal government for assistance. His funding request appealed to agricultural concerns, suggesting farmers would benefit from information about the food habits and economic impact of birds. Created in 1885, the Division of Economic Ornithology and Mammalogy of the Department of Agriculture researched the relationship between wild animals (especially birds) and agriculture. Food habits research carried out by the division demonstrated that although some birds did eat grain from farmers' fields, most birds did farmers a considerable favor by eating thousands of insects that damaged crops. The Division of Economic Ornithology thus made inferences about the value of birds based on economic grounds.

The same sort of research on the predatory birds showed similar economic benefits to the farmer, providing a scientific basis for the protection of hawks and owls. In 1895 the agency was renamed the Division of Biological Survey.

The first chief of the bureau, Merriam guided the agency away from its economic emphasis toward his own interests in mapping out the life zones of North America and conducting research on vertebrate fauna natural history. A close observer noted that 1886 to 1896 was a "decade of the steady subordination of the economic to the scientific."[37] Merriam never used the word "economic" in correspondence regarding his own title, and from 1891 to 1896, he dropped the term when writing agency reports, referring to the Division of Ornithology and Mammalogy. Beginning around 1905 when the agency was renamed the Bureau of Biological Survey, but especially evident during hearings in 1907, members of Congress who could not see the value of mapping the distribution of skunks in America pressured the agency to demonstrate its "practical value to the agricultural interests of the country." The bureau returned to its economic analysis and agricultural concerns, also taking up the federal government's enforcement duties regarding the importation of exotic species and the protection of migratory birds. Agricultural interests and sportsmen successfully enlisted the federal government in their campaign against predatory animals. In March of 1907 the Biological Survey followed on the heels of the U.S. Forest Service in publishing directions for killing wolves, contributing to a record kill of over eighteen hundred wolves and twenty-three thousand coyotes that year. The Bureau of Biological Survey quickly became the central federal actor in the campaign against predatory animals in the West. Merriam disliked the agency's new direction, so he resigned in 1910, working for the next thirty years on reclassifying bear species and conducting anthropological studies of California's Native Americans.[38]

In 1913, Bureau of Biological Survey Chief E. W. Nelson created an informal plan that he communicated to the governors of Montana and Wyoming and the Department of the Interior "to provide for the utilization of the increase of the elk herds in such a manner that the number on the ground shall remain the same from year to year."[39] If about six thousand elk died each year due to natural causes and hunting, then one to two thousand would be available yearly for distribution to other states. Significantly, during the early 1910s these experts conflated the northern Yellowstone herd with the Jackson Hole herd to the south. Actually, two great divisions of elk existed in the Yellowstone region, one in the northern part of Yellowstone Park, and another that migrated from the low country of Jackson Hole northward up to summer range in southern Yellowstone Park and areas east and southeast of the park. At the time, very little was known about the geographic range of these herds and their migratory habits. Estimating the numbers of elk was not straightforward; personnel from the USBS and the USFS conducting the first counts in 1915 and 1916 came up with such different numbers that they invited the Boone and Crockett Club to send a representative to the 1917 count to settle the discrepancy. Harsh conditions during the winter of 1916–17 caused an unusually large winter kill in the park.[40]

Although the Boone and Crockett Club desired a greater distribution of elk from Yellowstone, the Bureau of Biological Survey noted that Wyoming and Montana would oppose any attempt to limit hunting opportunity, thus placing an effective upper limit on the number of elk available for shipment. Additionally, E. W. Nelson thought that local sportsmen might eliminate the herd's yearly increase, if favorable hunting conditions occurred. On a single day during the fall of 1911, for example, forest officials estimated that hunters harvested fifteen hundred elk when a deep snowfall created favorable hunting conditions. Part of the reason for hunter success near Gardiner, Montana, was the easy road accessibility, but even more important was the location of the park's boundary line, clear on the map yet invisible on the ground.

The northern boundary stretched from the junction of the Gardiner River with the Yellowstone due east, crossing the Yellowstone three times in two miles. In this area, all within three miles from Gardiner, some of the northern herd left the park seeking low-elevation winter range. Hunting along the boundary line seemed to change the behavior of elk, and it also seemed to present some risks. Vernon Bailey, chief field naturalist for the Bureau of Biological Survey from 1887 to 1937, wrote at the time that the "present policy of raising elk in the Yellowstone Park to be killed as fast as they come out does not appeal to most of us as a wise conservation policy."[41] Bailey thought the same policy had failed on Yellowstone's western border, resulting in a virtual absence of elk in the southwest corner of the park. E. W. Nelson was hopeful that "some method may be worked out whereby a belt along this border of the park may be closed to shooting."[42] Thus by 1913 some scientific people thought a surplus number of elk might be removed without harming the herd. At the same moment, they seemed ambivalent toward Bailey's and Nelson's belief that the boundary line hunt might kill too many elk. This search for a safety zone for the elk along Yellowstone's northern border was later replaced by a search for securing winter range for the elk, an effort continuing today.

Jesse W. Nelson, grazing inspector for the USFS, thought it important that the concerned agencies "agree on the number of animals which the available winter range will carry and arrange to maintain the herds at approximately that size."[43] This directly opposed the approach of the Biological Survey, which started by asking how many elk agencies wanted to support, then determining how much land was necessary to furnish the required winter range. J. W. Nelson's approach essentially started with the range itself and proceeded to the animals. How many grazers and browsers could this place support? The question and concept soon became known as carrying capacity, a term whose origins are tied inextricably to the origins of range science.

Bigger questions involving land use and the role of state and federal governments in conservation loomed behind the problem of the elk and their winter feed. By 1912 conflicts between grazing and conservation interests arose. S. W. McClure, secretary of the National Wool Growers Association, complained to the secretary of agriculture that "the chief beneficiaries of our Western game laws are the game wardens and the pernicious political machines which they have fostered." McClure did not mention the political influence of the sheepmen. He worried about the possibility that elk would displace sheep on grazing ranges on national forest land surrounding Yellowstone Park. The state of Montana should act to provide "prosperous homes for its people and not to provide immense game preserves for the idle rich of Eastern States."[44]

Henry S. Graves, a local official of the U.S. Forest Service who later became Gifford Pinchot's successor as director of the bureau, suggested that the real question was how federal lands were to be utilized. He thought a "very serious question of public economics arises as to how much of these Yellowstone ranges should be devoted to domestic stock and what part should be held purely for the propagation of elk."[45] Graves urged the Department of the Interior to decide how many elk it desired on public land and to proceed with planning for the forest reserves from that point.

Officials of the Bureau of Biological Survey were also involved in the discussion. Vernon Bailey visited Livingston, where a rancher named Warner argued for sheep grazing along the southern boundary of the Absaroka forest, from Gardiner to Slough Creek, a landscape that Bailey thought of little value to either elk or domestic sheep. Bailey suggested that the Absaroka forest should choose a strip of land leading northward from the park along one of the few available river courses and designate it (in effect) a game refuge. In the summers, elk would wander so far out of the park that they would disperse into the Absaroka Mountains in time for hunting season in the fall, without interfering with stock range on the forest. Emerson Hough, who might be called the first conservation activist to work on behalf of national park issues, argued for limiting agricultural expansion in the interests of Yellowstone's animal life. He had been advised that the secretary of agriculture planned to issue permits to graze 28,000 head of cattle and 133,000 head of sheep for the 1917 season just west of Yellowstone Park on the Madison reserve, an action that meant "the ruin of all hope" for elk on the park's west side. Relationships between government officials and this early citizen activist hence assumed an adversarial tone. Hough sought to cast the onus for dispute on Nelson when he wrote: "Yet you blame us people, who are trying to do something unselfishly, for criticizing officials of the Government who will do things like this."[46]

Some people blamed the elk problem on a lack of foresight. In 1914 concerned citizen Mary E. Elliott wrote to the secretary of the interior, suggesting that the "Government is back of their starvation. It has permitted Settlers to take up or settle on their grazing lands and it has made no provision for these dumb helpless creatures." Elliott hoped that if the secretary brought the problem to the attention of President Wilson, "his good heart might suggest some way to relieve the situation."[47] Other people used distinctly populist tones in discussing the game situation. Mr. Rumsey at the Pinto Ranch near Cody, Wyoming, argued that "the game situation of Wyo. has been run and controlled—not for the preservation of the game—but for the preservation and pocket books of the people of Jackson Hole!"[48] The Wyoming Game Protective Association, established by Rumsey in 1916, argued that the game preserves were arranged in such a fashion that hunters drove the elk there; if only the elk were properly dispersed across the landscape, they would not starve to death.

Despite the widening belief that the elk herds of northern Yellowstone and Jackson Hole were too numerous for the available winter range, there lingered an uncertainty in many people's minds regarding how to secure the survival of the herd and the species. Like others, George Bird Grinnell thought the number of elk on Yellowstone's range ranged upward of thirty thousand animals. Even though the elk might be locally numerous, Yellowstone could not run the risk of losing its herd, because Grinnell thought that Yellowstone accounted for at least 75 percent of the total elk numbers in North America. Biological Survey chief E. W. Nelson thought that because of increasing demand for use of the forests for grazing, "adequate provision" would have to be made for summer as well as winter ranges for the elk of the Yellowstone region "in order that their future welfare may be guarded."[49] Writing on behalf of the Permanent Wild Life Protection Fund, William T. Hornaday in 1917 saw the establishment of game reserves as "absolutely the last chance of the West to bring back the big game to its now lifeless and desolate wastes of wilderness."[50] Organizations with related interests, such as the American Humane Association, worried that elk might become extinct, even in Yellowstone.[51]

During the mid-1910s state and federal agencies assumed increasing responsibility for game animals. The U.S. Forest Service warned that strict enforcement of the game laws was necessary to prevent the slaughter of elk for the "tusks," or upper canine teeth, used for pendants or cuff links.[52] The Forest Service and the Biological Survey claimed that hundreds of elk were killed yearly in the Yellowstone area for this illegal purpose, the carcasses of the finest bulls left to rot while "elk teeth were peddled openly about the hotel at Gardiner."[53] Until the Benevolent and Protective Order of Elks (BPOE) grew sensitive to the problem, the fraternal order comprised a large market for those teeth. The Progressive-era abhorrence for waste is clearly evident behind the Forest Service's enforcement of game laws.

Scientists, conservationists, and public land administrators advocated various solutions for the problem of insufficient winter range. E. W. Nelson thought that the danger of losses to the elk of Yellowstone could "be practically eliminated by having the local supply of wild hay in the park cut, stacked and securely fenced to be held for emergencies."[54] In the early 1910s the army administration at Yellowstone began to harvest hay in the vicinity of the entrance near the town of Gardiner. Vernon Bailey thought predators should be eliminated from the area. J. W. Nelson, grazing inspector for the Forest Service, recommended in 1917 that some of the elk might be slaughtered, "thereby reducing the herd nearer to the capacity of the winter range." The chief forester quickly rejected this notion, noting that "the responsibility for recommending the slaughter of a certain number of elk" belonged to the game associations and not the Forest Service. Those who think criticism of public agencies is a recent phenomenon should note Nelson's sensitivity to "the critics whose main object in life appears to be their attempt to discredit our efforts in protecting game animals."[55] Thus during the early days of game management, the NPS and the USFS responded to sportsmen's groups and the Montana and Wyoming game commissioners, although they had their own conceptions of proper management.

Several significant themes emerge from our examination of this era. First, early park administration set precedents and physical effects lasting for years. Yellowstone's caretakers created a physical infrastructure, the road system and hotels, that transformed habitats previously occupied exclusively by wildlife. Second, the way that early park administrations dealt with wildlife comprised a strictly reactive approach to wildlife management. There was no science of wildlife management—until this time, no one considered the inevitable result of mass slaughter of wildlife a problem. Wildlife problems were seen as relatively straightforward. If the elk were being slaughtered, the park should protect them. If the elk appeared to be close to starvation, the park must feed them. Because the American bison was on the brink of extinction, the park propagated remnants selected from several herds and guarded the results carefully. When sportsmen wanted abundant fish throughout the Rocky Mountains, federal and state agencies established fish hatcheries (including one at Yellowstone) to propagate and distribute trout. In each instance managers raced to catch up with a situation thrown in their laps. They appeared to have a good deal of success in dealing with problems that seemed self-evident. Congress and early park managers frequently created wildlife policies in haste and during a mood of crisis in response to a long history of excessive harvesting of wildlife resources.

Until 1916 the U.S. Forest Service and the Bureau of Biological Survey comprised the expertise of the federal government over wildlife in the region, while the army enforced the law within the park. On August 25, 1916, a third major federal agency entered the field when Congress created the National Park Service to administer park lands held by the federal government, including Yellowstone and Yosemite. Although the Park Service unified the administration of park lands that were previously under the jurisdiction of three different cabinet departments, the bureau did not avoid future policy disputes with other agencies, nor could the new agency ultimately escape strictures created by tradition and culture.

CONSERVATION THOUGHT AND YELLOWSTONE

1916–1930

> Ecology has no aim, but ecologists have.
>
> Charles C. Adams, *Guide to the Study of Animal Ecology*, 1913

During the 1920s scientists interacted with conservationists and the fledgling National Park Service in charting the direction and purposes of the national parks, in the process setting parameters for Yellowstone as well. The active participation of the scientific community in advising the NPS during the 1920s is striking. A lively interaction between early ecologists and the NPS furthered ecological research and education in Yellowstone. Scientists and conservationists attempted to steer the national parks during three important campaigns: for "national park standards," for educational uses of the parks, and for the reservation of primitive areas for scientific study.

The influence of newly formed ecological ideas on national park conservation during the 1920s can be seen most readily in scientists' efforts to perpetuate natural conditions within the national parks. Ecologist Charles C. Adams, along with Victor Shelford and other scientists, began a new way of looking at the national parks, advocating the preservation of "natural conditions." This alternative way of focusing on the landscape and its inhabitants eventually changed the way Americans thought about their national parks. While ecological approaches to understanding nature grew in academia, the day-to-day administration of Yellowstone fell somewhat short of the ecologists' ideal of an outdoor laboratory where natural processes continued untainted by human hand.

In the early days of the NPS, administrators continued to use a problem-oriented approach to many aspects of wildlife management. Managers fed the elk to preserve this game species from extinction and manipulated wildlife for effective presentation, for example, erecting a fenced-in section near the Mammoth thermal area where tourists could not miss seeing the bison. This problem-fixing approach can also be seen in the campaign against predators taken up by the federal government, including Yellowstone, in response to the request of stockmen. Cultural assumptions about "good" and "bad" animals played no small role in the early days of NPS management of Yellowstone. For many years Adams's ecological view of national park purposes coexisted in a state of tension with more traditional ways of viewing the park's wildlife. While the discipline of biology underwent great changes from the late 1890s through the early 1920s, natural history traditions remained strong in some scientific institutions and in federal and state agencies that dealt with wildlife. In June 1920 the California Academy of Science's hunt for grizzly bear specimens in Yellowstone exemplified this older natural history approach to understanding wildlife in the park.

During the 1920s, wildlife management, education in the parks, and academic ecology all became more professionalized as institutional forms were created in agencies, universities, and professional associations. It is ironic that a growing professionalization contributed to a split between naturalist and ranger divisions in the NPS. Ultimately, ecological thinking in Yellowstone was bounded by strong preservationist traditions in big game management that focused on single species, an emerging range management paradigm, a cultural ethic of control over nature, and the isolation of ecological knowledge within a politically weak arm of the NPS.

For years, J. Horace McFarland, leader of the American Civic Association, national park advocate Enos Mills, and the Sierra Club had advocated the creation of a bureau to manage the national park lands.[1] President Taft endorsed the concept in 1912, and in January 1915 independently wealthy borax tycoon Stephen T. Mather went to Washington DC as first assistant to Secretary of the Interior Franklin K. Lane. Starting at a conference at Stanford University, Mather facilitated a national publicity campaign to establish a formalized bureau, aided by the efforts of his assistant Horace M. Albright. Robert Sterling Yard prepared his *National Parks Portfolio*, which was distributed free of charge to thousands of people.[2]

Significantly, Mather belonged to the Sierra Club and had strongly opposed construction of the Hetch Hetchy Dam in Yosemite. Historian Stephen Fox has suggested that Mather brought "an amateur spirit" to conservation in the federal government, shaping the early years of the National Park Service.[3] Indeed, Mather guided the National Park Service on a different route from the utilitarian conservation course employed by other federal agencies such as the Bureau of Biological Survey and the U.S. Forest Service.

Another account of the early Park Service portrays Mather as "acting as a moderator between one faction of the parks' friends that wanted the reservations tricked out as luxury vacation resorts and another that wanted them left as close to the entirely primeval as possible."[4]

Representative William Kent of California sponsored the Park Service Act signed into law by President Woodrow Wilson in the summer of 1916. Congress designated the NPS to "conserve the scenery and the natural and historic objects and the wild life therein and to provide for the enjoyment of the same in such manner and by such means as will leave them unimpaired for the enjoyment of future generations." The legislation thus required the Park Service to protect the natural features of its domain, yet it also set the tone for the agency's more public function, providing for the enjoyment of those natural wonders by the public at large. Not until the postwar era would some scholars and conservationists identify this "dual mandate" as a fundamental problem. A recent view suggests that "From that bureaucratic fount has flowed 81 years of paradox."[5] For Horace Albright a close reading of the organic act revealed that "Congress intended that the National Park Service should be primarily a protective bureau."[6] Even while Yellowstone took a protective posture toward elk and bison, Albright and Mather leaned toward the "use" side of the equation, seeking publicity for the parks and setting an agency agenda that encouraged tourism and ultimately limited the influence of ecological ideas. Foremost among the concerns of Congress and those who lobbied for a Park Service were "the preservation of scenery, the economic benefits of tourism, and efficient management of the parks."[7]

During the early days of the Park Service the ways in which scientists, conservationists, and park officials viewed the purposes of the national parks greatly influenced the shape of the new bureau. Although the earliest motivations for establishing national parks centered around the protection of scenic wonders, by 1880 the logic of national park conservation had begun to emphasize wildlife protection. By 1916 a national enthusiasm for the primitive life had blossomed, emphasizing the salutary health and psychological effects of a good dose of nature.[8] Civilized life had benumbed the American people, and what the desk-weary and factory-bound workers needed was some vigorous exercise and contact with primitive nature. Teddy Roosevelt's advocacy of the strenuous life exemplified some of the ideas that fed into national planning for recreation during the 1910s and 1920s.

Joseph Grinnell and Tracy I. Storer, of the University of California's Museum of Vertebrate Zoology, echoed the opinion of urban park advocates, noting the recreational element of parks' raison d'être. Modern people, they wrote, were not only overwrought by the tensions of civilized life, but they also were physiologically out of balance. A few weeks in open country or in the mountains was the only prescription for a businessman's complete rest and relief. In natural surroundings "he may find entire relief from the nerve-racking drive of city life, and be brought once more into contact with primitive conditions." Grinnell and Storer thought about re-creating people as fully human, rather than in terms of simple amusement. The best aspects of nature for recreation "are those which most infallibly tend to revive our atrophied faculties and instincts." Primitive sounds such as bird songs or falling water, landscapes of subtle hues that relieved the eyes from paper work, and easily accessible mountains for exercise were important restorative parts of nature.

Yet the most important healing aspect of nature was "natural phenomena that make a purely intellectual or esthetic appeal, as do the conflicts between the great insentient forces of nature" and the "intimate inter-relations of plants and animals."[9] Thus the contemplation of nature played a crucial part in readjusting the overcivilized mind and body and retuning human balances upset by modernity. Because of "the commercial exploitation of nature," places bearing these natural qualities were becoming harder and harder to find, and so the regenerative potential of nature was to be found increasingly within the national parks.

The wildlife management policies of the early Park Service were shaped by the protective idea expressed by Yard and by cultural notions about animals. The elk in Yellowstone National Park exemplify the protectionist tradition. At the time that Congress created the National Park Service in 1916, concern over Yellowstone's elk was growing. Beginning in 1917, sportsmen and three federal agencies (the NPS, the Bureau of Biological Survey, and the U.S. Forest Service) began negotiations aimed at purchasing private lands to provide adequate winter range for the existing herd, an effort that has continued to the present day. In February 1917, Acting Superintendent Chester A. Lindsley suggested a withdrawal from entry and settlement by presidential proclamation for a few sections of land north of the park. Shortly thereafter the Forest Service advised the General Land Office that it recommended deferring opening sections for settlement along the Yellowstone River until the issue had been decided. The chief of the Biological Survey supported the Park Service and Forest Service, and on April 16, 1917, only one day before the lands were to be opened for entry under the grazing homestead law, Executive Order 2599 temporarily withdrew the area from settlement until March of 1919.[10] Conservationists nationwide supported the purchase of land to create a state game refuge. When addressing the 1919 national meeting of the Grand Lodge of Elks in Atlantic City, New Jersey, forester J. W. Nelson urged the Elks to support the program, noting the cost of land acquisition was still increasing.[11]

Ranching interests in the Yellowstone River valley resisted the provision of more winter range. M. R. Wilson of Bozeman wrote to his senator, complaining that the extension of the elk reserve had the effect of inviting hundreds and even thousands of elk to wander farther out among private lands, where corrals could not keep the elk from devouring the ranchers' carefully gathered winter feed. Wilson complained that the elk were protected at government expense only "to be a pest and a nuisance to these people."[12] Government purchase of one or two ranches, which could raise three hundred tons of hay, he suggested, might help avoid friction between the local ranchers and the park. The Department of Interior reassured anxious citizens in the Yellowstone Valley that nobody planned on purchasing all the cultivated land in the upper Yellowstone and dismissed rumors of a proposed state elk refuge north of the park encompassing a swath twenty-five miles wide. The Interior Department and the National Park Service were not set against the commercial interests of Yellowstone's neighbors; rather they would "do everything in their power to so develop this park as to make it each year more valuable to the West from the standpoint of commercial gain."[13] This desire to garner political support for the parks by supporting tourism ultimately determined some of the preservation limits.

Feeding the elk comprised another solution to the perceived problem. Conservationists, hunting enthusiasts, and agency people all supported supplemental feeding, beginning a tradition still carried on today in several Wyoming game refuges. Horace Albright assumed the duties of superintendent in Yellowstone on July 1, 1919. During his first winter in the park, severe weather created conditions right for a large winter kill. By November, Albright was back in Washington, seeking money from wealthy friends and the Appropriations Committee to feed Yellowstone's elk.[14] In 1920 Albright continued feeding hay to the northern herd in an attempt to keep the elk from descending down and out of the park to winter range and from the guns of Montana's hunters. Albright himself supervised the preparation of magazine articles to spread the news to the public and located news-papermen interested in the story. The American Humane Association covered the story of the elk in the February issue of *National Humane Review*.

By December of 1919 the park had spent thirty thousand dollars on a total of one thousand tons of hay, and Representative C. A. Newton offered to help find money from Congress to feed the elk.[15] Biological Survey chief Edward William Nelson assured the editor of *Outdoor Life*, J. A. McGuire, that his bureau was doing everything possible to help the elk. Nelson reasoned that the additional hay secured with the financial help of eastern sporting clubs might pull the herd through, although if severe conditions continued, "heavy losses of elk will be inevitable."[16]

Some observers proposed that government bureaus would have to work together to devise an efficient solution. Although officials such as E. W. Nelson had established early forms of cooperation between agencies, conflicts were perhaps inevitable. Some contention was caused simply by the friction between energetic and goal-directed people as they pursued separate agendas. Some of the people who rose to the tops of bureaucratic organizations had dominating or controlling personality traits, and hence when bureaus had conflicting interests, strong-willed personalities clashed. Nelson's habit of opening his staff's personal mail, for example, demonstrated his dominating style of management in the Bureau of Biological Survey. Ira N. Gabrielson was the first to stand up to him, saying that he had never heard of such a practice outside a penitentiary.[17]

In 1915 and 1916 the Bureau of Biological Survey and the U.S. Forest Service cooperated in the earliest counts of elk on the northern range. They hoped to secure information the Forest Service could use to reserve the proper amount of winter range for the elk herds. The chief of the Biological Survey sought to persuade the Forest Service to form cooperative management arrangements with the state game agencies; otherwise it would be "extremely difficult to prevent the eventual extermination of the elk and other large game animals in many sections."[18] During the 1910s the highest levels of the federal administration initiated cooperation between agencies. In 1917 the secretary of agriculture wrote to the secretary of interior, suggesting that "definite planning in advance and a coordinate administration of the elk by the two departments are essential."[19] Despite the stated desire for cooperation, actually coming to agreement and effecting coordinated management proved problematic over the years.

Federal officials proposed several plans of management. Forest Service grazing inspector Jesse W. Nelson devised the very first one, but it was quickly superseded by a more comprehensive analysis. In 1918 chief forester Henry S. Graves devised his suggestions for management, which he called a "program" for the Yellowstone elk.[20] Assistant to Division of Forestry chief Gifford Pinchot from 1898 to 1900, Graves quit the bureau to direct the Yale School of Forestry. He returned to the U.S. Forest Service in 1910 as chief forester, serving until 1920.[21] Graves sent his ideas on the elk to Biological Survey chief E. W. Nelson for comment. Nelson had made his career as a naturalist, never actually graduating from a college program but capitalizing on his *Report upon Natural History Collections Made in Alaska between the Years 1877 and 1881.* Joining the Bureau of Biological Survey in 1890, he spent much of the next fourteen years carrying out research in Mexico, publishing his *Revision of the Squirrels of Mexico* in 1899. Promoted to chief field naturalist in 1907, he took charge of the bureau's biological research in 1913 and became assistant chief in 1914. From 1916 to 1927 he served as chief of the bureau. Nelson was elected president of the American Ornithologists' Union (1908–11) as well as the American Society of Mammalogists (1920–21).[22] In 1919 Nelson and Graves proposed their elk plan as a joint program of the Biological Survey and the Forest Service.[23] These two agencies had started gathering information on the northern Yellowstone elk beginning in 1911, with the cooperation of the Boone and Crockett Club. As he wrote the first draft of his plan, Graves was worried about conveying the impression of a pervasive New York influence in agency thinking about the elk.

In fact, a variety of national conservation organizations centered on the East Coast did have an important influence on wildlife policies. The Boone and Crockett Club, founded in 1888 by wealthy sportsmen including Theodore Roosevelt, Elihu Root, and Henry Cabot Lodge, celebrated a primitivistic philosophy and the hunt as a regenerative activity for civilization-benumbed men.[24] Gun and ammunition manufacturers supported the American Game Protective Association (AGPA), the first sportsmen's group with a professional staff. G. O. Shields, a zealous advocate of hunting restrictions, organized the short-lived Camp Fire Club of America. These national groups regularly communicated with federal and state agency officials, forming an early network of formal and informal associations between conservationists, agency people, and scientists concerned about wildlife. Meetings, frequent lunches, and sometimes banquets with Native American themes and costumes in Washington and New York City were an integral part of the social interactions among these conservationists. During

1915 and 1916 AGPA organized meetings in New York City to discuss the Yellowstone elk, with representatives of the Camp Fire Club of America and the Boone and Crockett Club in attendance.

Popular wisdom, such as Mary E. Elliott's belief that homesteaders displaced elk, became unified with experts' opinions in an official diagnosis of the elk problem. In 1918 Graves and Nelson argued that the "elk problem is a land problem." As civilization pushed up from the plains to the edges of the Rocky Mountains, they wrote, settlers' fields steadily encroached on the usual haunts of the elk, making "the winter home of the survivors more and more narrowly restricted." Fences erected by ranchers obstructed the annual spring and fall migrations of the elk, and domestic stock consumed what for ages had been elk forage. The elk herds of northwest Wyoming had been gradually pushed farther and farther back into the mountains "until now there is scarcely enough winter range to take care of the remaining limited numbers during the average winter season." The situation had reached a crisis, wrote Graves and Nelson, and if the existing size of the herds was to be maintained, a "definite program" was required, perhaps including "certain radical actions."[25]

Graves and Nelson thought the herd should be maintained at its current size, which Graves initially believed to be forty thousand animals. Safeguards would need to be introduced to protect the elk against losses from overshooting, predatory animals, and starvation. Graves and Nelson recommended possible methods to implement those safeguards, namely an extension of the park to the south, enlargement of the existing state game preserve in the Gallatin Canyon just northwest of the park, a joint determination of hunting seasons by the state and federal authorities, the use of federal courts to strengthen the administration of state game laws, cooperation between the states and the federal agencies, making winter range in the park used by Yellowstone Transportation Company horses available to the elk, taking the lands withdrawn from settlement in April 1917 and adding them to the Absaroka and Gallatin National Forests, and the purchase of private lands north of the park. They recommended that officials study the elk's migration and observe the herd to determine the annual increase.[26] Finally, Graves and Nelson urged the "most vigorous campaign possible against predatory animals that destroy elk."[27]

Graves and Nelson worked together on the problem for several years, and their program represented the state of public opinion and professional understanding of the time. Their ideas and plan were also remarkable, because they formed the basis for management of the Yellowstone elk through the 1920s until new conceptions of the elk and their range emerged. Thus the U.S. Forest Service and the Bureau of Biological Survey endorsed protection of the elk. In early 1917 all the public lands south of Yankee Jim Canyon to the park boundary were withdrawn from settlement, excepting mineral lands. On May 26, 1926, Congress added those lands to the Gallatin and Absaroka National Forests, and appropriated money to purchase additional winter range.[28]

While their prescription on the desirability of additional range remained convincing, other facets of 1920s thinking on the elk seem contradictory today. Why would knowledgeable people, while concerned about enough winter food for the elk herd, also recommend that predators be exterminated? The answer lies in two places: cultural attitudes that condemned "bad" animals and a belief that predators took game from the hunter. Despite the great efforts to protect elk and bison, there were limits to preservation in Yellowstone; until the 1930s predators were persona non grata in the park. There is documentation of independent wolfers in 1877 poisoning ungulate carcasses, and by 1880 Superintendent Norris thought that wolves were nearly extinct in the park.[29] During the days of army administration, it was common practice to shoot coyotes, mountain lions, and wolves on sight. Scientists believed they had good reasons to support the elimination of predators on the public lands. In 1915 the U.S. Biological Survey's chief field naturalist Vernon Bailey wrote Lieutenant Elmer Lindsley at Fort Yellowstone, urging "no time should be lost in getting the wolves and coyotes out of that region."[30] In 1918 Yellowstone Park Superintendent Albright noted that a hunter of the Biological Survey would be assigned to Yellowstone to assist in exterminating predatory animals. Yellowstone's official involvement with predator control lasted from 1914 to 1926, during which time Yellowstone authorities removed at least 136 wolves, of which about 80 were pups.[31]

"Extermination," "destruction," and "depredation" were commonly used words in discussing predators during that time, when many people shared the assumption that predatory animals simply had no place in a progressive West. Yet nobody really knew much about predators. Graves asked Dr. H. W. Henshaw if it were possible to estimate game losses due to predators, because he suspected these were greater than previously reported.[32] The Biological Survey and the Forest Service in 1916 estimated a total of 14,000 animals in the northern Yellowstone elk herd, and guessed that

2. Ranger displays coyote carcasses, January 1929. Courtesy Yellowstone Photo Archives.

3. Hunters pose with mountain lion, c. 1925. For many years the federal government paid hunters to kill predatory animals in and near Yellowstone. This particular kill may have occurred just outside the park. Courtesy Yellowstone Photo Archives.

about 500 elk were lost yearly to old age, that 600 were trapped and shipped out of Yellowstone, and that predator wolves killed 1,400 annually.[33] The "scientific" justifications for elimination of predators involved simple economic calculations. Any loss of game animals was too much to bear.

Horace Albright, superintendent of Yellowstone from 1919 until 1929, shared William T. Hornaday's fear that the last elk herds in the lower forty-eight states were in danger of extinction. He perceived herds of ungulates precariously balanced on the brink of disaster, threatened by hunters as well as by the harsh winters that buried Yellowstone's high plateau region under deep snow. For Albright it was more than a question of just shepherding the Yellowstone herd through another winter; it was a question of survival of the species. In 1919 Albright wrote to Charles C. Adams, professor at the New York State College of Forestry in Syracuse, suggesting "if we succeed in saving the nucleus of the great herds that are now being slaughtered by hundreds or are meeting death through starvation we must bring the Country to a realization that our national elk herds are constantly facing extermination and that some means must be found of giving them perpetual protection."[34]

Albright thought of Yellowstone as "our greatest game preserve," the only national park serving as a true place of protection and refuge.[35] Montana's hunting laws, he wrote, were "unworthy of a civilized state."[36] Others joined in Albright's discomfiture with the hunt, including Robert Sterling Yard, leader of the fledgling National Parks Association (NPA), who lambasted the fall hunt on Yellowstone's northern border. Calling the boundary line hunt of 1919 a "disaster" for the elk, Yard castigated the hunters who "fired by volleys . . . scarcely taking time to aim, heedless of law or sportsmanship, carried out of their senses by greed of flesh."[37] Guessing that 6,000 to 7,000 were killed outright and 2,000 to 3,000 must have died later of poor marksmanship, Yard lamented that the proud northern elk herd had been reduced from 15,000 to 6,000. Despite Yard's gloomy assessment, the protection offered elk in Yellowstone was so effective that the size of the herd in the northern reaches of the park grew noticeably by the early 1920s, reassuring Albright that the Yellowstone wapiti would not become extinct.

Albright attributed this success to the creation of the National Park Service. When "competent and trained men" replaced political appointees in superintendent posts, and after the NPS organized a ranger corps to protect the flora and fauna of the park, then "game conservation" would become a reality in the parks.[38] According to Albright, restraining dogs and cats also helped, so by the mid-1920s visitors could view the "abundant" deer and bear in places where it had been difficult to see wild animals. Until the early 1930s, park officials welcomed the elk, motivated in part by their belief that tourists came primarily to see wild animals. This complete protection for the elk lasted until 1934, when a new view of the wapiti emerged, which would dominate park management for more than thirty years.

Despite the protection Albright and fellow conservationists offered the elk, proponents of preservation embodied contradictions that seem incongruous to us today. Cultural attitudes toward nature, shaped partly by people who wrote about nature, helped create the limits of preservation in Yellowstone. During the early twentieth century, nature writers penned books that portrayed animals in explicitly anthropomorphic terms. In 1898 Ernest Thompson Seton wrote *Wild Animals I Have Known*, featuring Raggylug the rabbit, Redruff the partridge, and Lobo the wolf, "King of the Currumpaw." In 1903 William J. Long went a bit too far when he suggested that a woodcock purposefully set a mud cast on its broken leg. The debate over animal stories was important enough that President (and naturalist) Theodore Roosevelt felt compelled to write on the issue, separating "scientific" nature writing from the "nature fakirs."[39] Anthropomorphizing animals led people to make moral judgments about them on human terms, rather than on natural parameters. Conservation was limited by these larger cultural attitudes and by available scientific knowledge. Utilitarian attitudes about nature and wild animals along with natural history traditions meant that conservation concentrated on preservation.[40]

As did others of his era, Albright separated animals into clear categories of "good" animals, such as the songbird and the elk, and "bad" animals, such as the cat and the wolf. In 1924 Albright's desire to protect the innocent creatures of Yellowstone prompted his decision to "finally eliminate cats entirely" from Yellowstone Park. Spurred by a national anti-cat campaign, Albright judged the domestic house cat "a dangerous animal" posing a great danger to the songbirds migrating through Yellowstone. He urged staff to dispose of cats to avoid any unpleasantness later on. These mental categories of good and bad animals helped shape the limits of preservation in Yellowstone during the early days of the National Park Service administration.

Many scientists and managers also saw these distinctions as logical and proper. During the army's administration and the early days of National Park Service administration, the cultural mandate to kill predators was reinforced by the fears of stockmen, who pressured federal agencies into conducting predator extirpation campaigns. The 1894 Act to Protect the Birds

4. "Coyote Jyp" pictured with naturalist E. J. Sawyer and tourists in 1925 near the buffalo corral at Mammoth Hot Springs. Unlike most Yellowstone predators, this particular coyote was perceived as tame and harmless, as an interesting encounter with nature. Courtesy Yellowstone Photo Archives.

5. Yellowstone Chief Ranger Sam Woodring feeds a fawn from a bottle, 1927. Woodring, like many of his time, had firm opinions on which animals were bad and which were good. Courtesy Yellowstone Photo Archives.

6. Woodring hand feeds elk, antelope, and bison in an enclosed area, 1927. In the early days of NPS administration, the elk were fed on an industrial scale, so great was the concern that they might go extinct. Courtesy Yellowstone Photo Archives.

and Animals in Yellowstone National Park had prohibited all hunting, killing, wounding, or capturing "of any bird or wild animal, except dangerous animals, when it is necessary to prevent them from destroying human life or inflicting an injury."[41] The National Park Service utilized a wide interpretation of "dangerous animals" as it joined the nationwide campaign to exterminate wolves and coyotes in the West.

In the spring of 1918, the Biological Survey detailed a hunter to help Yellowstone exterminate predatory animals. Ultimately, agents acting on the government's behalf killed 508 wolves from 1918–23 in Wyoming and South Dakota, and in Montana from 1918–30 agents shot or poisoned 413 wolves. Together with ranchers and bounty-hunters, the campaign to eliminate wolves in the West proved very effective, with the last wolves shot in the 1940s.[42] Albright thought that the parks could afford to be generous. In Yellowstone and Glacier, the NPS had not tried to kill all the mountain lions or the last wolves, because in those vast wilderness areas "we can afford the luxury of a few of even these cruel and destructive beasts."[43] For all practical purposes, wolves were extirpated from Yellowstone Park during the mid-1930s. While some members of government and scientific institutions helped eliminate the "bad" animals, a new branch of the life sciences started to crack the foundations of traditional attitudes toward wildlife.

During the first decade of the twentieth century, ecologists introduced ideas that eventually revolutionized how people thought about the national parks. During the 1920s a movement to preserve undisturbed "natural conditions" in selected locations throughout the American landscape comprised one of the most explicit and important connections between scientists and the National Park Service. Professional ecologists Charles Christopher Adams, Victor E. Shelford, and Barrington Moore, secretary of the Council on National Parks, led scientists' efforts to designate natural areas as scientific research reserves, writing and speaking on the subject during the late 1910s through the mid-1920s. Adams began by advocating protection of the "primitive" in America's undeveloped lands. During the 1920s ecologists modified the notion until it assumed a more solid definition as the protection of "natural conditions." Nonetheless, park defenders continued to use the term "primitive" through the 1930s.

Charles C. Adams was one of the most significant people in the scientists' movement to protect the primitive. Arriving from Harvard at the University of Chicago in 1899, Adams studied with Charles B. Davenport, Henry C. Cowles, and Charles Otis Whitman. He worked as a curator at the University of Michigan's Natural History Museum while completing his Ph.D., awarded in 1908. From 1908 to 1914 he served as an associate (i.e., a professor) in Animal Ecology at the University of Illinois. In December 1914 he attended the initial organizational meeting of the Ecological Society of America (ESA). The organizing committee included J. W. Harshberger, Shelford, Cowles, Robert Wolcott, Forrest Shreve, and Adams. In 1916 the New York State College of Forestry at Syracuse University named Adams assistant professor of forest zoology. Partly because of his experience as the director of the New York Natural History Survey, Adams stressed the importance of ecology in forming a basis for natural resource management. The ESA named Adams its president in 1923.[44]

During the early part of the twentieth century, zoologists followed the direction established by plant ecologists, applying the tools of ecological study to the world of animals. Shelford and Adams, who were classmates at the University of Chicago from 1901 to 1908, performed some of the earliest work in the field and went on to shape the discipline. Where Cowles had

7. Charles Christopher Adams. A well-known and active ecologist, Adams helped create the discipline of animal ecology. He played a significant role in bringing scientific study to Yellowstone Park, advocating the preservation of park landscapes so that scientists might study nature under "primitive" conditions. Photo from *Annals of the Association of American Geographers* 49 (1959), p. 165, copyright Association of American Geographers, courtesy Blackwell Publishers.

employed a physiographic method that emphasized the environment's role in plant succession, Shelford adopted an approach that investigated the organism's role in shaping its environment. In 1913 he published *Animal Communities in Temperate America*, which sought an explanation for succession by starting with physiography and proceeding to developing an understanding of the organism in its environs.[45] In 1913 Adams published *Guide to the Study of Animal Ecology*, also one of the first books in the field. He suggested that ecology concerned itself with fundamental biological problems, defining the object of ecological study as "the responses of organisms to their complete environments."[46] Shelford and Cowles participated in the nascent stage of research and analogy that eventually became known as the Chicago School, emphasizing "the organism-environment relationship as an interactive process."[47]

Thus the most important level of ecology for Adams was above the individual and aggregate (single species), in what he called associational ecology, which sought to describe the relationships among animals as well as between animals and environment. He traced this idea to the German naturalist Karl August Möbius, who proposed the term "biocoenosis" in 1877. Möbius had worked on oysters, developing his idea of the oyster bed as "a community of living beings, a collection of species, and a massing of individuals." It was not enough to examine the oysters, if one wished to explain what affected their population. Adams also used the word "biocoenosis" to describe a community where species and individuals continually possessed a certain territory. The important point is Adams's opinion that any "change in any of the relative factors of a biocönose produces changes in other factors of the same."[48]

Advocating the importance of ecological surveys, Adams pointed out the fact that experts in taxonomy traditionally designed the surveys used by museum expeditions and for purposes such as government surveys of fishery resources. The result was an economically useful list, but such surveys were of limited use for discovering relationships among animals. A descriptive element was still essential in ecology to study conditions and responses. Yet the scientist must do more than collect specimens; he must also gather "observations on the habits, activities, interrelations, and responses of animals."[49] Ecological surveys would have to be developed in a conscious and deliberate manner. Adams was self-consciously splitting away from natural history traditions as he helped create the field of animal ecology.

For Adams, field work was essential to ecology. He repeated the question posed by William Keith Brooks in 1899: "Is not the biological laboratory which leaves out the ocean and the mountains and meadows a monstrous absurdity?" Adams was certain that the answers to important questions would be found not in the laboratory but in the field. The ecologist must not simply collect, as was the wont of previous generations of naturalists, but learn to habitually "study in the field." By this he meant thinking, endlessly mulling over facts and observations: Had not Darwin and Wallace concocted the idea of natural selection while puttering about in the field? Evidence from the field helped the ecologist to arrive at the ultimate aim, "the interpretation of the responses of animals to their complete environment."[50] Adams wanted to arrive finally at explanation, not mere description. Ecologists today still struggle with this goal.

Adams gave the Park Service scientific reasons to protect the primitive, urging scientists to conduct ecological surveys to record animal "associations, their interrelations and responses to their environment—before they have become too much changed or exterminated." Adams suggested it might not be possible to save every type of environment, but he felt it important to at least preserve a record of the ecological relationships. Adams sought a study and documentation of "original conditions," which were vanishing with each succeeding generation. He wondered "if the naturalists of the future will commend our foresight in studying with such great diligence certain aspects of biology which might be very well delayed, while ephemeral and vanishing records are allowed to be obliterated without the least concern."[51]

Adams was not alone in his concern about preserving natural conditions on the American landscape. In 1916 E. W. Nelson addressed the National Parks Conference, where he made public his notion that Yellowstone had value "as a surviving picture of wild life as it existed over a large part of primitive [America] before the white man occupied the land."[52] Joseph Grinnell and Tracy Storer, scientists at the University of California's Museum of Vertebrate Zoology (MVZ) at Berkeley, also joined Adams in advocating the preservation of natural conditions.

During the early 1920s Grinnell became one of the instigators within the American Society of Mammalogists gathering opposition to the predator control policies of the Biological Survey.[53] Grinnell's career exemplified a period of transition in science. Starting out as a collector, he directed the MVZ at Berkeley for six years while studying for his Ph.D. He taught students in the traditional disciplines of taxonomy and vertebrate zoology, influencing an entire generation of scientists coming out of Berkeley. Although he used ecological concepts in teaching, recognized the role of competition, and made contributions to niche theory, he was not enthusiastic about some ecological studies proposed by his students. Storer later claimed that Grinnell resisted an ecologically oriented project he had proposed. This circumstance arose because Grinnell and other scientists were "living between two worlds," traditional natural history and the new animal ecology.[54] Natural history can be characterized as descriptive science that emphasizes information about the life history of animals. The tradition in America stretches back to the two hundred hand-colored prints in Mark Catesby's *Natural History of Carolina, Florida and the Bahama Islands*, published in parts from 1730 to 1743. Other famous American field naturalists include John and William Bartram, Alexander Wilson, and John James Audubon.[55] As used by systematists in museums, the natural history tradition embodied the world of taxonomy and questions of classification and distribution, in service to evolutionary questions. The new animal ecology sought to use quantitative methods to answer questions about the relationships between organisms and their environment. Grinnell's and Storer's 1916 article published in *Science*, "Animal Life as an Asset of National Parks," set forth their progressive ideas just as Congress established the National Park Service. The article suggests that their thoughts about the national parks reflected some of the latest ecological thinking but also reveals how widely shared concepts of their day limited conservation practices.

The balance of nature concept quietly underlay many other ideas naturalists and ecologists used when they described wildlife in the landscape. The idea that nature possessed a fundamental balance originated in ancient Greek philosophy. In 1749 Linnaeus wrote his essay "Oeconomia Naturae," putting a name (the economy of nature) to the balance of nature. The notion provided an unexamined background assumption well into the twentieth century, partly because it was poorly articulated, so it retained validity even when the evidence seemed to disprove the notion. With the introduction of Darwinian concepts, scientists started with traditional ideas about a static world and incorporated the notion of an evolving natural world. Yet as they acknowledged change in the biological and geological worlds, they generally failed to update the balance of nature. When scientists used the balance of nature concept during the early twentieth century in discussing wildlife, they implied some sort of population regulation—the numbers of elk or mice, for example, were kept in check by their predators. They also used the term to conceptualize larger issues such as the relationship between vegetation and wildlife. Scientists did not perceive the limits of the balance of nature idea, and so they made loose analogies to other concepts such as the biotic community.[56]

To "realize the greatest profit" from parks' native animal and plant life, wrote Grinnell and Storer, "their original balance should be maintained." Dead trees should not be cut down, because they "are in many respects as useful as living" ones; woodpeckers, which ridded the living trees of destructive insects, found sustenance as well as nesting sites in standing dead timber. They found downed timber also essential in maintaining a "balance of animal life," for decaying logs provided homes for mice and thus supported hawks, owls, fox, and marten. Undergrowth or thickets should not be destroyed in parks any more than necessary, because they provided "protective havens" as well as berries for birds, squirrels, and chipmunks. Nonnative species, they thought, should be excluded from the parks: "In the finely adjusted balance already established between the native animal life and the food supply, there is no room for the interpolation of an additional species." The well-known example of the English sparrow proved this point, that introduced species often competed so well that they displaced native species.[57]

Grinnell and Storer saw the predator situation very differently than did Albright, the NPS Ranger Division, and the Bureau of Biological Survey. The Berkeley scientists advised that predators in the national parks be allowed to "retain their primitive relation to the rest of the fauna," even if they levied a considerable annual toll on the other native animal life. These naturalists were convinced that prey species, such as mice and squirrels, had adjusted themselves to that annual and regular predation by carnivores. Like many other naturalists of their time, Grinnell and Storer thought of predatory animals, such as marten, fisher, fox, and golden eagle, as "exceedingly interesting members of the fauna."[58] In 1915 "interesting" meant that the animal was of considerable scientific curiosity, because naturalists knew very little about the species and were quite eager to know much more.

Grinnell and Storer argued for an absolute prohibition against the hunting or trapping of any wild animals in the parks. The principle was simple: "The native complement of animal life must everywhere be scrupulously guarded," especially along roads where the animal life was most likely to be seen by visitors, and thus had the "highest intrinsic value from an esthetic viewpoint."[59] Grinnell and Storer equated the removal of predators in the parks with the destruction of natural balance, and they gave an esthetic justification for preservation of that balance.

Yet their ecological understanding of the balance of nature in the national parks had limits. Nature might be adjusted, they suggested, so as to present the animal life of a national park at its best to the human visitor. Managers might increase native berry-producing plants, especially in the vicinity of camps and buildings, making up for thickets destroyed in building and road construction, allowing visitors to see a greater variety of bird life. They thought that local feeding stations during the tourist season would not alter natural conditions "in any serious degree."[60]

Other scientists shared the sentiment that wildlife should be made available to visitors. Vernon Bailey, chief field naturalist for the Biological Survey, wrote to Robert Sterling Yard, noting that the two had shared similar experiences when visiting Yellowstone. During his trip Bailey had seen very few animals: "I believe that the streams of huge, shrieking automobiles have driven these animals back some distance" from the well-traveled routes. Even chipmunks, numerous when oats had comprised the primary motive fuel in the park, were now seldom seen. Bailey believed that "it will become necessary to make a special effort to render the animal life more accessible" to park visitors, which might be accomplished by placing salt licks just out of sight of the roads and "distributing certain favorite foods for some of the smaller animals where it will bring them into conspicuous places."[61] Thus experts knowledgeable about wildlife advocated altering natural conditions in the interests of providing wildlife viewing opportunities for tourists. Nature by itself, they thought, did not accomplish the things that a park should provide for visitors.

In their ideas about manipulating wildlife for the benefit of tourists, we see the outer boundaries of Grinnell's and Storer's ecological thinking. Although visitors should be discouraged against destroying lizards and snakes in the parks, the rattlesnake was still fair game. Cooper and sharp-shinned hawks were destructive to small birds, and thus it might be advisable to reduce their number along roads and camps, so tourists would see the small songbirds. Their emphasis on the localized control of predatory birds to create roadside venues where tourists could see a variety of bird life demonstrates their conviction that naturalists might control nature, carefully arranging the wildlife for display.

Grinnell and Storer recommended that parks employ a professionally trained resident park naturalist, who not only would undertake educational activities for the public but would "familiarize himself through intensive study with the natural conditions and interrelations of the park fauna" and make practical management suggestions. Their concept gave each park the latitude to control predators under the sanction and direction of the resident park naturalist. They believed that naturalists were aware of the delicate interactions of nature and therefore would exercise the greatest caution in controlling predators.

Adams and his ideas about preserving natural conditions helped spark a larger movement originating in the ESA. In 1917 ESA President Ellsworth Huntington appointed Victor Shelford to head the new Committee on Preservation of Natural Conditions for Ecological Study, which functioned through 1946. By 1921 the committee identified nearly six hundred natural areas, many of them in the national parks, that deserved preservation. Emphasizing scientific rationales over recreational and aesthetic reasons for preservation, the committee's motto advocated "An Undisturbed Area in Every Natural Park and Public Forest." By 1921 about 10 percent of the ESA's membership enthusiastically joined the committee, which during the 1920s fought irrigation schemes in the national parks, including one intended for the Bechler Basin in southwestern Yellowstone. Scientists were concerned that logging and hunting were one step behind the farmers' dam, forever changing the original conditions found there.[62] Other organizations, such as the National Research Council, signed on to the campaign to preserve natural conditions. Perhaps scientists' most widely noted public statement on the subject occurred in December 1921, when the American Association for the Advancement of Science passed a resolution opposing the introduction of exotic plant and animal species into the parks. More importantly, the resolution opposed "all other unessential interference with natural conditions."[63]

Charles C. Adams remains central to this story, because he took a great personal interest in Yellowstone, and because he served as an early connection between science and the park, bringing ecological ideas to the National Park Service. Adams's central contribution to the development of rationales for park management was the idea that national parks provided a superb location for scientists to study ecological conditions. This notion proved attractive to scientists serving on advisory boards, who helped shape the Park Service mission.

Adams also contributed to science in the park in a very practical way. In 1919 he participated in establishing the Roosevelt Wild Life Forest Experiment Station, located at the College of Forestry at the New York State University in Syracuse, New York.[64] The idea of a biological research station was not unique to Adams or to his university. In 1888 scientists established the first American station for field research at Woods Hole, Massachusetts.[65] Based on European research facilities, the Woods Hole station provided a place for the study of marine biology, becoming a model for other field stations in the United States. The establishment of the early American field stations represented a movement to make biology a more quantitative science, effectively moving the discipline away from natural history traditions.

Parties journeying from Syracuse to Yellowstone National Park established their field headquarters at Camp Roosevelt, near the junction of the Yellowstone and Lamar Rivers.[66] Summer season housing at this location had been originally developed by the Wylie Permanent Camping Company, and the facility saw much activity during the early 1920s. Professor Alvin Whitney, also with the New York State School of Forestry at Syracuse, operated a Boy's Forest and Trail Camp from 1921 to 1923.[67] As director of the Roosevelt Experiment Station, Adams supported several of the earliest scientific studies of wildlife in Yellowstone. In 1922 Edward R. Warren published an article titled "The Life of the Yellowstone Beaver," while Richard A. Muttkowski's study on the food habits of Yellowstone trout appeared in the

Roosevelt Wild Life Bulletin in 1925. Edmund Heller, a staff member of the Museum of Vertebrate Zoology and co-author (with Theodore Roosevelt) of a book about African wildlife, turned his talents to a study of big game animals in Yellowstone in 1925.[68]

While some contributors to the *Bulletin* briefly visited Yellowstone, Milton P. Skinner spent much of his professional career associated with the park, working as Yellowstone's first park naturalist from 1920 to 1922. Skinner then secured an appointment on the staff of the Roosevelt Wildlife Experiment Station in August 1922 as one of two Roosevelt Field Ornithologists. He was promoted from "collaborator" to a "temporary appointment" as a Roosevelt Field Naturalist in February 1924.[69] In 1925 his voluminous study on Yellowstone's birds appeared in the *Roosevelt Wild Life Bulletin*, and in 1927 Skinner wrote a prescient article on predatory and fur-bearing animals of the park for the journal.[70] In 1925 Skinner also published *The Bears of Yellowstone*, in which he made some observations that shows him as a man of his time and others that presaged work done sixty years later. As did some other writers of his generation, Skinner assigned moral qualities to the animals he studied, writing that bears seemed to have some idea of personal cleanliness, so it was "probably true that the filthy specimens I have seen were the lazy, degenerate members of their race." He also defended the grizzlies against their undeserved reputation, writing "the more I know of grizzlies, the less do I believe that they were even the ravening monsters the nature-fakers would have us believe, or that they ever sought trouble unprovoked."[71] Skinner, a veteran of many days in the field, had observed the bears enough to make detailed comments on their food habits, information that became important later when biologists wondered how dependent these bears were on the park's garbage dumps. The bears ate roots and bulbs in the spring and berries at the end of summer, along with pine cones, timber ants, termites, and "fat juicy grubs," indeed "practically everything edible."[72]

In 1926 Adams became preoccupied as director of the New York State Museum in Albany, and no further projects were carried out in Yellowstone, although the station in Syracuse carried on scientific work, evidenced by publication of the *Bulletin* until 1941. Although the Roosevelt Experiment Station carried out investigations in Yellowstone for a relatively short span, Adams had successfully introduced the idea of preserving unmodified nature for scientific study within the boundaries of the park. Horace Albright, however, never embraced Adams's notion of preservation to protect an unmodified nature. Rather, he protected animals with the intention of providing tourists with the opportunity to see abundant wildlife. Yet the creation of the Roosevelt Experiment Station, and the connection between Adams and the advisory boards influencing national park policies, laid a foundation for later thinking about what the parks could protect and preserve. The great potential for ecological research in Adams's notions would be largely dormant for many years, reawakened from time to time when individuals undertook a specific ecological research project.

Barrington Moore, a professional forester elected president of the Ecological Society of America in 1919 and editor of the journal Ecology, also joined Adams in publicizing the need for preserving natural conditions in the national parks. When the Boone and Crockett Club published Hunting and Conservation in 1925, editors George Bird Grinnell and Charles Sheldon included Moore's essay titled "Importance of Natural Conditions in National Parks." Moore carefully explained the scientists' case for preserving parks in a natural state. People must see conservation in the broadest sense, wrote Moore, where the object was putting every acre of land to its "highest use." The importance of national parks for recreation was widely accepted, but the parks also offered an opportunity to study plant and animal life "in their natural surroundings."[73] Moore stated that scientists were becoming less satisfied with collecting and identifying, wanting instead to pursue new studies in heredity and environment. Laboratories were necessary but not sufficient; studying in nature's laboratory would enable scientists to study the processes of evolution and adaptation firsthand. Despite his recognition that the outdoor laboratory presented a world of constant evolution, Moore also saw a delicate balance of nature in the world he wanted to study.

Investigating the balance of nature made national parks important to science, thought Moore, as these were increasingly the last places left undisturbed. He argued that the "processes of nature are so delicately adjusted" that when people interfered with nature the results were entirely unpredictable.[74] Moore used Darwin's discussion of the chain connecting cats to clover as an example of the hidden links in nature. If cats ate the mice that preyed on bumblebee larvae, the bumblebee population would rebound, pollinate more clover, and thus the cats would inadvertently assist the growth of a field of clover. In America, Moore thought, species of animals had gone extinct precisely because people had upset the balance of nature by introducing nonnative fish and game animals to forests and parks and by removing dead trees.

Moore echoed Adams's thoughts on the usefulness of dead wood in nature. Where fallen trees gradually rotted, moss and ferns proliferated and created the most beautiful part of the forest. Parks must resist the urge to tidy up the forest, instead leaving the forest completely untouched. Yet the forest must be protected from fire, Moore believed. The place of fire as part of a natural regime was not part of Moore's thinking; it was simply outside the universe of possible ways to see fire at that time. Although Moore had progressed beyond the notion of rotting wood in the forest as waste, like most scientists he had not yet come to see the role of fire as a useful phenomenon in nature; it represented waste and tragedy.

Moore suggested that natural conditions in parks would add to people's enjoyment of the parks. Moore believed Yellowstone to be proof positive that when spared from hunting, wild animals in nature were not afraid of people. Without that fear wild animals approached people more closely in the parks, creating memorable opportunities for the tourist to observe wild animals in their native haunts. He also suggested a larger utilitarian objective for the preservation of natural conditions in the parks. Although civilization depended on the control of nature, Moore argued that it was safer and more effective to work with nature. Yet nature's laws must first be discovered, and the outdoor laboratory served best for the study of nature. The ultimate use of understanding nature's laws was in agriculture. Studies of natural conditions were "capable of adding to the sum of scientific knowledge which forms the basis on which rest the practical methods of cultivating crop plants and domestic animals."[75] For Moore there was an ultimately useful application for preserving natural areas in the parks.

Not only scientists but national park advocates as well spoke out on behalf of natural conditions in the parks. The best-known public advocate was Emerson Hough, author of *The Covered Wagon* and other western stories. In 1921 he suggested that the Park Service had done quite enough to publicize the parks in hopes of attracting tourists. Hough thought the "real question is how to retain the wilderness quality of these parks, so that there will be something worth selling to the public next year." For Hough there was something more than scientific interest involved as he advocated "sacred parts of the wilderness set apart by act of congress [sic] to be left unchanged forever." It could be argued that the idea of a national wilderness system originated from Hough's advocacy.[76]

Scientists' desire to study particular places free of human influence also established a powerful intellectual direction for thinking about America's wild lands. What was natural? The definition created during this time increasingly came to mean those places that humans did not inhabit. In the upper Yellowstone the first waves of the cattle and sheep frontiers had encountered only a very small group of Native Americans known as the Sheepeaters. Settlers in Bozeman and scientists in Washington could not imagine that the Sheepeaters had affected the landscape in any substantial way. Only very recently have scholars reexamined the role of Native Americans in the landscape history of Yellowstone. Hough's definition of the natural was common in American culture at the time, and by adding "wilderness" to his definition, he added cultural force to scientific justifications for the preservation of natural conditions.

During the 1920s wildlife research and management was institutionalized in the National Park Service in two organizational units: the Naturalist and the Ranger Divisions. The history of the Naturalist and Ranger Divisions tells us something about how the Park Service conceived its educational, research, and management functions, as well as the practical organizational difficulties in Yellowstone. A close collaboration between the park naturalists and the Ranger Division dates from the establishment of the first park naturalist position in Yellowstone. The park naturalist, often the holder of an advanced degree in some branch of the sciences, served as a park's expert on natural history, including wildlife. The Ranger Division was responsible for carrying out wildlife management activities. The rangers, who sometimes had a year or two of college science, possessed a high degree of practical knowledge and competence, which enabled them to gather some scientific data, carry out elk censuses, and perform other duties related to the management of wildlife. Shared assumptions of the naturalists and rangers as well as the occasional friction between them revealed the nuances of thinking about nature within the NPS.

Practical management of the elk was the responsibility of the rangers of Yellowstone, who had been trained by Horace Albright to protect the last of America's elk against the ravages of the hunter and the poacher. One of the rangers' functions was to patrol the northern boundary line, to protect the elk. As Ranger Peter Lawson herded elk from Hellroaring Creek into Slough Creek in late December of 1920, Chief Ranger James McBride reported so few elk had been killed that preservation of the herd was assured. Hunters from Gardiner had failed to get "their meat," because the rangers did such a good job of pushing the herds of big game back into the park. McBride noted that after rangers had herded the elk the entire month of December, "they seemed to have realized that it was impossible for them to get out of the park." The effort required rangers to be out in the "grazing districts" throughout the day, flagging the boundary line by day and building fires there at night. The work was difficult, and McBride noted that he needed more good men. Not actually more men, but men "dependable and fearless. The inconvenience of married men has been shown very clearly this month." Evidently the luxuries of married life had spoiled some rangers for the physically taxing duties of park ranger life. Counting 14,450 elk, Chief Ranger McBride personally supervised the feeding in Slough Creek.[77]

The Naturalist Division always remained the poor relative of the Ranger Division. Many of the features of the NPS interpretive program initiated in Yellowstone were utilized later by other parks. In 1895 Milton P. Skinner, while a college student, first visited Yellowstone. Employed by the Yellowstone Park Association as a hotel walking guide, he escorted visitors at the Old Faithful area, lecturing about the flora and fauna. Along with others, he advocated an educational program for the park, and in 1919 Superintendent Albright appointed Skinner a park ranger. In 1920 Albright named him park naturalist, creating the first full-time position for interpreters in Yellowstone National Park and thus professionalizing nature education in the park. The park naturalist represented a small fraction of the park staff, one person out of sixty-eight park employees, twenty-six of whom filled the ranks of the Ranger Division. Despite the efforts of John C. Merriam's Committee on Educational Problems in the National Parks, the educational function of the parks never materialized to the extent that they envisioned.[78]

According to personnel rosters, Yellowstone's park naturalist was expected to conduct scientific research—an indication that few boundaries existed between the interpretive and research missions of the parks during this period. The movement for educational use of the parks originally viewed interpretation and research as twin activities. Interpretive duties, however, limited park naturalists in the amount of original research they could accomplish. And few naturalist positions were created, so gathering the information thought necessary to game management became the province of the park rangers. Park Naturalist Skinner began work to establish a museum at Mammoth Hot Springs, exhibiting park fauna skinned and prepared by Chief Park Ranger Sam T. Woodring. In 1925 the park established a fenced area at Mammoth, so visitors would be sure to see the park's wildlife. Skinner also gave lectures about natural history, led nature walks, and created bulletins to be posted at points of interest. He was assisted by a few rangers detailed to help during the summer tourist season, institutionalized as seasonal ranger naturalist jobs in 1926.[79]

The genesis of interpretive work and the establishment of museums occurred in Yellowstone and Yosemite simultaneously. In 1920 Steven Mather invited Dr. Harold C. Bryant, economic ornithologist and educational director for the California Fish and Game Commission, to organize the Yosemite Free Nature Guide Service, which conducted nature walks and evening lectures. In 1921 Ranger Ansel F. Hall established the first park museum in Yosemite as well as the Yosemite Museum Association that would solicit donations for the museum. In 1923 the Park Service created a chief naturalist position, filled by Hall. At that time the Park Service established a Division of Education headquarters at the University of California at Berkeley.[80] After creating the naturalist positions, the Park Service sought to provide standardized training for naturalists based in the sciences. For admission, the field school required two years of college work or equivalent experience for all candidates.

In November 1929 the Park Service convened the first park naturalists' training conference at NPS Educational Headquarters in Berkeley. Here scientists and Park Service employees sought to define the role and duties of park naturalists. The naturalists' most important duty was to give information to the public, but who would compile the material? And how could scientific facts inform park administrators? Much discussion revolved around how ranger naturalists might add to the knowledge base in each park, conduct original research, and make scientific information available to rangers, administrators, and the interested public.

George Ruhle, Glacier National Park's first park naturalist, noted that research in parks could serve the educational program, but he also saw research as an appropriate part of "maximum utilization" of the parks, yielding "prestige and decorous advertisement." Participating in scientific research, he thought, prevented "mental stagnation" on the part of naturalists. Joseph Grinnell pointed out that scientific research was valuable in a practical sense, because the park naturalist was best placed to pass information to the park visitor. Grinnell added that some people were naturally better at teaching than at research; therefore, it might be advisable to develop two types of naturalists for the parks. Research specialists might be assigned to the headquarters branch, and specialists in information might be assigned to the educational staff.[81]

Dorr G. Yeager, appointed park naturalist at Yellowstone in 1928, spoke on creating species inventories for the parks. Either outside agencies or the park's own educational staff might undertake the task of making "a complete inventory of the floral, faunal, archeological, historical and geological features contained within our respective parks." Complete lists of birds, animals, and plants would be useful to park staff as well as visiting scientists. Other naturalists commented that such an inventory of natural park assets would make it possible to protect important features during the construction of park improvements such as roads, camps, and buildings. Scientists might also list unsolved scientific problems in the parks and search for solutions.[82]

The conference participants proposed a program of scientific research for the parks, in which the naturalist would have a significant role. C. Frank Brockman, Mount Rainier National Park's naturalist, suggested that eventually the park naturalist might take an active role in a park's research program. As a specialist, the naturalist should conduct research in his own field, recognize when research was needed in another taxa or subject area, and then carry it out with the advice of a university professor conversant with appropriate methods. Brockman argued that a naturalist should take on one major technical problem a year and perform associated research. It was not enough to pass along information gathered up from myriad resources. The park naturalists would not gain the respect of the Park Service or other scientists if they merely read others' work and assembled the information. Naturalists should "take a very decided, definite part in the research program," gathering firsthand knowledge and facts about park conditions and features, building a foundation for the park's educational work. Naturalists were recruited, noted Brockman, from colleges and universities, the position application clearly stating expected requirements, hence "very rarely does anyone enter this work without the desire to do original work." The naturalists focused on the problems with carrying out Brockman's vision. Contemporary staff levels had difficulty handling administrative problems, therefore adding the additional work of a research program was problematic. Nevertheless, the feeling was that each naturalist should enter into some sort of research activity, no matter how limited. The conferees proposed that the director of the Park Service should engage park naturalists in research as soon as possible.[83]

The conference revealed a general recognition that very little was known about the natural resources in the parks, an acknowledgment that there was a desire among educated and motivated NPS employees to perform more research in the parks, and a feeling that research could directly aid administrative decision making. Yeager spoke on how recorded scientific information might inform park administrative programs. It would be best to have scientific information available for ready access when problems arose, said Yeager. If park flora and fauna were to "be maintained in the best possible conditions" parks must utilize scientific information. If a species was decreasing in a park, information was required before any ameliorative action could be taken. Yeager suggested that before "beginning work on a predatory animal problem" all the scientific facts should be "carefully accumulated."

Yeager's proclaimed caution about gathering information before beginning any predator control was belied, however, by the conscious effort of Yellowstone rangers to exterminate coyotes and mountain lions, even as Yeager spoke to his fellow naturalists. The information he had published only months before in Yellowstone's *Ranger Naturalists Manual* explained the park naturalist's position quite clearly: Mountain lions and coyotes, killers of big game, were to be shot or trapped. Policy on predators was created from popular knowledge and an attitude justifying human control over nature, not from direct scientific inquiry.[84]

A gap existed among ecological understandings in academe, the naturalists of the NPS Educational Division, and the Ranger Division. The Educational Division served as the birthplace and nursery of ecological ideas within the National Park Service. Grinnell, an active participant in the movement to revise predator control policies in federal agencies, attended the first NPS naturalists' meeting. His presence was much more than symbolic. At the time of the conference, Grinnell was struggling to preserve Yosemite National Park from excessive development, advocating the idea that Yosemite become an "open-air classroom, a sanctuary where every native resource . . . would be protected and studied in its natural environment."[85] Grinnell, along with a well-known field biologist from Berkeley named Joseph Dixon, attended the conference intending to shape the Educational Division along lines they believed scientifically up-to-date as well as advantageous to the Park Service. Partly as a result of the conference, in 1930 the NPS reorganized the Education Division as the Branch of Research and Education under the leadership of Harold C. Bryant. This was one of the roots of scientific research within the NPS.[86]

Did the most avant-garde ideas of the Education and Naturalists Divisions filter through to the rangers? One way to answer this question is to examine attitudes toward predators among the naturalists and rangers. In 1922 Rob-

8. Assistant Park Naturalist Dorr Yeager poses with Barney the bear cub, 1931. Courtesy Yellowstone Photo Archives.

ert Sterling Yard wrote an article about America's national parks for the *Survey*, in which he remarked that wildlife in the parks remained "untouched." The national parks were "national museums of the original American wilderness," embodying the American ideal of nature conservation.[87] Yard was fundamentally mistaken about the preservation of an untouched nature in Yellowstone. The National Park Service, despite Albright's protectionist stance on other wildlife, killed predatory animals in Yellowstone until at least 1933. The habit was deeply ingrained. Albright noted that issuing permits to government employees to hunt predators on days off "caused considerable trouble among the men without permits." In 1920 fur prices were so low that the operator of the Cooke City stage stopped carrying a rifle, but the incentive pay for predator skins evidently kept the park employees motivated. In 1921 Superintendent Albright reported the continued efforts of Ranger Henry Anderson "to exterminate coyotes, wolves, and mountain lions."[88] In April rangers killed a large male wolf and then located and dug out a den and killed the eleven pups. Other animals also found Yellowstone unwelcoming during the 1920s. A family of otters at Fish Lake (present Trout Lake) had found the fish planted by the Bureau of Fisheries an abundant source of sustenance. Arno B. Cammerer, assistant NPS director, notified Albright that because the otters were classified as predatory, they could be removed by a Mr. Clarence Olsen, who had applied for a permit to trap them.[89]

In 1927 Yellowstone compiled its first *Ranger Naturalists Manual*, and in 1929 the park produced the volume in hardback. The manual reveals what park naturalist Dorr Yeager expected his summer assistants to know, as well as some aspects of Yeager's thinking on wildlife. Ranger Naturalists could read up on tourists' most common questions, as well as specific information on botany, Yellowstone's geology, the history of the park, and how to be an effective nature guide. A section on zoology was divided into three parts: birds, reptiles, and predatory animals. The information on predatory animals was written not by Yeager but by Sam T. Woodring, former chief ranger at Yellowstone and, by 1929, superintendent of the newly created Grand Teton National Park. Many species of predatory animals and birds were known to exist in Yellowstone: cougar, wolf, coyote, lynx, bobcat, otter, marten, bald and golden eagles, osprey, horned owl, and pelican. In February 1928 National Park Service officials shortened the list, officially designating only a few of those as predatory, namely the cougar, wolf, coyote, and bobcat. In other words, these four species remained on the list of "bad" animals that had no place in Yellowstone. The complaints of stockmen and the idea that predators "destroyed" big game created this categorization. Common knowledge did not assign a significant role to bear predation on wildlife or stock.

Woodring called the mountain lion "our most destructive predatory animal," which was "fortunately, very scarce in Yellowstone Park." After the last known kill by a lion in 1929, the offending "killer" was tracked and shot the following day. Woodring noted that mother lions trained their cubs in "the art of killing," and when game was plentiful perhaps six big game animals might fall prey in twenty-four hours. The wolf was "another destructive animal in the game fields." Woodring thought they had migrated out of

Yellowstone, because the last authentic report he knew of occurred in 1923. Woodring noted that the trappers of yesteryear knew that wolves migrated to new places every few years. "Certainly," wrote Woodring, "if the wolves were as plentiful as coyotes, we would have no deer, sheep, or antelopes in the park today."

The coyote killed more animals than the other predators because of its slyness and its high rate of reproduction. Since the time when settlement had pushed the coyote up into the mountainous regions of the West, Woodring argued, the species had become "one of our most cunning destroyers of big game animals." During winter seasons he claimed to have counted 50 deer carcasses more than once that were "the unmistakable victims of coyotes." Coyotes had adopted the tactics of wolves, hunting in pairs or in packs, ev-

9. Ranger Sam Woodring poses with a group of wolf pups that rangers had dug up out of their den, c. 1920. These pups were destroyed after a series of photos was taken. Courtesy Yellowstone Photo Archives.

10. Sam Woodring, superintendent of Grand Teton National Park, 1930. Courtesy National Park Service, Harpers Ferry Center.

ident from the many tracks seen around carcasses. Coyotes were ravenous: They devoured "whole carcasses of full grown antelopes and deer." Although for eight years park rangers had shot and trapped about 250 coyotes annually, it seemed that the coyotes' reproduction kept up with this toll on their numbers. Woodring thought northern Yellowstone contained as many coyotes as ever. Ranchers adamantly stressed the negative role of predators, but many professionals in state wildlife agencies, the Bureau of Biological Survey, U.S. Forest Service, and National Park Service shared those views.[90]

The NPS Ranger Division did not embrace the attitudes of the Branch of Research and Education. The Educational Division and the Ranger Division were organized separately, and no mandate for communicating scientific information between the divisions existed. Information from the naturalists went on demand to the park superintendent, but communication with the Ranger Division was informal. Park rangers at Yellowstone did communicate with the chief park naturalist, Dorr Yeager, but acceptance of new ideas in Yellowstone was limited by cultural conceptions of nature. The park naturalist would have faced an uphill struggle in advocating the protection of predators when the entire ranger corps was paid bonuses for shooting them. Indeed, a park naturalist operating too far outside contemporary cultural norms risked removal by the park superintendent. C. Frank Brockman noted that during the 1920s and 1930s, science did not have the cachet it had later. The early park naturalists were considered impractical, and were often referred to as "posy pickers" or "nature fakers" by other Park Service personnel. Brockman wrote that the naturalists were "neither fish nor fowl." They were different enough from members of the Ranger Division to be labeled "Sunday supplement scientists," yet they also lacked full status in scientific communities.[91]

The founders of the Park Service did not emphasize the new ideas from ecology embodied in the "preservation of natural conditions" during the 1910s and 1920s. Rather, Albright's and Mather's interest and emphasis was developing tourism in the parks. Yellowstone's actual creation as a park owed much to the influence of railroads, and the two men's early interest in promoting tourism set precedents for the park. An additional reason for tourism development may have been Mather's desire to build up a political constituency for the parks. Building the bureau and defending the parks from commercial development meant encouraging use of the parks, primarily focusing on increasing support for the NPS. Biographer Donald Swain paints Albright as participating in "unabashed boosterism." When driving through the park, he sometimes stopped to flag down buses so tourists were sure to see the wildlife. Albright visited campgrounds at night, regaling tourists around the campfire with stories about Yellowstone's history. His booster tactics were "all part of his and Mather's strategy to increase Park Service appropriations by increasing park usage."[92]

During this time a regional movement encouraged tourism in the western United States. Beginning in 1902 a group of businessmen associated with the Salt Lake City Commercial Club initiated a campaign to unite the mountain states in a "tourist trust." In 1905 Fisher Sanford Harris published a headline that became the movement's calling card: "See Europe if You

11. Superintendent Horace Albright, a perennial booster for the parks, undoubtedly fed the bears on more occasions than the one pictured here in 1923. He remained convinced that the park should try to make wildlife easily accessible to tourists. This endearing custom came with significant costs, including damage to automobiles, injuries, and the removal of "troublesome" bears. Courtesy Yellowstone Photo Archives.

Will, But See America First." Harris and other boosters used nationalistic and patriotic themes, as they sought to utilize the West's scenery as an economic asset.[93] The western national parks functioned as important draws for a budding tourist industry. The concomitant development that enabled and encouraged the Park Service to develop its landscape with tourism in mind was the widespread availability of automobile transportation. First admitted to the park in 1915, the automobile quickly dominated. After only one year authorities decided it was best to simply cast aside horse-drawn transport in favor of Fords and Buicks. A growing segment of the American public found their new auto-mobility enabled them to visit Yellowstone, where the Wylie Permanent Camping Company helped meet their needs for low-cost lodging, while "sagebrushers" brought their own camping gear.[94] The growth of automobile tourism and auto-camping contributed to the origins of the twentieth-century wilderness movement, as gentlemen such as Robert Sterling Yard objected to Park Service plans for skyline drives in the eastern parks.[95]

Another reason the early administrators of Yellowstone focused on tourism was the entire rationale behind public parks. The American Civic Association and the American Society of Landscape Architects were both early twentieth-century advocates of the parks. Those who produced the rationales for public parks were closely allied with those producing the grand designs for the parks, and with the people administering them. From the early days of the Park Service, the professions of engineering and landscape architecture held sway in the organization and power structure of the NPS. Mather's division chiefs, Charles Punchard, Daniel Hull, and Thomas Vint, were all trained in landscape architecture.[96] To Mather and his associates, there was no conflict between preservation of natural resources and human use of the parks. In their minds development properly designed and executed carried out the purpose of preserving the park's resources for the future. They assumed tourism would proceed apace and that their role was to create facilities that blended in with the landscape, rather than intruding on nature. Ultimately, the direction and momentum established by the founders of the Park Service and by Mather and Albright predisposed the NPS toward emphasizing tourism first and placing other ideas and agendas further down their list of priorities.[97]

Another important limitation to embracing ecological notions and the preservation of natural conditions was the sheer weight of natural history traditions that pervaded some scientific institutions and their applications of science in Yellowstone. Practical science in Yellowstone reflected disciplinary concerns and boundaries of the time, as well as the personalities engaged in science and park administration. Science in Yellowstone also exemplified unsettled relationships between scientists and the wildlife protection movement. An incident in Yellowstone involving a bear-collecting expedition from the California Academy of Sciences demonstrated the strength of natural history traditions in institutional settings as late as 1920.[98] The episode is important, because the resulting bad press made Park Service administrators reluctant to permit further scientific collecting in Yellowstone and made Albright rely more on his own judgment rather than consult with scientists outside the Park Service.

Barton W. Evermann, an ichthyologist and the director of the California Academy of Sciences, first applied to the secretary of the interior in 1915 for permission to collect four grizzly specimens for a museum exhibit. The secretary demurred, writing that gathering specimens for museum display or collections was against park policy, but permits were issued to institutions needing bears for live exposition in public zoological gardens.[99] Four years later Evermann wrote to Steven T. Mather, regretting the extirpation of the California Grizzly, the most appropriate bear for museum display because of its large place in California history. The next best thing would be to exhibit a group of Yellowstone grizzlies. Evermann was under the impression that the grizzly was so abundant in Yellowstone that "it is desirable to reduce their number somewhat from time to time."[100] The academy would need "an adult male (the biggest we can get)" plus a female and two cubs. Although such a display would have an educational and scientific value, Evermann used one more argument to kindle Mather's interest, suggesting that a group of Yellowstone grizzlies on display in San Francisco "would prove a very fine advertisement of the Park."[101]

Actually, there was already some question about the relative abundance of bears in Yellowstone. In 1910 G. O. Shields, founder of the Camp Fire Club of America, publisher of *Outdoor Sport*, and self-styled "pioneer in the sledge hammer method of game protection," noted his conversations with photographer W. H. Wright, who was familiar with Yellowstone Park. Wright thought that soldiers and "privileged attaches of the park" were killing bears in large numbers, suggesting that in only a few years the number of bears had been reduced by more than half.[102] Nobody really knew how many bears existed, but impressionistic estimates were the only sort of figures available.

Relations between the California Academy and the National Park Service started out on a friendly basis. In March 1919 Albright (as NPS assistant director) visited Evermann at the San Francisco museum with Joseph Grinnell of the University of California and National Park Service landscape engineer Charles P. Punchard. In February 1920 Mather himself granted a permit for Evermann to collect a representative group of four bears—one male, one female, and two cubs. Evermann selected the team that would actually carry out the work, which consisted of Dr. Saxton Pope, a San Francisco surgeon and principal agent for the California Academy; his assistant Paul Young; W. J. Compton; taxidermist Paul Fair; Pope's brother, Gus, from Michigan; Judge Hobert of Detroit; and cook Art Cunningham—all a rather dubious selection by the California Academy. Ned Ward Frost, for whom Yellowstone's Frost Lake was named, provided the local guide and outfitting services.[103] By mid-June, shortly after the expedition's arrival in Yellowstone, embarrassing news accounts and criticism of the park appeared. It seems that this adverse publicity for the park started when the expedition's cook gave his account to a local newspaper.

Few creatures in the world are more aggressive than a mother grizzly with cubs, especially when she is surprised, approached, or disturbed. Saxton Pope and Young began their collecting efforts by maneuvering as close as possible to such a sow with her cubs, so they might employ bows and arrows; there were "a few minutes of uncertainty in the world of science as the arrows failed to stop the onrushing mass of fur and muscle."[104] Frost stepped in with his rifle to save his clients from an early demise, and Pope collected the sow and one of the cubs. A telegram to Evermann from the field describing this first encounter also precipitated public news from the West Coast of a bow hunt for bears in Yellowstone.

Because Evermann was particularly interested in small cubs, Pope's party began to look for another specimen, which they encountered with the cubs' mother. As if he did not know what would happen, Pope later explained to Director Mather that "the bear attempted to attack my brother, G. D. Pope, of Detroit, and he was obliged to shoot her with the rifle."[105] Now Pope had three bears, and when Albright encountered the party as they shifted about the park, he warned them that their permit called for four specimens and he would allow no more. Pope asked for the assistance of Ranger Henry Anderson in securing a large male grizzly, which rumor placed on the eastern edge of the park in the Absaroka Mountains. Albright had specifically "refused to permit any of the Canyon Hotel bears to be killed, because I felt that this would spoil the amusement for the tourists."[106] Pope now gathered his party and headed not for the east boundary, but directly toward the area around the Grand Canyon of the Yellowstone, and Canyon Hotel.

Pope did not require many days to discover the habits of grizzlies in the area of the Canyon Hotel. Every night bears followed a well-worn path as they came to feed at the garbage heap. Using an old, abandoned cabin for cover, Pope and Young waited there on a bright moonlit night. A sow and cubs appeared, and believing they "must secure the type of animal wanted by the Museum," the men of science again let fly with arrows. When the sow grizzly charged, Pope saw well enough in the moonlight to strike home "with an arrow in the heart at a distance of less than forty yards." Just at this moment a large male grizzly appeared, making "demonstrations of a very alarming character. Not only were we endangered, but he was a very desirable specimen."[107] Pope again let fly, and so near the Canyon garbage dump the team collected a male, a female, and a cub grizzly. In total Pope killed and skinned seven grizzly bears in the interests of science, exceeding his permit by three specimens. The expedition collected one adult male, three adult females, two two-year-old cubs, and a small yearling cub. Before they were able to leave the park, rangers seized and impounded all the specimens.

Once the news hit the press, the fact that someone was killing Yellowstone's bears completely overshadowed any information about the intentions of the expedition and the scientific and educational benefits that had motivated granting a permit. The Interior Department received many public complaints about the deaths of the bears. Director Mather was demonstrably livid, promising that he would confront Evermann personally if presented with an opportunity. Assistant Director Arno B. Cammerer regretted the bad publicity; after all, Mather and Cammerer had intended for the whole thing to be accomplished quietly and had always assumed rifles would be used. Albright wrote to Evermann, advising him that the park was "particularly anxious that no general statement of the final results of Doctor Pope's hunt should be given to the press."[108]

The immediate result of the publicity was that tourists began asking Superintendent Albright and the rangers if Yellowstone had embarked on a campaign to exterminate the grizzly. Albright complained that "not a day goes by that we do not receive protests from tourists, who come to the office and to the ranger stations and ask if something cannot be done to stop the killing of Grizzly bears." For the public, the roles of rangers, wildlife, and the park were very clear. The park should be a haven of protection and shelter against the guns of the hunter, and in the public mind there was not much scientific value in these dead collections. For visitors, Yellowstone bears belonged in the forest, not in a faraway museum. Albright believed he was in a "tangle that only a lot of explaining will clear up."[109]

Saxton Pope wrote to Albright in mid-July, a very brief letter of only six lines, asking the park superintendent to simply forgive and forget, promising he would never do it again, and regretting any trouble. Pope thought that criticism of the Park Service was coming "from longhaired men, or shorthaired women. . . . All we want now is the hides. Ask [Park Ranger] Scoyen if he sent them."[110] This terse reply to Superintendent Albright did not endear the California Academy of Sciences to the hearts of National Park Service officials. Pope also offended Charles C. Adams. Responding to Adams's letter of protest to Barton Evermann, Pope informed Adams that his excessive love of animals probably had "its origin in subnormal endocrin [*sic*] secretion." Pope further suggested that his account, written "in the vernacular of the sportsman," would continue to thrill "when all your monographs crumble on the dusty, forgotten shelves of time."[111] Albright wrote to Director Mather, suggesting that the episode with Pope comprised the "basis for recommending that under no circumstances shall the National Park Service grant another permit for killing animals in this park for museum purposes."[112] Albright now considered collecting a dangerous policy, because it would inevitably bring criticism of the Park Service. Albright clearly based his new collecting policy on what it meant for the park's public image. This was Albright's first major fiasco with wildlife and administrative policy, and not his last embarrassment.

The "scientists" from California had abused the trust extended by Albright and Mather, never to regain it. Yellowstone shipped four of the bear skins to San Francisco, but soon Saxton Pope and Barton Evermann were writing conciliatory letters seeking the remaining three specimens. Evidently educated by Evermann in the arts of gentlemanly deportment, Pope now wrote a very long missive, assuring Mather that the expedition had "tried to observe the spirit of conservation," and related their feelings at the time of the expedition that the success of the museum's collecting expedition should outweigh any small infraction of the permit. Pope asked Mather to "give your official pardon to our excess of Zeal, believing that we did it in the interest of science and with no other motive."[113]

These words proved hollow when the October issue of *Forest and Stream/Rod and Gun* hit the newsstands. It contained an article by Saxton Pope titled "Hunting Grizzly with the bow: that the age-old implement of the chase still holds its place among modern weapons is conclusively proved by two California sportsmen." Pope described: how his team had lured the bears with bait; tracked wounded bears through the forest, finding pools of blood along the way; the sudden "roar like dinner-time in a menagerie"; maddened beasts milling about in pain and surprise; the surprise charge of an enraged sow; and the kills by bow and arrow. Pope reported a most gratifying feeling, having killed the bears "fair and clean with the bow and arrow." Even guide Ned Frost was impressed: "Now I know that you can shoot through and kill the biggest grizzly in Wyoming."[114] In other words, it was a lurid account aimed at hunters pining away the closed season and dreaming of bigger adventures. Notwithstanding Pope's pretensions about being a connoisseur of hunting technique, this article sealed the fate of museum collecting missions in Yellowstone for quite some time.

Employing the influence of mining executives and friends who knew Yellowstone's concessionaires as well as Mather and Albright, Evermann pushed and prodded for another year, seeking possession of the entire lot of seven specimens. Indiana Senator Harry S. New asked Mather to overlook the excess number of specimens, claiming that after years of hunting together he knew Gus Pope was not a game hog: "This trip of theirs was a great big outstanding sporting event with which we can all afford to be pretty liberal."[115] Evermann worried that the skins in Albright's possession might be in better condition than the ones in California, and the academy promised to send three back. In the same letter, however, Evermann suggested that because the bears were already dead and they would be in the hands of scientific men, how could Albright really object to sending them on? But Albright was willing to discuss only which skins would be sent to California, clearly unwilling to trust Evermann with all the specimens at one time. Mather and Albright held the California Academy to possession of only the originally permitted number of specimens. Four years later the indefatigable Evermann still attempted to secure permission to reenter the park to secure another cub and a yearling.

Mather believed that for Barton Evermann, the only issue was skins, ostensibly for scientific study and practically for display. But for Mather, ethical questions as well were involved. Those questions started with the fact that Pope had betrayed not only the technical letter of the collecting permit but also an implied trust. In 1921 the main issue was not killing seven individuals of a rare species, for the numerical status of the grizzly bear population simply never came up as an issue for naturalists or administrators. The problem with the bear-collecting expedition involved the Park Service mission, and tourists vociferously brought it to Albright's attention. For both administrators and the public, Yellowstone represented a place of protection for animals, although a human-centered ethic proved the driving force. The special nature of the national parks had been violated, their unique purpose of protection and preservation cheapened.

The negative publicity surrounding this episode undoubtedly sensitized Albright to issues surrounding the protection of wildlife in Yellowstone, as well as the concerns of conservationists and the general public. The bear-collecting expedition made Albright a more ardent preservationist and even more sensitive to criticism than he already was. In 1921 his regrets about the Pope expedition centered on the embarrassment to the Park Service—Albright suggested that Evermann delete any reference whatsoever to Yellowstone National Park from the display in San Francisco. Albright regretted issuing the permit in the first place and wished he had detailed park rangers to collect the specimens rather than allowing any outside party to conduct the work. Albright's feeling that no one could be trusted with a gun in Yellowstone set a lasting precedent.

Three years later, however, a new concern entered Albright's correspondence when he denied additional collecting permits to the museum. Albright wrote to Stanley A. Easton, manager of the Bunker Hill & Sullivan Mining and Concentration Company in Kellogg, Idaho, who was lobbying on behalf of Barton Evermann. Albright explained that neither Mather nor the secretary of the interior would be inclined to permit the killing of any more bears in the park, partly because "there are not many grizzlies in the Park, and we do not want to disturb what we have."[116] This is the first indication in written records showing any concern over the number of bears. Although Albright had worried about Yellowstone's visible big game for some time, until the second proposed collecting expedition, the possibility of harm to the bear population was not an issue.

During the 1920s national conservation groups became more organized and sought to influence the management of the national parks. At the same time, the Park Service built connections with the institutions of conservation and science. Conservationists, scientists, and National Park officials worked together very closely. Conservation groups in the early 1920s included the Camp Fire Club of America, organized by the mercurial anti-hunter G. O. Shields. On its subcommittee on parks were T. Gilbert Pearson, president of the National Association of Audubon Societies, and Frank R. Oastler, an ornithologist who participated in several other public service organizations. During the 1920s the Izaak Walton League was the largest and one of the most active conservation organizations. Many Yellowstone park employees belonged to an active chapter that met in Mammoth Hot Springs, with Superintendent Horace Albright often in attendance. While the Sierra Club, the American Game Protective Association, and National Audubon Societies had memberships under seven thousand, the Izaak Walton League boasted more than a hundred thousand members nationwide.[117]

The National Conference on Outdoor Recreation was not a nongovernmental organization per se, but it attracted a wide variety of people interested in progressive ways of dealing with the problems of a modern technological society. In effect, it continued a movement that began during the

Progressive era: Theodore Roosevelt chaired the first conference in 1924, and it met on at least two more occasions, in 1926 and 1928. The conference convened, according to Robert Sterling Yard, as a result of the need for clear thinking amid a great boom in enthusiasm for outdoor recreation, partly brought on by the automobile and the popularity of motor touring. Yard pointed out that "recreation" meant more than diversion; it was the only word that could encompass "Conservation, preservation, purification of polluted waters, restoration of disappearing species, education, mental and physical health, and spiritual inspiration."[118] All these were the concern of the National Conference. John C. Merriam, director of the Carnegie Institute in Washington DC, addressed the first convention to discuss the values of wildlife. Also speaking out for wildlife were Frank M. Chapman, an ornithologist at the American Museum of Natural History in New York City, Charles C. Adams of the New York State College of Forestry, William T. Hornaday, Robert Sterling Yard, and Barrington Moore, secretary of the Council on National Parks, Forests, and Wild Life. Printed as a Senate document, the first conference's proceedings in Washington revealed the widespread interest in natural areas as therapeutic agents for a modern nation.

The National Parks Association, established in 1919 by Yard, successfully influenced thinking about the national parks' purpose. Yard was associated with the National Park Service from its inception. When Stephen Mather went to Washington to take charge of the new Park Service, he brought Yard at his own expense to serve as the bureau's publicity director in Washington. An experienced journalist, Yard wrote articles that brought favorable publicity to the Park Service. Together with Mather, Yard established the National Parks Association (NPA), but soon friction developed between them.

Yard's ideal vision of the parks was embodied in his campaign for "National Park Standards," an effort to restrict the national park designation to only landscapes of truly national interest. The National Park Standards defined the parks as large land areas that were essentially in their "primeval" state, superior in quality and beauty, lands that quite naturally deserved to be preserved for people's education, inspiration, and enjoyment. Of particular interest was the NPA's idea that parks would be "a sanctuary for the scientific care, study, and preservation of all wild plant and animal life within its limits, to the end that no species shall become extinct." This urge to preserve species on the brink of extinction was shared by many people of the time, including Horace Albright and conservationists with an interest in Yellowstone. The NPA urged that "wilderness features" in parks "be kept absolutely unmodified." The relatively natural conditions found in the parks struck knowledgeable observers as unique qualities worth preserving. Finally, National Park Standards urged that "sanctuary, scientific, and primitive values must always take precedence over recreational or other values." Thus during the 1920s the NPA saw not only the danger of industrial intrusions into the parks but already worried about the proper balance between use and preservation.[119]

The NPA also formed an important link between scientists, conservation organizations, and the parks. George Bird Grinnell served as president of the NPA during the 1920s, and its board included Irwin Laughlin, regent of the Smithsonian Institution, Vernon Kellogg, secretary of the National Research Council, Frank R. Oastler, member of the Executive Committee of the National Conference on Outdoor Recreation, and Charles Sheldon, vice president of the Boone and Crockett Club.

Scientists influenced the emerging character of the National Park Service through social networks and by serving on advisory boards. One good example of this sort of influence was the connection made between the Roosevelt Wild Life Experiment Station and the National Park Service. Yellowstone's association with the Roosevelt Station also points to the national context of park preservation during the first two decades of the twentieth century, which shaped the direction of park wildlife policies. The membership of the Roosevelt Wild Life Experiment Station's advisory board suggests the instrumental connections the Park Service was forming in its early days. On the Wild Life Station's Honorary Advisory Council sat Dr. George Bird Grinnell, Dr. Gifford Pinchot, Dr. Frank M. Chapman, and Colonel Henry S. Graves, among others.[120] This advisory board had a great deal of potential for influencing the direction of the NPS, because these gentlemen were leaders of conservation in Washington. Brought together at events such as the National Outdoor Recreation Conferences convened by President Calvin Coolidge from 1924 to 1929, scientists shared ideas with governmental leaders of conservation and attempted to shape the direction of the NPS.

Hermon Carey Bumpus, an eminent naturalist and from 1902 to 1911 director of the American Museum of Natural History in New York, occupied a central role in the early interaction between the scientific community and the National Park Service. He made lasting contributions to park philosophy and the interpretive function of parks. Bumpus was an enthusiast for the outdoor study of nature, which fostered his portrayal of national parks as outdoor laboratories. In 1919 the American Museum appointed him chair of its Committee on Outdoor Recreation. Bumpus was convinced that conservation required public education, and hence he sought financial support for the first trailside exhibits and museums in the national parks. That support came from the Laura Rockefeller Memorial Fund, and the first museums were built in Yellowstone beginning in 1930. In 1928 the secretary of the interior appointed Bumpus to serve on a special committee that would consider educational problems in the national parks, and he served through 1931. He also chaired the National Parks Educational Advisory Board from 1929 to 1935. These two committees formulated the national park interpretive mission.[121]

Bumpus was a great enthusiast for conservation. After his first trip to Yellowstone, Bumpus proposed a "Temple to Conservation" be built near the junction of the Yellowstone and Lamar Rivers, where Teddy Roosevelt had reputedly camped. A long hall would feature the statue of Roosevelt at one end, and the statues of other conservationists such as Grinnell along the sides. Wings jutting from the building would hold a conservation library and Albright's papers concerning the beginning of Yellowstone Park. Displays of Yellowstone's rocks and plants would surround the building. Although his ideas on trailside museums were well received, Bumpus did not succeed in persuading others to embrace the Temple of Conservation.[122]

Bumpus presented his program for Yellowstone museums to the 1928 meeting of the Committee on Outdoor Education. His plan called for a series of trailside museums, rather than one central museum such as the one at Yosemite. The proposed plan also called for a memorial to conservation to be erected on top of a hill near the thermal terraces at Mammoth Hot Springs. Robert Sterling Yard indicated to Carnegie Institution President John C. Merriam that he was not absolutely opposed to such a memorial, but the time was not yet right. Only with the passage of time would the meaning of Yellowstone in conservation history become clear. Roosevelt and Grinnell had only a peripheral relationship with Yellowstone; if there was to be any statue, it should be of the Montana lawyer Hedges, who reputedly had dreamed up the national park idea. But the statue was unnecessary, because National Park Mountain loomed over Hedges's campground and thus already served the purpose of a monument to conservation as embodied in the national parks. At a convention of museum experts, Bumpus asked Yard what Merriam's board might object to. Yard told Bumpus that Merriam's board was "not objecting to things doing, nor rivaling anybody's building; that we were interested in great underlying principles upon which every educational undertaking must depend for real success."[123] Indeed, in setting up a framework for public education in the parks, the committee attempted to shape the parks toward something more than tourist attractions. Mather and Albright utilized tourism as a method for building the agency, encouraging tourism in the parks, participating in the "See America First" campaign, and finally building campgrounds designed to facilitate automobile touring in the parks. By devising an educational function in the parks, the American Museum's Committee on Outdoor Recreation fashioned an important adjunct to the promotion of tourism. Educational purposes for the parks also represented an important avenue through which scientists and conservationists influenced public expectations for the national parks. The parks became places not only to view inspirational scenery but also to learn about nature.

In 1927 the National Parks Association formed an Advisory Committee on Educational and Inspirational Use of National Parks, soon containing twenty members including James R. Angell, president of Yale University; Clarence Cook Little, president of the University of Michigan; Ray Lyman Wilbur, president of Stanford University; Frederic Delano, chairman of the Joint Committee on Bases of Sound Land Policy; Vernon Kellogg, secretary of the National Research Council; Frank R. Oastler, National Conference on Outdoor Recreation executive committee member; George D. Pratt, president of the American Forestry Association; and Charles Sheldon, vice president of the Boone and Crockett Club. John C. Merriam chaired this committee and was also elected to the board of the NPA in 1927. Merriam's conception of the Committee on Educational Problems in the National Parks, as it came to be known, was a group established to gather the opinion and judgments from national leaders in education and science and from those who studied the inspirational values of nature. The committee would examine "fundamental questions in education and research which have bearing upon the great problems presented by National Parks."[124]

Significantly, these luminaries of the scientific world and leaders of conservation thought education, science, and inspiration to be the three main pieces of the national parks. Inspiration was not the least of their triad of concern. As he discussed the opportunity for parks such as Yellowstone to present the geologic history of the earth, Merriam noted that the "work of the Creator's hand presents itself here in such a way that all may comprehend."[125] Merriam waxed mystical when he addressed the trustees of the National Parks Association meeting at Washington's Cosmos Club in 1927, suggesting that if visitors to Yosemite gazed upon the great walls and only heard water falling, they were missing "the great essential." The stupendous waterfalls and sheer towers of rock lived not just in their physically evident forms today but also "in their great meanings." National parks must be more than mere places to study flora and fauna; after all, that might be accomplished in many places. In the national parks the public had the opportunity to not only see birds, flowers, and animals but also to comprehend "the vast thing which is behind them." The parks should be set up not only for teaching science, but also "for realizing whatever else it is behind these wonderful spectacles that we call inspiration."[126] Merriam and his associates took seriously the idea of encouraging the highest uses of the parks.

In 1929 as Merriam worked on plans for the new Parc National Albert in the Belgian Congo, the advisory group came up with the idea of closing sections of Parc Albert completely, not only from general visitation but from all entrance. Closing certain park areas would serve first to keep the primitive qualities intact, and second to maintain wild behaviors of the animals. There was a hazard that under complete protection, wild animals would become domesticated, behaving differently than under "normal primitive conditions." Places where hunting was permitted might be more similar to actual primitive conditions than would an area of complete protection. It was not enough to preserve the lives of animals; rather the "conditions of life" must also be preserved. Merriam suggested that people would find domesticated deer that wandered among park buildings very different from "the wild, sensitive creature seen in its native habitat in the wilderness."[127]

At the same time that the National Park Service sought connections with conservationists and scientists, the agency also sought to differentiate itself from other organizations. Yellowstone came into conflict with other agencies over boundary arrangements and wildlife policies. By 1926 Albright was in the process of rethinking his relationship with the land management agencies abutting Yellowstone. He wrote to the Wyoming Fish and Game Commission, suggesting more hunting outside the park "in view of the great increase of herds during the past few years." The second subject of his letter was a more delicate matter. Someone close to the Wyoming game commission had heard a nature lecture in Yellowstone that had criticized hunting. Albright for years had criticized the "game hogs" and went so far as to call Montana's game laws "uncivilized." Now Albright sought to patch things up with the people responsible for the game laws in Wyoming. He assured the commission that "any statements deploring the sport of hunting in this vicinity" did not have the approval of the park administration.[128] Yellowstone rangers had been instructed to say nothing derogatory about hunting, and if the commission liked, the nature lecturers would be instructed to encourage sportsmen to come to the surrounding areas to hunt. Historian Donald Swain credited Albright with an "intuitive political shrewdness," and indeed Albright cultivated the Wyoming Game Commission for a purpose. During the 1920s park advocates sought expanded boundaries for Yellowstone. Wyoming and the NPS started negotiations in 1926 and completed the first boundary adjustments to the park in 1929, when the eastern boundary line was redrawn to follow natural topographic divides along mountainous ridges at the head of river drainages. At that time Yellowstone gained a net seventy-eight square miles, but the Wyoming Game Commission and the U.S. Forest Service were satisfied with the arrangement, because it promised easier administration of the particular watersheds under their jurisdiction.[129]

The second proposed boundary adjustment at this time originated in 1926 when Montana Senator Burton K. Wheeler passed legislation securing funding for a new highway to the north entrance through Yankee Jim Canyon as well as authorization for adding approximately seventy-six hundred acres of land just northwest of Gardiner. This area reaching from the Yellowstone River up toward the high slopes of Electric Peak contained important antelope winter range and during the 1930s was referred to as "the Game Ranch."[130] Albright suggested in 1926 that perhaps the Wyoming Commission would like to reconsider its opposition to this proposed boundary adjustment. Albright sent a mixed message as he reassured the Wyoming Commission that lands north of the park acquired for a game refuge would be utilized "of course, only in bad winters" and be turned over to the Biological Survey or the Forest Service so that hunting could continue under the Montana Fish and Game Commission.[131] Formed in New York, the privately funded Gallatin Game Preservation Company acquired most of the Gardiner addition and deeded the land to the United States, and in 1932 President Herbert Hoover proclaimed the area part of Yellowstone Park. Because the land was added to Yellowstone, it was never opened to hunting. Thus by the 1920s relationships between the state game commissions and Yellowstone were problematic, and rivalries occurred for jurisdictional authority over wildlife management.

The first time people thought about Yellowstone as an ecosystem was not in the 1970s when the word was well known; rather it was during the 1920s when elk began to forage among ranchers' hay bales in the Yellowstone Valley north of the gateway community of Gardiner. Each summer the elk herd in northern Yellowstone tended to scatter into high elevation habitats in the park and to the north in the Absaroka forest. In winter the elk drifted down to elevations below seventy-five hundred feet, congregating in the Lamar River Valley and trekking as far as fifty miles down the Yellowstone River Valley to rangeland at five thousand feet elevation near Yankee Jim Canyon, seventeen miles north of Gardiner.[132] William Rush described the migrations as "slow, deliberate movements occurring largely at night."[133] A bunch of elk might take two to three weeks to move from Mountain Creek in the high country down to Hellroaring Creek and the immediate vicinity of the Yellowstone River. Many observers believed that natural migration routes and access to normally available winter range had been shut off by farms and ranches. Conservationists and neighboring ranchers advocated various solutions including feeding. The accepted wisdom of the day noted a land problem, and conservationists, government officials, and scientists all agreed that more winter range for the elk should be secured. Despite some common ground, perceptions of the elk and land problem did intensify early rivalries between the Forest Service and the National Park Service. Some of the land desired for elk winter range already had been incorporated into the Absaroka National Forest. The Forest Service was unwilling simply to give over its lands on demand, and the problem was of sufficient dimension to create official investigations. The National Conference on Outdoor Recreation asked the President's Committee on Outdoor Recreation (five cabinet-level officials, including Secretary of the Interior Hubert Work) to look into the matter of boundary adjustments to the national parks. On February 10, 1925, the President's Committee duly organized a commission that included Charles Sheldon of the Boone and Crockett Club; Colonel W. B. Greeley, chief of the U.S. Forest Service; Stephen Mather, director of the NPS; Barrington Moore of the Council on Parks, Forests, and Wild Life; Duncan McDuffie of the Sierra Club; and Arthur Ringland, secretary of the National Conference on Outdoor Recreation. In 1925 and 1926 the commission went to the field, investigating park and forest boundaries at Sequoia, Mt. Rainier, Rocky Mountain, Grand Canyon, and Yellowstone. In 1926 Congress authorized additions to the Absaroka and Gallatin National Forests, in 1928 appropriating $150,000 for the purpose.

From the beginning of the NPS, Albright had fought special interest efforts to chip away at Yellowstone. During the 1920s irrigationists in Idaho sought to build a dam and reservoir at Bechler Meadows in the southwest portion of the park, or better yet have Congress cede the land to Wyoming. In 1929 proposals to transfer 340 square miles from Teton National Forest to Yellowstone at the southeast boundary for the protection of elk and moose, eliminate 40 square miles at the southern boundary to permit the Forest Service to use the Snake River for the transportation of forest products, and eliminate 27 square miles at the southwest boundary for the water reservoir on the Bechler River brought the President's Boundary Commission to Yellowstone Park to investigate the situation. Olaus J. Murie, employed at that time by the Bureau of Biological Survey, was appointed coordinator of personnel from the Forest Service, National Park Service, and the state of Wyoming to make investigations for the Boundary Commission. Murie and the other game biologists visited Yellowstone in June of 1929. The commission sought information on elk and moose in the southeastern area of Yellowstone "to determine whether complete sanctuary is necessary under Park Service administration" by adding the upper Thoroughfare region (at the very headwaters of the Yellowstone River in the park's southeast corner) to Yellowstone Park, or whether "the public welfare will best be served" by continued hunting under the administration of the Wyoming State Game Commission. The central questions involved migration of elk and moose: Did elk in the southern part of Yellowstone migrate east, south, or north? Second, did hunting cause the elk in southern Yellowstone to migrate east, or did it push them north to join the northern Yellowstone herd, thus exacerbating problems there?[134] What is interesting about the public hearings held in Cody, Wyoming, on July 15, 1929, and in Washington DC on February 3, 1930, was the widely shared notion that the national parks served as game refuges. The land problem of winter range, the propagation of game animals, and hunting were all inextricably woven together. Sportsmen's clubs opposed the extension of park boundaries because they did not want hunting removed from the jurisdiction of Wyoming. Elk hid in parks and evaded their guns; because hunting was prohibited in parks, hunters opposed enlarging Yellowstone. Many observers thought that hunting made elk reluctant to come out of game refuges. Murie, on the other hand, thought that "migratory movements of animals are strongly fixed habits and I seriously doubt if hunting affects the ultimate winter destination of elk."[135]

From the park's perspective, elk and particularly moose near Bridger Lake needed "the complete sanctuary of national park administration," because by some estimates the number of moose had declined by 90 percent as the result of hunting pressure. Game refuges, thought Albright, were abso-

lutely necessary to encourage and protect a breeding number, ultimately
creating good hunting in the surrounding national forest areas. Adding territory to the park would include "a natural part of the Yellowstone Park, a
logical continuance of the natural lines of the Absaroka Range." Although
the protection and propagation of big game still dominated the thinking of
many people, wider views on the importance of nature's constituent parts
began to appear in Yellowstone during the early 1930s.[136]

The early days of Yellowstone Park set important precedents for wildlife
management. A national movement to protect big game species focused
on a Yellowstone Park thought to be one of the last refuges for elk. First the
army, then federal and state agencies responded to that movement, to
become part of the driving mechanisms of a protectionist (or "preservationist") form of conservation. Many people thought of Yellowstone in these
sorts of terms, as more or less a game refuge. Albright's attitudes about
hunting along with his fears about the possible extirpation of elk in the Yellowstone area made him a firm believer in the park as wildlife haven. Yet academia proposed changes in conceptualizing the parks even as the National
Park Service set up shop.

During the early days of the National Park Service, interactions between
conservationists, scientists, and bureau personnel influenced the mission of
national parks. Scientists advocated not only educational uses for the parks
but also the preservation of natural conditions so that a scientific bench-
mark might be established on the federal landscape. Charles Adams's experience in Yellowstone helped form ideas about scientific opportunities for
the study of natural landscapes found in the parks. Grinnell and Storer
brought ecological issues into a national discussion regarding park conservation. While Adams and others sowed the seeds of an ecological vision for
Yellowstone, the California Academy's bear-collecting expedition revealed
the strength of natural history traditions in the institutions of science and
conservation. The Yellowstone Boundary Commission, created in response
to political pressure from the USFS and irrigationists in Idaho, included the
expert testimony of Olaus Murie and opened doors for a wider audience to
think about natural or ecologically based boundaries. During the next thirty
years Murie became an important advocate of Yellowstone as an ecologically
whole wilderness. An ecological view of Yellowstone progressed by incremental adjustments in thinking about the parks as places to preserve natural
conditions.

THE WILDLIFE DIVISION AND THE ECOLOGY
OF INTERVENTION

In the early summer of 1930 a small group of men arrived at Yellowstone Lake. Launching rubber boats, they investigated a principal nesting area of the trumpeter swan, whose numbers had been reduced to a paltry few by reckless sport and market hunters. Representing the newly formed Wildlife Division of the National Park Service, George Wright, Ben Thompson, and Joseph Dixon brought with them protectionist impulses, a problem-solving interventionist style, and a dawning ecological awareness. The story of their presence in Yellowstone illuminates a time of transition for agencies dealing with wildlife in America, a period when actions and strategies changed from protection to management.[1] The activities of the NPS Wildlife Division in Yellowstone also demonstrate that management decisions resulted from a complex interaction between scientists, management imperatives derived from the agency's orientation to tourism, shared understandings of park purposes, and political pressure from outside the park, as animal lovers and hunters expressed their conceptions of Yellowstone's identity. The scientists of the Wildlife Division carried out two major wildlife research projects in Yellowstone: They acted to save the trumpeter swan and American pelican, and they investigated the feeding habits of the park bears. Additionally, they offered their opinions on the northern elk herd and entered an ongoing debate over predatory animals.

The Wildlife Division's involvement in Yellowstone during the early 1930s reveals several things about the state of science and of the parks.[2] First, the balance of nature formed an essential understanding of nature, widely shared at the time. That basic understanding of nature can be termed an "equilibrium" paradigm, an understanding of nature common to National Park Service administrators, biologists, and the conservation community at large during the 1930s.[3] The 1934 decision to control the population of the northern elk herd within Yellowstone Park demonstrated a general consensus among administrators, scientists, conservationists, and sportsmen about the need for perpetuating a stable balance between ungulates and range. Saving Yellowstone's pelicans and controlling the elk herd, beginning in 1934, served the larger purpose of restoring the ancient balance of nature so rudely disturbed by civilization's processes. Yet this common understanding of a balance of nature did not necessarily yield a harmony of action—a public controversy over Yellowstone's pelicans demonstrated tensions within the conservation community.

Second, the Wildlife Division embodied a growing ecological awareness, in large part thanks to a growing relationship between the National Park Service and Joseph Grinnell's Museum of Vertebrate Zoology at the University of California, Berkeley. In *Saving America's Wildlife*, historian Thomas Dunlap asserts that mammalogists of the 1930s developed relatively sophisticated ecological understandings that led them to appreciate the role of predators in a properly functioning natural system. Acting through professional societies, this group sought to change federal predator control policies.[4] Historian Richard West Sellars argues that Wildlife Division scientists created an ecological orientation in the NPS during the 1930s that declined during and after World War II. The story of the Wildlife Division in Yellowstone reflects these themes.[5]

Third, actions of National Park Service scientists during the controversy over the predator pelicans demonstrate that in the early 1930s they acted as much out of preservationist values as from ecological theory. Preservationist thinking identified crisis situations involving the potential extinction of a single species, such as the prairie chicken, the trumpeter swan, or the American white pelican. Ecological thinking, on the other hand, involved explanations of how elements of nature functioned or related to one another. Despite their ecological sophistication, biologists working for the NPS Wildlife Division also thought in straightforward ways about the preservation of single species in Yellowstone, with the trumpeter swan and the pelican the objects of their attention. While they did think about the balance of nature on Yellowstone's lakes in ecological terms, these biologists had no hesitation about interfering with natural processes in the interest of preserving a species in danger of extinction.

A fourth emergent theme was the confidence with which the NPS sought to manipulate and control nature. It was no coincidence that the profession of game management matured during the 1930s and that its birth was associated with Yellowstone. First convened in 1902 at Mammoth Hot Springs, the National Association of Game and Fish Wardens and Commissioners organized wildlife professionals. Protecting Yellowstone's elk represented part of their efforts to guard vanishing wildlife populations. George Bird Grinnell, William T. Hornaday, and George Oliver Shields led a popular movement for state hunting licenses, bag limits, and specified hunting seasons. The association supported such legislation and hoped to assist in prosecuting game law violators. The problem of migratory waterfowl came to dominate their concerns. Members of the society, many of whom also belonged to the American Game Protective Association, voted resolutions favoring passage of the Weeks-McLean Act (1913) and the Migratory Bird Treaty Act (1918). While helping assert state authority over wildlife, the organization also acknowledged federal authority over migratory birds. Success in controlling harvests contributed to confidence in a maturing discipline of wildlife management.[6]

Curt Meine writes that by 1925 some of the essential preconditions for the professionalization of wildlife management were in place: professional associations, the employment of state and federal game wardens and biologists, and professional programs offered by universities. During the 1920s Aldo Leopold formulated the basic theory of wildlife management. The sustained yield concept, similar to the basic principles of forest management, played a prominent part in his thinking. By the mid-1920s Leopold promoted a philosophy of "managing" game, partly by increasing production to produce a surplus that could be harvested. If a particular game refuge prohibited hunting, the game population would increase and overflow out onto the surrounding range. Hunting would take only the surplus and not endanger the core population. The states created refuges, most of which allowed hunting. A notable exception was the Jackson Hole refuge, established to provide winter forage that had been lost to agriculture.[7]

In 1930 the presentation of a comprehensive wildlife policy at the American Game Conference marked an important milestone in the professionalization of game management. A second indicator of the new professionalism in wildlife management was a growing number of graduate programs and the appearance of Leopold's *Game Management* in 1933.[8] During the 1920s Yellowstone Superintendent Albright manipulated wildlife, but his actions were either preservationist oriented (e.g., protecting elk from wolves), or aimed at presenting wildlife to the public in specific locales. In the 1930s the

Wildlife Division's manipulation aimed at bigger things: to control succession on the northern range, and to train entire generations of bears to new behaviors. At the same time that the Wildlife Division of the NPS incorporated new ecological ideas, it also embodied a managerial ethos.

Continuing use of the word "problem" indicates how scientists and administrators viewed their charge. Wildlife experts were convinced that human activities had played a large role in upsetting the balance of nature, and their job was to tweak the system back into a proper balance. Importantly, some administrators and scientists shared interpretations of what they perceived to be "natural." They were partly correct in their assumptions, yet ultimately they had too much confidence in their ability to understand and control nature. In this, the Park Service paralleled the U.S. Forest Service and the Bureau of Biological Survey, which also asserted that humans could and should shape landscapes toward desired purposes. Essentially, many ideas about how to manage wildlife in Yellowstone were as much derived from a growing culture of wildlife managers as from an ecological approach.

During the 1920s Charles Adams, Joseph Grinnell, Tracy Storer, and others had created the notion of preserving the primitive in national parks. "Natural conditions" described nature free of corrupting human influence, the factory and fence of modernity, a landscape in its original condition. The question of how to fulfill this purpose for the parks had now become understood in two very different ways. The men of the Wildlife Division sought to return the parks to their primitive state through the manipulation and control of nature. Although their scientific advice on bears and elk reflected a managerial ethos, a few NPS personnel doubted human ability to know enough about nature to proceed with an interventionist ecology of control. In the NPS Washington DC office, Arthur C. Bryant questioned the tactics advocated by other members of the Wildlife Division as he advocated the desirability of watching nature unfold in Yellowstone.

The case of Yellowstone's predator pelicans demonstrates a transition from tradition-bound ways of thinking about the parks in utilitarian terms toward a new emphasis on protecting all animals, regardless of their perceived usefulness. The newer view owed debts to efforts to preserve single-species and the growing ecological understandings of the natural world. Critics of Yellowstone's policies have portrayed the park as arbitrarily setting its own wildlife policies, but from the inception of the Park Service in 1916, Yellowstone was tied to a national network of advice and scientific authority that in the early 1930s included scientists of national stature as direct participants in policy decisions.[9] Products of their own time, these scientists sometimes offered advice embedded in the professional and popular cultures of that era. Significantly, scientists of the National Park Service's Wildlife Division during the early 1930s clearly envisioned the national parks' purpose and drew from that vision to bolster their scientific justifications for protecting the pelican in Yellowstone.

The episode also reveals schisms within the conservation community. Along with Horace Albright, the National Park Service's Wildlife Division considered themselves experts and resented the intrusion of a vocal outsider into their established domain. NPS staff viewed Rosalie Edge as a sentimental preservationist, a somewhat hysterical Cassandra, protesting over a small matter better handled by professionals. Ultimately, it was not science alone that saved the Yellowstone pelican but an interaction among scientists, Yellowstone Park administrators, and the radical tactics of Rosalie Edge, a conservation activist who shared NPS scientists' vision of the park's purpose.

Native to Yellowstone National Park, white pelicans established a breeding colony on one of the two small Molly Islands, located at the far reaches of Yellowstone Lake's remote southeast arm. The controversy over the Molly Island pelicans began in 1889, when the U.S. Fish Commission started a fish-stocking program for the waters in the western part of Yellowstone Park. By 1902 the commission established an egg-collection station at Thumb on Yellowstone Lake. Associated with a hatchery at Spearfish, South Dakota, the station collected eggs from the native or black spotted trout (Salmo lewisi) and by 1909 enjoyed a reputation for success. In 1910 the hatchery at nearby Bozeman, Montana, took over operations in Yellowstone, and by 1914, there were three egg-collection stations in the park as well as a fish hatchery near Lake Hotel.[10] Large quantities of trout eggs were taken from Yellowstone Park, five million in 1915 alone, and planted in waters throughout the country.[11] In the middle of the decade Yellowstone's trout fishery quickly declined, and fishermen's creels went empty. Three possible causes of the problem were identified: market fishing to supply the park's hotels, sport fishermen, and finally the native fisherfolk—the pelicans, osprey, otters, and mergansers. Note that the collection of native trout eggs by the fish cultural station was not entertained as a possibility for the fishery's decline. The park restricted the fishing operations of the Yellowstone Park Hotel Company in 1917 for the purpose of improving sport fishing, and in

1918 (as ecologist Charles C. Adams later told the story) "the pelicans and gulls were condemned for serious injury to the trout." In 1919 certain parties recommended that the number of pelicans be reduced; the people most interested in a reduction of pelican numbers were the men at the fish cultural station.[12]

Not only was the supply of fish faltering, but many fishermen complained that their catch in Yellowstone was "wormy." Filleting their day's limit, they discovered long tapeworms inside the fish, a most unappetizing sight, and the Fish Commission heard about this state of affairs. This particular parasite (*Diphyllobothrium cordiceps*) had been identified by Joseph Leidy when the 1872 Hayden expedition brought back specimens to Washington. In 1922 the U.S. Fish Commission employed Dr. Henry Baldwin Ward to study the pelicans to determine if they carried the parasite in its adult stage. Head of the Zoology Department at the University of Illinois at that time, Ward had already served as president of the American Fisheries Society in 1913 and founded the *Journal of Parasitology* in 1914. In short, Ward was a nationally known expert in parasitology but also was known for his solid work in fisheries.[13] Upon his arrival, Ward found concerns other than parasites commanding his attention.

12. The fish hatchery and its dock on the edge of Yellowstone Lake, at the lake development, 1928. Courtesy Yellowstone Photo Archives.

The men of the Fish Commission in Yellowstone had more pragmatic worries; they knew that pelicans ate fish, and the commission wanted to know just how many trout and eggs were consumed by pelicans each season. Hence Ward ignored the parasites and performed some of the first research into the food habits of pelicans. With Joseph L. Hyatt, an assistant in zoology at the University of Illinois, Ward spent approximately ten weeks in the park during the summer of 1922. Living at a cottage near the fish hatchery on Yellowstone Lake, Ward and Hyatt were "afforded many privileges and constant assistance" by the superintendent of the hatchery, C. B. Crater. Ward believed that the findings of his study were enough to direct policy and "support it if at any time it becomes the subject of public or official discussion."[14] Later events demonstrated not only how experts differed but also how scientific opinion changed through time and how science sometimes served the interests of the agency that employed it.

Ward and Hyatt visited Molly Island a total of eight times. They concealed themselves on the lakeshore near the island while observing the pelicans for days, watched in one-hour observation periods the birds feeding at creek inlets and along the lakeshore on a daily basis, and gathered information about pelican sightings from Park Naturalist Milton P. Skinner, several rangers, and visitors as well. Adult pelicans were shy to begin with and even more so after Ward's first visit to the island when he managed to catch two pelicans for captive study; thereafter, whenever Ward's party approached the shore the entire adult pelican population would rise up into the air, leaving their nesting areas undefended. Ward determined the rumor that young nestlings poked their bills into their parents' throats to feed was simply untrue. Parent pelicans, after feeding for half a day, would disgorge their catch in small piles on the ground for the young to feed on. After examining these piles and dissecting a few pelican stomachs, Ward concluded that the native trout comprised 98 to 100 percent of the pelican diet. Concealed on the shore of a creek or the Yellowstone River, Ward used a field glass to watch pelicans feed in the gravel shallows. Pelicans caught at least two large fish per hour, so in fishing for about six hours a day a pelican would consume about twelve fish. And pelicans could eat many more small fish: Ward learned from a game warden that a pelican had been collected with 235 young fish in its stomach; another dissection revealed 45 fish from three to six inches in length. If there were 500 pelicans in the colony eating 12 fish a day, that take of 6,000 fish per day would add up to 300,000 fish over the 50 days of the trout spawning season. Unfortunately, Ward wrote, the pelican nesting and hatching season coincided precisely with the trout spawning season. The future supply of trout was adversely impacted by the loss of eggs to the pelicans; from a daily catch of 6,000 trout, the loss of eggs would be 3 million. In two weeks, said Ward, the pelicans took more eggs than did the fish hatchery in a season. Additionally, sport fishermen only caught 25,000 or perhaps 30,000 fish in 1922, only 10 percent of the pelican catch. Ward's conclusion was that the pelican "probably contributes to the reduction in abundance of the trout more than all other influences combined." The recent decline in the sport fishery could not have been caused by excessive fishing, nor could the parasite be blamed, because S. A. Forbes's survey of Yellowstone Lake in 1890 showed the parasite Diphyllobothrium abundant. If the pelican were awarded the same strict protection afforded most other wildlife in Yellowstone, "the present difficulty might be considerably accentuated." Ward compared the pelicans to the lynx and wolf, suggesting that like other predatory animals the colony of pelicans should be controlled. This would be accomplished most easily by methods suggested in his own work; all the eggs over a previously determined number should be destroyed. Ward finally cautioned that the eggs should be taken carefully so that the colony was not chased away entirely from Molly Island: "A limited tax on the fish of the lake is justified to support so unique and interesting a bird as the pelican."[15]

Ward's analysis of the "problem" facing the U.S. Fish Commission and the National Park Service was constructed in wholly economic terms. The relationships that he saw between fish and pelicans, between fish and humans, and between pelicans and fishermen were entirely economic ones. In an age when the Bureau of Biological Survey used economic ornithology to prove the value of nongame bird species by demonstrating their insect-eating capabilities, some scientists as well as managers thought that a simple examination of what the pelicans possessed in their gullet would reveal what harm or good they did, and hence what value they represented. This kind of analysis that used economic terminology, reasoning, and values comprised an economic wildlife ecology that was manifestly anthropocentric in its management implications. This economic ecology had its roots in natural history traditions and a progressive managerial ethos.[16] Although Ward and others used very crude models that could not analyze complex ecological relationships, they believed they were on the right track and possessed confidence in their work. Differential mortality was still a gleam in some ichthyologist's eye. The goals of the men at the fish hatchery comprised the superimposed context for what Ward saw as an objective scientific examination of the pelican "problem."

In 1924 the NPS and the U.S. Fish Commission began activities aimed at controlling the number of pelicans on Molly Island. During this time Horace Albright was superintendent of Yellowstone. Information about the pelican culling was not assembled in any methodical way until late 1931. Harry J. Liek, former assistant chief ranger at Lake Ranger Station during the late 1920s, wrote to Yellowstone Assistant Chief Ranger George W. Miller: "Little did I think that I would have to account for the skeletons of those pelicans when I was killing them." Liek estimated that in 1926 about 200 eggs were destroyed, and in 1927 personnel had killed 83 young pelicans, because "a lot of the early hatch got away, and in 28 we killed 131 every young pelican on the island, [sic] that year nothing escaped."[17] Captain C. F. Culler, district supervisor of the Bureau of Fisheries based at LaCrosse, Wisconsin, who visited and worked at Lake Station from 1923 to 1930, estimated that "practically 80% of the eggs and young were destroyed to prevent any great increase in the flock." If there were 150 mating pairs, that would mean about 240 eggs and young were destroyed each year that he worked in the park. Culler reasoned in terms of economic relationships and utilized the logic of control. In the years before Lake Hotel caught fish for dinner and before the tourist traffic increased, "the pelicans were allowed there to keep the lake from becoming over populated." Culler evidently believed that control over the fishery resources of Yellowstone was entirely his domain. With the increase in tourist traffic brought by the automobile, it was "necessary to curb the predicious [sic] bird so that the [tourists] will continue to enjoy good fishing at all times."[18] Clearly, neither the Fish Commission, the park naturalist, the chief ranger, nor the park superintendent had ever kept a record of killing pelicans on Molly Island. No formal plan was ever devised or written; this was an entirely ad hoc management program carried out in a place largely hidden from public view. Off the shores of Yellowstone Lake, the U.S. Fish Commission had taken management into its own hands with the compliance of a cooperative Park Service.

The first scientist to question the purposes of the U.S. Fish Commission was none other than Charles C. Adams, director of the Roosevelt Wild Life Forest Experiment Station. In 1925 Adams publicized his views on wildlife's role in the national parks, addressing the pelican matter specifically. In the *Roosevelt Wild Life Bulletin* he reviewed the history of the trout egg-collection program at Yellowstone Lake, noting that so many eggs were shipped to neighboring states that "by 1917 the depletion of the small streams between the Thumb and the Lake Hotel was recorded." From 1918 the Bureau of Fisheries had blamed the pelicans for the noticeable reduction of trout numbers, but now Adams defended the pelicans. The trout depletion was "primarily due to the too extensive egg collecting, and to the commercial use of trout on tables; and secondarily, to excessive angling; and lastly, and least of all, to the pelicans and the gulls." Adams's analysis of the situation stood in stark contrast to Ward's, as did his solution. Adams suggested that fish culture activities, the collecting and distribution of fish eggs, had no place in a national park. The only safe way to preserve the supply of trout was "to absolutely prohibit the shipment of trout eggs outside of the Park." This was the first challenge to the Bureau of Fisheries, and it clearly influenced thought among Yellowstone's staff.[19]

In 1929 Fred Foster, described by Superintendent Roger B. Toll as the fish culturalist at Yellowstone Lake and by himself as the district supervisor of the Rocky Mountain Region for the Bureau of Fisheries, reported to Toll about the lake's trout status. He identified the pelican as one of the "chief enemies" of park fish. The pelican had some biological and aesthetic value, but "the disciples of Audubon should bear in mind that the trout are 'footing the bill' and that the fishermen will be 'good fellows' only up to a certain point." Foster castigated the otter and mink as "killers who frequently destroy far in excess of their needs" and were seldom seen by the park visitor. The park had allowed them to increase without control, and he had received reports "of serious depletion in certain waters through their activities." Foster said it was urgent that otter and mink "be placed upon the unprotected list" and that rangers should trap them until they were "reduced to proper numbers."[20] Foster used the anecdotal reports of fishermen to explain how it was that otters and mink were responsible for reduced numbers of trout hooked on the angler's line. Actually, there were no data on fishing success; and neither could he present any data on the food habits of nature's other fishermen, the otter and mink. Foster's reasoning encompassed the calculations of the fish culturalist and the production manager.

On July 30, 1930, Maurice C. Hall, chief of the Zoological Division at the Department of Agriculture's Bureau of Animal Industry, arrived at the northern border of Yellowstone to be greeted by Fred Foster. Hall had suggested that control of the tapeworm might be possible with anthelmintic treatment (destroying or expelling intestinal worms) of the pelicans. The very next day Hall and Yellowstone Park Ranger McCarty went to Molly Island, where

McCarty shot eight pelicans. On the first of August McCarty used a lariat to capture seven live pelicans, and one additional capture was made by Ranger Ryan with a dip net. Following these collections, Hall performed postmortem examinations, as well as anthelmintic and insecticide experiments on the live specimens. Hall found that 44 percent of the pelicans he examined harbored the tapeworm *Dibothrium cordiceps*, 19 percent harbored flukes in the small intestine, and 100 percent had nematodes in the stomach, as well as lice in their mouths and on their skins. He gave four pelicans a level teaspoonful of kamala (a powder from the capsules or seed pods of an East Indian tree) and washed it down with two ounces of water. One of the birds passed a tapeworm posthaste, and upon postmortem examination all four were found free of tapeworms. Hall also dosed two trout with kamala, and force-fed these trout to two pelicans that demonstrated little appetite. One of them passed a tapeworm, and again these pelicans proved to be free of tapeworms postmortem. Hall then turned his attention to the lice, swabbing the patches of infestation with cotton doused with kerosene. The pelicans "appeared to be very little disturbed" by this treatment, so Hall proceeded to the question of the practicality of treating pelicans. He thought that nesting pelicans might be fed trout dosed with kamala, the whole point of his second experiment. In his report Hall discussed in considerable detail the reasons why the tapeworm were injurious to the fish: The parasite might invade the trout's ovaries, causing a reduction of fish egg production that Foster had noted. Second, this parasite caused pathogenic effects among spotted brook trout at Elk Lake in Oregon. Although the Yellowstone Lake trout might have relative immunity to the parasite, it still might show effects in terms of stunted growth; and were the trout in Yellowstone not smaller than trout in other waters? Because of modern techniques of transplanting and stocking fish, Yellowstone Park was in danger of becoming a "focus of infection for the entire West." Third, Hall considered it a very serious matter that the parasite was giving the fish of Yellowstone Lake "a bad reputation," because the trout were becoming known as "wormy."[21] Some action to protect the fish was required. Although it was out of the question to exterminate the pelicans, Hall suggested that managers might be able to limit their numbers by capturing them with nets during nesting season.

It was no joke, wrote Hall: "We shall have to do many things with our wild animals that might have seemed amusing twenty years ago." Because agencies were trying to conserve wildlife "under highly artificial conditions," it was becoming necessary to dip elk for scabies, lure mountain sheep away from lungworm-infested ranges, and distribute medicated salt licks.[22] Hall's views were representative of how many scientists viewed wildlife in the parks: An active and interventionist management style was needed. Yet management wasn't simply a matter of producing a larger crop of any particular species; it must also aim at creating a new balance between humans and nature. Humans had irrevocably upset the natural order of things as nature yielded to civilization, and now only human action could restore a proper balance.

Second, Hall's report revealed how scientists as well as NPS administrators believed that wildlife was closely tied to the purposes of the parks. Which wildlife best suited the mission, however, was debatable. Since the days of Director Stephen T. Mather, the NPS had emphasized the touristic function of Yellowstone, perhaps partly to plump up its budget, always vulnerable to the depredations of other agencies and never reaching quite far enough. As did the fish culturalists, Hall placed the value of the trout to sport fishermen first on his list of priorities. Here, Hall's emphasis reflected the Albright administration's drive from 1919 to 1929 to encourage tourism in Yellowstone. The value of the pelican as part of the scenic landscape, or as part of a natural system, did not enter into his calculations. Hall advised that the pelican numbers should be controlled, even though he did not have necessary information about other fish-eating birds of Yellowstone Lake, nor did he know if otters carried the intestinal parasite. Hall's work, performed at the behest of the U.S. Fish Commission, seemed to validate Foster's position. If science is a social endeavor, then perhaps we should not be too surprised that Hall's recommendations were very similar to Foster's outlook on the proper relationships between fishermen, trout, and the pelican.

Yet Maurice Hall did not have the last scientific word on the pelicans. An underlying rift was beginning to open between two fundamentally different views of the purposes of the parks and the value of wildlife. During the early 1930s, bird watchers' quiet concern over the dwindling number and distribution of pelicans in the western states quickly escalated into national criticism regarding Yellowstone National Park's wildlife management policy, becoming an embarrassing episode for NPS director Horace Albright. The park was forced to change its policy regarding the predator pelicans. Two events in particular led to this outcome, the first involving the creation of a scientific arm of the National Park Service, the second an external prod from the conservation community.

In the summer of 1929 the newly created National Park Service Wildlife Division first arrived in Yellowstone. The division was created almost single-handedly by George Melendez Wright, a 1927 graduate of the University of California, Berkeley's College of Forestry. He studied under Professor Walter Mulford and received a minor in vertebrate zoology with Joseph Grinnell. While a student, he accompanied Joseph S. Dixon, economic mammalogist on Grinnell's staff, on a two-month collecting trip to Mt. McKinley National Park in Alaska. From 1927 to 1929 Wright worked as a naturalist and ranger in Yosemite. The genesis of the Wild Life Division was shaped by the Committee on Educational Problems in the Parks, headed by John Campbell Merriam. Dr. Carl P. Russell, the NPS field naturalist, originally came up with the idea of a comprehensive survey of wildlife problems in the national parks. In 1929 George Wright, Joseph Dixon, and Ansel Hall submitted a proposal to study wildlife in the parks, which fell into the lap of Park Service director Horace Albright, recently returned to Washington from the superintendent's post at Yellowstone. Albright presented the matter to the Committee on Educational Problems in the National Parks. Merriam responded by suggesting that Dixon's plan for a two-year effort to catalog the wildlife problems of the parks was not the best way to start off. Cataloging wildlife problems, even for two years, would not uncover all the difficulties parks faced. A first survey, suggested Merriam, should aim at discovering the most significant problem that could be attacked and solved within a few years. Albright suggested establishing an organization for central education and research to help define wildlife problems and administrative solutions. Merriam suggested that the Committee on Educational Problems had no authority to deal with the proposed study, and therefore, the Park Service itself should assume immediate authority over the survey.[23] Wright's and Dixon's study proposal thus created an immediate need for the orderly administration of wildlife research. Although the Park Service allocated no money for the study, George Wright committed himself to scientific wildlife study in the parks and funded the field work out of his own pocket. Not until 1932 did Congress fund the wildlife surveys to the tune of $22,500.[24] Wright's group was referred to as the Wild Life Survey until formalized in 1933 as the Wildlife Division, with Wright as its leader. The initial staff was small, including Wright, Dixon, biologist and former Grinnell student Ben H. Thompson, and secretary Mrs. George Pease. The National Park Service attached the survey to its Education Division (directed by Ansel Hall), housed at the University of California, which was becoming a vital center for National Park Service functions, including education, forestry, and landscape architecture.[25]

The investigations of the Wildlife Division began in 1929 when Joseph Dixon arrived in Yellowstone Park to study the status of the trumpeter swan. The following summer, Wright, Dixon, and Thompson came as a team to continue the research on the swan, which was thought to be declining in numbers due to human encroachments on its breeding grounds throughout the American West. The team paddled about in a rubber boat, found the nests of the rare trumpeter, and divided up to observe two of the nests. Wright and Thompson watched as a raven came to take advantage of the temporary absence of the brooding swan that had left to feed. The raven swooped down upon the nest, cracked open one of the eggs, and carried off the embryo. Dixon "took no chances with my swans and shot the raven when I saw him try repeatedly to steal the eggs."[26] Enterprising newspaper reporters picked up the story, spreading the news of this activist campaign of swan protection to city-bound Americans: "Ravens, otters, owls and coyotes are under suspicion. . . . The naturalists are going to suspend one of the rules of sanctuary and will kill any animal found guilty of eating the priceless cygnets. But the evidence must be conclusive."[27] It was not the knowledge of ecological relationships so much as a fear of the swan's extinction that motivated this scientist. The rare must be protected against the many, and extirpation was an option that could not be entertained. In a letter to the Park Service director, George Wright conveyed his notion of the National Park Service's responsibility to posterity: "Unless the Park Service is quick to accept the challenge to do everything within its power, we will surely suffer the opprobrium of our own and future generations for our *laissez-faire* attitude."[28] Timely intervention was the key to preserve a species in danger of local extirpation and perhaps irreversible extinction.

Dixon carefully approached a swan's nest during hatching to hold a day-old cygnet in his hand. He thought some colleagues "will probably say I'm a poor scientist because there is no known specimen of a downy trumpeter swan and I didn't collect him but the bird is too rare to spare even one at this critical time."[29] Dixon and the other men from the Wildlife Division still demonstrated strong connections to natural history traditions. Although some historians of science suggest that natural history was transformed around the turn of the century into an experiment-oriented world of laboratories and research stations, those scientists who worked with wildlife for the federal agencies still manifested concerns that embodied the traditional research agendas of systematists.[30] To collect the specimen was to enable science to study nature, but for Dixon, preserving the endangered took precedence over the demands of science. Although he was never known as an activist for conservation, Dixon was out in the field performing the hard work of a preservationist-oriented biologist.

The decline of other avian species also aroused the concern of ornithologists and conservationists. Thompson continued the work of the Wildlife Division in Yellowstone, turning his attention to the pelican problem. He gathered data reaching back into the late nineteenth century on the numbers of the white pelican on its known breeding grounds. Some of the places where the pelican had bred in profuse numbers at the turn of the century were now barren of pelican nests. In 1895 naturalists had counted fifty-five hundred breeding pelicans at Klamath Lake in Oregon, but in 1931 none were breeding there; a thousand birds had been counted at Miquelon Lake in Alberta in 1910, but by 1919 there were none. Thompson concluded that in the very recent past the pelican had suffered a drastic loss of numbers, from 50 to 100 percent, caused by the reclamation of wetlands and lakes, as well as by "local prejudice." He surmised that the pelican colony on Molly Island suffered from prejudice "typical of that against all pelican breeding colonies,"[31] which was the feeling that the pelican was an unwarranted competitor with the sport fisherman.

Food habits research performed during the 1920s by E. Raymond Hall, the Reverend S. H. Goodwin, George Willett, and A. C. Bent, particularly on the Gulf of Mexico, indicated that the pelican had an undeserved reputation for eating commercial fish exclusively. Despite previous introductions of exotic species to the Yellowstone plateau region, the cutthroat trout was still the predominant species available to the pelicans breeding at Molly Island, and thus many fishermen were inclined to see the pelican as a greedy competitor for the only fish in town. Thompson suggested that the Molly Island pelican was "somewhat omnivorous," eating all kinds of fish, not just game fish, as well as the oxylotl, a salamander found in Yellowstone.[32] Reviewing the effects of human disturbance of breeding colonies, he noted that visiting tourists had a devastating impact on nesting birds, because the brooding pelicans were so shy of humans that they would simply leave the nests for hours, and if tourists stayed on the island overnight, the eggs stood even more probability of loss through exposure and predation.

Thompson's report to Superintendent Toll offered several justifications for protecting the pelican. First, the opprobrium that the fishing community directed at the bird was undeserved. Second, the pelican was "a very old bird, having attained its present form in the course of evolution before man existed," and therefore, the pelican had not only great scientific but aesthetic value as well.[33] This argument demonstrates that scientific concerns were perhaps not foremost in Thompson's mind. He suggested to Toll that "the status of that particular colony should be gauged first by Park Service standards" and only secondly by the trend of pelican numbers nationally.[34] This emphasis on Park Service standards opens an important door into the Wildlife Division's philosophy.

Thompson, Dixon, and Wright possessed a conception of the Park Service mission. Because they were employed by the National Park Service, their sense of duty might seem a given, yet we must ask why they should have had any interest in the larger goals of the agency. After all, they were engaged in practical wildlife problems and scientific research, puttering around in boats, placing tiny bands on the legs of birds, and counting eggs. They had a clear sense that the mission of the NPS coincided with their own interests and concerns with wild animals—they worked for an agency that not only managed sizable lands but also seemed among federal or state employers the most able and willing to perform the actions necessary for the preservation of species in danger of extinction.

The Wildlife Division demonstrated a willingness to intervene if necessary to protect a species in danger of local extirpation. In 1935 Harlow B. Mills, a naturalist assistant in Yellowstone, found a pair of trumpeters nesting at Swan Lake. On June 5 he noted that the water of the lake had receded 1.5 inches, and it was his supposition that if the lake level continued to drop, the nest would be endangered by coyotes or tourists who approached too closely thus disrupting nesting behaviors. After discussing the situation with park naturalist Bauer and the assistant superintendent, Mills proceeded to create a sandbag dam at the outlet of Swan Lake to keep the nest insulated from the shore. Action and intervention was the imperative of the day, as Mills proceeded even before he received the proper clearance from George Wright in the Washington office of the Wildlife Division.

Wright's recommendations in the spring of 1934 regarding practical measures to ensure the survival of the trumpeter swan also exemplified the Wildlife Division's interventionist posture. Wright suggested that "local coyote control" be exercised at Trumpeter, Swan, and White Lakes to prevent the loss of cygnets. He also was enthusiastic about the flag system that Ranger Arnold had devised to prevent swans from making land crossings between lakes. Evidently, a number of vigorously flapping flags intimidated the swans enough to turn them back to the safety of lake waters. The Wildlife Division assumed an active role and interventionist stance in managing rare species, such as the trumpeter swan and the pelican, in the interest of propagating their numbers. Furthermore, in spite of a growing consensus in the scientific community in favor of protecting predatory species, scientists were willing to control predators where they thought necessary, throwing their weight onto the balance mechanisms of nature in hopes of bringing back a vanishing species. For the Wildlife Division, the parks were one important element in a greater system of places where wildlife still found refuge, and the park's purposes were particularly suitable for the preservation of rare wildlife.

Yet Thompson and Wright were lecturing the choir. By 1929 spurred in part by Charles Adams's analysis of the fishery decline, Toll clearly doubted the rationale of Foster and the Bureau of Fisheries. The superintendent commissioned an internal report on the pelican situation, this one to be conducted by the corps of rangers at Yellowstone Park. In the spring of 1931 George W. Miller, assistant chief ranger in Yellowstone, submitted his report to Toll, suggesting that the pelican deserved protection. Miller reviewed information gathered from professional biologists, such as C. C. Adams and E. Raymond Hall, as well as information gathered by Yellowstone naturalist M. P. Skinner, and summed up the essential controversy: "I am of the opinion that the elimination of any fish-eating bird is desired by the fish culturalist. On the other hand, the ornithologist is desirous of preserving the fish eating birds regardless of the damage they may do fishing."[35] Yellowstone Chief Ranger George F. Baggley responded to Miller's report, advising Toll that a thousand to fifteen hundred pelicans could be supported on Yellowstone Lake, and suggesting that they be allowed to increase until they reached "the maximum number that can nest on these two islands."[36] Toll also was pleased by the fact that the input of scientists seemed to help resolve an issue that had been under discussion for years, and he celebrated "how much easier it is to reach an agreement regarding action to be taken when all of the facts are available."[37] Remarkably, Yellowstone Park rangers were coming around to speak for the preservation of a species that they had helped suppress for almost a decade. Together with the men at the fish hatchery, they had actively participated in killing a native avian species, the Molly Island pelicans, an action contrary to the protectionist policies for other wildlife species within the park, except for the predatory species. But now they repudiated that killing.

One factor in developing new attitudes among the rangers was a changing of the guard. In 1928 Dorr G. Yeager became park naturalist, and in 1929 Chief Ranger Baggley replaced Samuel T. Woodring, who had served since 1922. Baggley was the first college-educated chief ranger in Yellowstone.[38] Also in 1929 Roger W. Toll was appointed superintendent of Yellowstone. The new group of people brought with them different values as well as a growing sense of a unique mission for the National Park Service. The change of personnel together with the catalyst of the Wildlife Division's work helped to initiate a new era of thinking and management in Yellowstone.

The second event that nudged Yellowstone toward a new policy regarding the predator pelicans was a verbal assault on the NPS launched by Rosalie Edge in New York City. In the early summer of 1931 a pamphlet titled "Last of the White Pelican" was published by a small group calling itself the Emergency Conservation Committee (ECC). The ECC was formed by members of the National Association of Audubon Societies who were dismayed by slow progress in conservation, disgruntled with particular policies, such as Audubon's leasing of its own Rainey Sanctuary in Louisiana for trapping fur-bearing species, and finally disgusted with the leadership style of T. Gilbert Pearson. Although journalist Irving Brant collaborated, Edge was the firebrand who led the ECC during the 1930s and epitomized its style and substance. Edge, a diminutive woman, was amiable and mild-mannered in conversation, but she blasted away in pamphlets criticizing Pearson as well as such federal agencies as the Bureau of Biological Survey, referring to it as the "United States Bureau of Destruction and Extermination."[39]

Only four pages long, the small pamphlet "Last of the White Pelican" caused a lot of trouble. The pamphlet noted that nationwide pelican numbers were decreasing at the major refuges and suggested that without action the species was in danger of extinction. Edge criticized the Biological Survey for failing to provide a guardian at the Nevada nesting ground, and she lambasted the Montana Fish and Game Commission for its publication of "a communication encouraging hunters to kill off the White Pelicans on account of alleged destructiveness to fish." California was chastised as well for removing protective regulations at the request of fishermen. To sport fishermen, the issue of fisheries and the impact of pelicans was of considerable importance during the summer of 1931. Edge took up the issue of the Yellowstone fisheries, suggesting that the "depletion of the trout in the park waters can be explained by other perfectly obvious causes with which pelicans have nothing to do, but even supposing the birds did affect the number of fish in the lakes, to what better use can a few of the Yellowstone trout be put than to enable these splendid birds to live and raise their young and escape extinction?" Thus Edge defended the pelicans partly in terms of their natural role as predator but more specifically in terms of the preservation of a rare and beautiful species. With a view that the parks should protect the endangered, Edge reasoned that especially in Yellowstone the pelicans should find shelter. Yet the pelicans were disappearing in Yellowstone, and they remained unprotected by federal law.[40]

Contained in the pamphlet was an ominous revelation. Edge wrote that the NPS "denies having issued permits for killing the Yellowstone Park pelicans," which suggests that rumors of control activities had reached her, and that she had queried NPS officials about the matter. In fact, since 1923, the year following Ward's exposé of the food habits of the pelicans, employees of the U.S. Fish Commission and the National Park Service had been engaged in a clandestine springtime decimation of the eggs and young pelicans on the Molly Island rookery. Although Director Albright and Yellowstone Superintendent Toll discounted the criticisms of Rosalie Edge, whom the mainstream conservation community characterized as an unreasonable sort, they were sensitive to that critique and found that Yellowstone was a very public place, suddenly occupying center stage of conservation's national concern.

Edge was not the only conservationist who knew something about NPS predator control policies; scientists joined in the criticism. W. L. McAtee, who served with the Bureau of Biological Survey from 1904 to 1934 and at one point directed its food habits laboratory, had become disenchanted with the bureau because of its support for predator control, and he was disturbed by the fact that the agency had lost scientific credibility.[41] In late 1931 McAtee published "A Little Essay on Vermin" in Bird Lore, the journal of the National Association of Audubon Societies. In the essay he defended road-runners and the pelican, stating that classifying these birds as vermin "could be termed a childish, if it were not a monstrous, absurdity." Historically, many hunters and fisherman have viewed predators as competition for game. During the 1920s this was a zero-sum economic game in which the wolf's or pelican's gain was the hunter's or fisherman's loss. After acknowledging that the pelicans might harbor parasites and that they did consume trout, McAtee took on the issue of exploitative use. He suggested that the recreational value of the pelican far outweighed that of the "submerged trout," simply because many more people saw the pelicans, "active and conspicuous, bizarre in appearance on land or water, and marvelous in flight." The number of people "interested in the total animal association" overwhelmed the number of people interested in taking game. His suggestion that "Trout-fishing is not essential" would not have endeared him to the readers of sporting magazines. Thus McAtee's argument used a simple-sum calculus similar to that of the fish culturalist, but his numbers added up very differently. His belief that "lovers of wild life" shared equal rights in conservation decisions with sportsmen was still anthropocentric and oriented toward consumer demand.[42]

The sting of outside criticism as well as the shifting opinion of scientists and rangers within the NPS encouraged a reassessment of the pelican situation. On November 11, 1931, Guy D. Edwards, acting superintendent of Yellowstone, wrote a confidential letter to Captain C. F. Culler, the district supervisor of the Bureau of Fisheries, asking for information that would help the NPS devise "a very definite control and management program for the pelicans in the park." Edwards informed Culler that well-known naturalists had visited the park during the summer and had disagreed on the subject of pelican control; nevertheless, "Director Albright felt that some control work was necessary in keeping the pelicans from becoming too numerous in the park."[43] Perhaps this language was meant to reassure him, but at any rate Culler supplied the requested information, estimating 80 percent of the pelican young and unhatched had been destroyed. As a fish culturalist he was inclined toward "the elimination of any bird feeding upon fish life," but because Yellowstone presented a special case, a flock of three hundred birds was acceptable but required "strict measures" to prevent enlargement of the colony. Over the next few months the administrators of Yellowstone gathered further information about the control activities that had been carried out during the previous decade. In January 1932 former ranger Harry Liek put his estimates on paper. In this way Toll discovered the pelican control program he had inherited.

Although in the 1920s the NPS and the Bureau of Fisheries seemed to agree on the relative importance of trout and pelicans, during the early 1930s this consensus broke down. Park Superintendent Toll soon led Yellowstone on a radically different path in the methodology of valuing wildlife. In April Toll edged toward a decision; he had gathered information from former rangers and collected the reports by Thompson and Miller. The publication of "Last of the White Pelican" in 1931 and McAtee's essay also spurred Toll toward redefining the relationship between Yellowstone Park and its predatory pelicans. During the 1930s considerable agency brainstorming took place via memoranda. In one memo Toll suggested to Chief Ranger Baggley that the Molly Island pelican colony should be left unmolested until the number of birds returned to population levels thought to occur in 1922, before the control measures began. Toll informed Baggley they would need to have a little chat with Fred Foster of the Bureau of Fisheries, get him onboard, and then place the islands off-limits to boating parties from either the Bureau of Fisheries or the tour boats of the Yellowstone Park Company.

But Foster continued to defend the bird reduction policy, protesting that he did not desire to exterminate the pelican, and all along he had in mind "the welfare of the National Park Service rather than the Bureau of Fisheries." He suggested limiting the Molly Island colony to two hundred birds, ample numbers "to guard against possible untoward conditions." Foster offered alternatives: If the park would feed the pelicans frozen herring or some other "cheap fish," then he would have no objection to raising the numbers of pelicans, partly because the life cycle of the *Diphyllobothrium* parasite might be broken. Foster wrote Edwards that the commerce department was working on a hatchery on the Madison River, with the intention that all the eggs would be used in the National Parks. Foster lectured Edwards on the fact that the fish of Yellowstone Lake got very little protection from fishermen or from predatory animals. Considering the toll of pelicans, gulls, mergansers, osprey, otter, and mink, "It is really quite remarkable that the black spotted trout has been maintained in present numbers in Yellowstone Lake."[44]

Yet opinion within the NPS continued to mount on the side of protecting the pelican. The National Park Service had created a supervisory post associated with the Wildlife Division labeled the Supervisor of Wild Life Resources based in Salt Lake City, Utah. David H. Madsen, expert in fisheries and president of the International Association of Fish and Wildlife Agencies from 1928 to 1929, filled the job during the early 1930s. On a practical level, Madsen thought it was possible to augment the fishery resource to satisfy the sport fishermen without using highly intrusive measures that quickly tipped the existing natural relationships. In a memo dated May 10, 1932, Madsen invoked the purposes of the NPS: "to maintain as nearly as possible primitive conditions within the Parks." He thought it was the parks' duty to maintain the native species of fish and questioned the artificial stocking of park lakes and rivers, because these programs in the past had introduced exotic species into park waters. The fact that pelicans ate fish of value to sport fishermen was insufficient reason to question their right to existence; both trout and pelicans needed protection. Madsen thought there were alternate ways of enhancing the sport fishery, "much more in keeping with Park policy than the destruction of so called natural enemies of the fish." The first course of practical action Madsen advocated was the revision of open season; the sport fishermen insisted that the park be open to fishing early in the season, because fishing outside the park did not pick up speed until later. This early season in the park unfortunately coincided with the trout's spawning season, causing a concomitant loss of fish production. Sport fishing itself was one cause of the depletion of the fishery, noted by Charles C. Adams in 1925, yet never addressed by the U.S. Fish Commission. Madsen wrote that the only reason a native species should be controlled was if another native species was in danger of extinction, a circumstance clearly not applicable here. "In my opinion," he wrote, "no efforts should be made to control the number of birds and animals within the parks." Although control measures were tolerated at fish hatcheries, the NPS should "attempt to balance the wild life supply . . . only after very careful study and as a last resort to protect a vanishing specie." Like the osprey, heron, merganser, otter, and mink, the pelican was bestowed with an undeserved reputation as an unduly voracious and harmful agent to the supply of native trout. Madsen's solution was "the intelligent stocking of the park waters with desirable species, without resorting to the destruction of the so-called fish eating birds and animals."[45]

On May 12, 1932, Horace Albright wrote to Toll, noting the studies indicating a decrease in the national population of the pelican. Albright asked Toll: "How would you feel about giving full protection to the Yellowstone Lake colony?" It was Albright, as superintendent of Yellowstone from 1919 to 1929, who had cooperated with the Bureau of Fisheries. He had played a preservationist role with the elk, feeding and nurturing the endangered elk herd, but with the pelicans Albright had acted as the gardener of nature, controlling conditions and yield. It was Toll's turn to put on the preservationist mantle. This was a species in trouble, grand forces conspiring to extirpate the victim, and finally Yellowstone the rescuer, one of the few safe refuges remaining. From 1932 to 1935 Toll expanded on the theme, extending protection from furry and friendly animals, such as the elk and bison, to include species previously persecuted, the pelican and the coyote. On May 21 Edwards replied on the park's behalf, advising the director that "we have planned full protection" for the Molly Island pelicans.[46]

When Toll decided to protect the pelican, he essentially redefined Yellowstone's purpose in concrete terms. On May 21, 1932, Toll committed to complete protection of the pelican. He had collected the reports by Thompson and Ranger Miller, the pamphlet "Last of the White Pelican" was tucked away in a file folder, and for all we know, a copy of *Bird Lore* magazine containing McAtee's widely read "A Little Essay on Vermin" might have graced his coffee table. Yellowstone Park would protect the native wild animals not only when convenient for visiting fishermen but in every instance. Nature, in other words, took precedence over human uses.

The exchanges between the offices in Washington and Mammoth Hot Springs demonstrated the relative independence of Yellowstone's superintendent, within a context of close agency communication and a new network of professional advice in the work of the Wildlife Division. Arno B. Cammerer, acting NPS director, praised Toll's decision to protect the pelican colony and noted prohibiting all boat landings with the exception of scientific observations was "exactly correct."[47] On June 4 Madsen visited Molly Island with Wright, Thompson, and Ranger Baggley. They counted 126 occupied nests and estimated a total of 250 to 300 birds in the colony, a figure that led the men to believe that the number of pelicans was not increasing, and due to outmigration, at this population level the number never would increase. When Madsen wrote to Director Albright shortly thereafter, suggesting that no population control activities should be undertaken, the Wildlife Division spoke unanimously for the protection of the pelicans.

Although it was after Toll declared protection for the pelican, the September 1932 publication of Rosalie Edge's pamphlet "Slaughter of the Yellowstone Pelicans" embroiled Yellowstone in controversy. Toll and Albright were correct in assuming that the pelican control measures only hinted at in the first ECC pamphlet "Last of the White Pelican" (June 1931) would eventually become public knowledge. This pressure forced them to take a position, rather than settle for a de facto policy. On October 15, 1932, Acting Yellowstone Superintendent Guy D. Edwards received a copy of Edge's new broadside, sent to him by Dr. Frank R. Oastler, a New York physician and ornithologist who had served on the Committee on Educational Problems in the National Parks. Edwards hastily replied to Oastler, explaining that two disgruntled employees who had recently quit the employ of the Park Service were "doing everything possible to cause us trouble."[48] One had been a confidential file clerk, the other an assistant in the chief ranger's office, and before they left they had copied incriminating correspondence. The whistleblowers appealed to the American Legion and the Veterans of Foreign Wars,

13. Roger W. Toll with
bobcat. This 1931 photo-
graph was taken at Carls-
bad Caverns. Courtesy Na-
tional Park Service, Harpers
Ferry Center.

who refused to render any assistance. They then gave information to a newspaper in Jackson Hole, Wyoming, "which has since its origin published vi-
cious statements regarding the Park Service."[49] The former employees were
not done yet, for soon Rosalie Edge of New York City had the documents in
her hands.

The "Slaughter of the Yellowstone Pelicans" accused the National Park
Service of making a concerted effort to exterminate the pelicans that nested
on Molly Island. Yellowstone and Washington officials realized the sensitive
nature of this topic, and in 1931 and 1932 they were reluctant to make public
the figures about pelican control coming to light. But information about the
yearly raids did indeed leak out of the park. Edge asserted that she had possession of an anonymous letter from a former park ranger who claimed
knowledge of control measures against the pelicans taken since 1923, although the park had never publicized any such action. The anonymous
whistle-blower said that Park Service personnel destroyed eggs and clubbed
the young to death, further stating that this action was ordered by none
other than the park superintendent. The former ranger enclosed a letter

14. Chief Ranger George Baggley took this photo of scientists banding pelicans on Molly Island, June 1932. Courtesy Yellowstone Photo Archives.

15. Boating party on Molly Island, 1932. Commercial excursions to the islands were eventually suspended because they disrupted the brooding habits of the pelicans. This group may have had some connection with the scientists banding the pelican chicks. Courtesy Yellowstone Photo Archives.

from a former park naturalist, who was irritated by three things: the shooting of 42 bears in 1931, the 1932 policy allowing hotels to pick wildflowers, and the controlling of pelicans on Molly Island. This anonymous letter stated that in 1930, 171 pelicans and 70 nests were counted, but only one year later only 54 young pelicans and no nests were observed. The charge that the information was omitted from the park publication *Nature Notes* at the request of the superintendent's office added to the sense of conspiracy. The writer had been told that the killing was carried out by men from the fish hatcheries. The plot thickened, because Edge's informant passed along a memo to National Park Service Director Roger B. Toll from Yellowstone's chief ranger, suggesting that Yellowstone could "well afford to keep 100 or 150 pelicans *until further study has shown that they are too destructive to have in the park at all*" (emphasis in original). Finally, the anonymous writer included a "pelican report" sent from the assistant chief ranger to Chief Ranger George Baggley that proposed to "*destroy all their eggs* and in a couple of years I think they would hunt another breeding place. Second, *detail a ranger who could keep his mouth shut, and with a shotgun he could exterminate them in one season*" (emphasis in original).[50] These memos clearly supported Edge's accusation that the Park Service was purposefully destroying a rare and strangely beautiful bird, and furthermore, performed the task in a brutal manner. Ranger Harry Liek's words "nothing escaped" revealed the intent of the men who visited the Molly Islands.

Professional scientists and managers both within and outside the National Park Service resented the intrusion of outsiders, whom they characterized as sentimentalists. Assistant Director of the Wildlife Division H. C. Bryant told Albright it was best to simply ignore Edge: "All she wants is material for publicity."[51] T. Gilbert Pearson also suggested ignoring the ECC. The editor of *Outdoor Life* did not approve of the "agitations" engaged in by the ECC, berated the organization as a group of "publicity seekers," and opined that the committee did "the cause of genuine conservation" little or no good.[52]

The Wildlife Division's Washington office staff circulated among themselves a three-page parody of ECC literature, which revealed their view of Edge: She was an extremist, a busybody who actually knew very little about wildlife. Printed entirely in capitals, the tongue-in-cheek pamphlet stated: "EVERYTHING IS BEING DESTROYED—THE WORLD IS COMING TO AN END." What was the purpose of the committee? "TO OPPOSE EVERYTHING THAT WE CAN THINK OF, FIND FAULT WITH ANYTHING BY CONSTANT CONVERSATION AND UNLIMITED SCRAWL. IN OTHER

WORDS KEEP HER GOING AS LONG AS THE INK HOLDS OUT. DECON-
STRUCTION NO CONSTRUCTION." How extreme was the ECC? "WE ARE
OPPOSED TO THE USE OF POISONS FOR ANY PURPOSE. LET THE
COCKROACH LIVE." The Wildlife Division staff believed that the sentimen-
talists overreacted to problems in conservation. The manuscript described
the ECC's base of authority: "WE DEPEND ON THESE GREAT OUT-DOOR
FIELD NATURALISTS WHO HAVE STUDIED THE LIVES AND HABITS OF
BIRDS AND MAMMALS BY CONSTANT OBSERVATION IN PET SHOP
WINDOWS FOR THE INFORMATION THEY FORCE UPON THE UNSUS-
PECTING PUBLIC."[53] This spoof was circulated among six scientists of the
Wildlife Division, including Demaray and Bryant, the top brass. Yet their de-
rision reveals that the jibes of the ECC were irritating the scientists of the
NPS. Who were these sentimentalists to question the most protective of the
federal agencies, the NPS? In their view Edge had a lot of audacity to challenge the authority of scientists who knew their jobs and understood wildlife. If the criticism meant nothing to them and if the ECC critique was entirely specious, the Wildlife Division could have ignored it. Yet Edge's blasts
at the NPS in effect criticized the very professionalism of the scientists
whose mission it was to know and protect the wildlife in the national parks.
Rosalie Edge and the Wildlife Division both believed in a preservationist
purpose for the parks, but they differed in their evaluation of Yellowstone
Park's performance.

The ECC's public criticism of the National Park Service also stung Albright. After all his efforts to protect wildlife and portray the NPS as a leader in conservation, the accusation that Yellowstone was destroying a rare
species of bird life was a great embarrassment. This was not the first time
Albright had been embarrassed over the killing of animals in Yellowstone.
One of his primary concerns had been the protection of wild animals, specifically that the public would have the opportunity to see those animals in a
natural setting. He had acted vigorously during the 1920s to protect and feed
Yellowstone's northern elk herd, which he thought on the verge of extinction because of hunters and winter snows.

The pamphlet was also embarrassing because by 1931 it was not clear to
Toll or to the Wildlife Division, and certainly not to the general public, how
controlling the population of pelicans fit into the protectionist traditions of
the National Park Service. From the turn of the century through the 1930s
the cause of bird protection found an enthusiastic American audience.[54] In
1932 Albright's friends in conservation circles were convinced that the

status of pelicans, trumpeter swans, and other birds was declining steadily. Albright's acquaintances from every province of the conservation and scientific communities flooded his office with a barrage of protests. Each and every letter insisted that the pelican should be protected. Frank Oastler traveled to Yellowstone in July to check into the condition of the pelican colony. Although he had visited the park since 1909, Oastler had "never heard of 'officially conducted pelican killing.'" He thought that breeding pelicans were so sensitive to human disturbance that anyone desiring to reduce their numbers would simply have to visit the colony on a regular basis; killing the young and taking eggs was not necessary. He surmised that the population was about the same size as he had noticed in previous visits and noted that the order for complete protection was "faithfully obeyed."[55]

Frank F. Gander, secretary for the Natural History Museum at Balboa Park in San Diego, notified the secretary of the interior that the fellows of the museum "most strongly protest" the killing of white pelicans in the park.[56] H. C. Bryant replied that the Park Service indeed had a policy of protecting "all forms of life within a national park," explaining that measures of control were employed only after scientific reports had been made on a particular situation.

Other park supporters seemed to express the ambivalence that resulted from new ideas meeting traditional attitudes. Walter B. Sheppard, a citizen of Jackson Hole actively involved in the land acquisition process that created Grand Teton National Park, informed Albright that he had already written to Edge, "suggesting that she turn her batteries on some abuse [such as the federal policy of grazing on national forests] about which there can be less controversy." He agreed with Albright that a park's purpose should involve "preservation of the balance of Nature, to a degree as nearly pristine as possible." If there was a fault in Albright's reasoning, "it lies in the fact that man's intervention and activities have seriously disturbed that balance." If conditions were yet pristine, nature could easily restore her balance, yet the intrusive activities of mankind had "thrown his weight in the balance against all living creatures the killing of which appeals to him for any reason." Yet Sheppard was not a sentimentalist, nor a categorical preservationist. He perceived a thorny dilemma: "To what extent is it justifiable to conserve an undoubted nuisance, like the pelican and coyote, for sentimental reasons?"[57] Sheppard divided conservationist thought into two categories, most of it sensible but the remainder sentimental in nature, of lesser value. Because the pelican in the end might share the fate of the great auk,

Sheppard thought the conservative policy Albright indicated was probably the best. Although most of Albright's acquaintances were immediately supportive and defended the NPS, Sheppard required a bit more assurance.

In late October 1932 Albright wrote a lengthy letter to T. Gilbert Pearson, president of the National Association of Audubon Societies, explaining and defending park policies. Albright took pains to explain what the NPS had done and why. Albright reviewed the history of the pelican, explaining how pelican control was initially suggested to protect the fish from the parasite, and later justified in terms of increasing the supply of fish to the sport fishermen. Although the "eminent zoologist" Ward had recommended control measures in 1922, Albright claimed that advice was not acted upon. At that time NPS Assistant Director Cammerer had conferred with Pearson, who vigorously defended the white pelican, noting it was not a voracious consumer of game fishes and, withal, was declining in abundance. Soon thereafter, Albright talked personally with Pearson in New York City. Nevertheless, beginning in 1924 "without consulting any organization outside of Government circles, the National Park Service and the Bureau of Fisheries did conduct, from time to time, experiments in the control of the colony by withdrawal of some of the eggs from the nesting grounds at Molly and Gull islands." Albright testified to the good intentions of the NPS, writing "we never lost sight of the fact that it was and is our fundamental duty to protect the primitive country in the national parks and the wild life therein, that even predatory species . . . must be given all possible consideration. We have never leaned very far at any time toward the control of predatory species, whether bird or mammal." Since Ben Thompson's report the NPS policy had been to "prohibit any disturbance whatever" of the pelican colony. Finally, Albright informed Pearson that although the pelican had been given "complete protection," the NPS "has in no way been influenced by the Emergency Conservation Committee."[58]

Why was Pearson not offended by the fact that following his conversations with Albright and Cammerer, when they had evidently been sympathetic to his cause, the Park Service soon began to experiment with controlling the numbers of pelicans, a species on the decline? Why did Albright think it important to assure Pearson that the NPS was not listening to the ECC? Part of the answer is found in the ties of culture and professionalism that bound Albright and Pearson together. For Pearson, the important fact was that the National Association of Audubon Societies was at the bargaining table with important government functionaries. By 1932 the social circles of conservation seemed well established when Albright, Pearson, and others dined at the Cosmos Club in Washington DC. They viewed ECC critiques as an emotionalism bent simply on attracting attention to itself, best ignored by level-headed men of good intent who must stick together. They resisted sharing control over the policy-making process with sentimentalists who exaggerated the gravity of any particular situation.

Yet Albright did not reveal the whole truth to Pearson. The words of Harry Liek, "nothing escaped," revealed the intent of the operation. Did Albright know the extent of the control actions? Given that no records were ever kept of the yearly operations, pelican control was apparently an informal and local decision. The relative autonomy of Yellowstone in the early days of the National Park Service meant that the chief ranger and the park superintendent had complete control over wildlife management. From 1919 until early 1929 that superintendent was none other than Horace Albright. Considering his propensity toward micromanagement (Albright made hotel reservations for VIPs himself) and the fact that he took a great interest in presenting wildlife as a tourist attraction, it is probable that he was aware of the control measures from the beginning. Publicity from the ECC pamphlets and his association with Pearson forced Albright toward reversing his stand and offering public protection of the pelican. Albright now faced the embarrassing situation of attempting to explain to the president of the National Association of Audubon Societies how the NPS, a preservationist agency, could have killed individuals of a species that was known to be in danger of extinction. How could he explain the willful campaign, effectively directed by the Bureau of Fisheries? The cat was out of the bag, and the new director had to put the best face on the predicament. Albright described the events to Pearson as an experiment, carefully contrived and controlled, which never placed the colony at any risk. He leaned on the crutch of prudent management as he reassured Pearson that the measures of control were themselves capable of being controlled with precision and foresight. Actually, such fine adjustment never was attempted. With the 1932 cessation of pelican control, Toll seized the reins of wildlife management back from the Bureau of Fisheries, and the NPS faced the necessity of creating a clear and more consistent policy, which, in turn, forced a redefinition of Yellowstone's purposes.

Pearson offered to help Albright by sending copies of Albright's letter to two hundred interested individuals. Albright soon received letters of support and understanding from many who had earlier written him scathing letters after reading the pamphlets issued by the ECC. Paul Bartsch, the mollusk curator at the U.S. National Museum, Seth Gordon, president of the American Game Association, W. M. Bell, acting chief at the Bureau of Biological Survey, Herbert Evison, executive secretary of the National Conference on State Parks, and others wrote in support of the NPS and offered muted apologies that anyone might give credence to the hysterical antics of the ECC, which was undoubtedly seeking only attention and notoriety.

John B. May, director of ornithology at the Massachusetts Department of Agriculture, had visited Molly Island in 1930 with the Appalachian Mountain Club. After observing two abandoned cormorant nests, he learned that the eggs had been collected for scientific purposes. What disturbed May was his perception of a general understanding among personnel working in the park that cormorants "would not be allowed to establish themselves in Yellowstone."[59] While May thought it odd to exclude a species of potential interest to the public, he expressed to Albright his sympathy for control measures aimed at a species "over-abundant" in any one place. Yet the size of the pelican colony was not large enough to necessitate control measures, and he was glad to know the park's policy was to protect the white pelican. A. Brazier Howell, a faculty member at Johns Hopkins Medical School who became active in the campaign against federal predator control, wrote to Albright, expressing his sympathies for the pelicans and arguing that "park visitors derive more units of pleasure from watching pelicans than catching trout." Albright replied that there had been good reasons for controlling the pelicans; after all, they ate up large quantities of cutthroat trout infected with parasites, swooping down at Grouse Creek "just like a fleet of ships closing in on a beleaguered enemy fleet shut up in a landlocked harbor." He reassured Howell that the Park Service "strictly adheres" to the May 1931 American Society of Mammalogists' statement deploring the control of predators. He argued that the park only destroyed predatory species "where it is absolutely necessary in order to protect other species more valuable to the park."[60] Yet never did the NPS reduce their numbers so that there was a danger of extinction, wrote Albright, instead, only aiming at stability and control. Albright's ambivalence between protection and control served his larger interest of creating a showpiece of animals in nature. Toll, who made the decision to protect the pelican, did not exhibit that ambivalence.

Looking back on that era, it is evident that Toll's decisions from 1931 to 1935 that protected the pelican and the coyote comprised an important watershed. The Molly Island pelicans episode was part of a longer and wider debate about extending wildlife protection to include mammalian predators. Even in the preservation-oriented National Park Service, actual adoption of the change in predator policy took time. Although Park Service Director Horace Albright declared protection for all animals in the May 1931 issue of the *Journal of Mammalogy*, it was not until 1935 that Yellowstone ended coyote trapping.[61]

Historians do not believe events are inevitable, and they shy away from simple explanations. From 1930 on, although biologists in the Wildlife Division were united and forceful in advocating protection of the white pelican in Yellowstone, they did not create a momentum for a decision favorable to the pelican by themselves. Several factors impelled Toll to declare protection of Yellowstone's predator pelicans: the publicity caused by the vigilant Emergency Conservation Committee, the opinion of Wildlife Division scientists who wanted to preserve rare species, the invocation of the parks' purposes by the Wildlife Division and by conservationists, and finally, Toll's own willingness to challenge the influence of the U.S. Fisheries Bureau in Yellowstone. The controversy over the predator pelicans helped preserve the white pelican in North America, shaped wildlife management policy in Yellowstone, and together with the debate over mammalian predators propelled Yellowstone and the National Park Service toward redefining the purposes of the parks. Toll gradually agreed to protect the pelican, and his decision was based partly on a very traditional preservationist orientation toward conservation, partly on his realization that the predator was a natural part of nature's operations in Yellowstone, and partly on the philosophical idea that all animals held a rightful place in lands administered by the NPS.

In 1931 the "bear problem" seemed to be the most nettlesome to Yellowstone's administrators, involving a risky interaction between increasing numbers of tourists and Yellowstone's resident populations of black and grizzly bears. Each year during the tourist season, black bears appeared by the roadsides, and tourists obligingly stopped their vehicles and fed them snacks of every sort. In the early years it seemed humorous; Albright himself as well as tourists found the roadside "holdups" by bandit bears a delightful encounter with the park's denizens. The bears of Yellowstone eventually became immortalized in television cartoons as Yogi and Boo-Boo, forever devising new methods of stealing picnic baskets. In a sense, it was classic Pavlovian response: The bears had been trained over many years by the tourists to associate snappy Fords and shiny Hudsons with a food supply, so the result was "begging" bears by the roadside.

Bears also found food in tourist camps, at the housekeeping cabins, and at auto campsites. They came into campgrounds at night, searching in garbage cans for food, tipping them over, and banging the cans about. Bears helped themselves to any unsecured food, and the noise of campers banging pots together as they chased bears away from their camp and into the next spread sleeplessness throughout the campground. Bears also ripped holes in canvas car tops as they detected and searched out odoriferous foods people left in automobiles. Guests at Canyon angrily sought parking places safe from bear damage, and some simply avoided overnighting at the attraction. Although many people reportedly had the thrill of a lifetime in their encounter with a bear, a serious downside materialized during the 1920s, when the park staff started to collect regular reports of damages to property and personal injuries caused by bears. The National Park Service had an additional problem, because many of these people began filing tort claims against the government, expecting full reimbursement for damages to their automobiles.

Bears inflicted injuries on many tourists who did not recognize the wild nature of these animals. A few bears became very well known in specific locales. Stopping daily at the same cabins to be fed by the tourists, these bears appeared quite tame. One such bear named Bruno did not always return the affection of park visitors, sometimes inflicting a scratch on the unwary. A. M. Drew of Fresno, California, wrote the director of the Park Service, noting that "childhood cannot be held responsible for Bruno's temperament and the fact that he will injure anyone that trespasses upon his good nature is fact sufficient for the park management to do everything in its power to keep childhood and foolish people from that danger." Injuries became almost a daily occurrence. One gentleman reported that he stopped his car near the outlet of Yellowstone Lake for a begging bear, but when no food was offered the bear "stuck all four of his tusks through his arm laying him up in the camp for nine days; and he says that while he was there [there were] seven other people in the hospital, all victims of the bear ferocity, and one of them hopelessly disfigured for life."[62] Naomi Crowlin was packing her truck when a bear pushed her with its forepaws, biting her arm and tearing the flesh. Such incidents were so common that when she walked into the superintendent's office to report the incident, the staff (not seeing her arm) burst out laughing. While being treated, Crowlin discovered the same bear had recently bitten six other people.[63] By 1929 injuries and damages were frequent occurrences in Yellowstone. Several boxes of these injury and damage reports occupy shelf space at the National Archives. In 1931, for example, tourists reported 76 cases of injury and 163 cases involving damages in Yellowstone, with 82 individuals seeking monetary compensation from the federal government for damages. The furry creatures that had boosted tourism now posed an irreconcilable dilemma, as delighted tourists became infuriated overnight.

Although most letters from park visitors complained about damages and injuries, a few complained that the overall park experience was lessened by their experience with the bears. In 1929 E. L. Quinn, a professor of chemistry from Salt Lake City, found many more bears in the campground at Fishing Bridge than he remembered from a previous trip to the park. The bears created so much noise as they tipped over garbage cans and stole food from neighboring camps that Quinn found it impossible to sleep. He wrote Superintendent Toll: "The bears are not wild animals in their own habitat but are partially domesticated much on the order of hogs."[64] Quinn suggested that the excessive numbers of bears really spoiled the park experience for the visitor, and thus the number of bears should somehow be reduced at the lake. Quinn and a few other visitors noticed that these were no longer wild animals, and he was among the first to imagine that it would be much more interesting to see just a few of the creatures.

From at least 1921, park rangers warned visitors about approaching or feeding the bears. As Park Ranger Milton P. Skinner put it in 1921, "No matter how friendly they seem, all bears are subject to dangerous fits without warning. LEAVE 'EM ALONE!"[65] Park rangers verbally warned people whom they saw too close to bears, and rangers posted notices at several locations in the park. Despite warnings from park staff, tourists throughout the 1920s and into the 1930s continued to feed the bears at the roadsides, dangling a morsel above an interested black bear as humans and bears posed for family photos of Yellowstone.

During the 1920s, park rangers tried various methods to chase bears out of campgrounds and away from cabins. In 1930 Ranger Baggley tried moving bears from Canyon to Madison Junction, but by 1933 some judged it useless, for the bears simply returned to the original location. Bears normally wander dozens of miles in a few days, and many male grizzlies have home ranges larger than a thousand square miles.

The Yellowstone bears ended up paying a price for searching out food in automobiles and campsites, and for the minor and major injuries they inflicted. A central axiom of bear management developed during the 1920s

16. Assistant Chief Ranger George W. Miller stands near this early-model bear trap, used to capture troublesome bears in 1931. Although managers tried moving black bears to different locations in the park, the bears often traveled back to familiar areas. Relocation of grizzly bears was initiated in later years and encountered similar problems. Courtesy Yellowstone Photo Archives.

was the notion that a very few bears caused all the trouble of tearing up automobile tops, while the vast majority of bears behaved in an ideal manner, showing up at the feeding grounds and disappearing back into the woods at night. The "bad" bears could be disposed of. Some thought the problem would disappear, and other people thought that some control would always be necessary. In 1931, for example, thirty-five black bears were killed by rangers. Horace Albright, Yellowstone superintendent from 1919 to 1929, believed the real problem in bear management was in ascertaining which bears were "actually doing the mischief."[66] During his administration the park "always made it a practice to kill bears when such responsibility was fixed," but identification was problematic.

Tourists feeding the bears at the roadsides and claw marks on late-model Hudsons were just the visible manifestation of a systemic problem. The larger difficulty was that feeding the bears had been institutionalized at Yellowstone on a grand scale. From the beginning of the tourist industry in Yellowstone, each tourist camp run by a concessionaire produced garbage that was dumped out for bears. Bears also found a regular supply of food at "bear feeding grounds," which consisted of hotel garbage. At Lake, Old

Faithful, and Canyon, tourists came to sit on bench seats arranged in an amphitheater and watch bears feed on trash dumped on a special platform. Very little separated the bears from the tourists, perhaps 150 feet at most, the boundary between human and bruin delineated by a simple rope. In 1926 the Yellowstone Park naturalist began to give lectures at these bear feeding grounds, thus institutionalizing the "bear show" as part of the park's educational program. The "bear pits" at Canyon were established within walking distance of the hotel. But by 1936 the park moved the Canyon bear feeding grounds farther from the hotels and cabins to "reduce the possibility of danger to the public," and erected stout wooden barriers around the feeding platforms.[67] Although some guests complained at the high cost of one dollar for transportation to the bear show, other tourists drove over themselves from nearby campgrounds to watch every night; bears as well knew the feeding schedule and showed up on a regular basis.

Beginning in 1929, Yellowstone sought a more definitive solution to the bear problem. Joseph Dixon, representing the Wildlife Division, visited Yellowstone from September 10 to 24, 1929, seeking information about bears and answers to the park's problem. His research with the bears got off to an exciting start when he followed a mother black bear and her cubs into a timber stand. He hoped to get a photo of them crossing the meadow beyond. Loud noises in the brush, possibly a large male grizzly, sent the black bears scrambling up trees and Dixon running for the safety of his automobile. His friend expressed surprise on his rapid return, remarking he thought the biologist was herding bears around in the forest, to which Dixon replied that "no, they were herding me."[68] Dixon later surmised that this grizzly was the same one breaking into locked boxes of oats in a barn on a regular basis.

Early on Dixon realized that the problem of damages and injuries was mixed up with food. After careful examination of bear tracks one morning at Canyon Lodge, Dixon concluded that most of the damage to autos was created by only 10 percent of the bears. A single bear had torn holes in the canvas tops of three vehicles to better smell out these potential food storage units. The bear in question was most probably the "show bear of the camp," the same black bear that greeted tourists and appeared in hundreds of home photo albums. Dixon thought it possible to track down "the culprit in bear damage cases" if rangers spent enough time on the task.[69] Dixon had very practical advice to offer a woman who asked what to do to prevent damage to her automobile. He advised her to not leave any food inside, and when she

17. Feeding bears from a wagon, probably at the bear-feeding area near the Fountain Hotel. From early on, hotels made their garbage available to bears. Tourists therefore had ample opportunity to view the ordinarily reclusive animals. This photo may have been taken as early as 1891, or as late as 1912. Courtesy Yellowstone Photo Archives.

came up with the idea of leaving a car door open, he advised fastening both doors open. In the morning, tracks revealed the bear looked into the vehicle but because of the easy access departed without leaving a scratch.

Dixon found that in most cases of personal injury, the people rather than the bears were to blame. Most incidents of biting or scratching resulted when people were "feeding the bears or teasing them by giving them food and then withholding the remains."[70] Only one man admitted to Dixon that the fault of injury lay with himself; he had fooled a bear into posing for a photo with an empty chocolate wrapper, but teased a second time the bear turned and bit him. If people would simply stop feeding the bears, as they were verbally warned, most of the trouble would disappear. Dixon thought that tourists would not stop feeding the bears despite any regulation, hence prominent signs advertising that feeding bears out of hand was at the tourists' own risk would at least free the park of the excuse that no one had warned the tourist. The park should also take care to inform visitors not to leave food in their cars, he advised.

Dixon also considered the bear feeding grounds. He speculated that the bear population followed the tourists; as the tourist season drew to a close, the bears began to drift away from the several tourist camps and cabins toward the three remaining places in the park where human garbage accumulated and was made available: Lake, Canyon, and Old Faithful. Dixon recommended that these three feeding grounds be moved a greater distance from hotels and campgrounds. People and grizzlies did not mix well, he noted. Additionally, it was questionable whether the feeding grounds at Lake, Canyon, and Old Faithful needed to support twenty to thirty grizzlies. Perhaps Yellowstone was overemphasizing the bears: "I do not see the necessity of duplicating this attraction at each camp ground," wrote Dixon.[71] He thought that the park might well have only one feeding ground where the public might watch the bears, well removed from hotels and camps to reduce human-bear conflict.

The Wildlife Division worked on the bear problem for the next four years. In general terms, Dixon thought the bear problem was getting worse instead of better, and that the bears might become more of a liability and less of an asset to the Park Service. In 1931 David H. Madsen, supervisor of wildlife resources with the Wildlife Division, argued that immediate action was required to convince the visiting public that the NPS was doing something to protect them while in the park. Negative publicity stemming from bear damages, he felt certain, reduced visitation in 1931. Actually, the Great Depression had more impact on visitation than complaints about bears. Madsen judged the park's policies to be unfair to the animals themselves. Because the older and stronger bears dominated the feeding grounds, younger bears might not be getting sufficient food and therefore ransacked vehicles and campsites. A good proportion of the bears might be entering hibernation not fully prepared for the winter. The number of black bears the area could naturally support, wrote Madsen, was on the order of twenty or thirty, yet now rangers estimated Yellowstone had about five hundred, up from an estimated two hundred in 1928. Two ideas are important here: Madsen's notion that a natural number of bears had been disrupted by human action, and second, his low estimate of the number of bears Yellowstone could support.

How to deal with these bears that broke into cabins and automobiles, and injured visitors? George Wright notified Toll that a combination of methods must be used to "effectively guarantee the Yellowstone visitor against annoyance in the various centers and still not deprive him of the assurance that he will see a bear during his stay in the park."[72] The bear feeding grounds would have to be moved away from human habitations, buildings and garbage cans could be bear-proofed, some bears would be trapped and moved far away, dogs might be employed to chase bears up trees, and tourists would be notified more effectively not to feed the bears. Accordingly, park staff and Joseph Dixon drew designs for bear-proof garbage cans and bear traps, as well as plans for a new bear feeding ground at Lake. Lake District Ranger Allyn F. Hanks suggested each visitor at the park gate be issued a card with emphatic warnings not to feed the bears.

The Wildlife Division communicated with Park Service personnel in Washington DC, in Yellowstone, and in other national parks, gathering expertise and opinion. In a sense, Yellowstone's policies were the result of a consensus-building process. Although the Wildlife Division's opinion carried significant weight, so did the practical expertise of the rangers, while ultimately the park superintendent had the last say in management decisions. Although his primary project was studying the elk, biologist William Rush chimed in on the matter of bear management. In Mammoth tipped garbage cans seemed to be the major source of complaint, said Rush. Yet bears did not bother with cans that contained no food, just as they "never bother an auto that contains no food." Rush opined that "food is the key to the bear situation."[73]

Rush also conducted a few practical experiments with the bears. Using a police tear-gas gun firing a .38-caliber cartridge, Rush fired away, watched the bear, then offered food. The two bears he experimented on remained unaffected by the tear gas, he thought, due to an eye structure insensitive to the gas. He also experimented with three different narcotics to determine how to put bears to sleep. Rush found that mixing three ounces of chloral hydrate with a quart of honey, then putting it on bread gave very good results. Yet these experiments, he noted, did not address the central problem of how to keep bears out of particular areas.[74] In September 1931 Rush received several bear carcasses from the rangers performing the control work and soon made a significant discovery. The bears were heavily infested with the tapeworm *Diphyllobothrium latum*, interestingly enough the same genus as the parasite infecting the trout. One bear yielded a full pint of the worms; no wonder the bears were "ravenously hungry."[75] Allyn Hanks, district ranger at Lake Ranger Station, thought that if some remedy could be found, the bear situation might materially improve.

Superintendents at other parks had similar problems and were canvassed for their suggestions. E. T. Scoyen at Glacier National Park had "very little sympathy with the average tourist and his troubles with the bears," because the entire problem was the collective fault of the visiting public. The only solution was "an absolute and impartial enforcement of the regulation of feeding bears" whether people fed the bears out of their hand or threw food to the bears. It would be better to train the tourists to obey the regulation by fining many people a small amount of money, than to continue sentencing many bears to "the death penalty each year for something which is not their fault in the first place." Waiting would not do any good either, wrote Scoyen, "we have got to face the facts and sacrifice a little publicity value and cause considerable hard feeling which we will deserve, due to our laxness in the past, in order to solve this problem."[76] O. A. Tomlinson, superintendent at Mount Rainier National Park, reported that efforts to feed bears did not come close to satisfying their ravenous appetites. The park would need a much bigger supply of oats if feeding was to work as a method of control. If 75 percent of a bear's appetite was satisfied by such feeding, property damages might be minimal. Tomlinson reported a large black bear had ransacked the superintendent's Christmas party food supply, including fruit cakes. Two nights later the raider was killed outside the park by a store owner. Notably, Tomlinson commented on the bear's old wounds (three .22-caliber bullets found in the animal's front quarters and a .30-caliber bullet lodged in the bear's side): "All of this evidence of the Chief Rangers [sic] attempt to frighten this particular bear show the futility of such control methods."[77]

During the tourist season of 1931, Dixon offered a remedy not essentially new, and yet it caused debate within the Park Service for the next two years as well as some serious thinking about the park's purpose. Based partly on estimates of bear numbers that suggested an increase in number from 1925 to 1931, Dixon suggested that a surplus of bears existed in Yellowstone, and that the Park Service should begin removing them. Despite the fact that troublesome bears had been removed continually during the 1920s, his recommendation was not universally embraced.

Rangers in Yellowstone thought that "bad" bears could be identified and disposed of. The idea originated in the 1920s and lived on as common knowledge throughout the 1930s. The entire problem centered around the issue of "finding some way to impress upon the bear population the fact that they are not wanted in the public camp grounds at Canyon and elsewhere."[78] In 1933 Park Ranger Francis LaNoue made this argument: "We will have to gradually eliminate this class of bear by disposal," and suggested "We can teach the bears that the feeding grounds are the only places where they can get garbage and other artificial foods."[79]

The Wildlife Division shared the idea that most of the problem belonged to individual bears and believed that control could be exerted over them. Wright supported Dixon's point of view, suggesting "that the consistent bad actors among the bears be quietly dispatched to bear heaven."[80] Madsen also concurred with Dixon, suggesting to Toll that troublesome black bears be identified by knowledgeable park rangers. Fifty bears should be removed that very year. If there were no outlet in zoological parks, then bears would have to be transported to the surrounding forests to be hunted, or the "surplus" killed under the close supervision of the Park Service.[81] Wright suggested that "the elimination of those bears too thick-skinned to be otherwise impressed, should make it possible to get every bear out of designated areas."[82] Here we see the limits of the Wildlife Division. Although trained at Berkeley with the most forward-looking group of zoologists in the nation, their conception of an individual bear's learning and behavioral patterns ultimately clouded the division's understanding of the bear problem. Even as they suspected that food had something to do with their dilemma, they were prone to see the problem on an individual rather than a systemic basis.

Yellowstone rangers and Wildlife Division scientists believed bears would show up at particular feeding grounds, yet stay out of patrolled campgrounds within five miles. Over the ensuing years this idea proved naive. The Wildlife Division simply continued the diagnosis and solution devised by Albright and Yellowstone rangers during the 1920s. In the matter of Yellowstone bears, these scientists offered more natural history than ecology. In essence, the Wildlife Division offered managers an ethic of control, a solution derived from common sense and ultimately from balance of nature concepts.

Dixon had reason to believe the numbers of bears in Yellowstone were increasing. Although he sought information on bear reproduction rates and numbers of bears, he did so in a way that did not guarantee accuracy. Based on a one-day count by the Park Service, he estimated the grizzly population at 130 and the black at 350, less than the park estimate of 424 black bears.

Rangers from each district wrote down the actual number of bears they observed, then gave an estimate for the number of bears they thought extant in the area. In the 1933 census, for example, the Riverside ranger district counted 3 adult black bears and estimated a total of 11, and it counted no grizzlies yet estimated 4 living in the vicinity. The Soda Butte station counted 9 black bear adults and estimated a total of 30 in the woods, and it counted 7 grizzly adults and guessed that 15 was the true number. There is no way of knowing how accurate this information was, but at the time many people trusted the information gained by this technique.

More importantly, Dixon thought that the bears had reached their "natural" plenitude, and that "their numbers must be artificially limited" so they would not expand indefinitely.[83] Based on the litters he observed (one litter of four cubs, and three litters of three cubs) Dixon concluded that Yellowstone grizzlies had high reproduction and survival rates. In short, on anecdotal evidence gathered in a few sites while in the park, Dixon was willing to make sweeping generalizations about numbers and reproduction rates throughout the park's thirty-four hundred square miles.

Dixon's logic of control and his suggestion that the Park Service plan on reducing the number of bears encountered opposition. William Rush informed Toll that the bear "is the most misunderstood and most wrongfully handled animal we have." Was it so surprising that bears would forsake expending the energy to turn over logs and rocks for a few grubs when they might more easily rip open a car top to secure several pounds of food? He saw, perhaps more clearly than anyone else, the central paradox of park practices and policy. In play and in family quarrels, bears inflicted more forceful blows on each other than all the "childish means" Yellowstone staff had used in hopes of chasing bears or modifying their behavior: thrown sticks and stones, ammonia, firecrackers, and electric shocks. Rush noted that at the same time, "we feed them delicacies from the other hand, which vitiates the little offered in the way of punishment. We have taught the bears during the past forty years how they can obtain an easy living and at the same time tried by very amateurish methods to discourage him in one or two things such as ripping auto tops and upsetting garbage cans."[84] Only with extensive training did hunting dogs learn not to act in certain ways, and yet the park expected the bears to avoid one or two specific behaviors. Rush suggested that only individual training would ever yield such results. Madsen, like Rush, understood that the habits of bears did not mix well with the habits of tourists. These sleek and fat bears that stole food had been judged by tourists and administrators to be bad: Bears "are expected to forget the training of three summers, and the instinct of ten thousand years, and eat like well trained boys. The truth is, . . . there are no bad bears. It is the system that is all wrong."[85] Rush and Madsen thus pointed out the conundrum that went unsolved for another thirty years.

Horace Albright found the idea of eliminating bears troublesome. Yellowstone was noted worldwide for its bears, and the idea of anything interfering with the tourists' opportunity to see bears was distinctly uncomfortable for Albright. Noting that in 1925 Ranger Keate at West Thumb logged almost one hundred reports of scratches and bites in one summer season, Albright told Dixon he did not believe the problem was much worse than prior years. As for numbers of bears, while superintendent he had noted that during some seasons many bears were sighted, but the next year they might be very scarce. Although the available food from garbage had doubled due to increased visitation since World War I, even more might be available if camp operators would efficiently separate the edible garbage from the cans. Despite the increased availability of food, Albright did not believe there were actually twice the number of bears. He surmised "the very fine protection in the park has probably made the bears tamer," just like the ducks and geese.[86]

In 1931 Albright disagreed with Dixon's idea that Yellowstone had surplus bears available. From the national parks' standpoint, he found the term "surplus" problematic: "The abundance of wild life goes through a cycle and I think it is preferable to speak of maximums and minimums rather than of surpluses."[87] Although Albright had shipped elk, bison, and bears out of the park during the 1920s for various purposes, such as zoological exhibition or restocking depleted game ranges, in 1931 he expressed ambivalence on the subject of surplus animals. The context of his thoughts was important here. Albright had been fending off another effort by Barton Evermann to return to Yellowstone for the purpose of collecting more grizzly specimens. If the park allowed the California Academy to collect specimens, then every museum in the country would expect the same, wrote Albright. Second, central to Albright's conception of Yellowstone's purpose was creating a place where visitors could see wildlife. Although it was fortuitous if animals appeared in a natural setting, the roadside was perfectly acceptable, and if two thousand people could crowd into an amphitheater to witness a number of grizzlies feeding on carefully separated garbage, the scale of the attraction simply attested to Yellowstone's preeminent place as a showpiece of nature.

What influenced Albright the most? Was it his preservationist instincts, lingering anger at the arrow-slinging hunters from the California Academy, or was he beginning to look at the park in ecological terms? Based on other communications, we can conclude that Albright was protectionist in thought but equally concerned with providing tourists an opportunity to see wildlife. Did Albright's ambivalence represent a fundamental change toward thinking about bear populations in an ecological sense of food supplies, territories, and shifting populations, or a wariness concerning possible adverse publicity? Although Albright worried over bad publicity and was willing to manipulate nature to the tourists' advantage, his thinking also reveals a gradual infiltration of ecological notions into even the most preservationist of NPS staff.

The most compelling critique of Dixon's calculations to remove bears was offered by Harold C. Bryant. Bryant received his Ph.D. in ornithology at the University of California, Berkeley, after investigating the diet of meadowlarks, proving their dietary habits were of assistance to the farmer and fruit grower, rather than a hindrance as many believed. Appointed economic ornithologist at Berkeley as well as named to the California Fish and Game Commission, Bryant penned more than two hundred publications during his career, including the imposing *Game Birds of California* with Joseph Grinnell and Tracy Storer. Bryant was singularly responsible for the initial development of nature-guiding services in the national parks beginning about 1920, organizing the Yosemite School of Field Natural History in 1925. By 1930 the interpretive program was so large that the NPS devised a branch of Research and Education, placing Bryant at its head.[88] Bryant's influence in the Washington office can be detected in the many documents he signed as an acting assistant director.

Bryant found the Wildlife Division plan to remove fifty black bears and up to twenty-five grizzlies very disturbing. To his mind, the Park Service should be working toward presenting wildlife to the public so that it might be viewed and appreciated. But the proposal of the Wildlife Division seemed to lead toward a different ideal, "that of making a park a huge game farm to produce a game crop that must be disposed of." Would the same procedure have to be followed with every abundant animal in Yellowstone? Bryant noted that the park had been recently "forced into marketing bison and elk," due to supposed surpluses, and now the first harvest of a bear crop loomed before them. The matter of ideals was not ephemeral to Bryant; the Park Service had spent years building ideals consistent with its land management

18. Harold C. Bryant was instrumental in the creation of nature education and interpretation within the National Park Service. Photo most probably taken in Yosemite National Park. Courtesy National Park Service, Harpers Ferry Center.

responsibilities. He realized compromise and reasonableness were sometimes necessary, and he did not want to "force a swivel chair viewpoint on to those of you who have been spending months in the field studying these problems on the ground." Bryant reminded Wright that the Park Service's fundamental purpose was to administer the parks as primitive areas; indeed "they are the only government-owned areas where emphasis is placed upon keeping unmodified conditions." Bryant felt uncomfortable with Dixon's heavy-handed solution, and he worried when the Wildlife Division at the same time guardedly endorsed predator control. He asked Wright, "Do you not think that there will be justified criticism if we begin advocating artificial control measures of every bird or animal that gives temporary trouble in a park?"[89] Bryant was correct; in his easy chair in Washington he did not face the practical difficulty of what to do next with bears that were ripping into automobiles nightly. Yet Bryant's thoughts on the purpose of the parks and how that translated into wildlife policy proved prescient. The Wildlife Division advocated management that intruded, rescued, and solved problems.

H. C. Bryant was one of the few who tried to match maintaining primitive conditions with practice.

Dixon responded to Bryant's misgivings by sharing his own conviction that "the present bear situation in Yellowstone is anything but natural."[90] Dixon had discussed the bear situation with an engineer who supposedly had been in Yellowstone since 1880. During an entire summer of field work during the 1880s, his crew had seen only seven bears, far too few to use as a food supply as they had hoped. Published travelers' accounts also pointed to the same conclusion, said Dixon, that the number of bears in 1931 was many more than in the early days of the park. Yellowstone Park staff noted that although the number of rail visitors (and therefore food from the hotels) had dropped, the bears were nonetheless increasing and coming into conflict with the increasing number of automobile tourists who used campgrounds and cabins. Superintendent Toll's office notified Director Albright that "we are all agreed that there is a surplus here and we must get rid of some of them."[91] Yellowstone's scientists and managers failed to address the apparent increase in bear population. Because tourists were feeding bears, the bears became more visible. To what extent human-supplied sources of food increased bear populations is not easy to estimate; methods of estimating population size have improved since then but remain hotly debated. What is important is that the Wildlife Division *thought* Yellowstone had a surplus of bears.

Toll, Albright, and the Wildlife Division confronted a related conundrum, this one highly visible. Albright appointed a committee, chaired by Joseph Dixon, to consider the bear problem on a park system-wide basis. Dixon asked Madsen the question that bothered both managers and scientists: "How can we have a good bear show and still protect visitors and their property?"[92] Director Albright noted one of his guiding principles: "One of the duties of the National Park Service is to present wild life 'as a spectacle.' This can only be accomplished where game is abundant and where it is tame."[93] Indeed, the park used various methods to present wildlife. For example, rangers placed salt in a strategic location in the Hayden Valley starting in 1929 to attract elk to a location where tourists could view them.[94] Mather and Albright never saw a great conflict between the Park Service's dual mandates, to preserve natural features yet also make it possible for people to visit the sites. Wildlife was a movable attraction that seemed particularly suited to manipulation. Albright thought that the feeding grounds at Old Faithful needed to stay right where they were: The "bear show there and the lecture are too important not only to Yellowstone but to the entire park system to justify removal of feeding grounds to a more distant place."[95]

Madsen, on the other hand, suggested that the park discourage the competition that had developed between the various hotels and camps, all endeavoring to attract the most bears to their own feeding ground. To decentralize the bear population, animal carcasses might be left near roadways, out of sight yet giving the opportunity for tourists to see the bears. Could the Park Service have some sort of perfect system where all the bears behaved and yet tourists still enjoyed a "good bear show"? Although a perfect system was not possible, Madsen thought conditions could be much improved. Whatever Yellowstone did, "the Park Service, can never excuse or live down any action on its part either by commission or omission, that will result in removing the bear from his present position as a Park attraction."[96]

Pressure in favor of the bear show continued for the next few years. In 1934 C. Max Bauer, Yellowstone Park naturalist, agreed with Ranger LaNoue that feeding bears at Old Faithful was "not necessary but perhaps undesirable." Yet Bauer believed that the bear shows had such high attendance that three points on the loop road were not too many to give tourists the opportunity to see the bears. Sometimes the parking lot at Canyon was completely filled, and at Old Faithful as many as two thousand people showed up at one time to see the bear feeding, "even with the show as poor as it has been there this season."[97] In 1934 Bauer suggested that a feeding ground was necessary at Mammoth Hot Springs. Thompson replied that Bauer's suggestion had stimulated more thinking about the bears at the Wildlife Division. The division was increasingly of the opinion that bear feeding was not very desirable: "We do not know what effect this artificial feeding of concentrated foods will have upon either the anatomy or the habits of the wild bear." The only mitigating factor in bear feeding was the pleasure and educational value derived from the public witnessing the grizzly bears at the feeding grounds. The grizzly shows at Old Faithful and Canyon were unique, "far more thrilling than fifteen or twenty blacks at the garbage heap where you see only a mass of shoulders and backs and hear the sloshing of garbage and the crunching of tin cans."[98] Tourists could see black bears at other parks, but only Yellowstone had the grizzly show.

Some had misgivings about eliminating the bear show. Rush thought that bears could be driven away from areas like Old Faithful, but the park would lose its greatest attraction. The damage incurred to automobiles was not too much, considering the great educational and recreational benefit de-

19. The bear show near Canyon Village, 1936. A park ranger, sometimes astride a nervous horse, would lecture on the natural history of the bear. This activity was very popular for park visitors, who would drive to the bear feeding grounds and special parking lot. Courtesy Yellowstone Photo Archives.

rived from watching the bears. Rush argued there was no practical way to reduce the damage "without greatly reducing the attraction of the whole wild animal population."[99]

In the spring of 1932 Ranger George F. Baggley assembled a plan for control of the bears. Baggley called for feeding all available garbage in the park to the bears, holding it at the incinerator until late in the day when it would be made available to the bears. Collecting it twice a day would ensure that bears would find no food during the day or night at campgrounds and cabins. At camps other than Old Faithful, Lake, and Canyon, Baggley wrote that no new feed ground need be established, as the garbage could be hauled three miles away and "dumped for the bears." Employees, especially the kitchen help who violated the "do not feed the bears" rule, should be dismissed. Baggley assumed that bears increased their numbers rapidly, and that some would have to be removed. A few troublesome bears would always remain, so five portable traps should be constructed and be made available to move first-time offenders. We know that Baggley had already lost faith in moving bears about, so we must assume that Toll still thought the technique worth a try. Baggley finally urged a concerted effort to warn tourists not to feed the bears but did not think more signs were necessary.[100]

At the end of the 1932 tourist season, Toll and Wright generally agreed on ideas for a plan that they hoped would establish "a bear population approximately normal for the area under natural conditions, with artificial feeding at two points only." Bear feeding grounds would continue only at Old Faithful and Canyon, "where every effort will be made to produce the best possible show." Achieving that normal bear population was the problem. Managers exuded a confidence in knowing bears and the necessity of control: "Any considerable bear population in the vicinity of Fishing Bridge, Lake, Thumb or Mammoth is unnecessary since there will be no bear feeding at these points."[101] Toll was correct in his assumption that eliminating feeding at Mammoth would create different conditions for bears, yet the natural food sources at Fishing Bridge and Thumb were considerable. Toll and Wright did not realize that campgrounds and human food supplies overlay great quantities of fish available to bears.

Not all the scientists and managers agreed on what should be done with the bears or why. Baggley's plan was to some degree the best consensus that could be reached among people who disagreed, but it also reflected the fact that the superintendent had ultimate authority in setting policy. Toll noted that the grizzly population had increased at the Old Faithful and Canyon feeding grounds, dominating black bears, and furthermore outstripping the artificial food supply. Yellowstone accordingly planned to "dispose of approximately one-third of the grizzlies," hopefully, by shipping them to zoos or supplying specimens for museums.[102] Yet Baggley's "Outline of Method for Bear Control," dated May 1932, noted there were not too many grizzlies. Clearly, Madsen and Dixon successfully convinced Toll that control measures were necessary, while the misgivings of Baggley, Rush, and Bryant lost out.

Bryant's questions about the park's purpose underscored the issue of what was natural. The idea of bad bears got mixed up with the notion of reducing the number of bears to establish a more natural number. In 1932 Toll wrote that the black bear population would be "brought down to a proper number by disposing of destructive bears." This effort to reduce the size of the population had to be carried out during the summer tourist season to single out the destructive bears, because if done in the late fall it "would be a reduction of population rather than an elimination of the criminal element."[103] In 1932 Toll was not thinking so much about a reduction in bear numbers but rather the removal of the problem bears.

In 1933 Madsen recommended to Toll that the Park Service calculate the number of bears supported by natural food in the area, then figure how many bears the park thought necessary to produce "the desired spectacle." The park then might "supplement the natural food with artificial food to the point where there is no starvation among the Park Bears."[104] Bears causing damage and injury would be eliminated. Madsen responded to LaNoue's report on garbage and reduced tourist travel by suggesting that with falling visitation, the bears couldn't find enough to eat, and to prevent property damage the park should make up the difference in food supplies. Madsen thought the bear population should not be reduced too much in an effort to balance the population with available food. Rather, Madsen agreed with Toll's suggestion that a supply of oats might see the bear population over depression-era drops in visitation.

Although forward-looking in many respects, the Wildlife Division demonstrated a good deal of continuity with ideas and management methods devised by rangers in the 1920s. In methodology Dixon exemplified a traditional natural history approach to the wild bears of Yellowstone. He never gathered any original data on the bear populations, but one could hardly expect that he would be able to do so in two weeks. Yet his confidence in making estimates about the numbers of bears and their reproductive success based on his personal observations and on a one-day bear census conducted by park rangers demonstrates what was considered adequate information in 1929. Much of the evidence he used seemed self-evidently important; rangers, administrators, and scientists thought there were many bears that were easily counted at the dumps and at the feeding grounds. Tracking the black bears around the hotels one could get a very good idea as to how many bears had come around during the night and damaged exactly which vehicles. While the nineteenth-century naturalist's estimate of bear numbers was more unreliable than Dixon thought, we should note that into the 1990s conservationists have vigorously disputed bear numbers in the Yellowstone country. It remains very difficult to know the whereabouts and hence the numbers of reclusive wild animals.

To his credit, Dixon rather quickly discerned the basic elements of the system involving bears and the garbage supplies issuing from the hotels, as well as the basic reasons for conflict between bears and humans. Dixon and Rush had intuitively sensed that the entire system of food availability was responsible for the bear "problem." In their description of a natural balance thrown awry by human activity, they recognized how hotel garbage had entered the ecological patterns of the bears' habitat. Their solution of eliminating the casual feeding of bears and secure storage of food in campgrounds eventually reduced much of the conflict between bears and humans. Their idea of reducing the availability of garbage to a few locations away from tourist-frequented areas foreshadowed a more radical solution adopted many years later.

When Dixon carried out his bear investigations for the Wildlife Division, managers began to see the potential for scientific examination of wildlife. In 1932 Baggley noted the need for research on bears. He called for gathering data on each "bear episode regardless of its character," and for pathological data. Baggley rightfully opined that there were "without doubt many things not now known about the Yellowstone bears in regard to their rate of increase and association with man." It remained a mystery why "bears do some things and their reaction to man-made plans for their betterment."[105] Very little was known about the life histories of bears, much less ecological relationships involving natural and artificial food sources. Yellowstone started collecting information on bears by requiring rangers to record every bear sighting. Those reports are now voluminous file folders full of brief records noting the time of day a ranger saw a bear along the roadside or sticking its head into a trash can. Staff thought the reports of bear activity might be useful, but these reports actually revealed little but the clash of nature and a human landscape. The most scientifically informative work was Park Ranger Frank W. Childs's studies of black bear hibernation from 1933 to 1934.

Director Albright came close to the truth when he confided to Dixon: "I don't think we have come anywhere near solving the bear problem in the Yellowstone."[106] For all practical purposes, ecological research on bears was not initiated until the 1950s. One reason for the lack of emphasis on bear research was a perceived need to address another pressing problem in the park, that of the northern Yellowstone elk herd.

In addition to the trumpeter swan survey, the public controversy over Yellowstone's predator pelicans, and the dilemma over what to do with the problematic bears, the Wildlife Division joined a scientific investigation of the elk already under way. In 1927 William Rush, biologist and assistant forest supervisor on the Gallatin National Forest, stood on the sagebrush-covered slopes north of the park headquarters at Mammoth, looking out over Mount Everts to the east and northward to where the Gardner River cut through ancient gravel deposits on its way to the Yellowstone. With the toe of his boot,

Rush thoughtfully poked at a bunch of cheatgrass, kicked at the bare soil between clumps of sagebrush, and knelt down, carefully placing his knee between a small rock and one of the cacti adapted to the cold winters of high country. The tufts of grass Rush took in his hand and the specific places on rabbit brush and horsebrush where ungulates had browsed on buds and shoots yielded clues regarding the recent passage and dining habits of the wapiti.[107] In 1928 Yellowstone hired Rush full-time to study the condition of the range, which he did until his departure in April 1932. Yellowstone was the first national park to hire a full-time scientific investigator to gather information regarding a specific species or resource. In 1932 Rush summarized his study in a 131-page document published by the Montana Fish and Game Commission.

In this monograph Rush quoted extensively from a report by Park Ranger Milton P. Skinner, written for the 1927 *Roosevelt Wild Life Bulletin*. Skinner echoed the common knowledge about elk in the West, theorizing that during the great slaughter of game animals on the plains, elk had retreated up into the mountainous regions, including Yellowstone. Skinner quoted parts of the accounts of early explorers and the official report of the 1872 Hayden Survey to demonstrate that during the early days, game was scarce in the Yellowstone country. The hunters supplying Hayden's party with meat, for example, did not have much luck around Yellowstone Lake. Skinner and Rush accepted the idea that in the days before civilization, game was scarce in the mountainous region of Yellowstone. They bought the notion that regional settlement in nearby valleys of Wyoming and Montana had pushed the remnants of once-great herds into the mountains, yielding an historical explanation for the contemporary good-sized herd found in northern Yellowstone. But Skinner overlooked other accounts of the Hayden Survey that mentioned or discussed wildlife in more detail. Today, historians acknowledge a considerable amount of evidence pointing to relatively abundant wildlife in and about the park area during the mid–nineteenth century.[108]

In 1914 Rush rode on horseback through the Lamar Valley, noting heavy use in only one particular location where a buffalo herd had congregated and where horses used for commercial operations were pastured. Rush thought that winter range north of the park had been heavily used, mostly by domestic cattle and horses. Since 1911 elk had left the park in numbers from five hundred to seven thousand and had done their share in depleting the range outside the park.[109] Returning to the park in 1926, Rush perceived changes in the vegetative landscape.

Rush believed that winter range inside the park had "deteriorated fully 50 percent since 1914 due to overgrazing and drought."[110] Rush had forty-one years of weather data available, which showed annual precipitation ranging as low as 7.95 inches. Yet drought was mentioned only peripherally in Rush's report. The signs of overgrazing, on the other hand, were very clear to Rush. He noted that sheet and gully erosion affected the winter range in the Lamar Valley, estimating that perhaps as much as two inches of topsoil had been lost. The undesirable Yellowbush (Chrysothammus sp.) became more prevalent, he thought, because the grasses were not competing effectively for water. Other indicators of overgrazing he noticed were Western wheat grass (Agropyron smithii) and dwarf Muhlenbergia (Muhlenbergia sp.).[111]

Borrowing from the 1931 work of M. W. Talbot, who was employed by the U.S. Department of Agriculture's Bureau of Plant Industry, Rush listed twenty-four nonforage plant species in Yellowstone Park, thirteen introduced from overseas, and only six of them native to Yellowstone. Imported along with hay and oats, these plants got the title "weed," because ungulates found them unpalatable. Cheat grass (Bromus tectorum) was the worst of the lot, an exotic from Europe that was spreading not only over Yellowstone's winter range but across thousands of acres of western range lands. Downy chess, in Talbot's words "a very inferior, almost worthless grass, has overrun large acreages on the lower foothills."[112]

Just as important as his impressions and conclusions was the methodology Rush employed. Although Rush's 1932 report analyzed the chemical composition of forage plants and gave indices estimating their palatability, it offered no quantitative assessment of changes in vegetation composition. Range managers identified species as "increasers" or "decreasers." Rush in essence simply walked or rode through the range and checked species off on his list, present or absent. The presence of certain species gave warning signs of overgrazing. Ungulates obviously ate the plants they found most palatable, but it was thought that they ate so much that plant reproduction would suffer and hence unpalatable species grew in number and extent. Proper range management sought to avoid such overgrazing to maintain the best forage production. When Rush wrote that cheat grass was expanding its range, however, he had no numbers to quantify his observation. The 1932 monograph was mostly based on this sort of use of a species list and the characterization of range condition by the presence of increaser and decreaser species.

The second important method Rush used consisted of building exclosures, or tall and stout fences that prevented elk from grazing on a particular plot of ground.[113] What would the vegetation look like if it were not over-grazed? By excluding all grazing animals, the fences did reveal that grasses and browse species freed from grazing and browsing pressure did indeed grow and remain more verdant appearing. The problem was that it was an either-or proposition: It was not possible to simulate a slight or moderate grazing pressure. Nevertheless, comparison of vegetation inside and out-side the fence line was thought a valid indicator of overgrazing.

Although plant ecology incorporated new methodologies during the early twentieth century, Rush's methodology reflected traditional tech-niques of range assessment. As Rush put it, he "depended a great deal upon his experience in dealing with domestic stock on mountain ranges" as well as on his familiarity with the northern range. Rush admitted that his tech-nique was "not the scientific method of range study and was adopted only for the sake of expediency."[114] Beginning in 1898 plant ecologist Frederick Clements had developed a new technique to introduce more quantitative methods to grassland studies. Clements and his students began measuring off a series of plots, one square meter each, across the Nebraska grasslands, noting the species, and counting the number of plants within each plot, or quadrat. With the invention of the quadrat came a "profound epistemo-logical shift."[115] This methodology helped lead Clements to his particular view of the prairie, which became known as the grasslands school of ecol-ogy. Publishing his ideas in *Plant Succession* (1916), Clements argued that grasslands naturally changed in composition over time, evolving through a series of stages toward an ultimate steady-state known as a "climax stage." Under certain adverse conditions, however, landscapes could fall backward on the successional pathway. By the early 1930s the succession theory be-came widely accepted, hence we might understand the "common knowl-edge" of the time as a Clementsian paradigm.

Not until 1931 did the introduction of quadrats bring the first use of quan-titative technique to assess the range in Yellowstone. Rush established test plots on the northern range to attempt a more concise determination of how fast cheat grass was spreading. He also recommended a "complete range study along scientific lines," disease studies, "studies in experimental pas-ture," and improvement of techniques for taking the elk census. To really get a sense of what was happening on the range, Rush noted, the park should use the "quadrat or mille-acre method for the study of plant succession, quadrats for volume studies, fenced and marked unfenced plots of browse for growth studies, phenological observations of forage plants, studies of exotic weed invasions and plots for erosion study."[116] Rush was learning fast about range methodology, and his successors used most of these methods.

Rush suggested that Yellowstone's northern range was changing, and not for the better. "Non-forage plants are taking the place of valuable forage plants." If this trend continued, the elk of Yellowstone would cause changes in the vegetation: "All browse species are heavily overgrazed by elk and will eventually disappear from the range" unless the situation improved.[117] He predicted browse species would disappear in fifteen to twenty years if the range did not improve within five years. Erosion and vegetational changes meant that the range would one day no longer support these grazing ungulates. Rush's ideas and predictions fit neatly within prevailing ideas about range and grassland ecology. Instead of progressing in the normal sequence of succession or maintaining an equilibrium, the range was retrogressing, going backward in effect as it gained unpalatable species.

Rush recommended artificial reseeding of the winter range inside the park as the "only practicable method whereby this range can be quickly brought back to a high forage producing capacity." Rush knew of a place just north of the park ideal for irrigation and the removal of sagebrush. Experiments at the Colorado Agricultural College demonstrated that sagebrush eradication improved forage plants 160 to 262 percent, and rodent control likewise increased production 344 to 1,445 percent.[118] Clearly, Rush had few qualms about manipulating the landscape, although he realized irrigation would stop at Yellowstone's border.

Rush's feelings about sportsmanship as well as his concerns about the range influenced his recommendations for hunting north of the park. Though he thought that five hundred elk per year might safely be taken from the herd by hunters, he also decried the boundary line hunt near Gardiner. Each year near the town of Gardiner, hunters greeted elk as soon as they left the park, traveling north down the river valley in search of more winter range. On opening day of hunting season, hunters lined up just north of the boundary and at the opening hour let fly volleys at the groups of elk. Many animals were killed outright, so many hunters were relatively pleased with an easy and successful hunt, even if they did not experience the pleasures of a wilderness hunt. The problem was that many animals were not killed but wounded by poor marksmanship, and as some hunters eagerly went forward to claim their kills by placing a permit on the elk, they found themselves in danger of being shot by other eager hunters. Another problem with the boundary line hunt was that many people thought the animals stopped at the border, knowing there was danger on the other side. Olaus Murie, who started work with the Bureau of Biological Survey in 1920 and stayed on through several agency name changes to retire from the USFWS in 1945, began studying the elk of Jackson Hole in 1927. Weighing in on the boundary line hunt, Murie disagreed with Rush: "In the face of a great array of guns, cars and general bombardment, when the time comes the elk will leave the park and work northward to their winter range. Other examples can be given, showing the stubborn and often stupid determination of these animals."[119] Although some animals always came out, hunting was viewed as a force holding the elk within the park.

In December 1926 Rush and Forest Supervisor Abbot witnessed a group of elk pinned against the park boundary fence near Gardiner by hunters who shot fusillades into the group for over an hour. The hunters were such bad shots that they wounded and maimed many of the animals. At one point seven of the elk had "one leg shot off."[120] Rush urged a revision of Montana's hunting laws to create a "limited license system," which would specify the hunting locale (district), sex of elk, and prohibit the killing of elk calves. He also recommended that a strip of land two miles wide just north of the park, from the Yellowstone River east to Jardine Mountain, precisely the location of the boundary line hunt, be closed permanently to hunting. Rush noted that under current hunting laws it was "very undesirable to attract elk from the Park early in the fall season."[121] This conclusion reflected not his scientific thinking so much as his ideas on sportsmanship in hunting.

Manipulating the herd and concern for the range also influenced Rush's ideas on elk hunting. Modeled on Utah's system, a limited license arrangement would end concentrations of dozens or even hundreds of hunters on the park line "and the fall migration would not be halted on the park line with the resultant damage to the Park range. Enough elk to more fully utilize the outside range would pass out, the hunting would be in the rear of migration instead of in front and pot shooting would be eliminated to a large degree." In the 1932 monograph Rush did not recommend reducing the size of the herd but stated: "No means should be taken to increase the present size of the elk herd until range conditions materially improve."[122] Estimating herd numbers at twelve thousand to fourteen thousand animals, his recommendation that hunters harvest five hundred elk per year aimed at taking the yearly increase of the herd. This concept of limiting the herd proved highly influential over the following thirty years.

20. William Rush in the laboratory at Mammoth, Yellowstone National Park, 1931. Like most park scientists in the early days, Rush was a generalist. He not only examined the northern range but also felt at home dissecting specimens like this bighorn sheep. Courtesy Yellowstone Photo Archives.

Rush recommended placing salt blocks over the range to manipulate the distribution of elk, spreading the animals over a greater portion of the range. Another way to manipulate the herd movement would be to increase forage production north of the park by means of irrigation and seeding, encouraging elk to leave the park earlier in the spring. Outside the park he suggested the control of "range destroying rodents . . . to secure the maximum amount of forage" as well as the control of coyotes and other predators preferably by trapping and hunting. Rush also suggested that the range be artificially reseeded along with the removal of all domestic stock from the winter range, and he called for an end to feeding hay at Game Protection Ranch, for when animals crowded together they fell victim to disease, and because elk became dependent "and do no rustling for themselves, thus becoming 'paupers.'" Yet at the same moment, Rush urged that feeding continue at Slough Creek "until winter range shows marked improvement."[123]

At the heart of Rush's management recommendations lay his definition of game management: "the production of the largest number of game animals, consistent with the carrying capacity of their range, and the best possible utilization of the surplus over the carrying capacity." Starvation of elk, for example, was "a preventable loss" that would be solved by the acquisition of more winter range and by range improvement. He thought that deer, antelope, mountain sheep, and moose "should be allowed to increase in numbers." Coyotes, however, might be reduced in number "to save the deer and antelope." Regardless of the fact that all animals supposedly found protection in Yellowstone, predators had to be carefully watched: "No doubt the bear and coyotes kill many elk calves but the balance that should be maintained between the predators and grazing animals requires a great deal more study than has been given it. My opinion at this time is that no bear should be killed solely because of their depredations on the elk herds but if museum specimens are required it might be well to locate and kill bears that are doing damage to the elk." Because coyotes developed a system of ambushing deer on the Yellowstone River near Blacktail Creek, Rush argued control was justified, because the deer might be extirpated. Although it was impossible to carry out studies thorough enough to "scientifically give each animal its place," broad principles could guide management. Though coyotes would keep the range-destroying rodents in check, mankind must exert a check on coyotes at the point where they killed "excessive" numbers of deer and antelope. Similarly, "the saturation point" in the bear population was when they destroyed too much property or killed too many elk calves.[124] Finally, Rush noted that managers would recognize overpopulation by the sign of overgrazing. Along with the assumptions of game management came presuppositions regarding proper balances, certain signs of imbalance, and the need for people to provide a cure.

Despite his suggestions about range improvements, changes in hunting laws, and salting, Rush had an intuition that the situation in northern Yellowstone was different from managing cattle on the Absaroka forest: "Scientific range management, while badly needed on the elk range, is impracticable because of the peculiar nature of the animals using the area." Elk wandered about, thus underutilizing some portions of the range and overutilizing other sections. They could not be herded, and salting and hunting "are not sufficient to effect the desired distribution on the range." Techniques used with cattle grazing, such as "seasonal use, rotation and deferred grazing, so essential to proper range management, are obviously impracticable" with wild elk on a large landscape. The answer was not terribly complicated: "Compared to the forage actually consumed, elk should have a larger acreage than cattle to allow for the uncontrollable habits of the elk."[125] Despite Rush's intuition that salting and hunting would not effectively move the elk into their proper places, such manipulative techniques were precisely what he suggested.

Rush was not alone in his assumptions about range management. In the 1920s the discipline of range management started to emerge, measured by the fifteen colleges teaching courses in the subject by the middle of the decade. The first textbook, written by Arthur Sampson, became available in 1923. Research during the 1920s focused on how various rates of stocking a range affected cattle production, and the first work on changes in plant composition was performed during that decade. The discipline included a growing group of scientists, including plant pathologists, agronomists, and grassland ecologists who by 1948 formed their own professional group, the Society for Range Management. Several concepts of range management, including carrying capacity, derived in large part from Clementsian notions about grassland succession.[126] If ungulates grazed too much, the climax vegetation of the range would be altered. Gradually, the composition of range species would retrogress, backward down the successional pathway to something less than the climax state. Range science concepts also reflected notions of equilibrium in nature. With excessive grazing the delicate balance of nature would be upset with the potential for disastrous consequences, including extensive erosion and a range that simply would never recover its former productivity. The lessons of the dust bowl became compelling examples of what could happen. Along with others, Rush knew about "carrying capacity," defined by range managers as the density of cattle providing maximum sustained production. Similarly, carrying capacity for Yellowstone's range was defined as the maximum number of herbivorous animals the vegetation could support over time.[127] If the number of grazing and browsing antelope, deer, elk, or moose exceeded that capacity, their grazing would adversely affect or damage the range. The concept retains its validity today among range managers, describing a general fit between animals and the range they inhabit. Theoretically based, carrying capacity remains a difficult parameter to estimate in real ecosystems.

Violation of the balance of nature became manifest during the late 1920s in Arizona's Kaibab National Forest. After zealously protecting deer on the northern rim of the Grand Canyon for years, wildlife managers were rewarded with the product of their labors: Deer herds increased dramatically. But the managers had not anticipated that the vegetation on the range could not possibly support so many animals. As winter gradually covered the dry landscape with cold winds and thin, almost transparent layers of snow, the deer exhausted the supply of grasses and herbaceous vegetation and finally began to strip trees of their bark in a desperate search for food. Massive numbers of deer starved to death but left a legacy in an apparent lesson for the managers of nature.[128]

Land managers of the 1920s and 1930s created the myth of a simple answer to the problems of ungulate eruptions and subsequent population crashes. In their view, the elimination of predators (especially the wolf) had caused the problem of ungulate eruption, and substituting human hunters for the missing predators provided the solution. Managers had a hard time convincing the hunting community of the need to reduce the size of ungulate populations, because for years wildlife managers had worked to increase the size of the herds, and the hunting public expected a bounteous harvest each year, not unnecessary and permanent herd reductions.[129] Wildlife managers, biologists, and range scientists grew more worried about the numbers of elk on Yellowstone's northern range.

The balance of nature concept provided one of the most influential guiding elements in Rush's thinking. The origins of the idea date back to Greek philosophy, thus lying deep in western culture. Well into the twentieth century, the concept continued as an important element in scientific and popular descriptions of nature. In general, the balance of nature concept posed elements of nature working in harmony, maintaining a general state of equilibrium, much like a smoothly functioning machine that never ran out of fuel.[130]

While some perceived the balance of nature to represent a static nature, the whole notion of change encompassed in Darwinian thinking undermined the notion of a perfect and unchanging nature. In 1913 Charles C. Adams described the balance of nature as "only a relative condition," moving like a pendulum, "sometimes showing considerable amplitude in its swing" and sometimes it barely moved at all.[131] From time to time, a local catastrophe overturned the normal course of affairs, and gradually a new balance developed. Adams and his generation revised the balance of nature. Only much later would this view become codified in the scientific literature as "perturbations" among "multiple equilibrium states."

By 1929 Adams understood the balance of nature in a yet more sophisticated way that foreshadowed later development of similar ecological concepts. When advocating land reserves for the preservation of natural conditions, wrote Adams, ecologists "do not mean, and certainly do not expect, the conditions to remain indefinitely 'balanced,' fixed and unchanged."[132] Adams argued that the parks could not be isolated or kept free of outside influences. Factors out of the control of parks, as well as the constant flux of evolution and adaptation, meant that parks would change through time. Did this detract from the scientific merit of studying these natural conditions? To the contrary, Adams thought that research in forest ecology conducted in natural areas was "needed to supplement controlled experimental studies." Adams's fundamental purpose was to set aside preserves "*to allow nature to take her own course with as little interference by man as is possible,*" a purpose unaffected by change in the landscape.[133] The preservation of natural areas would reveal how the balance of nature operated on its own.

Rush's version of the balance of nature was not radically different from Adams's. After all, it seemed obvious that weather conditions in any given year affected the size of the herd. Yet the concepts of succession and retrogression, as well as the possibility of a radical upset of the balance, captured the imagination of most scientists and administrators. Rush believed that the necessary precursor to herd eruption was a bountiful vegetative environment, that a subsequent glut of animals devastated that environment, and that a precipitous drop in population resulted. The scientists of the Wildlife Division shared Rush's climax-stage ecology, balance of nature scheme, and most importantly, his logic of control.

From 1929 to 1933 Rush and the Wildlife Division consulted together on the elk investigations. In 1933 Joseph Dixon and Ben Thompson reported the northern range in "deplorable" condition. They thought the range had deteriorated noticeably since they had last seen it in 1929, noting the trails left on hillsides, the hard-browsed *Chrysothamnos*, the browse line on trees where elk had eaten everything within reach, how elk had stripped the bark from aspen, and finally the sagebrush and willows they surmised killed by overbrowsing. To Rush, Dixon, and Thompson, the herd had clearly exceeded the carrying capacity of the range. The Wildlife Division agreed with other observers that the elk herd was "hovering on the brink of disaster" as the hungry times of winter approached; the first hard winter would bring "hideous starvation and wastage."[134] These words are an important clue to the Wildlife Division's motivations and their view of nature. Wasting na-

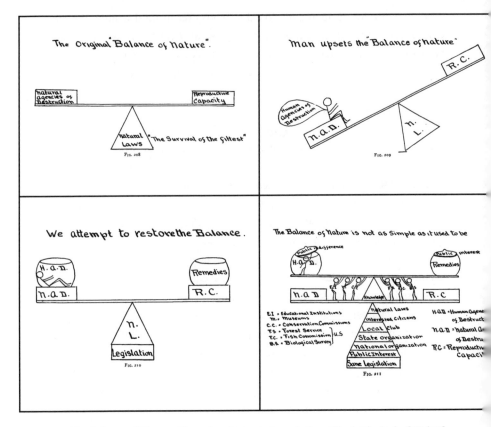

21. The Balance of Nature. These drawings are from Arthur Allen's *The Book of Bird Life* (New York: D. Van Nostrand Co., 1930). The notion that managers could restore a disturbed balance was widespread during the 1930s. Courtesy International Thomson Publishers.

ture's products was simply wrong. The manager's task was to rationalize the use of nature as well as to prevent inhumane deaths of wildlife.

Like Olaus Murie, who had studied elk food habits in Jackson Hole, the Wildlife Division believed that the size of the herd should be reduced. Considering the yearly increase of two thousand head, if the park removed three thousand elk per year, after approximately three or four years the elk herd would be about the correct size. Two available methods could effect the reduction: increasing hunting in Montana, or slaughtering elk within the park and distributing the meat to Indian tribes. Unfortunately, the Montana legislature would not be able to pass new game law legislation until the 1936 season, but then it would be possible to adjust bag limits, season length, and develop a system of open and closed seasons. Yet in mild winters the elk would not come out in sufficient numbers, they noted. Hence the park "must be prepared each season to slaughter elk as it does buffalo."[135] The Wildlife Division suggested that the prolonged overgrazing of the range endangered the elk as well as other species, and the solution would be to remove about half the herd.

Taking the advice of Rush and the Wildlife Division, Superintendent Roger W. Toll used the word "overgrazing" for the first time in his 1934 annual report. A shortage of precipitation and "heavy overgrazing on the winter range, which has caused serious depletion," said Toll, "will require stringent measures to bring about proper rehabilitation."[136] Yellowstone Park managers accepted the common wisdom of the day and adopted the judgments shared by range science and wildlife biology. In the early 1930s concern with the condition of the vegetative cover encouraged Yellowstone's managers to reconsider their handling of the elk herds they had so carefully protected and nourished toward greater numbers.

When scientists located the cause of a deteriorating range in an oversized elk herd, managers faced the practical question of how to eliminate elk. Yellowstone initiated a program to reduce the size of the herd that lasted over twenty-five years, yet in the end seemed to have little effect in rehabilitating the range. The program varied little over this time and incorporated three major elements: hunters took a harvest just across the border in Montana every autumn, park personnel trapped elk and shipped them out of the park, and if those methods did not cull the herd down to a proper size park rangers performed a "direct reduction" by shooting the excess population.[137]

Park personnel began to herd and trap the wild elk on a systematic basis, much as cowboys on the range lands surrounding Yellowstone managed their charges. Herding elk into the traps was always a problematic affair. The park built large corral-like structures, with a fence on one side running a third of a mile, to force a moving group of elk into a wooden fence funnel, and finally into a corral where wide gates swung shut behind the nervous animals. For wild animals unused to human proximity, the trapping procedure was traumatic—park rangers seized bulls and cut their antlers off with a saw to prevent harm to other elk as they were shipped. The trapped elk were dispatched to zoos, depleted game ranges in national forests, and state departments of fish and game for restocking purposes. To carry out direct reduction after the yearly Montana hunt, rangers traveled to places where segments of the herd pawed through the snow to find sustenance on their winter range in the Yellowstone and Lamar River Valleys. After rangers shot the elk with high-powered rifles, horse teams (and later Sno-Cats) dragged off the carcasses to be butchered as quickly as possible so that the meat would not spoil before its shipment to Indian reservations.[138]

From the first direct reduction in 1934 to the last in 1967, 67,440 elk were removed from the Northern Yellowstone herd. Over that span, 13,753 elk were shot by rangers, while hunters shot 41,400, 6,700 were live shipped, and 5,541 were counted as the victims of bad weather and insufficient winter forage.[139] Although direct reduction was continually used during that period to remove elk, the method took relatively few animals when compared to the Montana hunt. If live trapped elk are included in the total, the Montana hunting season generally took twice as many animals as did the NPS direct reduction. Hunters and outfitters resisted direct reduction from the 1930s to the 1950s, and, finally, during the early 1960s direct reduction came under fire from a wider national constituency.

The Wildlife Division also confronted the issue of mammalian predators in Yellowstone.[140] The division visited Yellowstone during the culmination of a national campaign by scientists aimed at changing federal predator control policies. A group of mammalogists were instrumental in educating people about the ecological role of predators and in lobbying key government officials. National Park Service policies on predators changed during the early 1930s. Curiously, the NPS safeguarded pelicans in parks after coyotes. Protection of the wolf (already extirpated) and coyote technically came with Albright's declaration of protection for all animals in 1931. The Wild Life Survey had suggested in 1932 that part of the range problem was a lack of predators, which should be addressed by "the restoration of the natural control factor in environment."[141] In reality, even when the new policy was decided and declared, the park found it difficult to shed old habits. Evidently, coyote poisoning went on in the park for another year before that practice finally ended. Historian Richard West Sellars argues a "cavalier attitude toward eliminating coyotes" continued, citing the example of Curtis K. Skinner casually shooting a coyote in 1935.[142] Ranchers north of the park subjected Toll to unrelenting pressure over the next five years to resume poisoning in the park, while they persuaded Bureau of Biological Survey agents to place poison baits as close as possible to the park border. In *Wildlife in the National Parks* (1935), the Wildlife Division endorsed "judicious control of coyotes by proper selective methods . . . where it is demonstrated to the satisfaction of the Director and the Wildlife Division that coyotes are endangering the sur-

22. Hauling elk carcasses by horse team out of the shooting corral at Slough Creek, 1935. Courtesy Yellowstone Photo Archives.

23. This photo of men preparing to cover elk carcasses with tarps prior to shipping conveys the production-line quality of the butchering associated with the elk reductions. Courtesy Yellowstone Photo Archives.

24. Cutting an elk's horns off, 1946. This was performed on elk
that were translocated, so the animal would not hurt itself or
other elk in the train car or truck. The procedure was not as pain-
ful as it looks. Courtesy Yellowstone Photo Archives.

vival of some other species."[143] Thus even the most forward-looking elements of the NPS did not extend absolute protection to the coyote. Similarly,
the Canadian national parks found it very difficult to end control of predators. At the same moment that Canadian parks were helping the public realize the place of all animals in nature's landscape, entrenched attitudes about
predators as well as a scientific viewpoint allowed managers to look at animals as individual units that could be experimentally controlled.[144]

By 1937 sentiment against the coyote on Yellowstone's northern border
proved so strong that in keeping with the policy that no "interference with
biotic relationships shall be undertaken prior to a properly conducted inves-

tigation," the NPS authorized a thorough study of the coyote's relationship to its prey species.[145] Adolph Murie, serving the Wildlife Division from 1934 to 1939, was selected to study coyote food habits in Yellowstone.[146] The Wildlife Division published his report in 1940 as part of its *Fauna* Series. National Park Service scientists H. C. Bryant, Carl P. Russell, Victor Cahalane, and Clifford C. Presnall supported and encouraged Murie's research. Carrying out his field studies from May 1937 through the spring of 1939, Murie analyzed almost nine thousand individual items from five thousand coyote scats. Murie's interpretation of his data indicated that the coyote was not as detrimental to the stockmen as was traditionally believed.

During summer months rodents were the major item in the coyote diet. Pocket gophers (*Thomomys fuscus fuscus*), for example, comprised 21.6 percent of the coyote menu, and Murie noted the coyote to be "one of the chief checks" on the pocket gopher population.[147] Field mice (*Microtus* sp.) represented a full 33.9 percent of the coyote diet, while snowshoe hare, marmot, and muskrat combined made up about 6 percent. Murie identified over 9 percent of the food items as grasshoppers and crickets. Coyotes also ate very small amounts of grass, fish, birds, other small mammals, and miscellaneous items scavenged from trash, such as cellophane and curtain material.

During the winter months carrion from the big game herds predominated in the coyote diet. Elk represented the largest source of food material among the large mammals, approximately 16 percent of the items identified, while deer comprised 1.03 percent, antelope only .54 percent, and mountain sheep a scant .02 percent. The proportion of domestic stock in the coyote's diet was so small, suggested Murie, that the coyote should not be viewed as an enemy of the ranchman. Murie found only five droppings containing domestic cow, and these were gathered near the Game Ranch "not far from one of the ranches still within the borders of the park."[148]

Murie's assessment was not welcomed by the Bureau of Biological Survey, but it comprised important evidence for Yellowstone's new policy protecting predators. Superintendent Toll found himself and the policy at the center of turmoil within the NPS. As Olaus Murie later described the situation, Adolph's studies of the coyote "met opposition at every step. In fact, it looked as though he would lose his job. . . . A former director did all he could to stop the investigation."[149] That former director was Horace Albright, who voiced his opposition to Director Cammerer. Albright's continued concern was for the tourist and for good public relations between Yellowstone and its neighbors, ranchers to the north of the park. Stock growing interests embodying traditional attitudes toward predators also exerted continual pressure on Yellowstone Park during the following three decades.

The Wildlife Division's study of the pelicans, bears, and elk, and Adolph Murie's work on the coyote comprised an important period of transition in thinking about wildlife in Yellowstone. This was not a radical revolution that established a new paradigm of understanding overnight, but rather a movement that incorporated continuity as well as significant changes in attitudes and growing ecological understandings. The larger purposes of Yellowstone comprised a major thread of continuity from the past; the purpose of the parks figured prominently in how administrators, scientists, and the public thought about Yellowstone. As several writers have noted, the problems parks face today are remarkably similar to the problems of the 1930s. This is not to say that the NPS has been negligent, but rather points to the deep and intractable nature of those situations.

The first important contribution of the Wildlife Division was its assessment of wildlife problems in the national parks. Published in 1932, *A Preliminary Survey of Faunal Relations in National Parks* was the first volume in the NPS *Fauna* series, described by historian Richard Sellars as "the threshold to a new era in national park thinking."[150] In 1935 Wright and Thompson continued their assessment of wildlife problems in *Wildlife Management in the National Parks*, the second volume of the *Fauna* series. The Wild Life Survey's initial investigations in Yellowstone proved influential in shaping its assessment of park wildlife problems. Wright thought it was important to understand the original conditions before Euro-Americans settled the area, as well as the history of wildlife conditions since that time. The first sort of wildlife problems, said the Wildlife Division, were created by humans before some parks were established. Settlement, logging, and agriculture had affected the wildlife populations in some parks, creating a problem of historical origin. Second, some parks did not have complete year-round habitats for some animals. These geographical problems were "traceable to the insufficiency of park areas as self-contained biological units."[151] A good example of this was northern Yellowstone's winter range problem. The third major problem was competitive in nature, a conflict between animals and humans that more often than not led to an animal's death, the bear problem in Yellowstone providing a vivid example of this type.

The second important influence of the Wildlife Division lay in creating the first clearly stated policies and rationale for wildlife management in the parks. The old policy of noninterference with wildlife had not yielded good results; the tradition of protecting wildlife was in itself not enough. The central thrust of the 1932 policies set up by the Wildlife Division was an interventionist sort of management strategy. Like the new generation of people trained in the new programs in professional wildlife management, Wright and company saw active wildlife management as a new form of conservation, superior to simple protection. A traditional objective, such as protecting the trumpeter swan from extinction, would profit from a new, active approach.

Third, the Wildlife Division introduced elements of ecological thinking into its rationale and recognized a role for natural processes. A good example of this ecological outlook can be seen in how the Fauna series pointed to wolves and coyotes as natural controls on ungulates. Ben Thompson suggested that the Kaibab disaster might not have happened if people realized "the organic character of the wilderness." Management of one segment of wildlife had inevitable implications elsewhere; shooting cougars resulted in too many deer, which, in turn, affected the range. "It is this very thing, the organic character of wilderness life," Thompson argued, "which makes it impossible for any national park or other wildlife refuge to stand alone, unharmed by factors outside of it." It was futile "to attempt to compute the recreational or game value of a wild animal on the basis of the number of times it may be seen by visitors," or how many might be harvested.[152] No one animal could be valued over another—that sort of thinking created the Kaibab disaster. Nor could park wildlife be managed without considering human influences outside the boundaries. Thompson's recognition of external effects on park resources proved prescient. In the 1980s the concept gained considerable cachet as environmentalists and managers recognized that outside threats were as dangerous as what occurred inside the parks.

The fourth major influence of the Wildlife Division can be found in its statements about the purpose of the parks and the relationships between wildlife and park visitors. In the 1930s the Wildlife Division applied the idea of preserving primitive conditions in Yellowstone. Performing scientific research in such places provided a utilitarian justification for preserving the primitive. The purpose of the wildlife reports, Wright said, was to provide "research in one branch of the science that is the very foundation upon which the National Park Service is built, namely, the preservation of the native values of wilderness life." This ideal, thought Wright, distinguished the NPS from the other federal and state agencies. In advocating the "preservation of the primitive," the Wildlife Division subscribed to the same purposes devised for the parks by scientists in the 1920s.[153]

The Wildlife Division addressed questions posed by the NPS dual mandate. George Wright asked: "How shall man and beast be reconciled in the conflicts and disturbances which inevitably arise when both occupy the same general area concurrently?" A failure to "maintain the natural status of national parks fauna in spite of the presence of large numbers of visitors would also be failure of the whole national parks idea."[154] The Wildlife Division dealt with the ambiguity of the dual purpose of the parks by suggesting that although both nature and visitors must be accommodated, the true success of parks would be measured by the preservation of their wildlife. Again, scientists' interpretations of the purpose of the parks had a formative influence on how Yellowstone would use ecological ideas.

Part of the fundamental difficulties of the national parks were found in cultural perceptions of wildlife. When visitors came to the park they expected to see animals in concentrations such as found in zoos, counted on the same convenience in seeing animals in a particular place at any time, and assumed the same safety people enjoyed in feeding tame animals. Thus, claimed the Wildlife Division, some park problems took root in "man's efforts to force the animal life to actually fit his concept instead of developing his concept to fit the wild life as it really exists in its natural setting." A "galaxy of bears at the garbage platform" satisfied the tourists' desire for the spectacular but was essentially a false image of nature. National Parks would offer a different kind of thrill, and tourists would learn to appreciate a new conception of wildlife, in essence a "realization that the unique charm of the animals in a national park lies in their wildness, not their tameness, . . . an appreciation of the characteristics of a real wild animal, notably, that each wild animal is the embodied story of natural forces which have been operative for millions of years and is therefore a priceless creation, a living embodiment of the past, a presentiment of the future." The role of Yellowstone's Educational Department, renamed the Naturalist Department in 1933, was to aid visitors in the "art of appreciation of wilderness life in national parks."[155]

The presentation of wildlife to the public must be natural, argued the Wildlife Division. This concept, established as a wildlife management policy in 1932, proved an important influence shaping the history of the National Park Service. The bears of Yellowstone provided one of the best examples of how artificialities introduced into the primitive environment had not only upset the bruins' feeding habits but also created a false image of nature, which interfered with the interpretive and educational functions of the parks.

To achieve the preservation of primitive wildlife conditions, the Wildlife Division advocated manipulation of wildlife and habitat, as well as restrictions on human actions. There was a certain irony in preserving the primitive by controlling the animals. While Toll and Wright protected the pelican from harm, they established a policy of removing elk and continued disposing of bears that damaged too many vehicles. Where was the park's mission to preserve primitive conditions? The Wildlife Division saw itself as preserving a threatened vegetative landscape, in today's terms a habitat. Because the division sought to remove artificial patterns of bear feeding, it saw itself as progressing toward the goal of preserving the primitive.

The Wildlife Division shared with state game departments and the USFS the assumption that manipulation and control of nature were desirable and would lead directly to the division's goals. The Wildlife Division saw conservation as "a means for securing the maximum cropping of natural resources without destruction of the productive capital. The forms of cropping include the realization of sporting, economic, esthetic, and scientific values."[156] These were men unafraid of meddling in nature to preserve it, and they saw such action as necessary because of the anomaly of trying to protect the primitive from thousands upon thousands of visitors. No similar situation or precedent had existed before. Conservation faced a task that would "challenge the conscientious and patient determination of biological engineers."[157]

The influence of the Wildlife Division on the historical development of the National Park Service suffered a blow on February 25, 1936, when George Wright and Roger Toll died in an automobile accident near Deming, New Mexico. At the time the two were serving on a commission investigating the possibilities of creating international parks. The Wildlife Division officially operated under Wright's leadership for only a little less than three years. Including the initial period when he had funded research out of his own pocket, Wright had worked on national park wildlife issues for seven field seasons. During that time the Wildlife Division progressed in terms of its own thinking about nature and made an important contribution to science in the Park Service that would not be replicated for thirty years. Clearly, Wright's personal leadership drove the contributions of the division. Harold C. Bryant noted that Wright had the "happy faculty of infusing into his writings, as well as into his contacts, an intellectual discipline and a vitality" that made the division a progressive force within the NPS. After Wright's death the National Park Service moved the Wildlife Division from Berkeley to the Washington Area Service Office under the guidance of Victor Cahalane, and in 1939 the division was transferred to the Bureau of Biological Survey Section on National Park Wildlife.[158] The division published a few more reports under the *Fauna* series, but with the transfer to the BBS the group's influence faded.

Significantly, the Yellowstone superintendency of Roger Toll and the creation of the Wildlife Division under George Wright coincided in time and in place. It is symbolic as well as tragic that they were together on the day of the fatal accident. Toll and Wright proceeded together on an intellectual journey in thinking about nature and about the National Park Service's mission. In the interactions between Wright and Toll we see the development of an ecological orientation to conservation in Yellowstone. Harold C. Bryant thought Toll's most significant contribution to Yellowstone was "the development of a more effective technique for the restoration and protection of natural ecological conditions."[159] Toll and Wright did not actually develop a specific technique, but the ideas they developed formed part of a lasting goal or ideal for the Park Service. Together with Bryant, they looked to science for information. While Toll and Wright advocated a logic of control to achieve natural conditions, Bryant offered an alternative vision doubting the wisdom of continued manipulation.

MANAGING THE NATURAL DURING
THE POSTWAR ERA

The park ideal is not yet completely accepted.

Olaus Murie to Newton B. Drury, 1951

During the 1940s and 1950s Yellowstone continued trends in wildlife management and national park conservation established during its earlier days.
The Wildlife Division had established a basis for scientific research within
the National Park Service, and its wildlife policies created for predatory animals were visionary. During the postwar period, however, the NPS did not
emphasize scientific research in the parks. Managers tended to see problems as having rather obvious solutions, rather than as conundrums requiring scientific research. Management directions previously created by the
Wildlife Division seemed to address these conspicuous problems. Naturalists and wildlife technicians were located far down the Park Service's list of
priorities, and budget allocations reflected this. Management strategies and
ecological understandings developed during the 1930s were still being used
by park managers.

There was good reason why administrators' concepts of wildlife management should have remained relatively constant during this time. The common wisdom of the day incorporated an orientation emphasizing productive range lands, maintaining equilibrium, and human control of wildlife
populations. An overall consensus regarding the northern herd existed
among range scientists, state game management officials, U.S. Forest Service officials, managers in Yellowstone, and sportsmen's organizations. Representatives from these groups met semiannually as the Absaroka Conservation Committee (ACC) to discuss wildlife issues concerning Yellowstone and
the surrounding areas. Discussions held at the ACC included virtually all the
local players in conservation and public land use, thus opening a window on
the context of park wildlife management at that time. The winter range of

the northern Yellowstone elk dominated the discussions year after year, followed by concerns over coyotes and other wildlife issues such as fisheries. National Park Service biologists working in the 1940s and 1950s were among the more emphatic, arguing that the number of elk on Yellowstone's northern range must be lowered.

Resistance to the idea of reducing the northern elk herd came from two sources. Sportsmen strongly opposed the direct reduction of elk within the park, as did George Kern, a railroad employee and conservationist from nearby Livingston, Montana. Kern doubted the range experts and argued that wildlife managers must consider Yellowstone's national constituency, who had an interest and a stake in park policies. Ultimately, Kern called into question the entire idea of controlling wildlife in a national park. In his statements to the ACC, he gave voice to the purposes of the national parks as an important guiding principle for wildlife management.

At the same time that Yellowstone actively controlled the number of elk, the park introduced important changes in other areas of wildlife management, based on the idea of presenting a more natural Yellowstone to visitors. Much of the direction for this came from the Washington DC office of the NPS, influenced by Director Newton Drury and Victor Cahalane when the USFWS section of National Park Wildlife was transferred back to the NPS in 1944. In 1943, for example, Yellowstone Superintendent Edmund B. Rogers shut down the "buffalo ranch," which had been established to propagate the once-endangered herd. The NPS faced considerable resistance from former Director Albright to returning the bison and bears to a more natural existence.

The conflict between creating a natural scene and solving the bear problem can be seen in USFWS biologist Olaus Murie's suggestion to build a fence around the entire Fishing Bridge development on Yellowstone Lake. Murie felt ambivalent about his solution, a scheme that pointed to the larger problem of Yellowstone. Drury perhaps best summed up the essential dilemma for the Park Service: The purpose of the parks was to preserve nature, yet the parks must intervene in nature to achieve that end. This inescapable irony became institutionalized. Yellowstone's managers continued to control and manage the park landscape in substantial ways, yet presented the park to the public as a primitive landscape. Scientists as well as managers continued to believe that management could reestablish primitive conditions. The question of what was natural for Yellowstone's elk, bison, and bears was a common one as managers discussed what to do. It is remarkable that from the time when Charles C. Adams and his colleagues first identified parks as places to preserve the primitive, this purpose for the parks remained relatively constant, while the tactics for achieving natural conditions changed.

Finally, the national movement for wilderness preservation shaped thinking about Yellowstone and its wildlife. Wilderness Society President Olaus Murie's correspondence with NPS officials continued in the tradition of scientists of the 1920s, who urged ecological awareness as part of thinking about the national parks. During the 1950s Murie's "wilderness" came to encompass meanings previously associated with "primeval" and "primitive." Although the Park Service resisted the designation of wilderness areas in parks that administrators considered the best examples of wilderness preservation in America, one practical result of wilderness advocacy was the zoning of Yellowstone Lake to create large sections where canoeists could experience a wilderness without the noisy intrusion of motorboats.

Park management during the wartime era presented particular demands on the NPS. Pressured by vital war needs, Congress lowered the priority of NPS funding. From 1940 to 1951 Newton Drury served as director of the NPS. George Hartzog later noted that the Drury administration was clearly oriented toward preservation of natural resources, especially when compared to the Mather-Albright years when public use of the parks enjoyed particular emphasis. Drury was notably sympathetic to the preservationist side of the use-preservation equation; he had helped organize the Save-the-Redwoods League, and coined the phrase "crown jewels" to describe the large, scenic wilderness parks of the West.[1] Drury considered John C. Merriam his "mentor in park conservation matters," and Drury's administration did reflect Merriam's preservationist aspirations for the national parks.[2] This preservationist phase of NPS administration lasted only ten years, when in 1951 Secretary of the Interior Oscar Chapman pressured Drury to resign in the wake of a battle over a proposed dam in Dinosaur National Monument.[3] Drury's tenure was also characterized by a wartime lack of funding for scientific wildlife research in Yellowstone.

Yellowstone Park rangers participated in both management tasks and a limited research program during the 1940s and 1950s. After the Department of Interior shifted the Wildlife Division's research responsibilities to the Bureau of Biological Survey's Section on National Park Wildlife in 1939, the practical responsibility of managing the park's wildlife fell to the park rangers, who consulted with the park naturalist as before. Rangers carried out resource management tasks under the NPS Branch of Forestry until it was reorganized as the Branch of Conservation and Protection in the early 1950s under Lon Garrison. Rangers proved very competent at the work of managing wildlife, and yet a distance grew between ranger, naturalist, and wildlife researcher. Perhaps it was inevitable with the professionalization of wildlife management, yet the separation of functions seemed to impede the adoption of ecological approaches, which were strongest in the naturalists. During the war interpretive functions had been separated from research when C. P. Russell became head of the Branch of Interpretation in 1941, re-named the Natural History Division under J. E. Doerr in 1946. In 1944 re-search functions were transferred from the USFWS back to the NPS under the Wildlife Branch led by Victor Cahalane, and it was renamed the Biology Division in 1948. Rangers carried out research through the 1950s in consul-tation with a NPS biologist from the Biology Division. During the 1950s scientists outside the Park Service initiated a growing number of projects in Yellowstone.[4]

Throughout the 1940s the Yellowstone rangers included men such as Rudolph L. Grimm, who served in the army during World War I, engaged in farm work after the war, and secured a permanent appointment in Yellow-stone in 1928. Grimm had spent a year in college, studying botany, forestry, and range management.[5] By 1939 Yellowstone promoted him to district ranger. Curtis K. Skinner had been introduced to Rocky Mountain National Park via a summer job between junior and senior years at the University of Colorado. After a stint as the city editor for Leadville's daily newspaper, he became a Yellowstone park ranger in 1930. Promoted to assistant chief ranger in 1938, Skinner served during World War II and was promoted to chief park ranger in 1948. These rangers personified the hands-on wildlife management expertise in the Park Service during the 1940s.

The elk on the northern range presented Yellowstone rangers, conserva-tionists, and agency officials a central problem of the 1940s and 1950s. Ex-perts from several agencies judged the winter range to be in poor condition. From the beginning of the direct elk reductions in 1934, sportsmen's groups had objected to the slaughter of elk within the park. Examining the proceed-ings of the Absaroka Conservation Committee, a consensus builder during the 1940s and early 1950s, allows us a unique window into the attitudes and thinking of conservationists in the period. Participants had confidence in generally accepted postulates of range management and believed that natural systems should maintain equilibrium. Again, people who advocated ecological viewpoints found special resonance in the park's purpose.

Some sources suggest that the NPS created the ACC in large part to create support for its direct reduction program.[6] Although the NPS did seek endorsement of its views, it should be noted that the Montana Fish and Game Department also had an interest in creating public support for the elk management program. Park Ranger Rudolph Grimm noted that a very large kill of elk during the winter of 1942–43 by direct reduction, winter kill, and hunting outside the park caused public criticism of the state and federal agencies in Montana. Some people worried that the herd would be reduced so much that it would no longer come out of the park in hunting season. Grimm commented that this public interest following the winter of 1942–43 "demonstrated the need for public support of a sound game management plan." Thus not only the NPS but the state game agencies sought public support. These agencies, together with local conservation groups and public land users, created the Absaroka Conservation Committee.[7]

On May 8 and 9, 1943, the NPS conducted a "show-me" trip over the northern winter range. Representatives of the Absaroka and Gallatin National Forests, USFS Region One, the Montana Fish and Game Department, Dude Ranchers' Association, Park County Rod and Gun Club, Upper Gallatin Conservation Committee (UGCC), and Livingston Chamber of Commerce inspected the range with Yellowstone Superintendent Rogers, Park Naturalist Dr. C. Max Bauer, Assistant Chief Ranger W. Leon Evans, District Ranger Rudolf L. Grimm, and other rangers. The party proceeded on horseback from Jardine (east of Gardiner) over Deckard Flats and down the Yellowstone Valley, crossing the river at Corwin to visit the Armstrong Ranch where they inspected damage incurred by elk the previous winter. The group also visited the "Game Ranch" where Grimm explained the value of study plots. That evening, Fred B. Williams, chairman of the UGCC, described the work done by his committee over the previous twelve years and recommended that the gentlemen from Park County form a similar organization. A. H. Abbott, supervisor of the Gallatin National Forest, and Dr. J. S. McFarland, Montana State Fish and Game warden, spoke highly of the UGCC, and so those present unanimously agreed to form a similar committee. Dr. R. A. Hamilton, chairman of the Park County Rod and Gun Club's Big Game Committee, nominated Wesley A. D'Ewart, a prominent stockman and Park County state senator from Wilsall, for chairman. D'Ewart, a conservative Republican with strong ties to other stock growers, went on to occupy the Montana eastern district's congressional seat from 1945 to 1955. George Kern, district accountant for the Northern Pacific Railway and active civic leader, was promptly nominated secretary.[8]

In a sense the ACC represented a town meeting in which federal agencies, major conservation groups, and other parties interested in problems associated with Yellowstone's wildlife discussed issues and attempted to reach consensus on management policies. ACC organizers noted that Yellowstone Park, the National Forest Service, the Montana Fish and Game Department, the Bureau of Biological Survey, and later the U.S. Fish and Wildlife Service had tried various measures to rectify the problem of the winter range, but some of those actions brought criticism from elsewhere. Before a policy satisfactory to everyone could be created, the interested parties would have to meet together and consider information in "a clearing house of ideas."[9] Although the agencies expressed their differences and remained independent actors, recommendations of the ACC virtually set wildlife policy during this time for the four agencies in this specific locale. Yet the composition of the ACC also determined its limits. The considerable influence of stockmen in this town meeting shaped the group's outlook and recommendations, making the assembly at times more of an undemocratic pressure group than an objective and deliberative body.

On May 9, 1943, the ACC held its first meeting at Mammoth Hot Springs. In all, twenty people attended, almost everybody on the "show-me trip." By 1946 ACC attendees numbered forty-nine representatives from twenty different organizations and interest groups, including government bureaus, businesses such as dude ranches, cattle grazers, sportsmen's associations, chambers of commerce, along with the park photographer, a few newsmen, and a district judge. At the first meeting, W. Leon Evans summed up the elk situation from Yellowstone's perspective. During the 1942–43 winter authorities estimated the northern herd at thirteen thousand elk. Because officials of the federal agencies thought the carrying capacity of the range was about six thousand animals, the NPS and Montana Game Commission had agreed to reduce the herd by seven thousand over three years by allowing hunting outside the park and by direct reduction within. Winter conditions were so tough that many elk left the park seeking winter range, and Montana hunters killed over sixty-five hundred elk during that one winter, far beyond anyone's wildest expectations. The ACC proceeded to hatch a three-year plan to keep the herd at its new size by using hunters outside the park to harvest the net increase of the herd. Calculation of the net increase of the herd included not only births but also losses due to winter kill and live trapping. Hunting alone would take all of the net increase, about 17 to 20 percent of the herd's numbers, or about sixteen hundred elk. Yellowstone Park would not slaughter any elk over the next three-year period and promised no direct reductions after that trial without first consulting the committee. The ACC noted that sportsmen should be pleased by the plan, with its potential for substantial yearly harvests.

Three things are worth noting about the first meeting of the ACC. First, the fact that the park suspended its direct reductions was remarkable. The park was convinced that the herd must be reduced, so the cessation of direct reduction reflected a willingness to compromise and experiment in seeking a solution to the problem. Second, the suspension of direct reductions points to the powerful influence of sportsmen's groups in these discussions. During the 1940s and 1950s hunters formed the core of the conservation activists, but by the 1970s, their relative influence in conservation activism waned. Because the ACC sought a broad consensus, it took the hunters' opposition to direct reductions within the park very seriously. It was not only hunters, however, who took exception to Yellowstone's direct control measures. The general public felt uncomfortable with national park personnel shooting wildlife *en masse*. In 1944 ACC acting chair Dr. R. A. Hamilton suggested that elk and bison symbolized to the public "Nature's original picture which Man has gradually destroyed" until a few fragments remained in the national parks. In the public mind there was "something inherently barbaric about a policy of mass slaughter of these magnificent animals, without even the excuse of 'hunting.'"[10] Thus from the early 1940s the general public as well as hunters opposed direct reductions of elk within Yellowstone.

Third, the ACC's notion that hunters could take all the net increase implied their belief that the harvest would tend to reduce winter kill and take elk usually lost to other sources of mortality such as predators and disease. Labeled compensatory mortality, the concept was derived from Paul Errington's work in the 1930s on muskrat populations and remained widespread for many years in wildlife management circles. Errington proposed that a wildlife habitat offered an animal population a certain amount of food and protection. A given number of the population would be able to make use of those resources to survive over a winter season, but a smaller percentage would not survive because of a lack of resources. That portion of the population might be harvested by humans without harm to the population's reproductive potential. The popular rendition of the concept reads: They're going to die anyway, so you might as well shoot them! Today, game managers are more careful in judging the effects of hunting, pointing out that Errington's ideas have been misapplied to species that reproduced in ways very different from muskrats. Biologists now suggest that hunting represents additive mortality, as well as compensatory mortality, in population dynamics.[11] In 1943 the ACC's consensus regarding wildlife and elk management plans in Wyoming and Montana was based on an approach that emphasized the production of elk for harvest.

From the very first meeting of the ACC's eleven-year existence, stockmen, sportsmen, and federal and state agencies established their place at the negotiating table as major participants. Carrying capacity remained a central issue well into the 1960s. The ACC quickly developed an intermediary function, acting as the agent of negotiation between ranchers and hunters on the outside and managers on the inside of Yellowstone, as well as between the federal and state agencies. Importantly, almost everyone accepted an outlook that emphasized human control over nature, and an understanding of nature as something that might be carefully balanced through manipulation.

From early on stockmen played a large role in the ACC. The committee carefully avoided taking a position on the issue of land acquisition, and in fact the topic was seldom brought up. Visions of hungry elk surrounding carefully stacked hay bales made the issue very touchy with local landowners. On other pasture lands competition between domestic and wild animals was more easily addressed. Fred B. Williams of the Gallatin Conservation Committee shared his experiences with the ACC. Ranchers who ran cattle just northwest of Yellowstone came into conflict with elk migrating out of the park that began competing for forage in the Gallatin Canyon. The solution in the Gallatin was achieved by adjusting the boundaries and timing of grazing allotments so that both wild and domestic animals could get their fair share of forage. Members of the committee had negotiated with the stockmen and formed many friendships along the way, a result Williams predicted for the ACC.

Ranching interests did not necessarily coincide with sportsmen's interests. In 1932 the U.S. Forest Service set aside sixty-five thousand acres north of Yellowstone's Hellroaring Mountain as a primitive area. Forest Service officials hoped that this area would solve a twenty-year disagreement between stockmen and hunters, who had different visions of the land's proper use. Established as a buffer area between the park and grazing districts on forest lands to the north, the mountainous Absaroka Primitive Area did not allow grazing. Stockmen from Big Timber, Montana, exerted continuous pressure, especially in the early 1940s, trying to gain access to all forest lands north of Yellowstone. Only seven hundred elk and about fifty moose inhabited the area, claimed the stockmen, and so a considerable quantity of forage went unused where three thousand sheep might be pastured. Jack Parsell of the Montana Fish and Game Department countered by explaining that for maximum yields, domestic and wild game should not be mixed on a range.

Walter Nye of the Dude Rancher's Association said that if domestic sheep were removed from the Boulder Divide country near the Absaroka Primitive Area, elk might migrate up Slough Creek and Buffalo Fork to utilize the range. The corollary to this was the notion that domestic animals had depleted that range, and if freed from stock grazing "Nature would restore the range to its original state" and herds of elk would once again inhabit the area.[12] The ACC did not buy the idea, because general opinion questioned where the elk would go if they migrated as far as the divide. The stockmen, with the sympathetic Wesley D'Ewart presiding, held as much influence as the hunters in the ACC for the next eleven years.

Coyotes provided the ACC with their second continuing problem, demonstrating the pervasive influence of ranching interests in the direction of wildlife management policies on Yellowstone's northern border. At the September 1943 meeting, Walter Melin of the Park County Wool Growers Association stood up and asked: "With ranchers and stockmen throughout the state bending every effort toward exterminating coyotes, why have Yellowstone Park authorities abandoned their policies in that direction?" Ranchers expressed the concern that Yellowstone was acting as a breeding ground for coyotes, which radiated north to raid livestock. Dr. J. S. McFarland of the Montana Fish and Game Department supported that notion, noting that although ranchers had spent a million dollars for bounties and control measures, the number of coyotes seemed to be steadily increasing. Hunters also resented the coyote. The opinion of Montana Fish and Game and the sportsmen's groups was that the coyotes killed game animals, which meant that the hunters lost a proportionate opportunity for their own hunt. Jack Parsell of Montana Fish and Game said his organization's studies indicated that sometimes 70 percent of "natural" deer loss could be traced to coyotes.

Other members of the ACC defended the coyote by suggesting that the species was not uniformly aggressive. Dr. Max Bauer, naturalist in Yellowstone, observed that coyotes "actually observed in acts of destruction against game animals are simply indications of killer instinct developed in individuals of their species," just like bears and other animals whose daily life involved "tough problems." Bauer suggested that the apparent increase in coyotes around Yellowstone was due to the park's protective policy, which created "boldness" in the coyote.[13] Although this seemed to be true, people at that time thought the same protection produced "tame" elk, bears, and ducks.

The ACC's consideration of the role of predation on elk populations proved muddled. On the one hand, members noted that coyotes preyed on elk calves, and they considered this a black mark. At the very same time, some members of the committee wanted to reduce the number of elk on the range. In other words, the ACC was thinking in terms of enhancing an available supply to hunters, and the delegates seemed reluctant to share the bounteous herd with the canids. From the time of the Kaibab deer herd disaster, naturalists had theorized that an absence of predators would create an ungulate eruption, and only the substitution of human hunters could remedy the problem. Yet updated ecological thinking about predators in general, and coyotes in particular, was not mentioned during discussion about the coyotes on Yellowstone's northern border. Most of the talk focused on potential losses to stock; it was impossible, said the stockmen, to release herds of sheep and expect to find them intact when the owner returned weeks later. By the 1940s downsizing had already hit the shepherd's profession.

Clearly, everyone had forgotten or chose to ignore Adolph Murie's research on the food habits of the coyote in the Yellowstone, carried out from 1937 to 1939. By examining over five thousand coyote scats, Murie had demonstrated that in spring, summer, and fall, rodents represented the overwhelming majority of the coyote diet. ACC members were concerned about the effect of coyotes on big game. Murie had pointed out that although the coyote did rely on elk populations for its winter sustenance, its effect on elk as well as deer, antelope, and bighorn populations was negligible. Deer represented only 1 percent of the coyote diet, antelope and bighorn even less. Stockmen of the ACC worried that coyotes came out of the park to prey on domestic stock, but Murie had observed that most coyotes stayed with the elk herds on the northern range through the winter, and furthermore noted that trappers north of the park were quite happy when coyotes came out of the park. He also pointed out that the coyote population did not increase indefinitely, but was "subject to natural controls." "The problem of the big game species in Yellowstone is not one of predation," said Murie, "but of inadequate winter range."[14] It was not the coyote that threatened the deer population, but competition with elk and the problem of finding forage on a hard-pressed range.

25. Dr. Clyde Max Bauer, posing in front of Antler House in 1934. Bauer was the Yellowstone Park Naturalist from June 16, 1932 through October 1, 1943, when the position became known as the chief park naturalist. He served under that title until November 15, 1946. Bauer defended the coyote before the Absaroka Conservation Committee. Courtesy Yellowstone Photo Archives.

Two ACC representatives brought Murie's evidence to bear on the subject. Dr. C. Max Bauer, Yellowstone's naturalist, presented the rationale of the Park Service's policy. Nature intended coyotes "to serve a legitimate and useful purpose in her general plan, to act as scavengers in removing carcasses" thus preventing disease among the animal kingdom. Seventy-five percent of the coyote diet, said Bauer, consisted of rodents "which were also links in the Natural Chain." Fred B. Williams also defended the coyotes, speaking in terms of their "legitimate place in the Creator's handiwork."[15] Bauer and Williams in effect presented an ecological rationale for the coyote. Unfortunately, the ecological argument did not hold much sway outside the park border.

The ACC decided to set up a coyote committee, which included one sportsmen's organization, Yellowstone National Park, the USFS, and four seats for representatives of wool growers and cattlemen. In May 1944 the ACC endorsed the coyote committee's resolution urging Yellowstone to return to its policy of destroying two hundred coyotes per year in the park. The ACC facilitated the placing of Compound 1080 baits in two locations north of the park with the intention of killing coyotes moving out of the park. Agents of the USFWS placed carcasses of deer or elk laced with the deadly Compound 1080 at a location marked by a wooden pole with a warning notice. Coyotes would feed on the carcass, only to die a very short time later. One of the greatest problems was that dogs belonging to ranchers or hunters sometimes fed on the baits, so to prevent this the location of the bait was marked, placed in the same location each year, and usually removed during the summer. Outvoted on the control resolution, the NPS argued that the baits should be placed two to three miles north of the park border. Despite considerable pressure, the Park Service did not resume coyote control in Yellowstone.

The Absaroka Conservation Committee finally called for cooperative research between the NPS, the USFS, the USFWS, the wool growers, and the ACC. Evidently not satisfied with Murie's study of the coyote menu, the committee decided to ask science for a determination on just how many coyotes were heading north to feed on stock. In 1945 the ACC arranged for Weldon Robinson, a biologist with the Fish and Wildlife Service's Wildlife Research Laboratory in Denver, to carry out a study of coyote migration out of Yellowstone.

At the September 1950 ACC meeting, Robinson gave a summary of his five-year research on coyote migration in northern Yellowstone. His research involved tagging 419 coyotes over five years, yielding returns (solid information as to their movements, usually when coyotes were shot or someone discovered a carcass) on 172 of them. He noted that coyotes moved northward down the Yellowstone valley, with about 50 percent of coyote populations leaving the park during the winter. The maximum "drift" or movement had been 115 miles, and the average coyote traveled (or the tag was recovered) 25 air miles from the park. Robinson calculated that half the coyotes traveling north of the park stayed outside the park, and thus Yellowstone provided a "reservoir" of coyotes. "Much as all of us would like to say that the Yellowstone coyote population is a self-contained unit," the tag returns demonstrated that the park "supplies coyotes in large numbers to surrounding areas." Robinson spent considerable time at the ACC meeting detailing six instances when he observed coyotes killing game animals. He claimed he did not imply that coyotes only fed on game or that predation in a park with a range problem was a bad thing. "Instead, I simply would like to emphasize the fact that coyotes *do* kill game animals and point out some of the ways that this is accomplished."[16] Robinson was convinced that the "toll of game animals taken by coyotes each year in the Park is considerable—be it good in serving to alleviate the critical range problem, or perhaps not so good in holding down species which are not overly abundant."[17] In Robinson's views the stockmen had found science to support their position; Murie's interpretation was ignored in favor of the "fact" of coyote migration and six cases of predation on game animals, interpreted as bad news for the hunter, despite the overload of elk in the park.

In 1950 Dr. Robert A. Hamilton presented Superintendent Rogers with the recommendation of the coyote committee that Yellowstone control coyotes within the park, and that other agencies continue to place Compound 1080 baits outside the park. The committee worried that bighorn sheep needed protection from coyotes, despite the fact that Robinson's evidence only included deer and elk. The coyote committee also noted that any reduction in elk numbers might encourage more coyotes to come out of the park. The USFWS and USFS expanded the number of Compound 1080 bait stations in southern Park County to a total of fourteen, including one new station on Deckard Flats north of the firing line and two in Yankee Jim Canyon northwest of Gardiner. E. F. (Gene) Grand noted that the purpose of the USFWS Control Division out of Billings was "the general benefit of all game, livestock and poultry growers" in southern Park County. "Ninety percent of it," he declared, "is for game." Wool growers claimed their lamb losses due to coyotes were 10 percent, and Grand claimed that antelope herds had taken "a terrific loss."[18] He further speculated that because the coyote population was not as large as the rodent population, "it would be a physical impossibility" for coyotes to hold down a rodent population. The political balance of the ACC swayed against the coyote.

Surprisingly, Superintendent Rogers endorsed the recommendations of the coyote committee and asked the regional director to approve control measures for coyotes in the northern area of the park "to reduce unnatural concentrations, particularly in the Lamar and Mammoth areas, and to improve our public relations."[19] Occasional and slight reductions would not seriously damage the coyote population, noted Rogers. The national office of the NPS, however, balked at controlling coyotes in the park. Despite continued pressure from stockmen north of Yellowstone, the Park Service successfully fended off demands for in-park control. At the ACC meeting in spring of 1951 Leon Evans of Yellowstone sought assurance that placing three more Compound 1080 baits close to the park would be on an experimental basis, intended to catch migrating coyotes. To ensure that only the drifting coyotes were killed, Olaus Murie suggested the baits be placed four

26. Chief Park Naturalist C. Max Bauer and Yellowstone Superintendent Edmund B. Rogers at Everts Cairn, located on Blacktail Deer Plateau, in 1938. Courtesy Yellowstone Photo Archives.

or five miles from the park, as was done in North Dakota. Grand replied that in Glacier National Park the USFWS placed baits only a quarter of a mile from the park, which still had plenty of coyotes. There is some evidence to suggest that the stockmen, Grand of the USFWS, and the USFS had their way, placing at least one bait only one-half mile north of Yellowstone on Deckard Flats. If so, that situation lasted only a year or two, when a long-term arrangement was worked out with a bait placed on Deckard Flats approximately three miles from the park border. Most importantly, the Deckard Flats bait assured members of the ACC that the USFWS was dealing with migrating coyotes. This helped the NPS national office avoid initiating a second program of coyote control within Yellowstone.

Federal and state agencies were quite willing to meddle with the balance of nature. In 1951 Fred W. Johnson of the U.S. Forest Service noted complaints from cowmen elsewhere that the use of Compound 1080 caused an increase in deer populations, which stockmen thought competed with cows for forage. He notified the ACC that his agency was "heartily in favor of control of deer by hunters rather than by coyotes," and sought the advice of local clubs and the ACC so that when the anticipated deer increase followed the coyote control, the ACC could back up the USFS by supporting "a doe season or some control measure of that kind."[20] If the State Fish and Game would not grant some sort of extra season, the USFS could not support the extra Compound 1080 stations. William Carpenter of the Montana Fish and Game Commission noted that the state's policy was to reduce surpluses by harvesting all the animals possible. Thus increases in deer numbers were widely accepted as a consequence of using Compound 1080, and the agencies felt quite capable of arranging a new balance.

Yellowstone's endorsement of coyote control was hardly enlightened, ecologically influenced thinking. It seems that ecology failed to percolate down from theory to application in Yellowstone. Rogers's use of the idea of "unnatural concentrations" implies that wildlife managers believed they could decide what a natural number of coyotes was. For the stockmen on Yellowstone's northern border, "unnatural" was the number of coyotes crossing the park boundaries. Though Rogers used the idea of "unnatural numbers" to justify support for coyote control, lending the credibility of "scientific" rationality, Yellowstone's use of ecology was bounded by the stockmen's commerce just north of Yellowstone.

Ranger Evans of the NPS was not the only defender of the coyote. In May 1950 rancher Walter B. Hiller presented a petition from nineteen Yellowstone valley residents to the ACC protesting the use of Compound 1080 baits, claiming that they were "sneaked in on some of us."[21] Gene Grand of the USFWS denied that Compound 1080 had been sneaked in on anybody, and claimed that the poison was used only according to standard procedures including land owner notification. In 1951 Hiller again presented the petition, reasserting the position of valley residents. The coyote, wrote Hiller, "is a necessary part of our wild life, and takes his part in the maintenance of the balance of nature. He does his part in the control of mice, rabbits, gophers, ground squirrels, et cetera—many authoritative statements to the contrary notwithstanding. Those who seek his destruction are doing so solely for highly personal and selfish reasons."[22] Hiller and the residents of Trail, Mill, Meadow, and Strickland Creeks seemed more aware of ecological relationships than the experts of the USFWS.

While Grand was ready to place baits to kill the most coyotes, other experts did not accept arguments that coyotes had a severe impact on game animals. By the late 1940s Olaus Murie enjoyed a wide reputation as an authority on ungulates. Published in 1951, his book *The Elk of North America* was considered definitive for quite some time. Murie had concluded that if "an elk population is flourishing and affords a reasonable amount of hunting, predation can generally be ignored."[23] At several meetings of the ACC, which he attended during the late 1940s and early 1950s, Murie watched the proceedings and bit his tongue, seemingly unwilling to publicly battle the tide of opinion swelling against the coyote.

From 1943 to 1954 a balance of nature figured prominently in the ACC's thinking, just as nationally the concept dominated conceptualizations of many wildlife "problems." The coyote committee, for example, noted that Yellowstone's original policy of predator control was designed "to maintain proper balance between predatory and game animals."[24] The notion of too many predators was partly a holdover from the days when the park feared the loss of the last elk in the West. Hunters who saw a forfeiture when predators consumed game animals also contributed to resentment against the coyote. "Maintaining a proper balance" was one way of understanding how nature worked, based partly on scientific concepts, which could be used to justify a course of action motivated by utilitarian desire or sentimental protection. Considerable confidence and a degree of hubris can be seen in the belief of some wildlife managers and public land users in their ability to decide what constituted a proper natural balance.

But defining that natural balance proved a knotty problem for the ACC. J. S. McFarland of the Montana Fish and Game Department, for example, wondered if rodents would damage the range under a more effective scheme of predator control. Chairman Hamilton answered by suggesting there were more than enough coyotes in Yellowstone to keep the rodent populations in check, even if the park controlled their numbers. McFarland's caution epitomized the idea that if humans meddled with one species, another animal population would grow or diminish. Ecologists' understanding of the balance of nature was spreading—McFarland also noted that natural populations continually fluctuated. The usual policy on rodents, he said, was to let things work themselves out unless the damage became too great.

But in the case of the large ungulates, since 1934 the park actively intervened to effect a natural balance. As Rudolf L. Grimm stated in the September 1946 ACC meeting, "we must bring about and maintain an equitable balance between the amount of range forage produced and the number of animals using this range." The result would be the fulfillment of the park's responsibility "to maintain in a natural condition the range plant cover" as well as the wildlife. Balance was their business, and natural conditions their goal. Hillory Tolson pointed out that the only motive in advocating a particular herd level was to fulfill the NPS mandate to maintain the herds in a natural state.[25] Thus during the 1940s and 1950s, while hunting and ranching interests on the Absaroka Conservation Committee sought to manipulate park wildlife for benefits accrued outside the boundary, the NPS demonstrated the lasting influence of the Wildlife Division in attempts to manipulate wildlife and conditions toward the maintenance of natural conditions.

The northern elk herd problem occupied the ACC's center stage throughout its existence. During the 1940s and early 1950s the concept of a special (late) elk hunting season evolved through trial and error, despite the resistance of hunters who generally wanted to bag the game as early in the season as possible. In 1946 H. O. Mitchell of the Park County Rod and Gun Club was designated chairman of a special subcommittee to investigate the issue of hunting on the boundary line. On October 2, 1946, seventeen members of the ACC mounted horses to inspect the range firsthand. Meeting at the OTO ranch afterward, they drafted a resolution later submitted to the Montana Fish and Game Commission. The ACC endorsed the idea of what they called an "administrative closure" in the vicinity of Bassett, Little Trail, Phelps, Eagle, and Pole Creeks, effective November 15. In other words, the hunting season would close during late autumn in the vicinity of Gardiner's firing line, to facilitate the migration of elk northward out of the park onto winter range. The season would remain closed until a special committee with representatives of Yellowstone, USFS, Montana Fish and Game, and the ACC decided that enough elk had come out of the park to warrant a hunt. The Montana legislature customarily set the end of the hunting season, sometimes as early as January 31. Thus the boundary area would have a special closure, then open once again for the special season. The exact date of opening the late season was the contentious issue, with nervous hunters on the scene pressuring the special committee to reopen the boundary line as soon as possible, while the committee anxiously waited for more elk to come out. On January 11, 1947, the four committee members opened the area to hunting, whereupon a bounteous harvest ensued. In six days hunters dispatched approximately three thousand head of elk, and the committee closed the area on January 16.

George Kern, secretary of the ACC, noted that the remaining herd was smaller than the number killed in the winter of 1942–43, meaning that there was some risk the entire herd could be wiped out. The era of big reductions was over, he suggested, because the herd had been reduced by approximately 60 percent. Now the ACC should adopt a conservative approach, taking only the yearly increase, perhaps a thousand animals per year. Even though the range didn't look quite right, ACC planning "should look for remedies other than further reduction in herd level."[26]

By 1946 the ACC had vested range experts with scientific authority and the final say on range matters. Their opinion became the final word; although there were a few doubters such as Kern, committee members yielded to the range experts. In 1946 Fred Williams of the Gallatin Conservation Committee noted that the GCC had originally argued for a population of about fourteen thousand elk but conceded to the merits of special studies done by the range experts. Dr. F. M. Nelson of the Park County Stock Growers Association added his support for the experts, saying "the ability and findings of these men are unquestioned."[27]

From the inception of the ACC, the Park Service took the lead in deploring the condition of the range, in issuing dire warnings of potential disaster, and in urging drastic reductions in the size of the herd. The NPS assumed the duty of gathering information about the range, and so initiated most of the scientific research carried out. At every ACC meeting it was a biologist or ranger from the Park Service who gave the orientation concerning range conditions, the number of elk, and information about progress in the program. Their interpretation of the data followed a range management perspective.

Studies of the northern range began with William Rush's arrival in Yellowstone in 1927, and the Wildlife Division had cooperated with Rush through 1936. In 1930 the Protective Division established five exclosure plots, using a square meter quadrant within and outside each exclosure. More plots were established in 1933 and 1935 to include tall browse species such as willow and aspen. Park Ranger Rudolph L. Grimm undertook the range study work from 1933 to 1947. In 1935 he established fourteen vegetative growth volume plots. Grimm clipped half of a 200-square-foot plot in alternate years to demonstrate the weight of vegetation produced. From 1939 to 1941 Rangers Grimm and Gammill continued clipping these plots. Grimm also established an aspen status study and a sagebrush utilization study.[28] During the war years Victor Cahalane of the NPS Washington office repeated the park's assertion that elk control was necessary.[29]

In 1947 a new range expert arrived on the northern range, playing the role of Cassandra. During the next six years Park Biologist Walter Kittams carried out research and issued the most dire warnings yet. In the fall of 1947 Kittams set up twenty aspen study plots so he could study the browsing behavior of the elk. Growing trees had been nibbled on, reducing average height from twenty-nine to seventeen inches. If that sort of browsing continued, young aspens would continue to come up for quite some time, but never develop into mature stands. Eventually, the browsing pressure would reduce the stands of aspen and finally eliminate them because they could not reproduce. When aspen were browsed so heavily, "we are simply exceeding the limit of abuse which our range can absorb."[30] In May 1948 Kittams stood up before the ACC with a set of colored charts to outline the range situation. For the remaining life of the organization, Kittams and Grimm effectively presented the case for elk reductions, and the ACC accepted them as its experts in range matters. Kittams argued that the herd must be reduced below its previously calculated carrying capacity, down to sixty-five hundred animals if the range was to recover from its depleted condition.

As far back as 1931, William Rush had discussed the difficulty of conducting an accurate elk census. He found variance in single-year censuses as great as 65 percent, and between years he noted discrepancies of up to 173 percent.[31] It was not that the herd had increased that much; rather, it was difficult to count moving elk that numbered somewhere between six thousand and eleven thousand animals. Problems with the census included rangers (usually on skis) assigned to too large an area to cover in one day, counters' vision obscured as the sun set on short winter days, counters' unfamiliarity with the landscape or loosely defined areas, questionable estimates of elk crowded into forested areas, and elk moving between census sections.

Other members of the ACC noted anomalies that only much later were put together in an explanatory framework. In 1947 Park Naturalist David Condon noted that the winter range included areas of low productivity where "sedimentary rocks have come to the surface." Rush and Kittams acknowledged that seasonal precipitation had a crucial influence on range condition. Every year they hoped for bountiful precipitation to increase the forage for the ungulates. Kittams had at his disposal forty-one years of weather records compiled by Rush, which indicated that the average precipitation at Mammoth was 18.02 inches, ranging from a low of 7.95 inches to the greatest annual precipitation recorded at 28.61 inches. Snowfall, too, varied considerably, from 19.7 to 200.9 inches, affecting the amount of energy the elk needed to expend to paw down through the snow to reach forage.[32] Yet Kittams overlooked the generally dry climate and poor soil conditions, instead emphasizing elk population densities and carrying capacity.

Some members of the ACC recognized that they were working with systems bigger than a traditional one-species approach could encompass. Officials associated with the NPS Wildlife Branch and the Natural History Division provided an ecological outlook that advocated mindfulness of all the animals on the range. Victor Cahalane noted in 1944 that the NPS was responsible for more than just one species—elk represented "only one factor in a very complicated set-up here."[33] In 1948 Park Naturalist David Condon again reminded the ACC that elk were not the only creatures existing on the northern range. Additionally, noted Condon, the beauty of the landscape itself was sometimes jeopardized; a scenic landscape formed an essential ingredient in the parks and must be preserved. Occasional ACC conference-attendee Olaus Murie gave the larger issues of wildlife management attention in his 1951 book The Elk of North America. Although wildlife management meant "the maintenance of the wildlife supply," not only huntable game but nongame species must be considered. Elk management needed "to be integrated with management of other species, for the elk is only one member of the fauna."[34] At the same time that Murie as a traditionally oriented game biologist endorsed the reduction of the northern herd, he also embodied a cautious intuition about the limits of contemporary management strategies, and a growing sense that some interventions intruded on the greater purposes of the parks.

George Kern became the main voice of doubt within the ACC. In September 1948, members of the ACC responded to Kittams's warnings, in deliberations calling for a reduction of four thousand head. Kern said that he could not dispute the findings of the range specialists, that he had neither field studies nor research data. Although he worried that Leon Evans and the other range experts might think he was proceeding from sentiment, Kern nevertheless argued that "I seriously doubt if we can successfully operate without including public sentiment in our decisions."[35] Not only the hunting groups, but the nation at large expressed an interest in what happened on the northern range. A reduction of four thousand represented 40 percent of the entire herd and sounded like an awful lot; why not aim for only two thousand per year and thus spread the reduction over several years? Kern had to answer to a lot of people about what the ACC was doing, and he found it more difficult over the years to provide acceptable rationales.

Kern regretted that the 1947 experiment with the administrative closure of the hunting season had not been given another trial. That attempt to encourage the elk to migrate out of the park had been a "far-sighted humane and logical plan" that "simply aimed to prove that there must be some less drastic means of handling surplus than plain slaughter in one form or another." The whole idea was to get the elk to migrate farther north, spreading themselves over the entire available winter range. Yet opening the area to hunting just as the animals congregated and moved outside the park ended the experiment all too early, Kern argued. Re-educating the herd to migrate beyond the firing line would take more than a scant sixty days. "Surely," Kern admonished, "the Absaroka Committee is capable of something more scientific than that type of management."[36] Other places in Montana were dealing with elk herds by spreading them out on larger areas, yet the ACC had only just begun to try to encourage better distribution by dropping salt blocks out of a plane over large areas.

In 1949 Kern repeated his doubts, while again conceding the facts to the range experts. What the experts said about reduced carrying capacity and range deterioration was indeed based on scientific information, he admitted, "but I simply cannot concede that the method proposed for obtaining correction of the apparent over-population is backed by the same scientific knowledge as is used in computing carrying capacity." The range experts were correct in saying that one of the major purposes of the ACC was to solve the range problem. Kern argued that the ACC had other important objectives as well, such as improving the unsatisfactory conditions on the firing line. Kern again spoke about public perceptions of Yellowstone and the ACC's management: "In all our discussions at these meetings, I cannot escape the feeling that there are about 150 million people who feel that they have a direct proprietary interest in these valuable resources that we are trying to manage. I shudder to think what would happen if that general public of the country could just get one glimpse of the carnage that occurs at the Firing Line on any morning during our so-called 'hunting' season when the elk are moving down across the Park boundary in large numbers. My guess is that they would vote 100% for turning the entire matter back to Mother Nature and letting her kill off the animals in any manner she might choose."[37]

Thus Kern noted two problems: First, the ACC needed to try other methods of dealing with the range problem. The herd reduction was not proving effective, and he doubted that more of the same solution would cure the problem. People had asked Kern about the accuracy of carrying capacity computations. Experience, he believed, showed that the range experts could not accurately estimate the size of the herd within three thousand animals. Dr. Howard Welsh of Montana State University repeated the story of how the USFS in California had estimated a deer population at four thousand, but after twenty-two thousand deer were killed a good-sized population remained. Fred T. Johnson of the NPS agreed with Kern that carrying capacity was perhaps not calculable, and suggested that measuring the ungulate utilization of vegetation might be a better way to assess the relationship between elk and range. Welsh thought the calculations problematic, but found the pictures Kittams had shown of a reduction in secondary growth between 1926 and 1949 quite striking and convincing.

Kern thought Kittams's sense of urgency was overplayed: When a big kill of four thousand was recommended but not reached, there was really little cause for alarm. After all, the range conditions had been many years in the making, and the ACC had existed for a mere six years. Fred Williams of the GCC pushed Kern on the necessity of large reductions, arguing that the range continued to deteriorate. Kern pointed out that reductions had been carried out for twenty years, and still the range experts called for more reductions: "How far do you figure we'll have to go?" There seemed no end to Kittams's calls for reduction. Kern reiterated his intuition that the commit-

27. Wesley A. D'Ewart, stockman, state senator, and chairman of the Absaroka Conservation Committee (left), with ACC Secretary George Kern, who questioned the efficacy of the medicine conservationists administered to the elk "problem." At the old "Post Exchange" building in Mammoth, 1943. Courtesy Yellowstone Photo Archives.

tee should look beyond reductions: "I still cannot escape the feeling that there must be some more scientific method of solving the problem than simply killing off a third of them."[38] The political problem was also significant to Kern. Indeed, the ACC's entire existence was based on the fact that dealing with wildlife management problems on the northern boundaries of Yellowstone was political in nature. The agencies had inherited boundary lines on the map, but wildlife crossed the lines and entered a different set of land-use rules on the far side of the park's border.

In the spring of 1949 Kittams and crew brought alarming news to the committee. Leon Evans detailed the previous census, the most accurate one yet, which raised doubts about prior estimates of the number of elk on the range as well as the growth rate of the herd. It was now obvious why the ACC failed to see improvement in the range, and why Kittams was seeing deterioration on the range: two thousand extra elk had been browsing the range for the last six years. If the present herd grew at an annual rate of 20 percent rather than the previously assumed 17.5 percent, soon eleven thousand elk would populate the range.

The ACC's original three-year plan had turned into a six-year plan with no end in sight. Park Ranger W. Leon Evans claimed "simple arithmetic" showed that overuse of the range over the preceding years necessitated dropping the herd down to five thousand "if we are ever to attain the desired balance between herd and carrying capacity."[39] Kittams showed pictures of the range to the committee to support his program. First, he showed photos demonstrating the poor grass production that summer. Then he showed photographs of exclosure plots, which showed comparative forage production and vegetative composition. The plots had been established in 1930 and 1934, and consisted of tall, stout fences that kept the elk out. Since June grass was present inside the exclosures, Kittams concluded that it was a more palatable species for the elk than the needle and thread grass that predominated outside; the elk had eaten up the palatable varieties. Kittams next showed photos of plots where he had clipped the vegetation on half the plot to demonstrate the relative production over the last two years. Clipping the vegetation on a plot, Kittams would dry and weigh the plant material. Comparing the weights of forage produced off the same plots (data collected since 1935), he calculated the 1949 forage production on some plots to be one-fourth that of 1939. Here was an important piece of evidence for the range degradation thesis. Kittams noted that lack of rainfall had something to do with the lack of production but argued that "actual lack of vigor in the plants is partly responsible. Due to continued overuse and trampling, the plants have been weakened and this shows up in a poor growing season."[40]

In the late summer of 1949 Yellowstone administrators called for a reduction of the herd down to a total of five thousand elk, which required a removal of five thousand animals during the winter of 1949–50. A crucial factor necessitating this drastic reduction was the dry summer of 1949, which caused a shortfall in forage production. Superintendent Rogers called for a reduction "before deep winter snow brings disaster to our large wildlife species."[41] Although the ACC accepted the notion that a large reduction was necessary, the committee members only reluctantly approved killing up to fifteen hundred elk in the park.

After the September 1949 ACC meeting interested business people met in Livingston on October 28 in hopes of translocating more elk and finding ranges where the elk might be placed. This became known as the "elk lift," funded for a short time entirely by the Park County Rod and Gun Club. Yellowstone had trapped elk as early as 1892, and by 1949 shipped a total of 5,604 elk to thirty-five states for elk herd restorations. The elk lift was substantially different in that it sought to take surplus elk off the range. The organizers had trouble finding enough money for the project, even though all equipment and time were donated. Yellowstone managers also hoped to expand their trapping operations, in early 1950 constructing a large trap in the Crystal Creek drainage. By early 1952 the park had five traps in operation, capturing 1,176 animals in early 1952. The problem was finding places where the elk could be released. Although Yellowstone Park notified fish and game commissions and conservation departments in forty-eight states, only Montana and Pennsylvania had expressed any interest in receiving live elk, and then Pennsylvania never filled out the paperwork. The park faced a very limited market for live elk, and thus although most went to game ranges in Montana, a substantial number of elk ended up on large ranches in Texas and New Mexico, and in the hands of some individuals, including the president of Mexico, Miguel Aleman.[42]

Although the ACC hoped for a big reduction of 5,000 elk in 1950, it got substantially less. Park rangers shot 513 elk, and Montana Fish and Game collected 321 at the live traps within the park. Hunters managed to kill only 40 animals, and thus from all causes only 900 elk had been removed from the winter range. The herd might grow to 12,000, the ACC feared, with attendant worsening of the range condition. Acting NPS Director Demaray directed the park to prepare itself for direct reductions of 3,000 during the winter of 1950–51, removing the increase of 2,000 plus 1,000 more.

In 1952 the ACC moved to create a subcommittee to study the issue of hunting in the park, and during the next fifteen years, sportsmen argued loudly for this cause. Given Kittams's sense of urgency and the strong sportsmen's contingent in the ACC, this seemed like a natural solution. For years the sportsmen had argued against killing any elk in the park. But now retired Montana Fish and Game Commissioner A. C. Grande and ACC First Vice-Chairman Stanton J. Ware of Salt Lake City advocated hunting in the

28. Elk that were killed in direct reductions were often shot with high-powered rifles from a distance in the field. As this photo indicates, however, some elk were trapped and then dispatched. Courtesy Yellowstone Photo Archives.

29. The elk reduction becomes mechanized. This photograph of slaughtering teams using a tractor was taken in 1935. Eventually, helicopters were pressed into use to herd elk toward pens. Meat from the slaughter was most often shipped to Indian reservations. Courtesy Yellowstone Photo Archives.

park. For NPS Regional Director Howard W. Baker, this was ominous news. Baker thought "the Service will be in an embarrassing predicament if the Absaroka Conservation Committee should ultimately endorse measures for opening Yellowstone to hunting."[43]

Other ACC members opposed the idea. Dr. J. W. Severy, a former member of the Montana Fish and Game Commission associated with the University of Montana at Missoula, noted that although Grand Teton Park did allow hunting on a tightly controlled basis, that constituted a different situation, "an attempt to settle troubled waters." The ACC finally voted unanimously against recommending controlled hunting within Yellowstone. The ACC agreed that the best and most practical way to regulate the herd was "to let nature take its course and control the migration, then hunting outside the Park to control the size of the herd."[44] If the Montana Fish and Game Commission set the hunting quota high enough, the surplus determined by the ACC might be harvested. Elk migration would be encouraged by closing and then re-opening the hunting districts north of the park when a large number of elk had moved out.

The Absaroka Conservation Committee met only twice more. At the last meeting in May 1954, Kittams characterized the situation on the range as "very grave." An evening tour of the area across from Gardiner revealed a "desperate" situation.[45] Gene Sherman of Montana Fish and Game said that "after 25 years of trying about everything we know we can try, we have a rather pessimistic attitude."[46] Handling the elk situation in a systematic fashion from outside seemed fruitless, so it seemed that the issue would have to be addressed from the inside. Yellowstone Chief Ranger Otto Brown assured the ACC that "a direct control program can be carried on in an organized and humane manner if the means are provided to finance it."[47]

In October 1954 Kern notified members that basic recommendations had been constructed over the years, and now "a fair trial" by the agencies was required. Until that trial had been carried out, further meetings were not necessary. Thus the ACC suspended its meetings after eleven years of searching for a solution to the range problem. Kittams reasoned that the committee had never solved the problem. After eleven years of resistance the ACC yielded to the NPS on the issue of direct reduction.

Management of the elk in Yellowstone Park during the 1940s and early 1950s demonstrates how some managers had great confidence in their own ability to manipulate wildlife in the landscape, even while the problems seemed intractable. One of the reasons managers could not "solve" the "problems" was that professional resource management thinking tended to simplify natural systems.[48] As Olaus Murie noted, "There is a tendency for the administrator to oversimplify the task of the research man. . . . The biologist is too often looked upon as a trouble shooter. He is sent out to look into something, size it up and come back with the right answer—and that case is closed!"[49] The larger living communities and ecosystems that individual species inhabited were not well understood. This was a shortcoming of game management from its early days; the tendency was to think in terms of one species at a time and attempt to control conditions to bring about a desired result, usually the enhanced production of a desired sport species. When attempted solutions failed to bring about the anticipated results, most ACC participants advocated more of the same treatment, while a few questioned the effectiveness of the medicine. As long as the complicated interactions of these ecological systems remained hidden and unknown, those answers remained unclear.

Although the ACC's vision was rather limited in scope, ecological ideas had filtered into the committee proceedings in subtle and sometimes contradictory ways. The germ of one ecological view was contained within the range management perspective itself. Concern with the condition of the range reflected the certain knowledge that grazers and browsers had an ongoing interactive relationship. The limitation of the approach was that it viewed all relationships in terms of production. How much vegetation did the range produce, how did browsers utilize it, and how many cattle or elk could the land produce? Management technique sought to manipulate conditions to improve productivity. Although that technique and approach fit in well with the utilitarian practicality of the Forest Service, it also conflicted with the greater purposes of the parks. Although the ACC discussed additional subjects such as water pollution from mines northeast of Yellowstone, the group never discussed wildlife beyond the problems associated with elk and coyotes. In part, that omission was due to the fact that those problems did not impinge on the interests of sportsmen or stockmen, two of the largest players in the ACC body politic. Second, aside from Kern and the NPS representatives, the ACC was not overtly concerned with the greater purposes of the national parks.

Other conservation groups and individuals, as well as the NPS itself, however, did think quite a lot about the greater purposes of the parks, and their concerns markedly influenced the direction of wildlife management in Yellowstone. Ideas about creating a more natural presentation of the wildlife in Yellowstone proved as important as ideas derived from range science or ecology in determining the direction of park management during the 1940s and 1950s, gradually assuming more prominence in the objectives and rationales of Yellowstone and national NPS officials. Two examples demonstrate how Yellowstone administrators transformed wildlife management directions pursued in the 1930s into polices aimed at presenting wildlife to park visitors in a more natural setting. First, the NPS moved to eliminate the ranching methods used for many years to propagate the buffalo herd in the Lamar River Valley. Second, NPS and Yellowstone administrators decided to end the "bear shows" where bears were fed garbage on a regular basis for public viewing. These two episodes exemplified the idea of creating a more "natural" park, in other words, a park in which natural ecological patterns were allowed to function unimpeded. Finally, the national movement for wilderness preservation that began during the 1920s and 1930s and flowered during the 1950s and 1960s shaped thinking about Yellowstone in a more ecological way. The practical result of thinking about wilderness areas was the zoning of Yellowstone Lake into portions that secured the southern shores as a wilderness area. The notion of a more natural park, of the park as wilderness, was an applied 1950s version of ecological thinking in the national park system.

The bison in the Lamar River Valley appeared anything but natural in 1950. In 1907 Yellowstone created the "buffalo ranch" in the Lamar Valley on Rose Creek. A ranching operation complete with roundups nurtured the herd until it reached about a thousand animals. Beginning in 1929 Yellowstone slaughtered a portion of the bison herd almost annually. The Wildlife Division presented the rationale for a reduction in bison numbers: The winter range in the Lamar Valley was obviously overgrazed, and to bring about a proper balance the herd must be trimmed down to a proper carrying capacity. The Wildlife Division proposed reducing the herd from 1,128 to 1,000 animals. By the early 1940s the carrying capacity was thought to be about 350 for the Lamar herd and 300 in the "so-called wild herds" farther south in the Hayden Valley.[50] From 1908 to 1944, 691 bison were shipped alive to zoos, Indian reservations, and other ranges, and 1,863 were slaughtered, the meat sold at cost or donated to Indian reservations. Yet at the same time, Yellowstone still irrigated a hay field at the buffalo ranch on the north side of the Lamar River, producing hay to feed the bison during the winters.

Equally important was the Wildlife Division's 1934 vision for a new period of bison management. At first the bison had been hunted until practically exterminated, but from 1907 to 1929 the Yellowstone herd had been built up carefully. Now the Wildlife Division "will be devoted to the task of returning the Yellowstone herd to the wild state insofar as the inherent limitations of the park will permit." Castration of bison calves was discontinued, and instead of being corralled and fed, calves would run with their mothers. Artificial management would be limited to "a single round-up which will be necessary so long as there is a surplus to slaughter, to winter feeding at the Buffalo Ranch which will be necessary so long as the herd must be held within present park boundaries, and, to disease prevention and cure. When these things are accomplished there will be once again a wild herd of bison in the United States."[51] Although the wish for a wild herd existed, this "limited" artificiality came to appear rather heavy-handed twenty years later.

The idea of eliminating the artificial feeding of the Lamar bison came from the NPS director's office to Yellowstone in late 1939 or early 1940. Superintendent Edmund Rogers responded that he was in agreement with "the

30. At the buffalo ranch, bison were propagated like domestic cattle for many years. This photograph was taken in December of 1935. Courtesy Yellowstone Photo Archives.

31. Chief Rangers Francis D. LaNoue and Curtis K. Skinner inspect new chutes at the buffalo ranch, 1948. Courtesy Yellowstone Photo Archives.

general proposition that artificial management of the Yellowstone bison, along with that of other park animals, should be eliminated to the greatest practical extent." Rogers proposed the herd be reduced to match the carrying capacity of the range, and the amount and duration of artificial feeding be reduced gradually as the herd was placed on a "self-sustaining basis within a few years."[52] He wanted to retain the facilities at the buffalo ranch, because they housed a district ranger's headquarters and barns for maintenance equipment, and hay was also grown there for the park's herd of horses and mules, varying between seventy to ninety animals. Rogers believed that it would not be possible to do away entirely with artificial management of the herd, because human settlement in the Yellowstone valley had artificially limited the bison's range; "the environment of these animals can no longer be a wholly natural one."[53]

During the winter of 1942–43 a group of bison meandered across the boundary at Gardiner and proceeded north twenty-five miles before spring green-up returned them to ranges in the park. That December the NPS decided to reduce the size of the Lamar herd by four hundred head, or about 50 percent. Three ideas influenced the decision. Feeding the bison at the "buffalo ranch" in the Lamar Valley was thought "out of harmony with basic principles on which the Park is intended to function. All forms of wildlife within its borders are to exist in their primal state without aid or interference from artificial sources."[54] Second, the park experts thought the Lamar range had deteriorated. Biologist Victor Cahalane stated at the 1944 ACC meeting that the drastic bison herd reduction was "wholly an experimental attempt to meet the range deficiency." Third, Cahalane noted that park policy was not determined by the desire to propagate any particular species of wildlife, but rather the aim of "maintaining a proper balance or ratio between the various species."[55]

Cahalane drafted a more refined justification of the plan in the spring of 1944. He reviewed the history of the Lamar herd, pointing out that ranching-style operations had been successful in increasing the Lamar herd to a point at which the available range could not meet their needs. Propagation techniques had been dropped until the only artificial technique remaining was feeding hay during the winter months. Because the bison in the park were sufficiently numerous and well dispersed to minimize the risk of losing the entire herd due to any calamity, Cahalane planned to eliminate artificial feeding. He noted that fears of possible extirpation of the Lamar herd were misplaced. The proof of bison doing quite well on their own was seen in the wild herds of Yellowstone. While the original wild band consisted of 22 bison, by 1944 they had increased to approximately 395 animals, gathered in bands on Pelican Creek and in the Hayden Valley. This proved that "it is possible for buffalo to thrive in Yellowstone without artificial feeding."[56] The real problem in transforming the semidomesticated Lamar herd into a wild herd, wrote Cahalane, was the depleted state of the northern range and competition with other species for forage. Nevertheless, "surplus buffalo will always occur," and this might be addressed the same way surplus elk were dealt with, by hunting on the north side of the border.[57] Regional NPS headquarters resisted the hunting season on bison, because it did not want "continuous and increasing pressure to provide the trophies," and secondly, because killing the large animals was very difficult, even with high-powered hunting rifles, and could not really be called sport.[58]

Drury faced resistance to the idea of putting the Lamar herd on a natural basis. For a time Devereux Butcher seemed reluctant to endorse the scheme and resisted publishing relevant material from the Park Service in the *National Parks Magazine*.[59] Dr. T. S. Palmer raised objections based on his concerns that the herd might die out without artificial feeding. Yet the most important outright opposition to the scheme came from none other than former Park Service Director Horace Albright, who in 1943 had become president of the American Planning and Civic Association. Albright still had considerable influence in conservation circles, kept abreast of NPS affairs, and corresponded in an indefatigable manner with people in all sorts of positions and places. Albright's opposition, in other words, was significant and something Drury had to overcome. According to Olaus Murie, some Yellowstone administrators took positions based on their loyalty to Albright. This helps explain Yellowstone Superintendent Rogers's reluctance to eliminate the buffalo ranch and his endorsement of coyote control.

During late 1943 and early 1944 Albright waged a campaign to stop Drury from carrying out plans to eliminate the buffalo ranch, discontinue bear feeding of any sort and remove associated facilities, and remove fences designed to corral wild animals. To secure a more natural bison herd, Yellowstone Park planned to reduce the herd to 350 animals, and Albright and Palmer, an expert on Bang's disease, also opposed the annual reduction of the bison herd. Albright wrote Drury in October of 1943, advising him that the bison herd should not be reduced without consulting the organizations that had expressed interest in the Lamar herd for many years, such as the American Bison Society and the Camp Fire Club. There was no reason to reduce the herd, wrote Albright: "After all, buffalo are cattle."[60]

Albright claimed that while he served as superintendent of Yellowstone and director of the NPS, naturalists had never told him about any range depletion. The thing that impressed Albright the most about the Lamar herd was its size: "I can remember when the famous old editor of Field and Stream, the man who was for years the grand old man of wildlife conservation, George Bird Grinnell, stood on a hill in the Lamar Valley one day and saw 1,000 head of buffalo in movement at one time. Tears streamed down his cheeks. He said it was the greatest sight that his eyes had beheld since 1876 when he was a reporter attached to Custer's staff on the plains." Albright lamented that the park had dropped the "big shows of buffalo" held during the 1920s.[61]

Drury replied to the older gentleman's nostalgia: "I am afraid that our differences derive from somewhat differing concepts of the purpose and function of national parks in respect to wild life." Given the basic legislation and the policies approved by the secretary of the interior, Drury did not see "how we can do other than work toward the ideal of placing all species including the bison, as rapidly as practicable upon a self-sustaining basis, free from all artificial aids."[62] Albright confessed that it was hard to confront the idea that he, as well as his predecessor and successor at the National Park Service, were wrong in fostering the large bison herd. Albright's major concern remained the public use of the park and the tourists' opportunity to see wild animals. Drury responded that current policies did not imply a criticism of previous policies: "On the contrary, I think that you and the other directors have earned the gratitude of all who are interested in the perpetuation of the bison because of the expedients you were able to adopt successfully in a critical time."[63]

Despite this cajoling, Albright protested vigorously after the reduction was carried out in the winter of 1944. He wrote Drury, suggesting that he was making a serious mistake. Albright argued that the range of the Lamar herd "is not and never has been overgrazed." The natural behavior of the bison in the past led them down the Yellowstone River in a yearly migration, but now they met their own destruction when they crossed the border. Albright suggested that Yellowstone was "on unsound grounds in attempting to restore what you call perfectly natural conditions. It simply cannot be done in the case of Bison." Albright complained that Drury had not solicited his advice in his survey, suggesting "it was sent to college professors whose reaction to a large extent is theoretical, not being based on actual knowledge of conditions." Over fifteen years Albright had discussed bison with people such as Charles C. Adams, J. S. Dixon, William Rush, and Harold Bryant, but no one had suggested a large reduction in the bison herd. Albright did not surrender to Drury's efforts at persuasion. He reiterated his contention that the national parks were "not biologic units where animals can live on natural conditions the year round" and that the public should be entitled to "full opportunities to enjoy the animal life of the parks even if in so doing for their protection and enjoyment of the resource, some small measure of artificiality in living conditions of the animals has to be introduced."[64] Albright then took his case to the Camp Fire Club, which unanimously agreed that further killing of the bison should not take place.

Drury regretted that the two disagreed over the size of the bison herd, but "when you urged me to accept this post I warned you that we might not al-

32. Secretary of the Interior Ray L. Wilber, Horace Albright, and Roger Toll were among the observers viewing this buffalo stampede in 1929. Yellowstone's herd was a notable success in big game conservation. The park's bison herd was used to film westerns, and Albright thrilled in the spectacle. Courtesy Yellowstone Photo Archives.

ways agree." He reminded Albright of the laws and policies that guided him and pointed out that the reduction was nothing new; since 1929 an average of 113 bison had been removed every year. Although Yellowstone was not a complete biologic unit for bison, it was not a complete range for deer, antelope, or elk either, yet Yellowstone did not "feed them hay and otherwise manage their lives." Why should the park manage the bison differently? Drury and Albright had a fundamental disagreement on how they viewed the park's purpose. Drury could not "interpret our existing wildlife policy, as you apparently do, to permit us to perpetuate artificial manipulation of wild animals, when it can be avoided, so as to assure our visitors any specific experiences, such as the sight of 1,000 buffaloes in the Lamar Valley at Yellowstone. As I understand our policy (and I believe it is sound), our aim should be to place each wild species, insofar as this can be accomplished, on its own, without dependence upon man, and occupying its natural niche in the biota of the park."[65]

To bolster his position, in late 1943 Drury solicited the advice of ecologists, as well as that of scientific and conservation organizations about his plans to put the Lamar bison herd back on a natural basis by reducing the size of the herd and stopping the artificial feeding. Wilfred H. Osgood, emeritus curator of zoology at Chicago's Field Museum of Natural History, supported him: "It seems to me that the Park idea should be the maintenance of approximately natural conditions and anything that goes beyond this is certainly debatable. To make them into rearing grounds for wild animals merely for show or to satisfy sentiment may easily go so far as to defeat their real purpose." E. Raymond Hall of the University of California, Berkeley, Museum of Vertebrate Zoology suggested that bison be reduced to numbers present in 1800, and further that wolves be reintroduced into the park "to further approximate the original fauna" and provide a check on the large ungulates.[66] Drury found a wide base of support for his action from prominent scientists nationwide.

The director's concerns lay partly in the manner of presentation of wildlife to the public and partly in the management principles established by the Wildlife Division. Drury explained to Harold Ickes, secretary of the interior, that "Maintaining an artificial buffalo show is contrary to long established national park policy as to wildlife."[67] In other words, the presentation of wildlife should be as natural as possible. The buffalo ranch, by producing hay for feeding, went against the Wildlife Division's principle that species in parks would carry on the struggle for existence unaided.

Drury further explained to Ickes how discontinuing the ranching operations at the buffalo ranch would not endanger the survival of the species as Palmer feared. Fourteen other states now had herds of bison, totaling 5,000 animals in the United States, and Canada also had considerable numbers. The Crow Indian Reservation wintered a herd of 700 bison, the Wichita Mountains Wildlife Refuge had 542, and the National Bison Range a herd of 566. Hence, safeguarding the species had been accomplished.

As they tried to return the Lamar herd to a more natural existence, Drury, Cahalane, and Rogers could not abandon all traditional wildlife management methods and the propensity to intervene in wildlife conditions. Bison, like elk, carried on only too well, outpacing the ability of the range to support them. "Natural curbs do not check the growth" of the herd, Drury informed Ickes, hence an annual reduction of bison numbers was necessary. In attempting to persuade Albright on the necessity of reducing the bison herd, Drury quoted from Tracy Storer: "It is utterly irrational to go on protecting such species until 'they eat themselves out of house and home' or fall disastrously to the ravages of disease. Any population, bison or others, maintained by protection is under more or less artificial management and the latter procedure rationally must include removal of the surpluses that develop from time to time."[68]

Another concern during this time was the discovery that the bison herd carried Bang's disease, or brucellosis, which caused spontaneous abortion. Several ungulate species shared the disease, so ranchers worried that the disease might be transmitted to their cattle. Brucellosis was first diagnosed in the Lamar bison herd in 1930. William Rush noted it was "entirely probable" that the infection came from milk cows kept at the buffalo ranch prior to 1919.[69] Rush speculated that the disease did not seem to do any appreciable harm, because the herd had grown in size. By 1934 the Wildlife Division

33. The concern over transmission of brucellosis from bison to domestic cattle originated during the early 1930s. Here Dr. Don R. Coburn and ranger Walter Kittams test samples from the park bison for brucellosis in 1948. Ironically, domestic cattle may well have given the disease to the bison during the late nineteenth or early twentieth century. Courtesy Yellowstone Photo Archives.

thought that 38 to 43 percent of the herd was affected. In 1945 Dr. Don R. Coburn investigated the problem and recommended that the calves be vaccinated; all adults reacting to the brucellosis test should be eliminated from the herd, and emigration of bison from the park should be curtailed. Hillory A. Tolson, acting NPS director, thought it would be impractical to apply those measures to wild animals. Two other herds existed in the interior portions of the park, and corralling those bison for inoculation would be impossible. Even if the bison in the Hayden Valley were destroyed and rebuilt from a herd in the Lamar Valley, elk also carried brucellosis and hence a "clean" herd might be reinfected. Olaus Murie suggested that modern efforts to remove all disease would reach limits when it came to wild animal populations—getting rid of all disease might also entail the disappearance of the wild animals. To have a wild herd meant that some problems, like disease, would never be solved entirely.

As Yellowstone returned the bison to a more natural state, the park also sought to return the bears of the park to a less artificial life. It is not possible to divide historical thinking about the bears into neat categories of a matured ecological awareness or an old-fashioned descriptive approach. The first thing that stands out in the historical record is a long-standing and continuing concern with human injuries caused by bears. Reducing conflict with humans proved one of the most significant motivators in changing Yellowstone's policies. Building on the work of the Wildlife Division, Olaus Murie went to Yellowstone to study the ecology of the bears, specifically their food habits. Although his suggestions were oriented toward the practical, Murie's study refined knowledge about the natural habits of the grizzly bear. Also significant is that scientists and NPS officials gradually redefined "natural" as the term applied to the grizzly and black bear populations of Yellowstone. In the early 1950s Director Drury and Yellowstone Park decided to end the "bear show" in Yellowstone, not only because they thought it would reduce unnatural concentrations of bears and thus human injury, but also because they believed that to remain true to the purpose of the parks, a natural presentation of the wildlife was preferable.

Since the early 1930s when Joseph Dixon and Ben Thompson looked into the bear situation, the instances of injuries and damages due to bears colliding with tourists did not seem to abate. From 1931 to 1941 the park gathered reports of 59 injury and 74 damage cases annually. For every 6,336 visitors, there was 1 injury, and for every 5,052 visitors, there was 1 damage report. In

1941, 82 injuries involved scratches and such, needing only minor first aid, but 8 cases required stitches. Additionally, control measures to deal with the most troublesome bears had to be carried out year after year. Many bears were trapped in cages made from steel culvert pipes and towed or trucked to remote places in the park, but as Rush predicted, many returned to the scene of their infraction. Park authorities used strong measures on repeat offenders. From 1931 to 1941 an average of twenty-five black bears were killed by rangers annually, the consequences of the tourists' habit of feeding the bears. Park authorities also decided that some grizzly bears had to be killed to protect the visiting public from danger. A yearly average of thirty-two black and grizzly bears were killed in control measures.[70]

Even though bears caused many tourist complaints, enforcing the regulations against feeding was problematic. Until they had an unpleasant experience with a bear, tourists did not believe that feeding the bears was hazardous. As Olaus Murie put it, "the public has been 'shown' bears for so many years, partly deliberately, partly incidentally . . . that many people are assuming that this is one commodity guaranteed when the entrance fee is paid."[71] Some people found enforcement of the regulations all too strict. The sacristan of the St. Ita Church in Chicago toured the park with a few of the altar boys. When the boys threw some bread out of their car to a bear, the "park police came up and hit the bear in the head with large rocks and cursed at him. Then they used abusive language to me and my little boys."[72] Others found enforcement lax. In a letter to Joseph Dixon, his friend and professor of mechanical engineering Robert L. Daugherty noted that although it was against park regulations to feed the bears, no one seemed to enforce the regulation. Daugherty "found within a day or two that I could be sure of finding bears at certain spots along certain roads being fed by tourists and could depend upon it as certainly as I could a railroad train schedule."[73] The NPS had enough difficulty getting concessionaire employees to obey the rules, but enforcement among the public was almost a lost cause. Rogers considered a vigorous enforcement program but warned that rangers would have to arrest twenty, and perhaps up to fifty, people per day. The court could never handle that many cases, so Rogers asked the regional director to pursue obtaining authority for Yellowstone Park rangers to collect cash bonds from tourists on the spot. The NPS worried that the public would resent enforcement of the no-feeding regulation.

Gradually opinion built that something must be done. As Victor Cahalane noted in 1937, "destruction of more than a few individuals a year in any park is an indication that the problem is not being brought to a satisfactory solution."[74] Some of the answer was more of the traditional treatment. The park in 1941 proposed an educational campaign for the people, utilizing posters, information delivered in naturalist talks and at information desks, warnings included in the Yellowstone descriptive pamphlet handed out to all automobiles entering the park, and lastly the threat of prosecution for those who ignored warnings not to feed the bears. Over the years these warnings proved ineffectual. Just as the Canadian National Parks administrators had found, most tourists injured by bears were aware of the regulations or had a copy of them in their possession yet simply chose to ignore the rules. Isaias Garcia Enciso, for example, was teasing a bear with some food when the bear bit him on the face, inflicting lacerations. Mammoth Subdistrict Ranger Lee Coleman noticed that Enciso actually had the bear warning leaflet and broadside in his possession.[75]

In 1941 Yellowstone also proposed an educational campaign for the bears. In the early season, "when bears begin to establish themselves along the roadsides and in the campgrounds," park rangers would "use all known 'driving' methods to frighten them from lanes of travel or visitor concentration," hopefully making them afraid to approach humans. This technique would be discontinued when tourist travel picked up, "to avoid overwhelming public criticism."[76]

Yet the problem was not that of Yellowstone alone. In early 1941 Dixon wrote to Cahalane, warning him that in other parks bear problems might better be avoided in the first place, especially in places like the Cedar Grove campground in Kings Canyon National Park. The cause of current problems was obvious to Dixon: "Bear shows and bear feeding in national parks had their origin in the bears acquiring a taste for garbage, then learning to raid camps and to 'hold up' cars etc."[77] Dixon urged Cahalane to bring up the bear problem at the next superintendents' conference as a subject of system-wide concern. Superintendent Rogers informed interested members of the public that in parks animals had the tendency to "increase in numbers beyond that maintained under early or primitive conditions" and furthermore "beyond their available natural food supply." Although Rogers noted that "it may be necessary" to control bear populations just like it was necessary to control elk or bison populations, recent elimination of troublesome grizzly bears was "necessary for human safety."[78] Park Service authorities began to eliminate the scheduled bear feedings. At the end of the 1941 tourist season, Yellowstone closed the bear show located at Canyon.[79]

During the summer of 1942, a very bad season of incidents, injuries, and the killing of eighty-one black bears in control measures precipitated another effort to better understand the bear problem. Dr. W. B. Bell of the Fish and Wildlife Service assigned Olaus Murie to investigate the park's quandary. Murie estimated it would require two years to get a handle on the situation, including "what is necessary for the preservation of the grizzly in Yellowstone."[80] The heavy bear control during the same summer also precipitated a change in bear policy. In December 1942 Drury decided to "discontinue all bear feeding and bear shows," referring to them as an "unnatural feeding program."[81] By April 1943 the grizzly feeding grounds were permanently closed.

Murie noted a few things as he watched tourists interact with bears. First, the bears had lost fear of humans. Bears raiding garbage cans were not "unduly alarmed when hit with sticks or stones to drive them away, or when shot at, or otherwise harassed by irate campers who have suffered bear depredations." Similarly, tourists seemed to lose all fear of bears. Watching bears seek handouts from the roadside or appear at the cabin door "tends to dispel any previous impressions of a heroic or dangerous animal of the forest." Also, considerable publicity had portrayed Yellowstone's bears "not as a wild animal in a wilderness setting, but as a picturesque 'highwayman' begging from automobiles."[82]

Murie posed an important question. After years of procuring food from dumps, the stoops of hotels, bear feeding grounds, campgrounds, and tourist cabins, not to mention roadsides, could the bears survive without that food supply? Murie analyzed 243 bear scats (droppings) in minute detail. He confirmed that bears were mainly herbivorous, a full 81 percent of the Yellowstone bear diet consisting of grasses and sedges. Insects and associated debris made up 9 percent of the diet, and mammals accounted for 2 percent. The total of all natural foods in the diet was 92 percent, while garbage accounted for 6 percent. Murie's interpretation of the data was that "the bears don't *need* the garbage to live, but are attracted to it," because they have "carnivorous tastes, to be indulged whenever the opportunity presents itself."[83] Because garbage was so easily available, Murie thought it futile to enforce the no-feeding regulations. The government must first eliminate the availability of garbage.

Although park rangers had devised a sunken garbage container with a bear-proof locking device, tourists found it not worth the bother to open, and some people deposited their trash on the ground next to the special container. In the spring of 1943 personnel from the superintendent's office devised a new and improved garbage can, modeled on post office boxes. Murie urged that several such experimental devices be constructed and placed in a campground. In 1944 Superintendent Rogers noted that "the installation of these units awaits the end of the war when labor and material will be available."[84]

In addition to constructing experimental food lockers and garbage containers, Lawrence C. Merriam of NPS Region Two headquarters in Omaha suggested that all the parks with bears design their own progressive bear control program, "for the purpose of frightening bears with the ultimate view that eventually the bear population will revert to a more normal wild state," and look on people not as a food source but as an enemy. Most tourists, thought Merriam, would rather see a "fleeting glimpse of a bear retreating into the forest than having the bears congregate as so many domestic pets" around the heavily visited areas.[85] Merriam also noted that proper garbage containers were costly and only solved part of the problem. Bears would still damage automobiles if they smelled food.

Murie thought that a fence surrounding the entire Fishing Bridge area might reduce human-bear conflict. Fishing Bridge was really a small town, according to Murie, entirely commercial and not at all attractive. In such an atmosphere, Murie noted, a fence could not be considered an intrusion. There was a precedent—one regular Yellowstone visitor devised an electric fence, which he placed around his tent each year. Rather than encircling just the campgrounds, a more encompassing fence line hidden in most places by the forest would keep bears out of the entire area and offer protection to parked cars as well as tents. Starting east of Fishing Bridge, the barrier could go north through the woods, swing west enclosing the incinerator and the old dump ground, pass southward to gates at the road, and on to the lake shore. The fence could be led into the lake far enough to discourage bears from swimming around. Some might object to this enclosure on the basis that "it would be an entering wedge and eventually everything in the national parks would be fenced."[86] But a reasonable policy about building such fences could be drawn up. Grand Teton's Jenny Lake camp, for example, would be unthinkable as suitable for fencing, but in other places with a great deal of bear-human conflict the barrier solution might be desirable. Merriam acknowledged that fencing campgrounds would indeed protect visitors, but he added that such a remedy would be very costly and "tend to create a zoo-like aspect wherever such fences were erected."[87] Additional personnel would be necessary to man the gates, again driving up the expense.

Although Murie proposed the fence at Fishing Bridge, he had considerable reservations about it. What policy should govern this special type of land use, the national park? Enclosing a campground meant "introducing another artificiality into the picture." Murie pointed out how many people enjoyed "the adventure of having bears in camp. One cannot deny that there is a certain excitement in it. I have watched people scurry into their cabins at the approach of a bear with that delightful combination of fear and pleasure that we can all appreciate. They call to each other across the way, proudly relating their latest exploit with bears—such as enticing one into the cabin, having one come up and sharing their meal with him, or petting one. There is, I confess, something appealing to this kind of experience, if we view it impartially." Despite the adventure that many tourists felt, "the tame bear itself is an intrusion, man made," and while contact with these bears might be unavoidable "it is not the function of the federal government to foster or to encourage that type of enjoyment of wild animals."[88] Inevitably, with tame bears a ranger with a gun would arrive on the scene, and one more animal was removed from the population.

In 1944 Murie proceeded with proposed experiments with bear shocking devices. Using a six-volt battery and an electric fence controller, Murie selected a "promising garbage can," and attached a wire firmly to the rim of the can. While his son Daniel waited in the car manning the controller, Olaus Murie shooed bears in camp toward the proper can and the great experiment. It seemed to have promise, successfully dissuading several bears from the electric garbage can, but the fact that tourists might get accidental shocks from a self-actuating device precluded its regular use. The idea was to train bears who had become accustomed to raiding garbage cans. The idea of using aversive techniques had been floating around since the 1930s, and testing the electric garbage can fell to Murie, mainly because he happened to be in the right campground at the right time. He favored a systemic solution instead.

The purpose of the parks figured prominently in Murie's consideration of the grizzly. While the black bear was not shy and people would always find it easy to observe, the grizzly was by nature more nocturnal and retiring. The bear show altered the natural picture in a very fundamental way; changing the feeding habits of the grizzly resulted in "deliberately destroying the natural habits and reactions and the natural distribution of an important animal in a fauna that we set out to protect specifically for its primitive character and value." Murie wrote to Drury, sharing his belief that national parks had "not only a duty, but an opportunity" to preserve a "natural fauna" for the enjoyment of the general public, as well as for study by nature lovers and naturalists. "Natural food habits, reactions to environment, distribution as affected by the associated fauna and flora, and seasonal weather conditions, are all parts of the ecological story offered by an animal like the grizzly." It would be a misfortune, he wrote, to "destroy these values in an animal that has become so scarce in the United States, simply for showmanship and the satisfaction of an artificially created human appetite."[89]

Indeed, concern over the numerical status of the grizzly population was new during this time, first brought to national NPS attention by the Wildlife Division's publication of *Wildlife Management in the National Parks* in 1934, when the division suggested that the national parks held the "last hope for the grizzly bear in the United States proper."[90] Yellowstone Chief Ranger Baggley's report on the grizzly in 1936 noted that although Wyoming reported an increase in grizzly numbers from 1924 to 1934, a precipitous decline in numbers in the states of Washington, Utah, Colorado, Arizona, and New Mexico indicated a tendency "dangerous . . . for the future of the species."[91] Baggley noted that if the "silver-tip" was to survive, additional territory besides the national parks would have to provide protection for the bear. Superintendent Rogers, on the other hand, thought the 1945 grizzly population in the Gallatin to be nearly as large as the Yellowstone population. Rogers was not worried that hunting outside the park would impact the Yellowstone population of grizzlies. He was not aware that Yellowstone's bears ranged over a vast landscape and mingled with each other. Rather, he thought in terms of populations inside and outside the park. Although many suspected that bears left the park to fall prey to hunters or livestock owners, those numbers were thought to be minimal.

Based not only on practical necessity, NPS wildlife policies set up in the 1940s also influenced the direction Yellowstone took in attempting to show the bears under more natural conditions. In a publication titled "Wildlife Conditions in National Parks," reissued several times in the 1940s, the NPS listed its wildlife management policies. These had direct roots in the policies proposed by the Wildlife Division in 1932. One of the policies repeated the Wildlife Division's prescription: "Every species shall be left to carry on its struggle for existence unaided," as long as it was not in danger of being extirpated from the West. Even more importantly, the NPS proposed that "the presentation of the animal life of the parks to the public shall be a wholly natural one."[92] During the mid-1940s Drury saw one major objective of the NPS as making "the major scenic-scientific parks self-perpetuating natural reservations in which each native plant and animal species takes its appropriate place."[93]

Rogers supported Murie's idea of fencing off the Fishing Bridge development, hoping to eliminate troubles in one of the more problematic locations of the park. In March 1946 Yellowstone formally proposed to "bear-proof" Fishing Bridge; the NPS never actually built this device due to the exorbitant cost, but it demonstrates managers' search for anything that might offer a solution. However, it was not sheer desperation, as the park wanted to fence off one of its developed areas to take one step "in the probably long process of putting bears back upon their own, or of rehabilitating them."[94]

The most influential opponent of ending the bear shows was Horace Albright, who also opposed the bison reduction effort. Many years of experience, he claimed, had convinced him that an effective way to deal with the bears was to have one or two feeding grounds. In 1946 Albright predicted a lot of trouble with Yellowstone's bears, because "they are naturally coming out to the roads and the public will naturally feed them."[95] He felt very strongly about the issue: "I am more than ever convinced that Murie is not going to be able to give any satisfactory answer to the bear problem. He is going to persist in his belief that bears must not be fed, although he will never be able to give any suggestions as to how the people can be kept from feeding them."[96]

Feeding the bears had been tolerated and implicitly encouraged by concessionaires' publicity during Albright's administration of the park; it was simply a traditional thing for tourists to do while at Yellowstone, and what else could hotels do with trash but dump it? By the time Toll took over as Yellowstone superintendent in 1929, these customs were ingrained. Albright never backed off from his long-held belief that "the general public has a right to have an opportunity to observe animals in the national parks when they have neither the time nor experience to seek the animals in the wilds."[97] Albright voiced other concerns about the bears—it remained unclear what the consequences of closing the feeding grounds would be. In 1944 he noted that hunters were disturbed over an increase in the number of grizzlies killed outside the park, and he speculated that not having a regular feeding program was "responsible for the wide migration of the bears."[98] According to this line of thinking, bears were simply safer in the park. Although Albright fought it, on October 4, 1945, Director Drury approved the regional director's proposal to eliminate all the physical structures associated with the Canyon feeding grounds.[99]

As in the case of the bison, to solidify his case and bolster his position against the formidable opposition of Albright, Drury solicited comments from scientists and conservationists who almost unanimously supported his decision to abolish the bear show in Yellowstone. What is particularly interesting is that when thoughtful conservationists discussed ending the bear show, it was often in terms of defining the natural, and in terms of presenting wildlife to the public in a more naturalistic way. Charles C. Adams wrote that "a constant effort must be made to interfere as little as possible with wild nature, plant and animal in the Parks." Devereux Butcher, executive secretary of the National Parks Association, noted that his organization had always advocated "the least possible human interference with wildlife" in the parks.[100]

Many comments centered on the idea of the bear show as artificial. Rudolf Bennitt, professor of zoology at the University of Missouri, notified Drury that "from the first it has seemed to me an artificial way to treat any wildlife species in a large natural area. Perhaps it would do for the St. Louis Zoo," but in Yellowstone the spectacle was incongruous.[101] Lee R. Dice, director of the Laboratory of Vertebrate Biology at the University of Michigan, wrote that although he had witnessed and enjoyed the bear feeding show in Yellowstone, "from the standpoint of the welfare of the bears these shows are deplorable. The presentation of the bears as scavengers, living mainly on garbage and on handouts from man, does not give a true picture of the character of the bear species."[102] Tracy I. Storer, professor of zoology at Berkeley, thought that the bear show produced "an abnormal situation with respect to both bears and people."[103] Paul B. Sears, influential shaper of the Nebraska school of plant ecology and the widely respected author of *Deserts on the March* (1935), serving as a professor of botany at Oberlin College, wrote: "As an ecologist I have nothing but praise for the new practice. The sooner the feeding of bears and other interference with natural conditions stops the better, so far as I am concerned."[104] Lee Dice also discussed the matter of ecological balance in the park: "The general balance of the ecology of the wildlife of the national parks is destroyed when one animal is for a time given an artificial food supply. I therefore congratulate the national parks in having the courage to discontinue these very popular bear shows and to allow nature to establish a natural balance in the national parks free so far as possible from human interference." Like many others, Montana State College professor Harlow B. Mills believed that "the biological outweigh the educational factors in bear feeding." In other words, the costs to the bears had outweighed the educational benefits for park visitors, which had become the justification for their continuance.[105]

Staying true to the basic purpose of the national parks provided a powerful argument for some correspondents. Joseph S. Dixon, in 1946 with the Fish and Wildlife Service, noted that the bear shows were "contrary to the basic principles of the National Park Service." S. Charles Kendeigh, chairman of the Ecological Society of America's Committee for the Study of Plant and Animal Communities, wrote that although the shows were popular, "they are not in harmony with the purpose of the national parks as representing natural communities of plants and animals in an undisturbed condition, where each species is leading its normal existence."[106]

Along with the desire to see a natural bear population, the 1940s also produced a concern over the very survivability of the grizzly bear in Yellowstone. Superintendent Rogers responded to a letter from Rosalie Edge, informing her that seven grizzlies had been killed at Fishing Bridge during the summer of 1949. Rogers reassured Edge that careful consideration was given to each case before being acted on, because the park realized it did not have a "surplus of grizzly bears." Nevertheless, the park could not escape its responsibility to "take immediate action to remove grizzly bears which persistently frequent developed areas where they are a menace to human safety."[107] No animal was killed unless it was absolutely necessary, wrote Rogers. Concern over the possible extirpation of the grizzly population persisted and surfaced again in the 1970s, utilizing a new scientific language.

Late in the tourist season of 1958, Yellowstone Chief Park Naturalist David de L. Condon stood with John J. Craighead at the Trout Creek dump, watching the bears feeding on garbage and taking photographs they later exchanged through the mail. This amiable beginning ushered in eight years of close cooperation in bear research and management between John and his brother Frank Craighead and Yellowstone personnel. Condon told Superintendent Lon Garrison that a cooperative study under Craighead's leadership would be invaluable: "Unless we soon acquire some basic data on our grizzly population, including this species' social behavior, its breeding potential, distribution, and other pertinent information, we are running the risk of jeopardizing the perpetuation of this species as a member of our park fauna."[108] The original proposal for this study aimed to collect data on population dynamics such as reproductive rates, age-specific mortality, and mean life span information. Soon John and Frank Craighead began to perform the first research of this kind, introducing Yellowstone to a brave new age of population modeling and statistical inference. Not only conservation but science as well changed in fundamental ways we can see reflected in wildlife studies in Yellowstone.

From the creation of the National Park Service, scientists and conservationists influenced what the organization thought worthy of preserving, and similarly during the 1940s and 1950s, conservationists shaped new definitions of what the parks were about. Organized in 1935 by Bob Marshall, Robert Sterling Yard, Howard Zahniser, and Olaus Murie, the Wilderness Society influenced definitions of national park conservation during the 1950s. As early as 1943 Robert Sterling Yard, president of the Wilderness Society, began a correspondence with Newton Drury. While Drury found Yard's rhetoric a bit overblown, he also seemed to enjoy these discussions of wilderness. Drury also kept up a correspondence with Howard Zahniser, elected secretary of the Wilderness Society and editor of the *Living Wilderness* after 1945. Responding to the Society's advocacy of wilderness areas in the parks, Drury argued that many parks were not big enough to include a wilderness area under a special designation and objected that the parks had been set aside to protect natural resources in the first place, so "it seems futile to designate a tract within a tract." He hoped that "National Park Status is the safest classification wild land can attain for its protection in a natural condition for future generations."[109] He asked Yard what regulations might apply to a wilderness designation that did not already apply to undeveloped areas of national parks. Even the NPA, he pointed out, could not agree on whether the best terminology might be "primitive" or "primeval." Drury suggested that the preservation of intrinsic qualities of "'primeval' national parks" would be more problematic than simply assigning them a "special title."[110]

When Yard emphasized the scientific values to be found in wilderness, he found support from wildlife biologists. The American Society of Mammalogists in 1946 endorsed the movement for wilderness preservation, specifically drawing attention to the fact that civilization still encroached on the remaining natural areas. Furthermore, the Society of Mammalogists noted "the current pressing need of the science of wildlife management for check-areas against which the trends of artificialized game-producing lands can be measured." Likewise, the Wildlife Society, an organization of professional wildlife managers and wildlife ecologists, adopted a resolution endorsing "the movement for wilderness preservation." The Wildlife Society voiced a similar interest in the preservation of natural areas "against which the practices in game production on lands under management can be measured."[111] During the 1920s Charles C. Adams had called for natural areas as reference points to judge the larger effects of modern technological civilization. In the 1940s and 1950s leading scientists called for a reference point to measure management. Clearly, the idea of preserving natural conditions had not been a passing fashion.

During the 1950s the national wilderness preservation movement influenced thinking about Yellowstone. Olaus Murie resigned his position with the U.S. Fish and Wildlife Service to serve as president of the Wilderness Society from 1945 to 1957.[112] Although he utilized several rationales to argue for wilderness preservation, in this context it is particularly interesting to note how he used the term "wilderness" to express the continuing interest of science in preserving the naturally occurring ecological relationships in Yellowstone's landscape. Early in the winter of 1950, while a special committee of the Wilderness Society met in Washington DC, Murie sat down before his typewriter at his home in Moose, Wyoming, on the edge of Teton National Park. In his letter to Frederick Law Olmsted, who served on the Wilderness Society's board, Murie suggested that "we must do some thorough [philosophical] engineering, to set in motion self sustaining concepts and arrangements." The problem of sustaining wilderness in the parks, noted Murie, was deep rooted. In the early days the park administration worked to bring the comforts of home into the wilderness, resulting in swanky hotels crowding around the natural features. Creating the infrastructure to support tourists' journeys had placed a premium on engineering ability, and hence created a trend to select personnel "on the basis of ability to handle the mechanical problems of a park."[113] It was subtle, wrote Murie, yet definitely discernible.

Murie argued a new "influx of hordes of people" carried with them a danger that "in the heat of controversy and material complexity, the ideal will be subordinated" to solving the mechanical problems of the park. The ideal he referred to was wilderness values. Murie noted that Park Service landscape architects should have two goals in mind: first, to accommodate the crowds of tourists; but secondly, "to insure the protection of areas that contain the elements of wilderness for which our national parks were basically created." Many people left Yellowstone cursing the crowds. How might the Wilderness Society and the Park Service encourage people to experience the wilderness that lay not one hundred yards from the parking lot? "Are we such a decrepit nation that we can not get out of our cars to view outstanding scenery?" Roads did not have to cling to the very edge of a scenic canyon; instead, the road might approach here and there, with parking areas hidden from view at panoramic vistas. Murie did not resent or deplore the numbers of people, but he urged that parks exercise caution in development to "avoid sliding into the Holiday Magazine concept of outdoor recreation."[114]

Murie thought highly of Newton Drury, describing him as a director "who so thoroughly understands and believes in the original purpose of national parks." Yet some park personnel, Murie noted, did not understand or agree with park purposes. Additionally, the naturalist section had not exploited all the opportunities presented to it. That section could be the most important in reaching the public, showing tourists the opportunities for park recreation, and teaching the principles of national parks and wilderness. The superintendent, wrote Murie, "should be a man who is conversant with the stock-in-trade of the National Park Service—esthetics. He should not only believe in it, but be enthusiastic about it." The job of the Wilderness Society was "not merely to watch details of park management, but to strengthen park personnel in the basic park policy, in which wilderness stands out. In other words, to encourage a wilderness policy that will work automatically from within."[115]

In 1951 Freeman Tilden published a book titled The National Parks: What They Mean to You and Me. Tilden might be described as a popularizer of the parks, a writer who celebrated the parks and brought them to armchair travelers. Yet looking back on Tilden, we see once again links between the ideas of early animal ecologists, of those who followed, and of the wilderness movement. Tilden argued the purpose of the national parks was "to preserve, in a condition as unaltered as is humanly possible, the wilderness that greeted the eyes of the first white man who challenged and conquered it. It is to insure that the processes of nature can work, without artifice, upon all living things."[116] Tilden saw in "wilderness" what his predecessors referred to as the preservation of natural conditions. Twelve years later the Leopold Report would echo Tilden's notion of the pristine landscape that fur trappers encountered when they visited Yellowstone. This idea of a landscape unaltered before contact with Euro-Americans was certainly widespread during the postwar era.

34. Olaus (left) and Adolph Murie in front of Cathedral Mountain, Denali National Park, Alaska, c. 1960. The Murie brothers spoke to the greater meaning and purposes of the national parks. Photo by Steve Griffith, reprinted by permission of Louise Murie-MacLeod, and courtesy of the Harpers Ferry Center, National Park Service.

Thinking about wilderness values in the parks was manifested in Yellowstone by the creation of wilderness zones on Yellowstone Lake. Lon Garrison, superintendent of Yellowstone, recognized bird life on Yellowstone Lake as one of his larger problems. In 1958 summer Ranger Wayne Replogle noted that the osprey had "moved back" from the shores of Yellowstone Lake. Garrison surmised that osprey, very sensitive to disturbance, were being crowded by human activity on Yellowstone Lake. This same human activity affected bird life in places such as the Molly Islands, where Caspian terns, California gulls, double-crested cormorants, and white pelicans nested. The motorboat activity was disturbing to the rookery on the islands, where California gulls returned to shore before the other birds, raiding exposed nests. The wake of large motorboats washing up on the flat shoreline sometimes created havoc in the nests. Flooding from a storm could be mitigated by concerned avian parents, yet the unexpected and irregular washing from boat wakes seemed more difficult for them to cope with.

The "profanity, the hustle, and the oil drip of a normal American fisherman with a motorboat" altered the natural serenity of a place far from civilization. For Garrison, a "native wilderness should be a natural experience whose challenges arise when people confront natural hazards such as wind, cold, storm, or the effects of elevation."[117] Garrison was sympathetic to fishing and boating, but by 1958 it was obvious that the number of boats was increasing by leaps and bounds. The number of boats using the lake each year had increased from three thousand to almost five thousand. Garrison wondered if the park could preserve the lake's wilderness qualities, deciding to "create a water wilderness in the three arms, with limited access in rowboats or canoes."[118]

Garrison talked with Olaus Murie and Howard Zahniser of the Wilderness Society, Dave Brower of the Sierra Club, and Tony Smith of the National Parks Association, but he could not go as far as these visionaries wanted him to. Garrison noted that wilderness support would have to come from an urban political base, and this would take some time. That urban-based movement of the 1960s, focusing on quality of life issues, would serve to change the complexion of national conservation issues.[119]

Yet the parks were also for people. During the postwar era increased visitation to Yellowstone strained the available facilities, a situation repeated throughout the park system. Secretary of the Interior Oscar L. Chapman appointed Conrad L. Wirth, a landscape architect by training, to the post of NPS director in late 1951. Wirth bypassed the annual budgetary process by creating a ten-year plan for improving the parks known as Mission 66. Although the plan's emphasis on building and refurbishing trails, visitor centers, roads, campsites, employee housing, and other facilities was criticized as favoring the tourists over the resources, it should be noted that the program also sought to improve services such as interpretation.

For Wirth, the NPS dual mandate was not terribly perplexing. Use and preservation were not mutually exclusive categories: "To isolate and emphasize either use or preservation to the exclusion of the other can seriously distort park planning, confuse park management, and imperil the validity of the whole national park concept."[120] The parks, thought Wirth, had only one purpose. Combining both use and preservation, parks provided "knowledge, refreshment, and esthetic enjoyment" gained through "the intelligent and appropriate use of park resources by people." Preservation was not an end in itself but rather a means to an end. The real problem was not "in compromising use with preservation, but in the definition of use itself— permissible, appropriate, beneficial use." Wirth's administration noted that wilderness "cannot be defended indefinitely for itself alone, and to evaluate wilderness in terms of refreshment and esthetic enjoyment gives the most effective answer to the question 'why wilderness?'"[121] Wirth saw the entire scenic park as wilderness. Most park visitors enjoyed this wilderness from the roadside. But did they enjoy it any less or derive a smaller benefit than those who traveled far into the wilderness? Clearly, the Wirth administration valued public use of the parks, and in a way similar to the Mather-Albright era, did not view visitor use as a major infringement on preservation of park resources. Above all, Mission 66 reflected a modern need and desire to plan in a more comprehensive manner for the intelligent use of the parks. That some conservationists thought the NPS erred on the side of coddling the tourist demonstrated the still contested domain of park values, and uncovers old concerns about wildlife and preservation of the primitive assuming a new guise of concern over preserving wilderness qualities.

The net effect of ecological ideas on Yellowstone during the 1940s and 1950s was somewhat limited. Although conservation in Yellowstone had expanded its purview from its early style of big game preservation, Yellowstone's view of ungulates and range remained tied to an outlook emphasizing the production of forage. Experts said that a range should look like a verdant landscape. The feeling that Yellowstone's range should not look like the Badlands exemplified a qualm that was at once cultural and scientific. Rush, Grimm, and Kittams provided evidence convincing the ACC that the Yellowstone Range was changing, and they interpreted those changes in a negative light. Some members of the ACC began to doubt the pronouncements of the experts when continued reductions seemed to have no effects. It may be that "false assumptions about the 'state of nature' of the resources combined with a heritage of ambiguous lessons from past regulatory efforts" to confound effective management.¹²² Expectations of stability at a climax state and hopes for a verdant range that produced a controlled number of elk and bison went unfulfilled. The lessons from the ACC's history were indeed ambiguous. When the range problem did not improve, the ACC reluctantly validated the Park Service policy of direct reduction, but minority opinion within the ACC doubted that a solution involving slaughter inside or outside the park would ever solve the range dilemma. While George Kern believed something was awry in the whole approach, Walt Kittams was convinced of the need for more forceful action.

Ecological notions about the park were used in defense of the coyote. Walter Hiller, Olaus Murie, and Yellowstone Ranger Leon Evans espoused ecological conceptions of the park when they resisted efforts to extend predator control into the park. The USFS, USFWS, and stockmen drew a line at Yellowstone's northern boundary where (for them) the coyote's ecological role ended. USFS and USFWS officials, as well as stockmen and hunters, were willing to deal with the assumed consequences of coyote control; a doe season was the simple solution to the anticipated increase in deer. Again, a few individuals such as Kern or Hiller questioned human ability to calculate that balance. Thus a fundamental difference between two approaches to management became more apparent, one advocating human intervention to maintain a balance in nature, the other suggesting that nature could establish its own effective balance. These twin traditions provided problematic choices for managers.

During the 1940s and the 1950s ideas about the preservation of primitive conditions from the 1920s and 1930s were incorporated into new measures aimed at preserving a natural landscape. Kittams and Grimm, for example, argued for measures aimed at preserving the park's natural vegetation. Evans and the director of the Park Service advocated the park's purpose when they objected to the ACC's attempts to manipulate the park's carnivorous wildlife. The goals of restoring the bison herd to a natural condition, reducing bears' dependency on artificial food, and the zoning of Yellowstone Lake demonstrated how interpretations of the purposes of the parks combined with ecological ways of thinking about Yellowstone in the rationales of management policies.

A NATURAL YELLOWSTONE

1963–1974

During the 1960s and early 1970s wildlife management in Yellowstone continued the 1950s trend toward establishing more "natural" parks. Changes in park policies resulted from a fusion of politics, science, and vision about the purposes of a national park. Repeated pressure for a public hunt in Yellowstone contributed to continued tension over the northern elk herd. The Leopold Report and the Robbins Report once again connected Yellowstone to a national context of science and wildlife managers who advocated the study of ecological factors in the park as a prerequisite for management. Two major events, the 1967 cessation of park reductions of the northern Yellowstone elk herd, and closing garbage dumps to grizzly bears in the early 1970s, revolutionized Yellowstone's wildlife management policies. The development of the natural regulation idea and the introduction of theoretical issues from population biology demonstrate two ways in which ecological thinking and science found new applications in debates over management policies. Park Service biologists looked through the lenses of national park purposes as they justified new wildlife policies using concepts from population biology and ecology. These new ideas also shaped the meaning of nature for visitors to Yellowstone.

Beginning in 1959, research on elk and bears conducted by John and Frank Craighead upped the ante for standards of scientific study in the national parks. The Craigheads' work introduced radio-tracking techniques, but more importantly it represented comprehensive ecological research of a kind envisioned by the Wildlife Division many years before. Significantly, research on grizzlies made it apparent that Yellowstone's bears no longer belonged to the park alone, but to a wider ecosystem. Friction between strong personalities, however, made working relationships between the Craigheads and Park Service personnel increasingly difficult. Scientific disagreements over population trends and management of the grizzly bear population began in 1967, demonstrating how interpretations of data led to differing management prescriptions. While most parties put preservation of the grizzly first on their list of priorities, ideas about how to carry that out effectively and notions about the purpose of the parks have remained contested territory.

Despite the reductions of elk, mostly by hunters, by 1961 the "problem" still pawed, nibbled, and browsed its way through the northern range. Pondering their choices, managers, rangers, and wildlife biologists decided that a public hunt could not remove enough of the herd, due to the rugged conditions of winter in Yellowstone. Even if enough hunters could be found, their pack animals would create significant range damage. Grand Teton National Park had conducted a public hunt for many years, a legacy of political pressure exerted in 1950 when the Jackson Hole National Monument was abolished and added to Grand Teton.[1] In 1961 Grand Teton rangers distributed maps and copies of the rules and regulations to hunters, yet discovered illegal kills of several coyotes, eleven moose, two bears, and twenty-three elk.[2] Yellowstone managers therefore were not optimistic about enforcing hunter discipline. Moreover, a large public hunt in the park might induce elk to fear and avoid humans; summer visitors thus might not see elk, which now wandered in plain view unafraid of humans.

Biologists at Montana State College in Bozeman and at the University of Montana in Missoula urged Yellowstone Superintendent Lon Garrison to use the Park Service's authority to carry out direct reductions. The yearly decreases by live trapping and relocation had not reduced the herd enough to reach the presumed carrying capacity, so Garrison and Chief Ranger Otto Brown planned a significantly larger reduction for the winter of 1961–62. A herd containing an estimated ten thousand elk would be culled to five thousand to achieve the carrying capacity calculated in the early 1950s by biologist Walter Kittams. Managers hoped that a smaller herd would allow the range to recover.[3]

Yellowstone serves several publics, and first among them is the tourist. Local folks of northwest Wyoming and southwestern Montana used to stifle a chuckle when visitors to the park pointed to the native ungulates grazing in the hot spring basins and asked: "Pardon me, but what is that?" Twenty-five years ago automobiles would stop and back up on the road to watch a bear, but not elk. Today, elk jams are frequent on Yellowstone's roads. Locals may be getting used to an increasingly urbanized crowd of visitors. For many Americans who are physically and psychologically separated from wild animals and large expanses of wild land, Yellowstone becomes a powerful symbol of nature. The general public is fascinated by the nobility and wildness of the wapiti of the great northwest. What the urban visitors, in particular, do not often realize is that the elk grazing peacefully before them are not quite the essence of wild nature they think. The Yellowstone elk are partly the product of long human manipulation of the landscape as well. Many among this urban public of the 1960s did not understand the necessity of shooting the animals. The reduction of 1961–62, in which rangers shot 4,309 elk, inspired letters from schoolchildren in faraway places and caused a public uproar.[4]

Hunters were disgruntled, because if elk needed shooting, who was more qualified to perform the task? The parks were *national* parks, after all, owned by the people. Local and regional newspapers reflected the protests of sportsmen, who began to pressure their congressional representatives to change the federal laws outlawing hunting in Yellowstone. Pressured by constituents, the Wyoming legislature came out in favor of public hunting. Montana's governor, Donald G. Nutter, and Montana's Fish and Game Department advocated controlled public hunting in the park. The International Association of Game and Fish Commissioners "protested the proposed slaughtering of elk by hired killers" and proposed substituting sportsmen for rangers.[5] A group of Wyoming sportsmen considered seeking court action against the Park Service to halt the reduction. The secretary of the Powell, Wyoming, Chamber of Commerce urged sportsmen's clubs to unite to test whether "the will of the people will prevail over that of the park officials."[6] The outcry was so vociferous that Wyoming Senator Gale McGee convened hearings in Bozeman, Montana, to consider the issue.[7] Superintendent Garrison later described the direct reductions and the ensuing controversy as a "brutal, bloody, abusive process including threats on my life" and midnight phone calls threatening Mrs. Garrison.[8]

Dr. W. Leslie Pengelly, wildlife extension director at the University of Montana, defended the decisions of park managers. Speaking before the Kiwanis club in Billings, Montana, Pengelly explained the necessity of controlling the herd and pointed out the practical limitations of inviting the public to hunt within the park. Pengelly and other Montana wildlife biologists wrote to NPS Director Conrad Wirth, supporting the elk reductions as well as the park's position against hunting. This offended members of the Wyoming Game and Fish Commission, who considered themselves experts on wildlife management. University biologists had second-guessed their expertise and questioned their wisdom. When commission members met in Cheyenne on January 16, they in turn criticized the "few arm-chair game managers whose knowledge of wildlife management is confined largely to textbooks and the classroom."[9]

Managers had a difficult time convincing the hunting public that the practical difficulties of a large hunt in winter and the specific purposes of a national park precluded hunting within Yellowstone. In magazines such as *Sports Afield*, Arthur H. Carhart and others advocated public hunting in the national parks. Carhart thought that the solution to ungulate overpopulation was "thousands of sportsmen as the only possible number of operators to do the job fully."[10] Organizations like the San Diego Rod and Gun Club and the Casper Sportsmen's Association advocated public hunting in the park. But park biologists and managers staunchly resisted the idea, viewing public hunting within the park as a practical problem—it was physically impossible for sportsmen to harvest the desired four thousand animals, and public hunting might well teach the herd to flee humans and therefore disappoint the camera-bearing summer tourist.

Ultimately, managers and biologists relied on their own conceptions of Yellowstone's purpose. Yellowstone had a significantly different objective than did the surrounding national forests. The parks were intended as "inviolate sanctuaries for all forms of nature," wrote Yellowstone West District Ranger Elt Davis. "Once the bars are let down to hunters, how can we logically reject the stockmen and others who will soon demand that we manage our resources for the economic welfare of these groups rather than retaining them naturally for the higher purpose of public enjoyment." Thus Davis and others saw public hunting as simply incompatible with the end purposes of the park. The struggle against public hunting in Yellowstone was crucial: The Park Service was "fighting for their very existence. . . . Everything we have been taught and trained for over the years could be lost if public wildlife reduction ever takes place in the parks."[11] Davis feared that if a public hunt was allowed, state wildlife agencies would soon be setting the terms of management within the parks. Not merely the matter of agency independence, but the more important notion of the national parks as separate places with a unique mission animated Davis, other Yellowstone managers, and scientists through 1967, the last year of direct reductions.

Clearly, the Wyoming State Game Commission was at odds with Yellowstone administrators. On April 3 and 4, 1962, Yellowstone conducted a helicopter census of the northern herd, inviting several interested parties to participate. The Wyoming Commission balked when they were not guaranteed space for an observer on every flight (which was impossible due to the number of outside witnesses) and threatened to withdraw entirely. F. Howard Brady, Izaak Walton League executive board member, was present at the census and opined that the Wyoming Game and Fish Commission had been "unprofessional . . . in this particular problem this past winter." Brady thought that "the present Fish and Game Commissioner from Wyoming does not have full control over his field men, and as a result, a lot of nonprofessional statements and charges are being made that will do Wyoming no good."[12] This tension between Wyoming and Yellowstone Park officials continued through 1967, when controversy again arose about direct reduction. The practical management strategies of the states and Yellowstone differed, because their notions of the national parks' role and purpose sharply diverged. The commissioners thought of the parks as properly accessible for hunting, as places for the enjoyment of the people. Biologists on a special advisory panel and the park managers understood Yellowstone as a manageable wildlife preserve and a place where the public might view nature's handiwork.

Following the controversy of 1962, Yellowstone managers did their best to mend fences and explain the necessity of reduction. On April 16 Yellowstone conducted a "show-me" trip, hosting twenty-four members of rod and gun clubs, representatives of the Wyoming Wildlife Federation, the press, the Range Management Department of Montana State College, Montana Fish and Game Department, and the U.S. Forest Service. Examining the grass, sagebrush, and rabbit brush at a place near Gardiner they called Coalmine Flats, in the vicinity of Eagle Creek just north of the park and in the Lamar River drainage, most of the delegation became convinced that the park's reduction policy was necessary. Earl R. Nott of the Montana Wildlife Federation complimented Park Service personnel in their "handling of the problem in the face of extreme opposition by mis-informed but well-meaning individuals and groups."[13] Robert C. Sykes, president of the Montana Wildlife Federation, urged the public to accept the decisions of professional fish and wildlife managers. Sykes used this analogy: Although he was the beneficiary of indoor plumbing, he was by no means a plumber. Too many sportsmen thought that by virtue of their hunting skill, they also were expert in wildlife management. "One of our greatest needs today is an expansion of our biological phase of big game management and more plumbers and less plungers."[14] Meanwhile, the national meeting of the Izaak Walton League of America (IWLA) was unable to agree on a resolution regarding the northern Yellowstone herd. The Laramie chapter advocated "an energetic trapping and transplanting program," and another group staunchly defended the Park Service's actions. The chairman of the IWLA Public Lands Committee notified the Wildlife Advisory Panel that "no one questions the need of keeping this herd at a reduced size, but many of us believe it can be accomplished by other methods more satisfactory to the public."[15] Thus in 1962 wildlife biologists, range experts, and hunters generally agreed that the range was in poor shape, elk caused that condition, and reducing the herd was absolutely necessary.

During the two periods of controversy over the northern Yellowstone elk in the 1960s, Park Service officials became increasingly aware that scientific data were needed to help inform management. The superintendent found justification of management policies to a skeptical public increasingly difficult. But basic research on the park's wildlife resources had received a very low priority during the 1940s and 1950s. In 1955 Chief Biologist Victor Cahalane resigned in frustration with the lack of support for research from the Washington DC office. In 1958 the National Park Service initially responded to criticism, establishing its first official research budget of twenty-eight thousand dollars, close to the amount assigned to George Wright back in 1932.[16]

Park Service scientists believed that ecological studies promised to improve scientific understanding, which could inform wildlife management policy. In 1961 Lowell Sumner, the principal biologist of the National Park Service, noted that a constrained research budget limited the NPS to "emergency studies designed to counterbalance . . . gross disturbances." Sumner pointed to the NPS desire to get beyond problem-oriented research to basic ecological research that would give a database to inform proper management. The entire annual budget for research in the national park system in 1961 was still only twenty-eight thousand dollars, however, and given sixty-one major park locations, this small amount hampered significant ecological research.[17] In the early 1960s Howard Stagner was transferred from the Mission 66 program to become chief of the Natural History Division, where he attempted to make scientific research a central concern of the NPS.[18]

The existing NPS science staff in 1962 evaluated their research program. Their report suggested that NPS research was "piecemeal, designed only to solve immediate problems, and lacking in continuity, coordination, and depth," lacked an ecological perspective, and was "descriptive rather than analytical," cataloging problems but not providing ecological insight into the parks.[19] The report discussed parks as islands surrounded by intensively managed lands, in other words, in terms of fragmented landscapes. Stagner convinced Secretary of the Interior Udall to commission an independent review of the National Park Service's research program. Sympathetic to the problems of the NPS, Udall quickly asked the National Academy of Science to review the NPS natural science program, and secondly established an advisory committee to report on wildlife management in the parks.[20]

The controversy over the 1961–62 reduction of the northern Yellowstone elk herd was the most publicized problem in wildlife management at that time. Was the reduction of herds necessary and proper? If the numbers of elk must be reduced by direct methods, why not include the participation of hunters? Secretary of the Interior Stewart Udall reported that he was "under great pressure" to allow hunting during the 1962 elk reduction controversy. In response to Howard Stagner's 1962 internal examination of NPS research, and in response to requests from Wyoming senators Gale McGee and Joe Hickey, Secretary Udall assembled the Special Advisory Board on Wildlife Management to investigate herd reductions in the national parks.[21] The scientists who served on the panel, A. Starker Leopold, Ira Noel Gabrielson, Thomas Kimball, and Clarence Cottam, were well known and respected in wildlife management circles as well as in the land management agencies.

Aldo Starker Leopold became an influential figure in wildlife management of his own accord, and not by reliance on his father's (Aldo Leopold) reputation. Starker Leopold worked as a professor of zoology and conservation at Berkeley, by 1958 assuming the post of assistant director at the Museum of Vertebrate Zoology. His experiences ultimately shaped the views of the panel. As a young man he had visited the Rio Gavilan in Mexico, which impressed him by its wild character. That trip made him aware of the function of predators, the role of fire, and how healthy the landscape appeared. Returning in 1958, Leopold was dismayed by the intrusion of grazing and logging. The loss of Rio Gavilan's wild character made a deep impression, just as its image of a healthy functioning wild landscape had impressed him many years earlier.[22] His impression that a minimally managed landscape could remain healthy and productive and a sensitivity to the loss of such natural areas influenced Leopold's thinking about America's national parks.

The panel's recommendations, released March 4, 1963, unequivocally stated that the control of elk populations was necessary, and direct reduction was a proper method of accomplishing this.[23] Removal programs at several national parks had not been large enough, the report noted, and future removals would "have to be larger and in many cases repeated annually."[24] This panel of wildlife experts affirmed the notion of carrying capacity, in other words, the calculation of how many animals a range could support without causing retrogressive succession. The report also agreed with the concept that an original balance had been disturbed by human action, and compensating actions could restore the balance. The meaning of the Leopold Report was that virtually all wildlife experts in 1963 agreed with several widely shared assumptions of the 1930s, including the idea that the one way to prevent the utter depletion of range resources and a resulting mass starvation of ungulates was to remove deer or elk from the range. The biologists who produced the Leopold Report blessed active management of the Yellowstone elk herd.

The report also addressed the issue of public hunting in Yellowstone, which had created rifts in the professional wildlife management community. Professional wildlife managers had daily contacts with the sportsmen who continually lobbied Congress to permit some form of public hunting in the park. After all, Grand Teton deputized hunters as agents of the government as part of its elk management program; that provision had been a condition of the park's establishment. Some game commissioners and state game department employees also advocated public hunting. In September 1962 the International Association of Game, Fish and Conservation Commissioners met with the advisory board at Jackson Lake Lodge just south of Yellowstone Park. During their meeting the president of the Colorado Conservation Council, Edward Hilliard, proposed public hunting in all the national parks. Carl Riggan of the Wyoming Fish and Game Commission advocated that all the wildlife in the parks be placed under state control. Dane Conger of the South Dakota Game, Fish and Parks Commission blamed the National Park Service for creating the problems, then shirking its responsibilities. Bill Towell, director of the Missouri Conservation Commission, wrote to Leopold, arguing that in large western parks public hunting would not interfere with existing uses at certain seasons of the year. The states, he suggested, believed that they "have a game management interest and responsibility to be shared with the National Park Service within the Parks." The director of the Louisiana Wildlife Commission as well as the commissioner of the Maine Department of Game similarly wrote to advisory board member Ira Gabrielson, lobbying for public hunting in the parks. The pressure for public hunting culminated on September 13, 1961, when Senate Bill 2545 was introduced to legalize hunting in the national parks.[25]

The advisory board differed with many state wildlife agencies and professionals, rejecting their suggestions for public hunting in the park. This was not because the panel was unsympathetic to hunting. Starker Leopold, for example, had hunted since he was a youth and continued to hunt throughout his life. Other frictions created the advisory board's opposition to public hunting in the parks. Clarence Cottam, director of the Welder Wildlife Foundation and advisory board member, forwarded to Ira Gabrielson an anonymous letter from a fellow professional that opined: "While the Bureau of Sport Fisheries and Wildlife looks upon your committee as a threat to its present state of somnolence, I view it as a great opportunity to secure more adequate protection." The agency, in his opinion, was all too anxious to open "the entire refuge system to wholesale recreational use."[26] Cottam's sympathy toward this attitude demonstrates that some wildlife professionals shared a sentiment that the states were not doing enough to protect wildlife, that the state agencies had become too much oriented toward production and harvest to the neglect of other values. The national parks, for many people, embodied some of those larger values. Ultimately, Park Service arguments that public hunting was unable to carry out the task without causing severe disruptions to the other park wildlife and to the visitor experience persuaded the advisory board to support the NPS's opposition to public hunting in Yellowstone. The Leopold Report noted that the particular interests of the states did not necessarily coincide with national park values.

Yellowstone Park Management Biologist Robert Howe hoped that the Leopold Report would "make our management more acceptable," because it represented the opinions of widely respected wildlife managers. Howe had carried on the range studies initiated by William Rush thirty years previously. By 1964 Howe believed that the general public had come to understand and accept Yellowstone's wildlife management practices. Yet during the 1950s and early 1960s similar controversies plagued the state wildlife agencies, as the public around Yellowstone questioned the decisions of wildlife experts. Outfitters and sportsmen familiar with the Gallatin Canyon just northwest of the park objected to the repeated efforts of the Montana Department of Fish and Game to reduce the number of elk in the Gallatin herd. Sportsmen questioned the accuracy of game counts, advocated feeding the elk, and suggested a shortened hunting season. Some dude ranchers

35. Yellowstone management biologist Robert Howe followed in the footsteps of William Rush, Rudolph Grimm, and Walt Kittams in his studies and assessment of the northern range. Here he examines an exclosure plot near Tower Junction in 1961. Courtesy Yellowstone Photo Archives.

did not accept game managers' arguments about range depletion and even argued that the Gallatin could support more, not fewer, elk. The sportsmen seemed to think of the experts as academics who were disconnected from the real world. Some seemed to worry that too few elk would survive management plans, while others opposed what they called the slaughter sanctioned by the special season. In the early 1960s interested local outfitters and sportsmen formed the Gallatin Elk Protective Association (GEPA). They opposed the cooperative plan of the Montana Fish and Game Department, U.S. Forest Service, and National Park Service to use special seasons to reduce the number of elk in the Gallatin herd. In February 1964, GEPA filed suit against Yellowstone Superintendent Lemuel Garrison and Howe, seeking an injunction against herd reduction by hunting or by relocation. The suit was quickly thrown out of the U.S. District Court in Butte, Montana, which ruled that it did not have jurisdiction. The decade of protest demonstrated that not all sportsmen understood the problem as game managers did. The state wildlife agencies had to sell the idea that managers had to balance big game herds with available range. Despite the protests of GEPA, by 1965 the Montana Department of Fish and Game believed it had convinced the majority of the public that action was necessary.[27]

Finally, the Leopold Report urged the NPS to conduct a program of scientific research. The committee recommended that the NPS establish a permanent, mission-oriented research unit that planned and administered its own program. George Sprugel, chief NPS scientist, predictably used the report to support his arguments for the importance of more research in the parks. Sprugel reiterated the concerns of previous generations of scientists. If the Park Service was to respond to its legislative mandate, "every reasonable effort must be made to reestablish and/or maintain the natural conditions as they obtained when the national parks and monuments were authorized." Conservation groups such as National Parks for the Future called for more research in national parks, reflecting a growing public understanding that insight into park ecosystems would require more scientific research.[28] Starker Leopold argued that scientific research was an indispensable part of ecological management: "Until you know precisely what you are doing and what the effects are going to be, management could be risky indeed."[29]

Park Service director Hartzog found implementing this recommendation of the Leopold Report difficult because of limited funding. Hartzog approached Representative Michael J. Kirwan, chairman of the Interior Department Appropriations Subcommittee, to discuss funding scientific research in NPS natural areas. Kirwan told Hartzog that research was a function of the National Institutes of Health, but not something for the Park Service. Hartzog used the expedient of changing the name from "research" to "resource studies" and funded it out of an emergency reserve in park management funds.[30] In short, although the Leopold Report urged research, Congress was unwilling to allocate additional funds.

Today the Leopold Report is remembered not for its recommendation that direct reduction was necessary and proper, but rather for its expression of what the panel members thought about the goals of the parks. The "biotic associations within each park" should "be maintained or, where necessary, recreated, as nearly as possible in the condition that prevailed when the area was first visited by the white man. A national park should represent a vignette of primitive America."[31] Some authors imply this notion appeared in 1963, but in fact clear precedent for the concept existed previously. Since the 1920s scientists and conservationists had worried over the progressive loss of primitive or natural areas, places where the influence of modern civilization did not yet penetrate. In 1932 the Wild Life Survey had suggested that one of the NPS's tasks was "preserving characteristic examples of primitive America."[32] Thus the concept of the "vignette," which most people associate with the Leopold Report, actually had roots much deeper in NPS history. The advisory board's use of the word vignette has been used by later observers to imply that the report advocated re-creating a frozen or unchanging Yellowstone landscape. Starker Leopold later commented that if the committee had known how carefully everyone would read its report, they would have spent more time writing it. Leopold was a relatively sophisticated analyst of scientific issues, and it is evident that he did not envision nature as static and unchanging.

In a speech at the 1963 NPS administrators' "Conference of Challenges" held at Yosemite, Starker Leopold explained what he thought were some of the report's most important concepts. To achieve the goal of a vignette, the Leopold Committee had urged long-range ecological planning informed by science. Everyone knew, said Leopold, that "ecologic situations" in the parks always changed and never remained static for very long. In some cases operational polices had inadvertent or unintended effects on the changes and evolutions, or successions, in park natural areas. Leopold used the examples of park policies that suppressed all fires immediately and controlled forest insects. These programs had "ecologic implications of one sort or another and the aggregate effect of many such programs operating superimposed one upon another, has been the creation of ecologic situations frequently far from what was intended for preservation in the first place."[33] Nature also created new situations for managers. In McKinley National Park, for example, a successional stage of aspen and willow in an old burn area had encouraged a growing moose population, while the caribou population decreased as a result of the fire-induced changes. If the moose population was to be perpetuated, managers must protect the willow from overuse and rejuvenate the willow and aspen by fire or some other horticultural method.

This implied a very difficult job for management, of "manipulation of ecologic situations to preserve what it is that we have set up to display before the public."[34] Some sort of zoning might be used—some areas where no management would be employed, others where nature would be managed to some degree. The day-to-day operations of the park, for example, response to fire, insects, and regulation of game numbers, would all aim at achieving a long-term ecologic objective.

Leopold reviewed the committee's opinion that the control of excess ungulates was right and proper, using the case of elephants in Murchison Falls Park in Uganda as a worst-case example of too many animals. Elephants had become concentrated in the park, creating a severe impact on vegetation. The USFWS lab in Denver, he noted, had dropped five thousand stilbesterol-loaded baits on coyote territory, and the experiment promised success in animal birth control. Perhaps the same might be done with deer and elk. Leopold went on to advocate the reintroduction of native animals back into parks where they were missing. Wolves naturally introduced themselves to Isle Royale, where Durwood Allen's research seemed to indicate "an extremely interesting balance between wolves and moose." Could wolves or cougar be reintroduced in Acadia National Park? Although Leopold believed such action was out of the question in Yellowstone because of a hostile political climate, he advocated the restoration of native animals as a long-range goal wherever possible. The really tricky part would be the "complete restoration of a range," or the "reconstruction of ecologic situations" to make such reintroductions possible.[35]

A major purpose behind Leopold's thinking was that the national parks were places for public use and enjoyment. For Leopold that meant that amid "the great rush that is developing within the country" for creating material goods, with millions of people looking for various types of recreation, and with the national parks occupying less than 1 percent of the land area, the place of the national parks was "strictly a qualitative one based on natural values." The scenery, the wildlife, and the plant associations all made up a part of a qualitative experience that should be presented in its entirety to the public. Some of the most intensive management should occur right by the roadsides, thought Leopold. Although the great back country areas would not be intensively managed, the public viewed the parks from the roadside and thus roadside "ecologic management, including roadside wildlife management, may be the most important facet of all, in creating this vision I am talking about." To Leopold a tree was "no more sacred than an elk, and if it requires the removal of some trees to create or maintain natural scenes other than forest," then it represented appropriate management.[36] Thus Leopold urged the NPS toward thinking about the parks in ecological ways while advocating active forms of manipulation toward ecologic ends.

Although Hartzog thought Starker Leopold's address brilliant, some biologists remained uncomfortable with the language and philosophy expressed in the Leopold Committee's report. Adolph Murie thought the committee had been wrong in its opinion that the national parks had relied too much on protection and not enough on management. Murie commented that "the contrary is true—we have had too much *management* and not enough *protection*."[37] What the Leopold Report had critiqued as "protective" and "over-protective" activities in the parks, Murie suggested were really management activities. This was not mere quibbling but important, because the terminology could lead to different philosophical viewpoints. The control of predators, of fire, of insects, the manipulation of fish populations, the hayfield near Gardiner, the buffalo enclosure, the buffalo ranch, and the salting program were all examples of manipulative management that prevailed in previous times, which the report labeled as overprotection. Management, wrote Murie, should always "be the minimum needed to compensate for natural ecological conditions absent or not fully operating. In the past, and it will be true in the future, a part of the biologists [sic] program has been an attempt to prevent undesirable intrusions, some of which have been ill-advised wildlife management."[38]

Most wildlife studies conducted by wildlife biologists contained recommendations against common management practices, Murie noted. Murie and other biologists had opposed practices such as wolf and coyote control, insect and mosquito control, pine tree blister rust eradication efforts, aggressive fire suppression, and open garbage dumps. Why did the experts make so many management suggestions? Murie blamed "a lack of understanding of park objectives, and a desire to practice management techniques."[39] The central reason Murie disagreed with Leopold's opinions expressed at the Yosemite conference and the committee's outlook was that Leopold's views emphasized management and manipulation, ideas "so contrary to generally accepted wilderness philosophy."[40]

It is important to note a significant split among professional wildlifers on the subject of management. Murie observed that when the Wildlife Society was formed in 1936, some factions wanted the organization called the Wildlife Management Society, while others "opposed the use of the word 'management' in the name of the society . . . because they did not want words such as 'management' and 'manipulation' closely associated with wild and wilderness areas where much wildlife is found and where we want as little manipulation as possible." The less management in wilderness areas, the better, thought Murie. The misplaced "fetish of management" should not intrude into places reserved as wilderness.[41]

Additionally, the Leopold Report seemed to call for freezing nature in time, at some special moment when explorers or pioneers first set eyes on the landscape. Murie suggested the vignette idea was insufficient, especially when considered in ecological terms, and advocated phrasing the park concept so "as to imply the maintenance of a living organism." The parks should strive "to maintain all the natural ecological factors of an area and leave them as undisturbed as possible so that they may act and interact as naturally as possible." Murie urged that the successional stages, in his words "the life of the habitat," should be given "free play for in most areas the ecological factors affecting habitat are operating naturally."[42] A particular habitat would thus move forward toward climax or be set back to an earlier stage by a force such as fire. Murie argued that Leopold was wrong about moose habitat in McKinley National Park; the willow was part of the climax vegetation and did not need intervention, because it was self-perpetuating. Leopold's view on this particular point, rejecting the idea of a climax stage, proved more enduring than Murie's. Yet Murie got close to the essential question when he suggested that nobody could "precisely predict the ecological change pertaining to moose or other species in McKinley Park."[43]

Murie was shocked by the recent experiment with coyote birth control carried out by the USFWS and expressed dismay that intensive roadside management could be thought of as yielding a qualitative experience of high caliber. The idea of chopping down trees by the roadside to present a selected natural scene, wrote Murie, was "the most extreme anti-park policy statement I have yet encountered." This grooming and shaping would hardly represent a natural scene. Murie asked: "Do we want to make Disney Lands out of our Roadsides?" He preferred the philosophy of a rough-hewn friend, a logger and conservationist who visited the parks on a regular basis. Murie had the good fortune to be present when a tourist asked his friend where all the animals were. The gentleman replied without hesitation, "This ain't no zoo, lady."[44] Wilderness had to be accepted on its own terms, and it did not come on a silver platter. Nature had to be sought out, and the parks would be mistaken to attempt to provide easy express roads to overlooks of the natural.

While the Leopold Committee deliberated, the National Academy of Sciences panel carried out its work, investigating the NPS research program. Chaired by Dr. William J. Robbins of the National Science Foundation, the NAS National Park Service Research Committee also included Dr. Edward A. Ackerman, executive officer of the Carnegie Institution, Dr. Frank Fraser Darling Sr., lecturer in ecology at the University of Edinburgh, Dr. Noel

Eichhorn of the Conservation Foundation, and other scientists associated with major research institutes. The group met in Washington on three occasions, made a field trip to Everglades National Park in January of 1963, and a second field trip to Yellowstone and Grand Teton National Parks in June. The committee consulted with almost one hundred NPS officials, employees, and scientists such as Dr. John Craighead.[45] At the time the committee visited Yellowstone, John and Frank Craighead were conducting pioneering research on grizzly bears, and Dr. Mary Meagher was investigating bison populations in the park. Park biologist William Barmore continued assessment work on the northern range. During the 1950s and early 1960s a few outside investigators also carried out research projects on the fisheries, benthic organisms in streams, and other topics. Yet research in Yellowstone had suffered the same fate as in the national park system, generally neglected while the development of Mission 66 proceeded apace.[46]

The Robbins Report assessed the overall place of research within the NPS. Knowledge about the parks' problems could only come from research, especially in natural history, which had received "meager dollar support" from the NPS. From 1960 to 1962 the NPS devoted less than 1 percent of its budget to research and development, whereas similar government agencies invested about 10 percent. The committee believed that NPS policies demonstrated that "the potential contribution of research and a research staff to the solution of the problems of the national parks is recognized and appreciated." Robbins and his colleagues, all associated with scientific research, found it "inconceivable that property so unique and valuable as the national parks . . . should not be provided adequately with competent research scientists in natural history as elementary insurance for the preservation and best use of the parks."[47] Thus the problem was essentially structural in the context of the NPS's priorities. More specifically, the Robbins Report suggested that research in the national parks "lacked continuity, coordination, and depth. It has been marked by expediency rather than by long-term considerations. It has in general lacked direction, has been fragmented between divisions and branches, has been applied piecemeal, has suffered because of a failure to recognize the distinctions between research and administrative decision-making, and has failed to insure the implementation of the results of research in operational management."[48]

The report suggested that park research should be mission oriented to focus on park problems, and that research should be long term in nature so that it might warn of impending problems. The idea of mission-oriented research was not new in scientific thinking, nor was it new to the National Park Service. Albright recognized the need for more information to delineate and describe the deterioration of the range that Rush had perceived in 1927. Yet mission-oriented research also had its shortcomings. Olaus Murie pointed out managers' tendency to think of biologists as trouble-shooters, called on to fix a situation in a hurry and move to the next problem. The Robbins Report, however, did not emphasize the notion of basic research in the parks, something the scientists within the NPS thought valuable.[49] The committee made twenty recommendations, including ideas such as ensuring that funds were made available for advanced students, traditionally the essential workhorses of much wildlife research.

Several recommendations reiterated the ideas advanced by the Wild Life Survey in 1931: The NPS should plan and administer its own program, a permanent and independent unit within the NPS should administer the work, the natural resources of each park should be mapped, and consultation with the research unit should precede all operational decisions. The Robbins Committee also noted that in some parks, remote areas approached "primitive conditions," and should be preserved in that condition, because they held "scientific value as outdoor natural laboratories in which the working of natural laws can be observed to greater advantage than anywhere else and because each such area is a refuge [of] plant and animal species—a nature's biological bank in which a biological reserve can exist and from which species may spread to adjacent areas."[50] A zoning scheme separated various landscape uses into natural, undisturbed areas where only researchers could travel, naturalistic areas affected to some degree by management, and public use and facility areas. The parks as refuges and as great natural laboratories were in one sense very traditional ideas. Albright thought of the parks as refuges, and Charles C. Adams had advocated the preservation of natural conditions in the parks. Wildlife management policies were catching up with ecology in redefining wildlife refuges to include creatures other than big game animals.

Equally important as the specific recommendations about how to do better science were scientists' ideas about the parks' purpose. The Robbins Report started at the beginning, considering the NPS organic act and the purposes of the parks. Should the parks try to attract more visitors with recreational facilities? The committee thought not, writing "the purpose of the national parks should be the preservation of nature, the maintenance of natural conditions, the avoidance of artificiality, with such provisions for the accommodation of visitors as will neither destroy nor deteriorate the natural features which should be preserved for the enjoyment of future visitors who may come to the parks." Differences of opinion existed regarding the place of management in the parks, they noted. On the one hand, artificial control was contrary to the idea of leaving natural forces to their own devices, but on the other, some thought no national park was big enough or isolated enough to be a "self-regulatory ecological unit."[51] The committee believed that management to preserve or restore natural conditions was unavoidable. But what state of nature, or what natural conditions would the parks manage toward? The NAS committee cited the recently completed work of the Leopold Committee, adopted the vignette of primitive America, and noted that while the ideal was perhaps not attainable, nevertheless, it represented a desirable direction.

The Robbins Committee clearly stated its view of nature as a dynamic entity. Scientists had challenged the Clementsian notion of orderly succession toward a climax state, and by the 1950s the notion of nature as tightly interdependent had fallen from general favor. As a recent historian phrased it, "prior to the 1950s nature was simplistic and deterministic; after the 1950s nature became complex, fuzzy edged, and probabilistic."[52] The assessor-scientists on the Robbins Committee recognized that the national parks were not "museum exhibits in glass cases; they are dynamic biological complexes with self-generating changes. To attempt to maintain them in any fixed condition, past, present, or future, would not only be futile but contrary to nature. Each park should be regarded as a system of interrelated plants, animals and habitat (an ecosystem) in which evolutionary processes will occur under such human control and guidance as seems necessary to preserve its unique features. Naturalness, the avoidance of artificiality, would be the rule."[53] The ideas of the "outdoor natural laboratory" where natural laws could be observed, and of the parks as "dynamic biological complexes with self-generating changes" proved very influential during the next thirty years. These ideas in essence gave intellectual permission to park managers and park scientists to interpret the meanings and purposes of parks in new ways.

The Leopold and Robbins Reports had a significant impact on NPS wildlife research and management style, although the connections are not all straightforward.[54] One effect was that concepts from ecology further permeated the institutional thinking of the NPS. In 1968 two young Park Service employees wrote master's theses addressing how the ecosystem concept might be used in national park management. B. Riley McClelland, who later argued with the superintendent of Glacier National Park over the installation of an alpine boardwalk, wrote on the ecosystem as a unifying concept in natural area management.[55] The most important value for managing natural areas, wrote McClelland, was "not a single feature or species, but a complex system of physical and biological relationships."[56]

Robert D. Barbee, who later became superintendent at Yellowstone, also conducted a scholarly study on the subject of ecological management in the national parks. Barbee's 1968 thesis essentially aimed at translating the Leopold Report into management language. He noted the dilemma of the Park Service's mission: to protect park resources, yet provide for visitor access. The Park Service must manage with the end goal of "naturalness," although the very presence of people compromised the goal. "It is the 'compromise' that the Service is most concerned with minimizing," wrote Barbee. Indeed, the service still faced the familiar dilemma of preservation versus development, but in the 1960s critics shifted from pleas to save the scenic toward arguments about ecological conceptualizations of the landscape.[57] Barbee emphasized that the mission of the national parks had not changed in any significant sense; yet rather than protect individual species, parks would emphasize concepts of ecological management. Barbee noted that the Leopold Report recommended that the Park Service should not abandon active management, but manage so that "operative factors of the environment" became "the primary controlling factors."[58] Thus Park Service management rationales changed as scientific conceptions altered: Shifts in management policy were "directly related to the growing sophistication of the technology ('science') of ecological land management."[59] Barbee was partly correct. Ecology did have a great influence on Yellowstone's management practices and rationales for its actions, yet people's conceptions of what they expected from Yellowstone also had an important effect on how the park would manipulate nature. In the end the public decided that nature could be manipulated outside park boundaries, but it was not the place of the Park Service to kill elk, science or management plan notwithstanding.

Many writers see the Leopold Report as a watershed in land management philosophy, and with good reason. The report presented the views of influential wildlife management professionals and seemed to advocate a new view on the parks. The idea of the "vignette" drew the majority of popular attention, and this notion has seized people's imagination ever since. It is the vision in the document, rather than the technical expertise, that lends the Leopold Report its continuing importance. Some observers emphasize a new philosophy of management embodied in the study. Thomas McNamee, for example, identified a philosophy focusing on natural management adopted after the Leopold Report. For McNamee this led not to disaster but rather yielded a great benefit in creating "vast ecological laboratories, where the processes of life and death may be seen and studied in all their richly baffling complexity."[60]

Although the Leopold Report introduced the vision of managing for a "vignette" of pre-Columbian America, alternative forms of that notion had been percolating among Park Service managers for many years. Albright, for example, had written about the parks as places where nature would be protected, to where the urban-bound could escape to view a *primitive* America. When E. W. Nelson addressed the National Parks Conference in 1916, he made specific reference to a pre-Columbian landscape. Scientists of the 1920s dreamed up research reserves to protect natural conditions. Similarly, the Wildlife Division of the 1930s argued that parks should be managed to protect primitive nature. Yellowstone Superintendent Lon Garrison noted in 1962, before the Leopold Report was released, that Yellowstone was a "natural museum" where wildlife management actions were only justified "when man-caused events threaten the delicate interspecific balance among animals and plants."[61] These words were almost verbatim from the Wildlife Division's recommendations and the written policies of the 1940s. Park managers from Albright to Garrison viewed Yellowstone primarily as a place that protected nature. The history of scientists visiting Yellowstone reveals considerable continuity in thinking about the purposes of the parks over the years.

Humans have managed the elk in Yellowstone in different ways since 1872, when Yellowstone National Park did not protect elk against hunters. During the 1870s and 1880s a continuing and extensive slaughter by market hunters severely impacted the populations of many wildlife species in the American West, prompting Congress in 1894 to pass the Yellowstone Park Protection Act, prohibiting sport and subsistence hunting in within the park. The elk herd that migrated to summer ranges and back down into the Lamar River drainage grew in size, pleasing the rangers who fed them. During the late 1920s and early 1930s, however, scientists and managers began to wonder if too many elk damaged vegetation on the range. In 1934 Yellowstone rangers began shooting the elk of the northern herd to directly control their numbers. In 1967, after years of controversy, Yellowstone stopped using direct reduction, and shortly thereafter, ceased live-trapping and shipment of elk as well.

For the historian this fundamental policy shift stimulates several questions. Why did Yellowstone initiate this change in wildlife management policy? In what ways did science inform this decision, and how did management imperatives shape the opportunities for science? Why did Yellowstone's policy on range management and ungulates differ from that on the public lands of the Gallatin National Forest just to the north? Management strategies for ungulate management were shaped by biologists and managers who conceived of Yellowstone as an exemplar of nature at work, and as a preserve for nature. The officials who regulated the elk hunt in Montana had a very different set of goals; they needed to provide for traditional public hunting. The perceptions of urban visitors and elk hunters regarding nature and about the purpose of Yellowstone also had an important influence in the form of political pressure on management decisions.

Public protest about the Yellowstone herd reductions largely died down from 1962 until the winter of 1966, because the park did not shoot any elk, although it did employ live trapping, removing 4,543 elk during that period. Once again, however, during the winter of 1966–67 Yellowstone managers decided to employ marksmen to cull the herd. With no advance warning news of the imminent direct reduction seemed to take the public by surprise and raised the hackles of both sportsmen and state game commissioners. Public objections were strong enough to initiate a second round of congressional hearings on the issue.[62] On March 11, 1967, Senator Gale W. McGee of Wyoming convened Senate hearings in Casper regarding the Yellowstone reductions. At the start of the hearing, Senator McGee announced that as "a direct result of a conference that I just had with the Secretary of Interior, Mr. Udall, and director of the Park Service, Mr. Hartzog, as of today the direct kill of elk in the park is stopped."[63] Political pressure, not the arguments at the hearings, nor a scientific rationale, persuaded the Park Service to halt the reduction. Essentially, hunters' protests and a larger public ultimately based in tourism halted the direct reduction of elk in Yellowstone. People would not tolerate park rangers shooting hundreds of elk as a method of reducing the herd, no matter what the justification.

The Absaroka Conservation Committee had resisted direct control in the park, and state game agencies in Montana and Wyoming had made efforts to accept live-trapped elk from Yellowstone. After the big reduction of 1962, for example, the Wyoming Game and Fish Commission had agreed to take excess elk from Yellowstone. In 1966, however, Wyoming State Game Warden Earl M. Thomas wrote that his state accepted large numbers of elk simply to keep them from being slaughtered, but that action "should not be construed as meaning that we either need or even want them." In fact, the "fewer elk that we are asked to accept, the better we will like it."[64] Since the turn of the century, state game ranges across the country had been successfully restocked from Yellowstone, and the demand for more was virtually nonexistent.

In 1967 Wyoming game commissioners, the governor, and the hunting public simply would not permit "their" game to be slaughtered like Wyoming's cattle, even if the meat went to Indian reservations where people made good use of it. The game, they thought, should be trapped and moved to areas where sportsmen could have a chance at it. If the park could not trap enough elk, George Stanich, president of the Skyline Sportsmen of Butte, Montana, offered to come to the park and "show them how it's done."[65] After all, his organization had experience in these matters. Ranchers reluctant to share substantial portions of their crops with the elk in Montana's Big Horn range called on the Skyline Sportsmen, who baited portable traps with hay and moved the elk to nearby state land. If trapping wouldn't work, then the public should be allowed to hunt in Yellowstone. Groups such as the Izaak Walton League supported public hunting in the park.

Although representatives from several sportsmen's clubs spoke in favor of public hunting in Yellowstone, support for the park's ban on hunting came from a somewhat surprising source. Outfitters make a living by equipping and escorting hunters in their pursuit of game and might be expected to welcome any sort of hunt. Yet Nedward Frost of Cody, Wyoming, stood in front of Senator McGee and declared that the Wyoming Outfitter's Association was "unalterably opposed to any public hunting in Yellowstone National Park."[66] Frost's background gives some insight into his position.

Nedward Mahlon Frost was the son of Ned Ward Frost (1881–1957), the outfitter who had guided Saxton Pope's ill-starred bear collecting expedition in Yellowstone. Frost earned a bachelor's degree in history from the University of Wyoming in 1933, worked in the mining industry, then spent four years working with the Wyoming Game and Fish Department. After serving with the Tenth Mountain Division in Italy, he returned to the family business in Cody, outfitting and guiding parties on hunting expeditions near Yellowstone. Frost was a founding member of the Wyoming Guide's Association, and served as president during its early days. In 1967 Frost put his college degree to work as the first employee of the Wyoming State Historic Preservation Office.[67]

In his testimony, Frost eloquently argued that the national parks represented "the esthetic principle," and "must be kept inviolate."[68] He went on to suggest that direct reduction should continue at all seasons of the year and in all parts of the park; although he did not say so, such management might yield the positive result of pushing the elk out of the park into the national forests where outfitters pursued their trade.

Politics played an important role in the Casper Senate hearings. George Hartzog later related how the new Republican governor saw an opportunity to embarrass Democratic Senator Gale McGee. The governor forced McGee to hold the Casper hearings and demanded that Yellowstone stop shooting and start trapping again. During the hearing McGee asked how many elk the governor wanted removed to ranges in Wyoming, and the governor asked for one thousand: "In the back of the room you could hear the ranchers audibly catch their breath as they began to murmur among themselves." Elk hunting season was over in Wyoming, and the elk would compete with cattle for winter range and haystacks. Hartzog directed the Yellowstone superintendent to begin trapping, and when about half the elk had been shipped, the ranchers' complaints persuaded the governor to call Yellowstone and demand an end to the shipments. When Superintendent Garrison called Washington, Hartzog gave him these directions: "Tell the governor . . . if, in the future, he will stay the hell out of my wildlife management program, I'll stop shipping; otherwise, keep shipping, even if you have to unload them on the Capitol grounds." The governor agreed, and "the Leopold wildlife management recommendations were in place at Yellowstone."[69]

Although Hartzog agreed with Senator McGee to stop shooting, he did not promise that Yellowstone would never shoot elk again. Hartzog and his staff carefully reserved all their options for controlling the herd, relying first on natural predation, second on trapping and transplanting elk, third on the Montana hunt, and fourth on control by shooting within the park. In a communication to Secretary Udall, McGee expressed his belief that direct reduction would not be necessary, but acknowledged that it was still an option. If required again, at least sportsmen would have a better understanding of it as a result of the hearings.[70]

Yellowstone Research Biologist William J. Barmore believed that the cause of the protest against direct reduction was "widespread public misunderstanding" of the park's management program.[71] Actually, the public did not so much misunderstand as they disagreed with the policy. What urban people expected of national parks had not changed since the days of Horace Albright: They expected that wildlife would find protection within the borders of the national parks. On the other hand, most hunters resented the "slaughter" of elk inside the park's border, preferring the individualistic and sporting hunt outside Yellowstone. Additionally, some people thought that the Park Service had not wished to communicate with the public, that a federal bureaucracy was acting in a high-handed fashion. The outdoor editor of the *Casper Star-Tribune*, Chuck Morrison, exclaimed at the Senate hearings, "I have been your friend for many years, but if you people do not remove some of your empire building, political-oriented personnel and clean house from top to bottom, you will lose my friendship and my respect for what was, at one time, a fine service."[72] In the end wildlife biologists' efforts to educate the public about the need to reduce herds had failed to overcome urban attitudes about protecting nature in the parks, as well as sportsmen's conceptions of a proper hunt.

When Yellowstone stopped the elk reduction program in 1967, McLaughlin and Barmore considered their options. The public understood the basic notion of overpopulation and the visible signs of starving elk, so removal could still be carried out by trapping and transplanting, or by hunting over on the Montana side of the border. The previous practical limitations regarding hunting outside the park, trapping, and relocating elk still existed, however. After the Casper hearings, the National Park Service changed its methods, but claimed that it reserved the right to take elk if necessary.

In 1967 the National Park Service transferred Jack K. Anderson, superintendent of Grand Teton National Park, to occupy the hot seat at Yellowstone. Glen F. Cole, an NPS biologist who had studied the elk of Grand Teton, was transferred to Yellowstone as supervisory biologist at the same time; Anderson helped to effect Cole's transfer. Graduating from Montana State University's program in fish and wildlife management in 1955 with a master's degree, Cole worked as a biologist for the Montana Fish and Game Department from 1954 to 1962, and as a research biologist in Grand Teton National Park from 1962 until 1967. Cole used the notion of problem-oriented research to give park science direction toward addressing the park's unique situation. Problem-oriented research was nothing new in Yellowstone; Director Horace Albright had urged such practical research back in 1914, but only enough for the immediate purpose at hand. Beginning with problem-oriented research in the late 1960s and early 1970s, science in Yellowstone adopted a greater emphasis on ecological research, both on ungulates and on range resources.

36. Jack K. Anderson assumed the duties of Yellowstone's superintendent in 1967. Courtesy National Park Service, Harpers Ferry Center.

From 1962 through 1967 Cole had researched elk ecology in Grand Teton, located just south of Yellowstone, sharing borders as well as the southern elk herd. Grand Teton was the exception to the rule in the national park
system, because it allowed public hunting. The Jackson Hole area was also
unusual, because agriculture had taken up a lot of elk winter range, so in
1912 Congress appropriated funds to establish a national elk refuge that fed
elk to compensate for the lost forage.[73] In Grand Teton Cole's management
recommendations in 1965 suggested adjustments in the hunting season so a
quota could be set on a forty-eight-hour notice. His goal was to remove two
hundred to three hundred more elk than were produced in the calf crop. In
these recommendations Cole echoed the conventional wisdom of range and
wildlife managers. Ultimately, he wanted to restore "historical elk distribu-
tions and migrations." This emphasis on restoring the primitive echoed the
Fauna reports issued by the Wildlife Division in the early 1930s, the Leopold
Report, and the Park Service mandate to preserve natural resources. Cole
thought that restoring historical patterns of migration and distribution
would "eventually reduce the need for large yearly elk kills on Park lands."[74]

In October 1967 Cole thought he perceived a clue to Yellowstone's problem. He examined the history of elk harvests and controls both in and out of
the park and pointed out that, from 1934 to 1955, hunters in Montana had

effected 84 percent of elk removals, about seventeen hundred per year. The only problem with those hunting yields was that "consistent boundary line hunting" forced the elk to remain inside the park, where they exerted a heavy grazing pressure on the northern range.[75] Like Olaus Murie, Cole believed this was an essential key: Hunting pressure kept the elk within Yellowstone and away from their native winter feeding grounds, resulting in more intensive grazing within the park.

Cole reasoned that the number of elk were out of control after 1955, because "the development of political pressures" prevented proper coordination between state game agencies and the NPS, and that for effective control of elk numbers trapping and transplanting was simply unrealistic. In other words, since the demise of the Absaroka Conservation Committee, interagency coordination had gone downhill, along with the elk harvests. Cole thought that Montana Fish and Game was now willing to be more flexible in setting the dates of its hunt, with the important result that elk would not remain in the park out of range of the hunters' rifles. Cole's central scheme was the "restoration of control by hunting outside boundaries." He recommended to the superintendent a plan cooperatively developed with state agencies, similar to the program he had developed in Grand Teton. Herd size might vary between four thousand to six thousand animals during three-year periods. Communication and, therefore, cooperation would be enhanced by a new agreement among the state wildlife agencies, the state governors, and the secretary of the interior.[76]

Yellowstone and the Montana Department of Fish and Game continued to remove elk in the winter of 1967–68, reducing the herd by about eleven hundred by means of hunting outside the boundary, taking a few for biological study, and live trapping some for shipment. After about eight hundred elk had been removed, or the equivalent of the year's calf production, Cole recommended that the removal be halted, rather than continuing to bring the herd down to forty-one hundred. Cole believed that shipping the elk to Wyoming could become a political issue in Montana, and in "deference to Montana already participating in meetings" to work out management agreements with the National Park Service, the trapping should halt. The herd was at a sufficiently low level, and because Montana Fish and Game now seemed willing to institute a new type of hunting system, Cole thought the park had "a new ball game."[77]

Officials of the Montana Department of Fish and Game, Yellowstone National Park, and the Wyoming Game and Fish Commission met at Mammoth on September 27, 1968. Superintendent Anderson clearly stated that direct reduction was still an option for park policy, which was fully supported by the director of the park service and the secretary of the interior.[78] Nevertheless, Yellowstone discontinued reduction of elk numbers, ending its program of trapping and live shipment, initiating what resource management specialist Edmund J. Bucknall called the "total ecosystem approach to management of wildlife." The 1968–69 management program for the northern Yellowstone herd aimed to allow migratory patterns to develop as much as possible, and to "permit population adjustment by predation, reduced reproduction, natural winter loss, and outside hunting." Management would consider "artificial controls" only when "range damage is imminent," or when other species were harmed.[79]

Yellowstone signed a new memorandum of understanding with the Montana Department of Fish and Game and the U.S. Forest Service, which provided for modifications in the hunt that they believed would allow "unrestricted elk movements outside Yellowstone before hunting begins."[80] The key to the new agreement was the "variable quota hunt system," whereby yearly targets for the Montana hunt could vary from zero up to twenty-five hundred elk. The size of the herd would not be reduced every year, but when harsh winters forced the elk to seek winter range at lower elevations outside the park, the number of elk permits and, hopefully, hunter success would increase. During mild winters when more food was available to the elk at higher elevations within the park, fewer animals would be taken with the intent of keeping the herd habituated to its migratory path.[81] In this cooperation with Montana's state game agency, Yellowstone did not completely abandon active wildlife management. After the 1967 controversy Yellowstone continued to use hunter kill outside the park in its policy rationale.

Although the park enjoyed a reprieve from the public furor, now scientists questioned the new management technique. John Craighead, leader of the Montana Cooperative Wildlife Research Unit from 1952 to 1977, wrote to Superintendent Jack Anderson, reminding him of past support of the scientific community during the 1962 debate over park reductions.[82] Craighead noted that the annual increase of elk had not been removed, and he asked "on what biological basis the present management is founded."[83] Craighead suggested that there was no scientific evidence that demonstrated any need for a change in policy.

Park biologist William Barmore warned Cole that people would expect a scientific rationale for the new management that relied on natural control mechanisms.[84] So far, he suggested, the park had little ecological baseline data to support its new policy. Barmore proved to be a biologist caught between two worlds and two ways of understanding the northern range. During the late 1950s and early 1960s he had continued the range studies initiated by his predecessors and used exclosure studies to demonstrate that heavy browsing suppressed the park's aspen. He belonged to a range management perspective in arguing that managers could know what was the natural or proper mix of elk and aspen—elk should be reduced to a level that "released" the aspen to grow. His sense of park values also entered into his thinking. Quoting an ecological perspective in the Leopold Report's vignette, Barmore suggested that "the preservation of rare plant and animal species or minor biotic communities rightfully assumes" an important status. The fragile half of the equation, the vegetative environment, should be favored over the elk population that easily bounded back from hard times. Both elk and aspen, he argued, should be "restored to their primeval status," which he judged to include fewer elk and more aspen.[85] In 1967 Barmore was reluctant to embrace the idea of a naturally regulated population and found himself "crosswise" with Cole, in disagreement on several issues. Firm and straightforward in conversation, Barmore was slow and perhaps perfectionistic in writing reports and his dissertation, trying Cole's patience. Yet over the next few years, Barmore slowly and gradually came around to agree with Cole about the general parameters of natural regulation.[86] Barmore had already begun to ferret out parts of a puzzle that other biologists later assembled. He had started to experiment with prescribed burning, suggesting that using fire as a management tool would restore a crucial environmental factor in aspen regeneration. Barmore represents a time of changing views and scientific understanding of naturally functioning ecosystems.

Cole's reply to Craighead and Barmore, drafted for the superintendent, was brief and to the point. For Cole the Senate hearings in Casper showed that the NPS "was very much alone in its attempts to manage the Northern Yellowstone elk."[87] There was a very clear danger that the proponents of public hunting in the park might prevail. But it was not only the purpose of the park and the issue of hunting in Yellowstone that drew Cole's attention. He suggested that the interpretations scientists found amenable for the management of wildlife in the national forests were not necessarily appropriate for the management of natural areas in the national parks.

As Cole hiked among the bluebunch wheatgrass and the Idaho fescue grass, which covered the knolls rising above the Lamar River, and as he spent hours viewing the movements of elk through binoculars or a spotting scope, he asked himself what forces affected the population of the elk herds. Cole's study of the elk in southern Yellowstone and Grand Teton National Park during the early 1960s led him to believe that given an entire, complete habitat, elk numbers would maintain a general equilibrium, or be "naturally regulated" by factors such as food availability and disease.[88]

Population regulation is a concept within ecology that still stimulates a great deal of discussion concerning just how and to what extent populations are limited in number. Ecology textbooks for undergraduates begin examining this topic by noting that no animal population grows indefinitely. All animal populations eventually meet constraints (called biological resistance), such as competition with other members of their own species (intraspecific competition) or predation, that place upper boundaries on the size of a population. Ecologists have studied important internal mechanisms of regulation, including physiological stress and dispersal. External influences include harsh weather and predation. Physiological stress associated with intraspecific competition for food or space is thought to cause decreased fertility rates in several species.[89] The term regulation can be used in two ways; first, in the sense of forces limiting the equilibrium number of a population, and second, in the sense of keeping numbers within some range rather than wildly fluctuating.

The beginnings of population ecology have been attributed to Georgii F. Gause's work on the competitive exclusion principle. Using earlier models created by Volterra and Lotka, Gause carried out studies instrumental in defining competition. Depending on environmental conditions, one species of *Paramecium* in his test jars would outcompete the other—from this, he reasoned that if two species had the same requirements, they could not occupy the same niche. Gause then experimented with the colonization of glass plates by microscopic organisms. G. E. Hutchison and others used ideas from Gause, Lotka, and Volterra to demonstrate that competitive exclusion helped explain how communities were organized. The niche lay at the heart of a community structure, shaped by the dynamics of competition and symbiosis.[90] David Lack's work in evolutionary ecology emphasized the importance of adaptation in evolution and examined the role of competition as a force in determining community structure. Lack's work during the 1940s and 1950s on the evolution of clutch size in birds led to his book *The Natural Regulation of Animal Numbers* (1954). Much of Lack's work discussed ideas associated with the effects of food limitation, specifically how limitations on birds' ability to feed the young influenced clutch size. As did Alexander J. Nicholson, Lack aimed at the bigger issue of fitness by examining how animal populations were regulated.[91] Nicholson championed the idea of density-dependent regulation that kept population numbers within a relatively limited range. Another primary source of work on animal population regulation was that of Paul Errington, who clarified the often exaggerated role of predation in nature and discussed the role of automatic adjusting or compensatory mechanisms in animal populations.[92] Errington's studies of muskrat populations in the 1950s and early 1960s established a "classical understanding of density-dependent relationships in reproduction and survival."[93]

Population regulation continually presented contentious issues for ecologists. At the Cold Spring Harbor Symposium in 1957, ecologists were deeply divided over the relative importance of density-dependent and density-independent factors in the regulation of animal populations. Defining even the basic concepts of regulation proved problematic. W. R. Thompson argued that a population was a creation of the mathematically minded population ecologist, and the idea of self-regulation within a population was "merely playing with words."[94] The divisions expressed by ecologists at this meeting had not disappeared by the time Cole addressed the northern Yellowstone elk problem.

Cole entered the regulation debate as a partisan of those who emphasized density-dependent factors in population limitation.[95] Simply defined, a density-dependent factor becomes more influential as a population grows in size, depressing the growth rate of the population by affecting birth or survival rates. Density dependent mortality means that a higher percentage of a population is affected as numbers increase, not just a higher number of individuals. Many animal populations show density dependence. Muskrat populations, the subject of much of Errington's work, are a good example of a small vertebrate that displays the phenomenon. Large vertebrates are strongly density regulated, part of what population biologists refer to as K-selection. Simply stated, the survival and reproduction strategy of large vertebrates includes a low reproductive rate but a great input of energy in nurturing the young (K-selected), while small mammals use a strategy of more rapid reproduction (and less care of the young) and higher dispersal (r-selected). There are trade-offs involved; K-selected species survive a long time and are slower to mature and reproduce when compared to the r-selected species. A paradoxical problem in population biology is that although populations of large vertebrates may be strongly regulated by density dependence, it is hard to obtain good data demonstrating this because their population levels show less variation over time than do small vertebrates.[96]

One textbook example of density dependence is the African buffalo, which suffers greater adult mortality as higher population numbers coincide with drought conditions. A. R. E. Sinclair interpreted this trend as regulation of the population. There is evidence that grizzly bear populations experience reduced birth rates when forage resources are limited. Several ecology texts give the bison as an example of density-dependent regulation: as the bison population density continually rises, the birth rate falls off more rapidly.[97] There are data demonstrating density dependence in the Yellowstone elk.

Shortly after Cole arrived in Yellowstone, according to colleagues, he asked whether human control of the ungulate population was necessary. This question represented a major shift in thinking about elk on the northern range. For all their attempts to make the park a more natural place, his predecessors had always assumed that humans must intervene to establish (or reestablish) natural conditions. Cole thought very differently about the need for management and the desirable extent of intrusive measures. His attitude was not based so much on a "hands-off" philosophy but from a practical question of efficacy and a theoretical orientation suggesting nature itself was capable of managing situations of "imbalance."

While a field research biologist in Grand Teton in 1965, Cole objected to the pine beetle spray program, which in 1965 dosed forty-two thousand acres of the park with insecticide (EDB) and diesel oil. For many years the U.S. Forest Service sought to control infestations of forest insects, which were considered destroyers of good timber, and the Park Service as well sought to preserve good scenery by controlling insects. By one account, Cole suggested in a meeting between USFS and NPS personnel that for all the good the program did, they might as well spray water on the trees. In a humorous vein, he suggested water would actually do the trees some good. Cole then asked what they supposed would happen if the program simply stopped. Nobody had ever questioned the necessity of spraying forest insects before.[98] Cole also offered a formal and deliberate rationale to the superintendent of Grand Teton. The pollution caused by the spraying had progressed beyond the obvious destruction of young trees and shrubs, probably affecting organisms in the soil and the physiological processes of vegetation regrowth. For years the parks had applied DDT until the harmful effects became apparent. Cole said that the park now faced a similar situation with the latest insecticide. It would be safer "to live with the natural infestation of a native insect in overmature trees (that will die from one cause or another anyway)" until research proved otherwise.[99]

In 1968 Douglas B. Houston joined the Yellowstone staff as a research biologist. Cole, Houston, and bison expert Mary Meagher brainstormed together over the next five years as they formulated questions and hypotheses and ultimately devised a rationale for a management policy that emphasized the "natural regulation" of Yellowstone's ungulate population. Although Cole prepared the official documents (as supervisory biologist) and published several pieces, the rationale of natural regulation was a team effort. Cole set forth his preliminary ideas about elk and ecosystems in two documents: "Elk and the Yellowstone Ecosystem" (February 1969) and "Mission-oriented Research in Natural Areas of the National Park Service" (May 1969).[100]

A 1970 article in *Ecology* stimulated a crucial turn in Cole's and Houston's thinking about the elk population. Ecologist Graeme Caughley had studied an introduced population of Himalayan thar in New Zealand since the mid-1960s. Titled "Eruption of Ungulate Populations, with Emphasis on Himalayan thar in New Zealand," the article dealt with testing a population model proposed by T. Riney in 1964.[101] First, Caughley reviewed the available evidence concerning the 1920s deer eruption on Arizona's Kaibab plateau, dashing Aldo Leopold's interpretation of the incident to pieces.

Leopold simplified data taken from D. I. Rasmussen's 1941 account of the events on the Kaibab, producing an ominous-looking graph depicting an eruption of the population from four thousand deer to one hundred thousand deer. Intense grazing pressure reduced forage resulting in a precipitous decline when 60 percent of the herd starved to death in the succeeding two harsh winters. The capacity of the range to support ungulates, suggested Leopold, was damaged by the severe overgrazing. If the herd had been reduced in 1918, the range might have supported thirty thousand deer. As a result of the overgrazing, however, herd numbers decreased to around ten thousand. The trouble with Leopold's account was that he had generalized three more specific sets of data available in Rasmussen's work. That data varied greatly: Several observers made eight estimates, reporting a deer population much larger than the forest supervisor's yearly estimates. Rasmussen utilized the highest estimate of population, one hundred thousand deer, to sketch his hypothetical line of population eruption and crash. The forest supervisor's estimates, on the other hand, depicted a slow increase and decline in numbers of a much lower magnitude. Leopold's graph neglected to include the forest supervisor's figures. Caughley argued that the data on the supposed disaster were "unreliable and inconsistent, and the factors that may have resulted in an upsurge of deer are hopelessly confounded."[102]

If the eruption sequence did not explain what had happened on the Kaibab, then what might? Caughley explained T. Riney's model. When red deer were introduced into a new area, the population experienced four stages: initial stabilization, population growth and a change in vegetative conditions due to preferential grazing of certain species, decreased nutrition of the population and an increased death rate, and, finally, a population stabilization at a lower density. After liberation, a population spread out from the initial point of release. Riney found four concentric geographical zones surrounding the initial point of release corresponding to the four stages, a veritable "rolling wave of density."[103] From the time of initial release, the zone at the center had successively experienced each stage. At one point the ungulate populations in the four concentric zones exhibited these four stages of Riney's eruptive population.

Yet, noting that populations expanded in good conditions and declined in response to limited food did not explain population processes. Parameters such as age distribution, sex ratio, fecundity, and survivorship yielded the more easily observed rate of increase. Scientists could not understand the process of ungulate eruption until these demographic factors were investigated. Caughley hoped to examine some of these factors.

Himalayan thar, similar to goats, had been introduced in 1904 for sport hunting in the Alps of New Zealand's South Island. The population thrived in the high country and spread to nearby mountain ranges and valleys to occupy thirty-six hundred square kilometers of breeding range. Caughley mapped an area near the headwaters of the Rangitata, Godley, Tasman, and Dobson Rivers, identifying four concentric geographic zones expanding outward from the point of initial liberation. Caughley and his crew shot many specimens, carefully analyzing the fat reserves of the female thar, finding that indeed the nutritional condition of the population was lowest in the third zone. As the herd expanded it affected the vegetative environment by consuming snow tussocks (*Chionochloa* spp.). The depleted supply of snow tussocks probably affected the thar in late winter, as shown by a steep drop in fat reserves. Although other factors, such as behavior, summer food supply, and disease, might explain the differences in subpopulations, Caughley believed the availability of tussocks was the most influential. Limited availability of the snow tussocks forced a drop in population, mainly associated with first-year mortality. The decreased supply of winter food per animal, Caughley thought, was the most significant factor in reducing the herd's rate of increase toward zero. Caughley suggested that the population density would drop to a lower point of equilibrium, but he did not have the hard evidence to actually prove the point. He noted that Riney's model fit the case of the Himalayan thar very well, and speculated that the eruption sequence for established populations would not differ from introduced ones. Finally, Caughley proposed that the four-stage process of ungulate eruption be tested as a hypothesis on other ungulate species.[104]

Caughley's article provided an important stimulus for the work of park scientists and a plausible explanation for the Kaibab story. Additionally, the predictive power of the model may have attracted Cole. Although it was clear that an ungulate population would affect its vegetative environment, it did not seem likely that a population had the capacity to create some form of disaster on the range. The suggestion of a population equilibrating at a new density below its peak must have been a tantalizing thought. Cole reflected on his own prior research on the elk of central Yellowstone and Grand Teton National Parks, as well as Caughley's work. He suggested that given an opportunity to wander over an ecologically whole habitat, an elk herd's numbers could be naturally regulated without the benefit of human interference. The herd would not increase indefinitely, nor would an increased number of elk damage the range beyond repair. Something would stop the growth of the herd before it got that far—obvious forces such as limited forage supplies and winter mortality, and subtle effects such as a decreasing birth rate would exert natural limits on the size of the population. Cole's rationale for natural regulation emphasized nutrition as a limiting factor, while downplaying the importance of predators.[105]

As elk populations increased in number, density-dependent factors began to operate. As a larger herd grazed the available range, the nutrition level of individuals would drop, reducing the herd's birth rate, calf survival rate, and recruitment rate (age of young joining population or reaching sexual maturity), thus ultimately reducing the rate of population growth to zero. Cole noted evidence that wolves occasionally visited Yellowstone, but he never counted them as a significant factor. One of the limits imposed by nutritional limitation on a herd of elk had a name in common parlance, a blunt and brutal reflection of stormy winters on the northern range, "starvation." What the biologist found acceptable as an inherent consequence of nature seemed inhumane to hunters and to tourists as well. Yet the alternative, shooting elk in the park, had remained equally unacceptable.

As early as 1971, and more definitively by 1974, biologist Doug Houston called into question traditional assumptions about the northern range and the herd that grazed it. The traditional view, espoused by Yellowstone Park Naturalist Milton P. Skinner in 1928, William Rush in 1932, Ranger Rudolph Grimm during the 1940s, and more recently by biologist Walter Kittams, assumed that elk had not historically wintered in the park and that changes in the plant communities reflected intense grazing pressure. Houston combed management records, historical reports of elk in Yellowstone, and the scientific work previously carried out on the northern herd. He suggested that the upper part of the northern range in the Lamar River Valley constituted a complete year-round habitat for one segment of the herd. Houston did not find historical evidence to indicate that elk had migrated seventy miles north of the park, as the traditional account had it. Despite efforts to keep the elk in the park during the 1920s, and efforts to herd them out during the 1950s, it seemed that distribution patterns had not changed substantially. Traditional interpretations of the relationship between elk and range depended on a second assumption, that the population had erupted to thirty-five thousand elk and then crashed to ten thousand between 1910 and 1920. Houston argued that population estimates from the first sixty years of the park were suspect and therefore the assumption of the eruption and crash "wholly incorrect."[106] Houston also suggested that the carrying capacity had been underestimated for the range toward the northern park border.

In 1974 Houston used the work of M. G. Hornocker, H. Kruuk, and G. B. Schaller to question the role of predation in restricting the size of the elk herd. The rationale for the elk reductions had been based on the idea that, in the absence of large carnivores, humans must cull the population. In 1974 Houston questioned the idea that elk winter kill was a priori evidence of overpopulation (defined as ungulate density resulting in retrogressive plant succession). The death of some number of ungulates that could not garner enough forage seemed to occur independently of the number of native predators on the scene. Before the predator extermination campaign in Yellowstone from 1916 to 1923, for example, observers reported substantial numbers of winter mortality. This suggested to Houston that predation did not limit the population at a level below the carrying capacity delineated by forage availability. At most, wrote Houston, "this predation served to dampen population fluctuations or extend the interval between them."[107]

Traditional (and widely accepted) conceptions of range science claimed that too many ungulates could damage the range. During the 1960s, for example, park biologist William Barmore studied the aspen stands in Yellowstone using exclosures to examine the impact of ungulates on aspen communities. Barmore concluded that although some browsing pressure stimulated aspen production, on the northern range elk were browsing the aspen too much and therefore reducing the extent and number of aspen. Cole and Houston countered with the idea that processes of plant succession must be considered when scientists interpreted relationships between elk and vegetation. Grazing pressure could hasten the replacement of a seral stage of vegetation, if environmental changes also affected the range at the same time.[108] In other words, changes in plant communities might be initially caused by climate, and then quickened by grazing pressure.

Wildfire was a more dramatic and obvious influence on vegetation than was climate. By 1971 Houston advanced the idea that vegetative change was "rather limited and mostly reflects the direct or indirect effects of a reduction in frequency of natural fires."[109] The 1963 Blacktail fire had cleared a big sagebrush canopy from a large area of the plateau and allowed the growth of Idaho fescue and Richardson's needlegrass. Similarly, on Bunsen peak an aspen stand was known to have rejuvenated following a fire in 1939.[110] Houston was hardly alone in considering the role of fires in ecosystems. In 1962 the Tall Timbers Research Station in Tallahassee, Florida, convened its first annual fire ecology conference. Both scientists and land managers from across the country convened to discuss prescribed burning programs, the use of fire in forest management, the natural history of lightning, wild land, and range fire ecology. In other words, the discipline of fire ecology was well established by the early 1960s, and ideas about the natural role of fire were gaining considerable credence in forest and even range management circles.

Of particular interest is how Cole and Houston thought of ecological processes in terms of the greater purposes of the parks. Cole said that "preserving natural relationships between an interacting biota and its environment . . . requires a directly opposite approach from that of the applied field of wildlife management."[111] Here Cole declared independence from the conventional wisdom on wildlife management on the public domain. Managing a natural area had different objectives, he argued, the greatest being that natural area management did not call for the sustained yield of wild animals for hunting. The different purposes of Yellowstone would require different management, which, in turn, required different scientific questions and research to inform management. In writing about predation's role on elk, Houston suggested that winter mortality was to be expected: "Interpretations that this mortality represents a loss is wholly inappropriate within the park where dead elk become necessary food supplies for carnivores."[112] The flow of nutrients and energy in the ecosystem wasted nothing in this ecological interpretation. Thus Cole and Houston, as did their predecessors, called on natural area management, a new interpretation of a traditional notion of preserving the primitive, to inform their approach to wildlife management.

In 1972 Resources Management Specialist Edmund Bucknall criticized the "continued insistence . . . that evaluation of range conditions [in the park] be based on the economics of domestic livestock production."[113] People's expectations of a healthy range might not be the same as the grassland nature created. Here was an important key to understanding park biologists' perceptions of the northern range. Shifting public ideas about wilderness and transformations in scientific notions of ecosystems encouraged managers toward entirely new conceptions of the northern range. The controversies over elk reduction, the provisional halt in direct reductions, contemporary work on population dynamics, a new scientific paradigm of change, and the deep-seated ideas of preserving natural conditions and presenting a more natural park to visitors all met at a moment that encouraged park biologists to question traditional assumptions of range management.

The scientists employed by Yellowstone National Park did not directly seek to justify policy with science. Fundamentally, these scientists continued the problem-oriented research that began under Horace Albright. A widely shared cultural resistance to shooting elk in Yellowstone created political pressure that presented Cole and Houston with the opportunity to formulate a new policy. Cole's first impulse was to document the effects of that policy. After 1969 park science clearly moved away from the traditional assumptions of range science toward forming hypotheses on factors limiting ungulate populations and toward long-term ecological monitoring. Ultimately, science formed management techniques within the context of park wildlife policies that were created at a time when both public perception and scientific understanding of nature experienced significant shifts.

At the same time that shifts in ungulate management contributed to changing perceptions of how to handle the elk, attitudes toward grizzly bears changed. In 1959 John and Frank Craighead initiated a project in Yellowstone titled "A Study of the Ecology of the Grizzly Bear." Their concern that the grizzly was "moving dangerously close to extinction" provided a major rationale for the study. Coordinated through the Montana Cooperative

Wildlife Research Unit at the University of Montana (John Craighead was the unit leader), the ambitious six-year plan for study aimed at uncovering population dynamics, extensive natural history information, bear movements, chemical and disease factors, food habits, and habitat requirements.[114] The bear was not known scientifically as well as other species and taxa when compared to elk, coyote, or game birds during the late 1950s and early 1960s. Ranger Frank Childs's work on bear hibernation in Yellowstone in the 1920s exemplified how the little natural history that was known about the bears came mainly out of the national parks, well before the International Biological Program brought on the age of "Big Ecology" during the 1960s. The important point is that the work proposed by the Craigheads in 1959 brought modern ecological studies to Yellowstone. Some of the questions and the basic ecological approach were as old as Joseph Dixon's inquiries, such as the relationship between the bears and artificial food sources. The comprehensive information the Craigheads sought promised to uncover the intricate relationships between the grizzly and its environment in Yellowstone. The scope of the study was ambitious, and their later use of mathematical models in assessing bear population trends introduced Yellowstone to theoretical ecology.

One problem that concerned both scientists and the National Park Service during the early 1960s was the effect of closing off artificial sources of food to the bears. In 1963 West District Naturalist Charles H. McCurdy reiterated instructions for interpreters to issue warnings and citations to tourists who violated the prohibition against feeding the bears. He also insisted action be taken at "bear jams" to get the auto traffic moving again on Yellowstone's narrow roads.[115] Bear-proof garbage cans had been proposed in the 1930s, and by the time Olaus Murie was wiring up his electric garbage can during the war, the basic design was completed. Yet the installation of such garbage cans was delayed by a lack of money for construction. The garbage cans seemed to slowly creep across Yellowstone's tourist trail. In 1963 bear-proof cans were placed "on an experimental basis" in locations from the west entrance to Madison Junction, and from there south and north to the Lower Geyser Basin and to Gibbon Falls. In 1964 Park Management Biologist Robert Howe proposed to extend installation to Norris campground and stretches of road north and east of Norris. Although over 150 bear-proof lids were available at the old CCC camp, Howe proposed waiting until the following year to install bear-proof lids at Old Faithful, because 150 were not nearly enough to outfit all the cans. More importantly, Howe wanted to watch the effect of the bear-proof cans as they spread from the west "to learn the total effect of bear activity when access to all garbage is removed from them."[116] At the time, how the bears would respond when denied access to garbage was a great unknown. Howe's plan to watch bears' reactions shows that the park was well aware of the potential for some sort of behavioral response or effect on the population.

By June 1965, the sixth field season, John Craighead and Walt Kittams were "once again in a haggle over research contract details."[117] The dispute was over the terms of a research agreement, which, according to Craighead, implied "that we are neophytes in the business of research and that every kind of regulation and restriction must be written in the contracts in order to prevent us from either absconding with the information or misinterpreting our findings as it were."[118] The NPS was seeking too much authority over

37. Frank and John Craighead's research on grizzly bears in Yellowstone revolutionized wildlife research techniques and profoundly altered understanding of the bear and its prospects. This photograph was taken in 1966. Courtesy Yellowstone Photo Archives.

the work, an unjustified extent of control given the very small percentage of funding that came from the NPS, wrote Craighead. Several factors contributed to this dispute over the terms of a cooperative research agreement.

First of all, the Yellowstone staff was beginning to insist that all researchers have a contract that spelled out in more detail the terms on which they conducted research in Yellowstone. The number of scientists desiring to carry out research in Yellowstone began to expand in the early 1960s, and such elementary things as providing housing became more problematic. Other researchers, such as the leader of the Colorado Cooperative Wildlife Research Unit, Dr. Fred A. Glover, had misunderstandings with the NPS over the cost of horses, the availability of trailers for researcher housing, and the procurement of gasoline. Glover's research concerned black bears, and verbal agreements about the project had not clarified the placement of bear-proof covers on garbage cans in the study area. The biologists and rangers at Yellowstone realized that offhand discussions did not always ensure a smooth working relationship with researchers in the park.

Second, the Craigheads believed that NPS administrators infringed on their prerogatives as independent researchers. In 1965 the Craighead brothers were the premier authorities on grizzly bears; they had spent more time in the field than anyone else. The Craigheads taught rangers how to handle bears. Capturing and sedating them with powerful drugs, along with measuring and releasing these powerful animals, added up to a decidedly tricky business. During the early days of their research, park rangers frequently called on a member of the Craighead team to assist at the scene of a problem. Not infrequently, Frank or John Craighead was called on to drive long distances during the night to assist in capturing a problem grizzly in a campground. The Craigheads "often took on the riskiest and most delicate tasks themselves" as they assisted those responsible for bear management.[119]

John Craighead resented an NPS request to provide a "detailed outline and work schedule for research that we initiated, planned, and financed before the Park Service initiated its present research program." This was one of the fundamental roots of an increasingly problematic working relationship. Craighead judged the NPS efforts to tighten administration of the research program "an attempt by Park Service personnel to completely engulf our work into a rigid service program and to take credit for our accomplishments without even the courtesy of treating us as fellow colleagues."[120] Turning over the results of the study should not be demanded in a contract, thought Craighead, but rather the researchers should be given the courtesy of offering the data to the Park Service. These ecologists were used to calling their own shots and assembling their own research funding without supervision from an authoritative body. Restrictions chafed at their sense of scholarly independence. Thus later disputes over management policies and the science that informed policy had fundamental roots in a perceived violation of professional courtesies and a conflict over the independence of scientists doing research in the national parks.

In 1967 working relationships between the Craigheads and the National Park Service worsened. Frank Craighead noted that their rapport deteriorated with the arrival of Superintendent Jack Anderson and Glen Cole, the new supervisory research biologist. Indeed, conflict ensued between people with very strong-willed personalities over scientific issues, the interpretation of data, and management policies. This struggle over control of a large-scale research project ultimately involved professional turf and institutional territory. Harry V. Reynolds, a park ranger from 1947 through 1963 and a personal friend of the Craigheads, later claimed that Anderson and Cole were leaders of "a deliberate campaign to obstruct and to discredit" the Craighead study, employing "cutting remarks, disparaging innuendoes, and unsupported gossip adverse to the study in general and to the competence and integrity of the Craigheads in particular."[121] While Glen Cole "never trimmed his sails" for anybody, neither was John Craighead one to overemphasize diplomacy.[122]

Minor irritations such as trouble in finding housing made John Craighead wonder if the park was not engaging in "deliberate obstructionism."[123] Disagreements over research methods in the park, however, provided more serious impediments to doing good science. In 1969 the NPS requested that highly visible tagging of wildlife be reduced as much as possible. As Superintendent Jack Anderson put it, the "conscious marking of park wildlife seems to have reached the point where it detracts from the scenic and esthetic values obtained from viewing wildlife."[124] The colorful markers attached to neckbands used to identify elk and smaller tags on bears in the studies intruded on a supposedly natural scene photographed by thousands of tourists each year. Testing the new radio collars on elk to develop the radio tracking system might just as well be done on the Jackson Hole Elk Refuge, suggested Anderson. Not only the park but other scientists objected to the conspicuous marking of bears in the parks; in 1962 Adolph Murie suggested that tagging bears in Mount McKinley National Park was unnecessary and "especially disastrous to park esthetics; it would cheapen the esthetic standards of the entire park." Although the bears in Yellowstone were "already contaminated," assembling each evening around a garbage dump, it would be a better expenditure of time and money to simply separate the bears from the garbage than to mark them, wrote Murie.[125]

The upcoming Yellowstone National Park Centennial celebration in 1972 motivated Anderson to take action. How would the park appear if elk and bear wore tags like cattle or pets? Anderson ordered the identifying tags and colored streamers on elk (used in migration research), and the tags and radio collars on bears removed as the animals were recaptured in the course of studies. Park Service biologists claimed they could identify individual family groups of bears by pelage (markings on fur). Although a few "camp bears" were notoriously faithful in visiting particular places, identifying individuals in a population anywhere between 150 and 300 animals was very difficult and could not pass the test of scientific reliability. The use of radio collars, pioneered by the Craigheads, has proved an enormously important technique in wildlife research. Data on home range, seasonal use of habitat, and information used in constructing population estimates were all derived from telemetric methods. The radio collars put the modern ecologist miles ahead of the natural historian's estimates of wildlife numbers and deductions about animal movements. Because of the method's effectiveness, the use of radio collars returned to Yellowstone for grizzly research, although the elk were not festooned with ribbons again. Minor irritations, including this problem with research methodology, became magnified in the context of personality conflicts between the Craigheads and NPS people such as Kittams, Cole, and Anderson.

Finally, one of the root causes of disagreement was the fact that the Craigheads unabashedly criticized park policies they thought detrimental to the grizzly bear. They were part of a growing number of wildlife biologists who were frustrated over the very slow progress in American conservation. While Olaus Murie diplomatically had refrained from criticizing the Fish and Wildlife Service during ACC meetings, the Craigheads took their management suggestions to the popular press. Their firm criticism of Park Service policy was big news in the West where public land issues are of wide interest, and even the *New York Times* and *Washington Post* carried stories in which the Craigheads appeared as defenders of the grizzly. This public critique put the NPS in a defensive posture, which did not endear the researchers to the bureaucracy.

Originally, a memo of understanding between the Montana Cooperative Wildlife Research Unit and the NPS had called for management recommendations from the researchers. Rather quickly, by 1964, the NPS eliminated that requirement from the agreement. Although the 1967 memo of under-standing between the NPS and the Montana Cooperative Wildlife Research Unit had objectives, such as accumulating population data, evaluating the effects of closing garbage dumps, and using elk carcasses as attractants, the memo only covered the need for data and the unit's ability to supply it.

In 1967 the Craigheads issued a report titled "Management of Bears in Yellowstone National Park." Urgently concerned about preserving the griz-zly, the research team issued the report as a preliminary statement of guide-lines for management. Recommendations, however, were not required or requested in the memo of understanding outlining the work project. Their research showed that the grizzlies were not exclusively Yellowstone bears but occupied large ranges and traveled over a vast area, including the sur-rounding national forests. The Craigheads suggested that the various agen-cies create one management program for the region. They also discussed a zoning plan for the park, which would restrict human access to certain areas in the interest of the wildlife populations but also to "manipulate and con-trol animal populations with optimum efficiency."[126] They also recommend-ed that some of the dumps remain open, or additional nutrition be made available for the bears in the form of elk and bison carcasses procured by park rangers for that specific purpose. If the dumps were closed, the closure should be gradual, so that the bears might locate other food sources. The Craigheads believed that dump closures would result in dispersal of the bears, resulting in conflict with humans, and they were concerned that the natural food supplies were not enough to indefinitely sustain the grizzly bear population at its current level. The report urged a more systematic record-keeping system on bear management, improved visitor education, and additional research.[127]

NPS Deputy Chief Scientist Robert M. Linn noted that the work on popu-lation dynamics was excellent, but he had reservations about publishing the management recommendations. Granted, it would be desirable to establish grizzly bear populations on public lands outside the park to help secure large enough numbers for the population to survive. But providing *any* sources of garbage could lead bears to associate food with humans. A repeat performance of the incident in Glacier Park, where in two separate incidents on the same night a bear killed a camper, might affect public opinion ad-versely and bode ill for the bears. Linn wanted the national parks to remain the ultimate refuge for wild animals.

The Craigheads had recommended a step-by-step phasing out of the

Trout Creek garbage dump. For Linn this represented "an impossible research design for evaluating a practice which must either be *eliminated* or *continued*."[128] While the Craigheads thought the park policy should not emphasize the opportunities to see grizzlies, Linn believed that at the very least interpretive signs might be erected at overlooks in places such as Hayden Valley to encourage tourists to look for the wild animals. Linn disagreed with the report's criticism of the Park Service for killing several grizzly bears over the years in control measures, while overlooking the fact that the Craigheads' own grizzly bear study inflicted ten mortalities by drug overdose. Linn urged John Craighead as well as the Bureau of Sport Fisheries to publish the study's data with all due speed, but he judged the management recommendations to have no basis in the hard data available.

Linn's primary objection to the report involved his interpretation of the park's purpose. Although the Craighead report agreed that the park should maintain pre-Columbian ecological conditions, it also implied that "the Park Service should manage the resources to augment the grizzly population." To Linn it seemed "unscientific to recommend augmentation of population numbers when the entire idea is to present a natural population." He believed the park's objective was "to maintain or restore natural ecosystem relationships."[129]

Yellowstone Chief Park Naturalist John Good shared Linn's reservations; he was uncomfortable with the recommendation to kill bison and elk to feed grizzlies. The Craigheads' idea was to compensate for a reduction of food supply caused by dump closures and to concentrate the bears away from areas frequented by humans. For Good, the bigger question was this: "Do we really need intensive management of the many big game species in Yellowstone or is there some way we can get off of the road we seem to be on which leads to manipulative management of more and more species as time goes on? If we can't find another road Yellowstone's vignette of primitive America will be about as valid as Disneyland's Grand Canyon, we will be spending astronomical sums, and our claims to ecological management will be suspect to say the least." If Yellowstone managed for the purposeful expansion of the bear population, and the states coordinated their grizzly hunting, there would be continued pressure to produce game animals for hunters: "We will never get out of the nursery business."[130] They hoped that there was another way to preserve grizzlies.

In 1969 John Craighead sought the permission of the Fish and Wildlife Service to publish the 1967 report to the NPS in the widely circulated journal

BioScience. Director John S. Gottschalk replied that the 113-page document "would put the National Park Service on trial before the public, a public that may not be able to see clearly enough the connection between data and management recommendations." Gottschalk reminded Craighead that the current memo of understanding "did not cover or contemplate the offering of management advice to the Service."[131]

Nevertheless, wrote Gottschalk, inference was the natural inclination of scientists doing research in wildlife. He did not expect that the Craigheads would entirely omit management recommendations as they published the scientific material. What they should do, wrote Gottschalk, was to expunge the manuscript of "needlessly provocative statements and phrases," such as the accusation that the NPS "has consistently failed to follow any of the suggested management procedures." As it was written, publication would be "a pure case of sour grapes, easily seen through by readers."[132]

Gottschalk offered an important insight into the nature of scientific research and its application to public land management. He noted that "management recommendations and the decisions that follow can seldom if ever be backed up completely by data: at some point, judgment and educated guesses have to take over."[133] It was expected that those knowledgeable about the grizzly would have something to say about what policies might be adopted. Initially, it was the interpretation of data, and then the actual data that caused a continuing rift between the Craigheads and the NPS. Discord over management policies was a disagreement over the implications or future results of policy, something no one could predict. Science was not truth in management but rather closer approximations of truth found by continued research in habitat use and population dynamics.

In the fall of 1969 the secretary of the interior's Natural Sciences Advisory Committee met in Yellowstone to consider the question of closing the dumps. A measure of the intensity of dispute can be seen in the fact that Frank and John Craighead would not give their testimony until Park Service people left the room. A. Starker Leopold, Stanley Cain, and Charles Olmsted reviewed the Craigheads' and park biologists' opinions, concluding that predictions of population levels were a matter of judgment rather than data. The committee also reiterated that the goal of bear management should be one of encouraging bears to live out their natural lives with a minimum of interference.[134] This opinion on allowing bears to live in a natural environment reaffirmed the direction set by the Wildlife Division back in the 1930s.

In 1969 and 1970 Yellowstone closed the last garbage dumps, removing this source of food for the grizzly. The Park Service chose this option under considerable pressure—grizzly bears were visiting campgrounds on a regular basis, frequently enough that bears were observed mating in a campground. Despite frequent relocations of problem grizzlies, conditions were ripe for . a disaster. The nighttime mauling of a young girl on her way to the comfort station in a popular campground was one of the triggers impelling the NPS toward actions managers hoped would reduce human-bear conflict.[135]

Yellowstone authorities did make some attempt at a gradual closure. In 1968 the garbage at Trout Creek was separated into edible and inedible trash and reduced in quantity. In autumn of the following year the NPS closed the Rabbit Creek garbage dump, and in the fall of 1970 it closed the last dump at Trout Creek. Yet given the context of a long history of bears feeding on garbage, the three-year period that cut off the dumps proceeded rapidly and produced dramatic effects. The number of bears removed in control actions (relocated or killed) increased dramatically after the dump closures. From 1969 to 1972 there were 162 known grizzly deaths in the Yellowstone ecosystem, an average of 32 per year. In 1971 alone somewhere between 43 and 48 bears were killed, including Marian, the first bear the Craigheads had collared, along with 17 other marked bears.[136] In the four years following the last dump closure, events dramatically fulfilled one of the Craigheads' predictions. In 1970 Superintendent Anderson requested John Craighead to consider his study of Yellowstone bears concluded.

In the wake of the dump closures, the main area of disagreement moved into the realm of scientific dispute regarding population estimates and predicted population trends. First, researchers disagreed on the number of bears. Cole believed that the Craigheads' grizzly bear study had not counted all the bears. Park biologists maintained that between 50 and 100 bears remained in the back country, where they could not be counted at the dumps. They based their conclusion on data gathered by a team studying black bears in the back country and on computations of the ratio of marked to unmarked grizzly bears observed in the back country. Based on their study of bear movements, the Craigheads believed their counts at the dumps included most of the population. They countered that their estimate of about 230 bears more accurately reflected the park's true population.[137] But differing interpretations of the predicted future trend of the grizzlies provided the main bone of contention.

The Craigheads used mathematical modeling techniques to analyze the information they had gathered about demographic characteristics of the bear population, including factors such as natality, population age structure, natural and human-induced mortality, and so on. Their best guess was that the number of bears would decline from about 245 to 136 by the year 1974, with continued decline afterward. Cole and the NPS did not agree with the model, suggesting that the bear population would actually increase. When the dumps were closed, cub mortality would drop because the young bears would not ingest toxic materials nor be killed by aggressive adult males; the high concentrations of dominant male grizzly bears would end, creating a situation in which females would breed at an earlier age.[138]

Because the biologists disagreed, in 1974 the secretary of the interior sought an adjudicator, requesting that the National Academy of Sciences appoint a Committee on Yellowstone Grizzlies. The committee, chaired by ecologist Ian McTaggert Cowan, did not support either a particularly pessimistic or a rosy scenario. It concluded that available data could not produce any accurate estimate of the population trend. Given the fact that bear control actions had increased since the last dumps were closed, however, it seemed probable that the population had declined.[139] The Cowan Report was very critical of the park's research program since 1970, suggesting that it was inadequate for providing the data needed for sound management. The NAS analysis suggested that park estimates of bear population numbers had no supporting data and criticized assumptions that ignored a decade of data and the Craigheads' conclusions. Natural history writer Thomas McNamee called the Cowan Report "a nearly complete vindication of the Craigheads."[140]

The committee, however, did not settle the question of how many bears wandered over the landscape. The following year Cowan reversed his own position to side with the high-side estimates of the Park Service, around three hundred bears. But by 1982 additional research led bear biologists to conclude that perhaps less than two hundred bears roamed the Yellowstone area.[141] It is likely that neither the Craigheads nor the Park Service had reliable data.

The controversy over the grizzly population subsided (but did not disappear), due to the independent opinion offered by the 1974 NAS report, a remarkable drop in the number of bear control actions after 1971, and the creation of a special interagency working group. Established in 1973, the Interagency Grizzly Bear Study Team (IGBST) represented biologists from the NPS, the USFS, USFWS, as well as the state fish and game departments. The IGBST goal was to study population trends, determine the use of habitats, and examine land management policies in relation to preserving the bear.[142]

Throughout the 1970s and 1980s the IGBST's work influenced the maturation of an idea created by the Craigheads: The Yellowstone bears belonged not to the park alone, but to an entire ecosystem.

In 1975 Jack Anderson retired from Yellowstone and from the National Park Service. As NPS biologists Glen Cole, Douglas Houston, and Mary Meagher later noted, his tenure at Yellowstone had been one of remarkable changes in wildlife management. In many ways, Yellowstone during the Anderson years had embraced ecological concepts. Anderson had grasped the idea of an ecosystem, as well as the importance of scientific research and how it could be used within the context of the national parks' unique objectives as natural areas. Indeed, Anderson was willing to use science to bolster the park's traditional cause of establishing a more natural scene. During the Anderson administration the moratorium on elk reductions had been established, and bears had been weaned (albeit rather forcefully) from any dependence on garbage as a food source. Additionally, the park altered its fire management plan to include a role for naturally caused fire, and finally native fishes were given more protection in the form of catch-and-release fishing regulations.[143] A cutthroat trout fishery that had all but collapsed was on the road to recovery. These management trends reflected ideas espoused by scientists as early as the 1920s who advocated the preservation of primitive conditions in the parks. The latest ideas in science and in ecological thinking served to provide current justifications for the traditional goal of preserving natural conditions.

From 1920 to 1970 theoretical ecology and mathematical methods occupied a "central place in ecology."[144] Theoretical ecology made its debut in Yellowstone with the Craigheads' work on grizzly population trends and Glen Cole's willingness to question old assumptions about the elk. A member of the Ecological Society of America and the Wildlife Society, Cole shared the intellectual excitement and ferment among ecologists in the early 1960s, asking questions on a landscape level and incorporating new questions about population regulation. The Craighead team introduced the use of mathematical modeling to predict grizzly bear population trends, thus ushering Yellowstone into a new era of ecological research technique.

The Craigheads' research in Yellowstone reveals more than the regrettable results of personality conflict. First, it demonstrates that science occurs within a social context in which the interpretation of scientific data (and resulting management decisions) were influenced by extrascientific factors.

The Craigheads emphasized the precarious position of the grizzly population and took a very conservative approach to management dilemmas. They resembled the Wildlife Division in their willingness to intervene to preserve a species they believed in danger of extinction. Park Service biologists, on the other hand, desired to minimize human interference with the bear population, drawing on a management tradition stressing the preservation of natural conditions.[145] Second, park biologists and administrators saw the management situation in terms of a longstanding and intractable problem left unsolved by previous incremental remedies. Third, park administrators sought to preserve their institutional autonomy by establishing an in-house research program, but in the end the Department of the Interior devised an interagency research program, partly to ensure that the research results might hold wide credibility.

The cessation of elk reductions in the park and the development of the idea of natural regulation have led observers to comment on management styles in Yellowstone, most dividing general methodologies into two groups: a let-nature-take-its-course school and an active management approach. The reader will recall that in the early 1930s, the Wildlife Division thought its recommendations would lead the Park Service away from a let-nature-take-its-course approach toward a future of "rational" and scientific wildlife management. Writing about the 1960s, former NPS Director George Hartzog interpreted events of his own time in a similar way, arguing that Secretary "[Stewart] Udall embraced the Leopold Report and directed the National Park Service to implement its recommendations for ecologically based park management, replacing the historic policy of 'let nature take its course.'"[146] Thus writers have identified two different periods when the parks abandoned nature's carte blanche for an interest in science and a more active management style.

On the other hand, critics of the National Park Service have argued that managers adopted a flawed philosophy of natural regulation in the late 1960s. These accounts criticize natural regulation as a bankrupt philosophy, as hands-off management that damages park resources. Alston Chase, for example, identifies a philosophy of allowing nature to take the lead role in Yellowstone that is used as "a rationale for doing nothing." He essentially argues that nature must be managed in the parks.[147] Although this popular critique raises important issues, it also obfuscates and distorts issues that lie embedded within a complex history.

Continuity, as well as change, characterized park management style and philosophy over the years. From the inception of the NPS, Yellowstone intervened quite regularly and forcefully for various purposes. In the 1910s and early 1920s, for example, a preservationist agenda endorsed by scientists of the day created protection in the form of feeding elk and breeding bison. Yellowstone did not stop active management after the Leopold Report. The two best examples of continuing active management are bison and fisheries management. Yet a natural Yellowstone was often the goal of protection or manipulation, beginning in the 1920s with the ideas of ecologists including Charles C. Adams and in the 1930s with the Wildlife Division. During the 1950s, when Newton Drury revolutionized management of the bison, the park presented the bison herd to the public in an entirely different manner that emphasized the natural character of the animal. The idea of managing for natural conditions did not originate with the Leopold Report.

Chase furthermore suggested that Yellowstone used bad science to cover management's mistakes. The ecosystem concept in Chase's account "was just a fictitious axiom," and the scientific hypothesis of natural regulation "an attempt to make a scientific virtue out of a political necessity."[148] A careful examination of park history reveals a more complex story of how scientists operated within the larger context of management imperatives created in part by scientific, public, and agency perceptions of Yellowstone. After the halt of direct reduction, park ecological research maintained established traditions of focusing on problem-oriented research, and in attempting to answer managers' dilemmas, developed a concept simmering on science's back burner—the idea of natural regulation.

Ultimately, Yellowstone's biologists drew on an old and now forgotten Park Service mission of "preserving natural conditions" as they forged new wildlife management policies. Park biologists used new ecological understandings to redefine Yellowstone's landscape in terms of natural conditions. The Leopold and Robbins Reports had reinvigorated Charles C. Adams's vision of parks as places where natural laws might hold sway. Like their predecessors, Yellowstone Park biologists during the 1970s again possessed a clear sense of an ecological mission for the Park Service, and employed their own interpretations of scientific data in service of that mission.

A GREATER YELLOWSTONE

1975–1995

From the mid-1970s through the present day, scientists and conservationists shaped public perceptions of Yellowstone as a place that ranged beyond the park borders and encompassed a regional ecosystem. This period introduced some of the concepts about nature that Americans now accept as familiar and self-evident. Several specific areas of research and episodes of controversy produced an expanding awareness of the Yellowstone area as a large and complex ecosystem. The research performed on grizzly bear population dynamics and habitat initiated by the Craighead brothers and carried on by the Interagency Grizzly Bear Study Team (IGBST) during the 1980s helped create public perceptions of the Yellowstone ecosystem. In the context of preserving the grizzly bear, the problem of external threats to the national parks became more obvious.

The dramatic fires of 1988 provided an opportunity for the American public to learn about and think about the park in ecological ways, but media coverage depicting the "destruction" of forest areas did public understanding a disservice, only rectified in the years following the fires when tourists witnessed the regeneration of vegetation for themselves. Efforts to reintroduce the wolf demonstrated traditional concerns about preserving endangered species, as well as a public awareness of wildlife ecology. Wildlife biologists, land managers, and conservationists working on regional wildlife problems created new visions of public land management based on ecosystem principles. Although interagency cooperation was nothing new, popular opposition to ecosystem management demonstrated once again the limits of applying ecological knowledge on a regional basis.

Ultimately, modern-day ecological thinking about Yellowstone translated into modern terms Charles Adams's notion of preserving natural conditions

and primeval nature. New ways of understanding the natural world recognized landscape-level change and the role of chance events, reflected in
the concept of preserving ecological processes. Continued research on the
northern Yellowstone range during the 1980s, for example, developed notions of a complex and dynamic system. Some of this research reflected a
general shift in ecology from viewpoints emphasizing succession, climax,
and equilibrium states toward a nonequilibrium outlook that ultimately
undermined views of "nature's balance." During the late 1980s and early
1990s Yellowstone Park biologists and interpreters used notions of natural
landscape change in redefining how the park landscape fulfilled the park
mission.

Throughout the 1970s and 1980s scientific research on the grizzly bears had
the important function of solidifying new ecological ways of thinking about
Yellowstone Park and its wildlife. IGBST leader Richard Knight, described as
a "headstrong and irascible" scientist, truly fulfilled the leadership function
demanded of him as he forced the uncooperative pieces of two national
parks, five national forests, and three states into a working relationship.[1]
The research performed by the IGBST expanded the extensive knowledge
base developed by the Craigheads. In the early 1970s researchers documented the dependence of grizzlies on cutthroat trout as a food source. After the
IGBST finally reinstated the use of radio collars, the team demonstrated that
grizzlies' home ranges extended even farther than previously thought. The
group performed extensive work on food habits, clarifying the importance
of winter-killed elk in the bear's springtime diet, as well as their heavy use of
ants during early summer and white bark pine nuts during the fall. The team
performed scatological analysis, analyzed day beds, and examined bear predation's role on livestock. The researchers also invented an expandable radio collar for growing bears and studied the particulars of winter dens. The
IGBST studied habitat type preferences and the use of areas affected by forest fires, discovering grizzly use of forested places in the region was higher
than expected. Where the Craigheads had collared twenty-five bears and estimated the range of male and female grizzlies at 90 and 28 square miles, the
IGBST was able to collar ninety-seven bears over a twelve-year period (1975–
87), locating the bears 6,299 times. The IGBST learned that the home range
of male grizzlies averaged 1,450 square miles, and females averaged 341
square miles.[2] Of eighty-four bears tracked by radio-transmitting devices,
all but nine spent at least some of their time outside the boundaries of Yel-

lowstone. Clearly, these bears were not Yellowstone bruins, but creatures of a huge ecosystem. The upshot was an affirmation of the Craigheads' notion that Yellowstone bears were better described as ecosystem bears.

Environmental laws passed during the late 1960s and early 1970s played a crucial part in creating the mechanisms for preserving the grizzly and for the associated ecological research. In 1975 the U.S. Fish and Wildlife Service listed the grizzly as a threatened species under the Endangered Species Act (ESA) of 1973. Ironically, the National Park Service, the agency that had created de-facto game reserves free from hunting pressures, had also exercised control measures adding to mortality figures and risk to the bear population. Pressures on the bear outside the park (large-scale logging, human presence, resort and subdivision development) proved a limitation to the population so that its continued existence in the park became questionable. Significantly, it was research carried out by the Craigheads that ultimately pointed out the importance of habitat outside the park to the survival of Yellowstone's bear population. The Endangered Species Act required that the responsible federal agencies investigate the habitat requirements of a threatened population, designate specific areas crucial to the preservation of the population, and devise a plan for the recovery of the species to a level ensuring long-term survival of the population.

Looking back, observers render mixed reviews on the effectiveness and desirability of the ESA, and interested parties have approached Congress, seeking to strengthen or weaken the act. The legislation remains one of the most powerful and effective protective mechanisms for wildlife. Although a recovery plan cannot force action by private parties, the shooting, taking, or killing of an endangered or threatened species is prohibited. The U.S. Supreme Court "sweet home" decision in the mid-1990s expanded the meaning of this protection by ruling that taking or destroying habitat required for survival, even though not immediately harming individuals, amounted to essentially a slow form of killing and was therefore proscribed under the ESA. The ESA has been particularly effective, because it requires federal agencies to consult with the USFWS if there is a risk that an activity might affect a threatened or endangered species. In the American West, vast acres of public lands provide great opportunities for species protection but also room for controversy where forests are managed to include multiple uses. Vocal critics of the ESA have suggested protection required by the law threatens the ruin of traditional economic activities such as grazing, mining, and logging. On the other hand, some biologists criticize the act, because it focuses on single species, instead of habitat protection that might protect several or many species. Another problem is a limited pie—most of the federal dollars went toward protecting a few species on a much longer list of species that might be "listed" or officially designated as threatened or endangered. Some environmentalists seek to strengthen the mechanisms of habitat protection and suggest that communities and regions need to include the needs of wildlife in their development plans. Ultimately, the ESA proved to be an important tool in the preservation of Yellowstone's grizzly bear.[3]

When the USFWS sought to delineate critical habitat for the Yellowstone area in 1976, the public hearings brought a chorus of indignation from the locals, partly because they feared restrictions on their traditional activities. Yet the sad fact of the matter was that during the 1970s, illegal killing was the primary threat to the bear population, much of that occurring on sheep allotments located on Forest Service land.[4] Author Thomas McNamee calls the furor over designation of critical habitat "an excellently depressing illustration of the gulf between legislative idealism and social reality."[5] As a result, maps of the area began to show an "occupied" grizzly bear habitat, but the term "critical" habitat immediately fell out of common use. From 1979 to 1982 the USFWS worked out the required recovery plan that specified three areas where grizzly populations would be established: the Yellowstone ecosystem, the area in and around Glacier National Park, and the Cabinet Mountains area in northwestern Montana.

As the USFWS worked up the recovery plan, Shoshone National Forest chief biologist Steve Mealey wrote the set of guidelines for managing grizzly bears in the Yellowstone region. Mealy had written his master's thesis on the natural food habits of grizzly bears in the postdump world while working with the IGBST in 1973–74. Appearing in 1979, the Yellowstone Guidelines have been referred to as "the most far-sighted, scrupulous, and comprehensive grizzly management scheme in existence."[6] These guidelines divided the Greater Yellowstone Ecosystem (GYE) into five land use priorities or "management situations." Situation one habitat was the core of grizzly country, occupied habitat essential to a recovered population, where all land use conflicts would be resolved in favor of the grizzly. The remaining categories described other habitat areas in the region in terms of their relative importance in sustaining a population of grizzly bears.[7]

By the early 1980s IGBST leader Richard Knight used the term cumulative effects to describe the threats to Yellowstone's grizzly population. Besides illegal killing, habitat encroachment constituted the main threat to the bear. Proposals such as Ski Yellowstone and a condominium development to be located on grizzly bear habitat near West Yellowstone exemplified this sort of pressure on grizzly bear habitat during the 1970s and 1980s.[8] To the northwest of the park in the Madison Mountain range, the construction of the Big Sky ski resort during the 1970s, with associated suburbanization of both wooded and previously logged areas, effectively cut the Madison range in two, precluding the availability of the northern part of the range for grizzly bear recovery. People seeking to own their own piece of paradise encroached bit by bit on the grizzly's home as they built summer cabins in the ecosystem. Guided by a multiple-use agenda, national forest administrators planned for logging and grazing in occupied grizzly bear habitat on the Gallatin National Forest just northwest of Yellowstone. Oil and gas activities formed another potential habitat encroachment. In the early 1980s the USFS issued oil and gas exploration leases in mountainous areas to the south and southwest of Jackson Hole. Helicopter-portable exploration crews used both subsurface and surface explosives in their search for oil deposits on national forest lands. Although such exploration does not destroy habitat, it makes habitat temporarily unusable to those wild animals sensitive to disturbance and large enough to move out of the way. Oil companies applied to explore on sensitive areas in the Shoshone National Forest to the east and southeast of Yellowstone Park. Each activity, considered separately, did not appear to threaten the chances for grizzly bear recovery. Yet this was precisely the problem, said Knight. The IGBST had come to see the cumulative effect of all these piecemeal infringements on bear habitat as one larger problem.[9]

In 1982 Christopher Servheen was appointed as the grizzly bear recovery coordinator. Some of the more important work during the mid-1980s was the cleanup of hunting camps and better interagency law enforcement efforts. As historian Roderick Nash pointed out, irony clouded the victories of American conservation. In an age when nature appreciation was culturally widespread, more and more people wanted to visit wilderness areas, and at Yellowstone such use crowded the widely roaming grizzly bear. Within the park, increasing back country use by backpackers displaced bears from their usual patterns and places. In 1983 Servheen helped devise seasonal closures for 20 percent of Yellowstone's back country, to protect both backpackers and grizzlies.[10]

Significantly, the science of the grizzly bear carried on by the IGBST during the mid-1970s through the 1980s solidified the notion of an ecosystem larger than Yellowstone itself. Now clear data were available in the form of home-range maps demonstrating that a grizzly's front porch might be in Idaho and its backyard in Wyoming—Yellowstone was not a complete habitat. In the organized attempt to ensure the survival of the grizzly, both agencies and conservationists understood the ecological connections between Yellowstone and the surrounding areas of national forest and private lands. During the late 1970s and early 1980s "Greater Yellowstone Ecosystem" entered the common parlance and agency consciousness. As previously noted, scientists and managers had talked about the limitations of Yellowstone as a complete wildlife habitat from the 1910s, in the context of the northern elk herd. Other observers had pointed to a natural setting larger than the park itself; in the 1930s Rosalie Edge printed a map for the Emergency Conservation Committee showing the surrounding national forests, the caption suggesting that animals needed protection outside the park as well as within. The Wildlife Division also had noted the park did not provide complete habitat for all animals. The Craigheads and the IGBST pointed out the extensive habitat needs of the bear, and by the 1980s the issue finally received theoretical attention.

In 1985 William D. Newmark examined the habitat requirements of bears in eight western parks in Canada and the United States. Though Yellowstone's boundaries encompassed over 10,000 square kilometers, the smallest sized population of bears that might be expected to survive in the short term required more than 12,000 square kilometers of habitat. For the long term, a minimum viable population of five hundred grizzlies required a much larger area, over 122,000 square kilometers. Newmark quantified an idea that Yellowstone's northern neighbors had kicked around long before, the notion that the park did not provide a complete habitat for all its animals. The legal and biotic boundaries of the national parks, said Newmark, did not line up.[11]

According to author David Quammen, island biogeography originated in the work of Charles Darwin and Alfred Russell Wallace. Careful documentation of the patterns of presence and distribution of species on islands led these early biogeographers toward suppositions regarding the mechanisms of evolution. Evolution is the creative aspect of a process that in modern times ends all too often in extinction. As scientists witnessed the extirpation of species at an increasing rate during the twentieth century, concern emerged about shrinking natural habitats. Philip Darlington noted a relationship between area and the number of species found there in his 1957 book *Zoogeography*. His data suggested that with a tenfold increase in habitat land area, the number of species doubled. Frank Preston published several papers from 1948 to 1962, suggesting a pattern he labeled the canonical distribution of commonness and rarity. Preston's evidence suggested that natural communities were structured with only a few rare species, a large number of abundant species, and, finally, a few species high in number of individuals. But what is interesting is the insight Preston drew from this pattern: "If what we have said is correct, it is not possible to preserve in a State or National Park, a complete replica on a small scale of the fauna and flora of a much larger area."[12] In 1967 Robert H. MacArthur and E. O. Wilson published a book that marks a watershed in thinking about landscapes in terms of conservation. They applied the notion of equilibrium, suggesting that after a period of time isolated habitats (such as islands) would attain a stable number of species based on the area and the rate of colonization and extinction. Disturbances natural or otherwise would upset such an equilibrium, however. Discussion of these ideas reinvigorated island biogeography as a fruitful field of inquiry, manifested in a blossoming field of endeavor known as conservation biology. The application of island biogeography to conservation problems might be represented by the 1984 publication of *The Fragmented Forest*, a book authored by Larry D. Harris that discussed the difficulties involved in preserving biological diversity in landscapes splintered by human action.

Newmark drew on the concept of island biogeography, considering the parks themselves as islands, or isolated habitats, surrounded by a sea of multiple uses and habitats either unsuitable or made unsuitable by landscape changes, often human induced. Newmark's 1986 dissertation argued western parks were slowly losing some of their species. Bryce Canyon National Park, for example, had lost the red fox, *Vulpes vulpes*, and Mount Rainier had lost its wolverines and lynx. Newmark concluded that parks slowly lost species, because they did not provide habitats large enough to sustain the species present when the park was founded. Although he could not definitively prove his argument because some of the species inventories were based on anecdotal evidence, the basic argument rang true and caused a stir in the conservation world.[13]

Because bear biologists pointed to the importance of the habitat around Yellowstone Park to preserving the grizzly, conservationists and the NPS realized that threats to habitats outside the parks constituted a hazard as significant as any problem inside park borders. Another source of the external threats notion came from parks with obvious outside influences detrimental to park resources, such as Everglades National Park, where agricultural use affected water supply to the delicately balanced wetlands. In 1977 seven federal agencies commissioned the Conservation Foundation to examine potential conflicts regarding land management policies. Its report came out in 1979, the same year the National Parks Conservation Association published its survey of national park superintendents. These two reports documented the superintendents' concerns with external threats that imperiled the aesthetic quality and ecological integrity of the parks. The superintendents reported that parks were threatened by adjacent activities, including "residential, commercial, industrial, and road development; logging, mining, and agriculture; energy extraction and production; and recreation."[14] In 1980 the National Park Service published its own *State of the Parks Report*. The Park Service pointed out that the large western parks, the "crown jewels" of the park system, reported an above-average number of threats to their physical, aesthetic, and biological resources, their very reason for being.[15] Some of those threats, such as air pollution in Glacier and Grand Canyon National Parks, were undreamed of when Congress established the parks. Around Yellowstone, conservationists worried over proposed leasing of the Targhee National Forest for a geothermal power project located only fifteen miles west of Old Faithful Geyser and the bubbling Upper Geyser Basin. A 1980 environmental impact statement written by the USFS acknowledged the possibility that Yellowstone's thermal features might be damaged, indeed lost, if development proceeded. In New Zealand geothermal resources had been tapped near similar park geyser basins, resulting in a great reduction of thermal activity. The geothermal project on the Targhee never got off the ground.

The establishment of the Greater Yellowstone Coalition (GYC) demonstrated not only changes within environmental politics but also how the conservation community adopted ecological thinking from science and used it to advocate the preservation of natural conditions, now defined in terms of an ecosystem. As scientists pointed out during the late 1970s and early 1980s, wildlife habitat needing protection was not confined to the park, but comprised a series of connected landscapes totaling over 5.5 million acres, half that area extending outside the park. Founded in 1983, the Greater Yellowstone Coalition embodied the professionalism of a modern conservation enterprise. Its board of directors represented a variety of interests in the region, and Executive Director Ed Lewis and Program Director Louisa Willcox energetically plowed into major land-use issues. The coalition was just that—by 1987 the GYC had signed on thirty-four regional and ten national cooperating organizations. Membership of groups such as the Murie Audubon Society seem unsurprising, yet enlisting groups such as the Good Sam Club show an attempt by the GYC to reach out and forge alliances in unexpected places. The Montana Wildlife Federation also signed on, indicating an effort to create links with traditional conservation organizations such as sportsmen's groups. The GYC set a goal "to ensure the preservation of the Greater Yellowstone Ecosystem—one of the largest, essentially intact ecosystems in the temperate zones of the earth."[16] The group involved itself with issues that ultimately revolved around wildlife preservation. Individual matters such as mining, extensive logging and road building, the Montana Wilderness Bill controversy, motorized use of de facto wilderness areas, and winter snowmobiling in Yellowstone Park all had ultimate impacts on wildlife. But as the GYC goal of "preserving the ecosystem" implied, from the beginning the approach examined issues from a large-scale perspective.

The GYC sought to employ science in the name of conservation. In 1988, for example, the GYC sponsored a scientific conference titled "The Effects of Timbering and Roads in Greater Yellowstone." By 1990 the GYC established its own science council, an advisory group representing diverse fields such as ecology, wildlife biology, fisheries, botany, soils science, sociology, and economics. When addressing land use issues, the GYC utilized the latest concepts from a new professional grouping of scientists calling themselves conservation biologists. This new discipline focused on biodiversity, rare and endangered species issues, the development of computer modeling techniques such as population viability analysis, and refuge design problems. Fragmentation studies and habitat use analysis are examples of specific studies a conservation biologist might participate in. The Society for Conservation Biology (SCB), initiating publication of its own journal in 1987, also adopted advocacy as a professional responsibility, which pleased many but also made some professional wildlifers feel uncomfortable. The creation of the SCB was similar in some ways to the earlier formation of the Wildlife Society, when Olaus Murie noted a disagreement over the emphasis members wanted to give to the management ideal. In 1989 Frederic H. Wagner pointed out that many people viewed wildlife science as oriented exclusively toward consumptive uses of (hunting) and control over wildlife. Society's values had shifted, and professional wildlifers had missed the boat. Beginning in the late 1950s, Wagner noted, academic ecology and applied wildlife management separated paths, with significant advances in science coming from academic biology departments emphasizing sophisticated research methodology, mathematical modeling, the hypothetico-deductive approach, and improved statistical technique. Traditional wildlifers were not publishing in new journals such as *Ecology* or *Oecologia*, and significantly there were no wildlifers on the editorial board of the ESA's new journal, *Ecological Applications*. Wagner thought that although some traditional wildlifers viewed the new discipline's practitioners as "belatedly discovering a cause which the wildlifers have been committed to for decades," some conservation biologists looked at wildlife scientists as "too oriented to the consumptive uses, and not sophisticated enough scientifically." As a result of not keeping pace with these changes in social values and in science, the wildlife profession was "in danger of losing by default part of what should be its purview to people who have not come up through traditional wildlife programs and do not share its experiences and values." Wagner was correct in sensing some fundamental differences in approach—traditional wildlife science was generally geared toward single species and game management, while the new discipline worried over preserving rare species and just how many grizzly bears were necessary for the long-term survival of a population in Yellowstone. By 1995 some observers thought that the Society for Conservation Biology contributed vision and the Wildlife Society provided technique. The Greater Yellowstone Coalition made very effective use of concepts from conservation biology to bolster its advocacy.[17]

Although the NPS received its fair share of criticism, seeing the problems at an ecosystem scale meant that the GYC called to task the USFS and state agencies as well. According to the GYC in 1987, the greatest long-term threat to the recovery of grizzly bear populations was the implementation of forest plans. The situation was one of "continuing habitat fragmentation as a result of road building, timber harvest, mineral development and other activities—despite all the interagency coordination now underway in the Ecosystem."[18]

Together with the Montana Wilderness Society, the GYC continually advocated the inclusion of more roadless lands in proposals for a Montana Wilderness bill. Just across Yellowstone's border to the northwest, the Porcupine Creek drainage contained land frequented by grizzly bear, moose, elk, and coyote. The Forest Service had recognized its wildlife values during the 1930s, creating a special wildlife protection designation for land near the

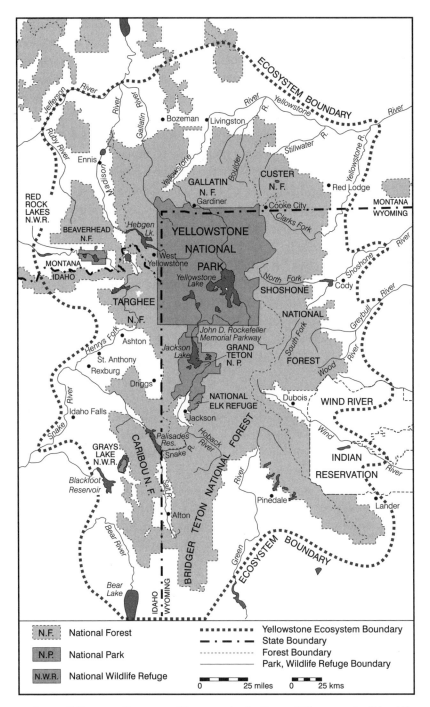

2. Greater Yellowstone Ecosystem. After a map by the Greater Yellowstone Coalition (Albert Harting, Dennis Glick, Chip Rawlins and Bob Ekey, "Sustaining Greater Yellowstone, a Blueprint for the Future," Executive Summary, [Bozeman MT: Greater Yellowstone Coalition, 1994], p. 3). Courtesy Greater Yellowstone Coalition.

junction of the Porcupine Creek and the Gallatin River. Special congressional action during the early 1970s had reserved 155,000 acres as the Hyalite-Porcupine-Buffalo Horn wilderness study area, some of which had been designated occupied grizzly bear habitat. This was the sort of place obviously suitable for wilderness designation, yet partly because of "historical" motorbike use, the USFS never recommended the area for wilderness. Indeed, a large portion of the Gallatin National Forest was already designated wilderness, including large areas of the former Absaroka National Forest north of the park. A larger and more problematic issue lay in the management of other Forest Service lands, including the few remaining areas that had not been logged and therefore had no roads. As Robert Keiter put it: "The fundamental question confronting the Forest Service in the Greater Yellowstone region is the appropriate level of development of its roadless nonwilderness lands."[19] Many biologists agreed that leaving roadless lands in the GYE undeveloped was essential to preserving the grizzly population. The advocacy of groups such as the Greater Yellowstone Coalition and the Montana Wilderness Society, books about the grizzly bear, articles in popular magazines, and finally the 1984 publication of the beautifully illustrated *Greater Yellowstone* by Montana Magazine brought ecological concepts to a wide public audience.[20]

The development of tourist facilities at Grant Village, near the shores of Yellowstone Lake's West Thumb, demonstrated the limits of the influence of ecological ideas in the face of cultural forces. Grant Village was originally conceived in 1936 as a replacement for antiquated facilities at West Thumb. During the days of Mission 66, Yellowstone completed Canyon Village in 1957, then turned its attention to its second planned development at Grant Village. Park Superintendent Lon Garrison encouraged the development, because like his predecessors, he believed it necessary to replace the facilities at West Thumb. The only adequate building was the Hamilton's store; the public campground was in poor condition, tourist cabins were in disrepair, and the small boat dock and marina were inadequate for the public demand. Although concessionaires seemed reluctant to undertake the project, the NPS began to construct the necessary infrastructure. The 1973 master plan for Yellowstone envisioned Grant Village as a staging place where people would leave their cars behind to sample the great outdoors: "Grant Village would become the wilderness take-off point."[21] The larger scheme of the plan called for limiting automobile transportation in the park and encouraged protection of fragile environments at Old Faithful and West Thumb by concentrating visitor accommodations at Grant. Yellowstone Park's master plan noted that Grant Village could serve to replace the facilities at Fishing Bridge, the area at Yellowstone Lake's outlet that Olaus Murie suggested fencing to separate bears from humans. An environmental statement found the plan's goal of restricting automobiles impractical and effectively discounted a large part of the rationale for building Grant Village. When John Townsley took over as Yellowstone's superintendent in 1976, he began to serve as the foremost advocate of the project, convincing the NPCA and the Sierra Club that Grant Village was a good idea and suggesting that lodging units would be removed from Old Faithful. In September 1978 the NPS sent the Office of Management and Budget (OMB) a request for fifteen million dollars for the purpose of buying out the Yellowstone Park Company, which the park claimed was not keeping visitor accommodations up to snuff. Three million dollars was allotted to build one hundred guest units at Grant Village.[22]

At first glance, the site did not appear particularly inviting to bears, but Grant Village proved to be situated on an especially valuable piece of wildlife habitat—five streams provided a good supply of cutthroat trout to grizzlies during the spawning season. An Environmental Assessment (EA) published by the NPS in June 1979 revealed that grizzlies intensively used the streams on the east and west sides of the Grant Village site. Increased use by humans would probably lead to conflict, which might be mitigated by blocking the center three streams to spawning trout. Only 5 percent of Yellowstone Lake's fish population would be affected, suggested the EA. Sanitation would also present a problem for the development of Grant Village. Sewage spilled from the existing development when pumps failed during power outages. Despite some misgivings of NPS engineers who evaluated the project in terms of costs and projected visitation numbers, in September 1979 the Park Service sought fourteen million dollars from the OMB for the project with future commitments for eleven million more.[23]

According to the requirements of the Endangered Species Act, the USFWS needed to rule on any activity by a federal agency that might impact threatened or endangered species on public land. In October 1979 the USFWS issued its opinion on the probable impact of Grant Village on the grizzly bear. First, closing the streams to trout spawning might violate the ESA. Second, the opinion questioned whether closing Fishing Bridge would be worth the environmental cost of building Grant Village. The

USFWS urged the NPS to reconsider building at Grant Village, yet in the end issued a "no jeopardy" decision, meaning in its opinion the development would not endanger the survival of the grizzly population. Concerned about the cumulative effect of developments at both Fishing Bridge and Grant Village, in 1981 the NPS and the USFWS agreed that Fishing Bridge would be removed, and those facilities and services provided at the new Grant Village. During the early 1980s the Park Service removed the tourist cabins at Fishing Bridge.[24] In the last days of the Carter administration the OMB told the NPS not to build Grant Village with public funds. The early Reagan administration discovered that Yellowstone had let a contract for the project, and partly because of the urging of West Yellowstone businessmen who feared losing motel business, the Interior Department stopped the construction on April 6, 1981. Montana Senator Max Baucus and Wyoming Senator Malcolm Wallop entered the fray, and with the support of people in the agencies they convinced the Interior Department to reverse course. Grant Village was back on line, and James Watt, "the apostle of free enterprise," interceded to make the Park Service a partner in the concessionaire business, signing a contract with TW Services in which the government owned the physical facilities.[25]

Unfortunately for the grizzly bear, the promised reduction or elimination of visitor accommodations and facilities at other locations stalled. In 1984 park staff put together a report explaining that the area at Fishing Bridge was a unique and rich food source for grizzlies; between the Yellowstone River and Pelican Creek bears found good fishing. The staff noted that persistent conflict between humans and bears occurred in the area; human injury rates were high compared to the rest of the park, and the resulting control actions removed reproductive age females from the population. Fishing Bridge was in ecological terms a "population sink" for the grizzly bear.[26] Despite the biological information, removing facilities at Fishing Bridge ran into political obstacles.

During the 1920s Hermon Carey Bumpus had worked with the American Association of Museums and the Laura Spelman Rockefeller Foundation to build "trailside museums" in Yellowstone, where park interpreters would educate the public about natural features of the landscape. Small yet beautiful natural history museums that employed native materials were designed by Herbert Maier for Fishing Bridge, Norris Geyser Basin, and Madison Junction, and constructed from 1929 to 1931. These structures characterized the rustic style, and their design was widely imitated during New Deal development of state and local parks throughout the nation.[27] The three museums had been listed on the National Register of Historic Places, and a group of advocates, including the Wyoming State Historic Preservation Office, lobbied to keep the Fishing Bridge Museum open. The Wyoming Travel Commission similarly objected to removing facilities at Old Faithful.[28] The Good Sam Club, representing tourists with trailers, complained that removal of the concessionaire-run 353-site trailer park would inconvenience those who needed the full hookups. Business interests in Cody, Wyoming, feared that closing the closest park facilities at Fishing Bridge would send customers to the other gateway communities. Acting through Wyoming Senator Alan Simpson, these interests were instrumental in blocking the removal of the Fishing Bridge development. Finally, by 1991 the NPS removed its own 308-site campground, but the remaining facilities stayed.[29]

The failure to remove the facilities at Fishing Bridge is an excellent example of how the regional and national political climate limited the parameters for ecological visions of the national parks. Traditional attitudes of some national forest users also limited the effectiveness of preserving an ecosystem oriented around the grizzly. In 1985 the Wyoming Fish and Game Department prepared a grizzly management plan, which envisioned a distribution of bears outside Yellowstone in suitable habitat in the drainages of the Greybull, Wood, and Wind Rivers. Local ranchers aggressively opposed the plan as burdensome to agriculture. Legal scholar Richard Schneebeck noted this example of how "effective state participation in decisions regarding the Yellowstone ecosystem can be frustrated by parochial interests and political pressure." The larger question was "whether the interests of these communities outweigh the national interest in the park itself."[30] That larger, national dilemma still represents one of the same concerns scientists espoused during the 1920s. The preservation of natural conditions, although redefined in method to consider whole ecosystems, remained a guiding principle for the parks. A vision of an ecosystem defined by bear habitat was limited in practice by human uses of the land both inside and outside the park.[31]

During the late 1970s and through the 1980s the northern Yellowstone elk herd continued to provide a subject for scientific discussions about the limitation of population density and questions about range conditions. More importantly, this issue demonstrated a congruence between park science and an emerging nonequilibrium paradigm in ecology, as well as a continuing, fundamental dispute over what sort of management was required in parks. The post-1967 management strategy of relying first on natural controls within the park for the northern Yellowstone elk proved remarkably durable, despite the herd's growth to an estimated population of over 16,000 by the winter of 1981–82, and 18,913 animals by 1988, more than anyone had anticipated for the carrying capacity.[32] Glen Cole's original question about whether elk really must be controlled was reframed as a testable hypothesis. In 1970 Douglas B. Houston began his research in Yellowstone, seeking to establish the cause of changes in the willow and aspen communities and to determine if natural controls were limiting the elk population. Published in 1982, his book *The Northern Yellowstone Elk* masterfully integrated information from recent biological research carried out by Hendrickson, Barmore, and Despain, and carefully critiqued past methodologies and assessments of range condition. *The Northern Yellowstone Elk* refined the information Houston presented in 1974 on the historical presence of elk in Yellowstone, and reiterated his judgment that the suppression of wildfires and climate had been more influential than elk in shaping the vegetative landscape.

Mary Meagher, an NPS research biologist, had been building an extensive collection of historical photographs of Yellowstone's range. Houston and Meagher utilized that collection in a re-photography project. Seeking out the exact location of the original photograph, they repeated the photo at the approximate time of year of the original. Houston interpreted the photographs as evidence that the range had changed relatively little in one hundred years. Photos revealed a slow but continuous invasion of lodgepole pine and Douglas fir into grassland, and sagebrush had spread in some places but declined in others. Bunchgrass communities had changed little, and although willows and riparian vegetation decreased, Houston claimed to find no evidence for "vast reductions in willow on the winter range."[33]

Second, Houston examined past methods of measuring vegetation and analyzed the resulting interpretations. Using original data, Houston suggested that herbage production studies from 1935 to 1963 showed crops of vegetation four times greater during periods of abundant precipitation. The data from square-meter quadrats and density transects (1930–43) revealed that an initial decrease and later increase in plant basal area corresponded not so much with elk numbers but rather with growing conditions. Quadrats measured in 1948 and on through the 1970s on harsh physiographic sites "did not show progressive changes in density, composition, or basal area over the study period." Parker transects and chart quadrat exclosure studies carried out from 1958 to 1974, in other words, inside and outside fences that excluded grazing and browsing animals, "showed little or no consistent difference between the treatments of nongrazing and grazing by native ungulates on species abundance, basal cover, and composition."[34] Aspen studies showed that regeneration failure occurred both before and after elk reductions. Even at low elk densities, aspens were heavily browsed. Similarly, even during the period of heavy elk reductions in the 1960s, willows were heavily browsed. At low densities, elk had also suppressed the crown cover of serviceberry and rabbitbrush on some sites. Aspens and shrubs seemed to be utilized extensively at any density of the elk population.

Previous narrative reports judged much of the winter range to be overgrazed, but when the 1930s drought occurred, Rudolph Grimm and W. H. Gammill stopped labeling the range condition retrogressive plant succession. Grimm was one of a few people who recognized that the drought had a great impact on the range. No data supported the assertion that herbaceous vegetation on ridge tops and steep slopes was in retrogressive succession, wrote Houston, rather the interpretation had been based simply on an assumption of what the landscape should look like. The presence of big sagebrush in the area of the boundary line, previously grazed heavily by livestock, and its later decrease were both labeled plant retrogression. The word "overgrazed" applied to everything from heavy utilization to retrogressive succession, representing "a subjective assessment that had little clear biological meaning." The earlier interpretations of range degradation, said Houston, relied on the decrease of aspen, the condition of herbaceous vegetation on steep slopes and ridge tops that only comprised about 3 percent of the area in question, and the decrease of big sagebrush in the "game ranch" area west of Gardiner. Houston opined that "departures of vegetation from pristine conditions on the winter range" were due to the influence of humans, resulting in "an increased expression of climatic climax vegetation through fire suppression."[35]

Drawing on the work of Graeme Caughley, S. J. McNaughton, and A. R. E. Sinclair, Houston pointed to the problem of using concepts from plant ecology and range management in considering native ungulates in national parks. Range managers and traditional wildlife experts thought in terms of economic carrying capacity, characterized by a large plant biomass and a small ungulate biomass. "A very different equilibrium occurs at ecological carrying capacity," wrote Houston, which involved a large ungulate biomass and a small vegetation biomass. Although the biotic effects on vegetation were greater, national parks needed to be judged according to the standards of ecological carrying capacity. The difficult question was "how great a biotic effect should be expected from populations near [ecological carrying capacity] and how should these conditions be distinguished from more intense effects heralding the destabilization of a grazing system through some influence of modern man?" No definitive answer to the question was available, wrote Houston, but studies revealed "surprisingly light biotic effects overall and suggest a relatively stable ungulate-vegetation system."[36] Some wildlife biologists agreed with Houston and Cole about carrying capacity. John Macnab (actually four biologists collectively submitting articles) noted that while terms such as carrying capacity, overpopulation, overharvesting, and overgrazing were commonly used, they engendered confusion and resembled shibboleths, or passwords that distinguished one group from another. Although carrying capacity had its roots in range management, wildlife management in natural areas had objectives entirely different from maximum sustained production. Macnab suggested that wildlife science was still a long way from a comprehensive theory on sustained yield harvests, and that scientists poorly understood the long-term effects of ungulate grazing on wild ranges. Macnab argued that "routine wildlife management can be treated profitably as scientific experimentation using appropriate predictions and tests."[37]

Houston's rationale for natural regulation involved scientific issues in population dynamics. His view of the limiting factors for ungulates was derived partly from the work of Caughley, McNaughton, and Sinclair.[38] In his examination of natality, mortality, and dispersal, Houston saw evidence for density-dependent influences on elk populations. In other words, as the density of an ungulate population increased, mortality would increase or the reproductive rate would decrease, effectively limiting the herd size. Mortality rates had a much greater influence on population regulation than did natality rates. Using population statistics gathered from 1951 to 1979, Houston demonstrated statistical relationships between calf recruitment (added to the population six or more months after birth) and the size of the elk population. The larger the population, the lower the recruitment rate, or, the higher the calf mortality. One theorist suggested that density dependence operated in a sequence, starting with juvenile mortality, and as the population size increased it affected age of sexual maturity, birth rates, and, finally, adult mortality: "Changes in elk nutrition with population size seem to be the ultimate cause of many of these density-dependent responses."[39]

Rudolph Grimm originally had calculated carrying capacity between 7,200 and 11,700 elk using the forage acre factor system. During the days of the Absaroka Conservation Committee, Kittams had suggested a carrying capacity of 5,000 elk over the winter. In 1974 Houston revised that number upward to around 12,000. C. W. Fowler and William Barmore predicted an equilibrium of 11,000 to 12,000 elk. In 1982 Houston suggested that the increasing number of elk throughout the 1970s meant that "density-dependent processes were operating to move the population toward an equilibrium" at the ecological carrying capacity. Houston had reason to believe that the elk population would find a new general level of equilibrium at a number higher than under the 1940s reduction policies. He suggested that "a stable equilibrium where the system returns to equilibrium when displaced" was a more likely scenario than stable limit cycles or unstable equilibria (increasing swings of the system when displaced).[40]

During the early 1980s wildlife scientist James M. Peek of the University of Idaho provided the Park Service a good-natured critique that stimulated the park's best thinking on natural regulation. Peek wrote a letter to Mary Meagher, expressing his appreciation for the work performed by the Yellowstone biologists and prodding them with his ideas about the problems of natural regulation. "Caughley's model," he wrote, "the current vogue, was developed from introduced populations where predators were absent. All I argue is that the removal of wolves from YNP long ago still affects the system, and think this should be rectified before we discuss 'natural regulation.'"[41] Writing in the 1980 Wildlife Society Bulletin, Peek summed up the essential issues and research regarding natural regulation.[42] Thinking about eruptions (Peek made a semantic distinction, spelling the term "irruption") had spawned a theory of ungulate-habitat interactions. He went on to review ideas on predator-ungulate interactions from research on Minnesota wolves and other work, as well as concepts regarding the associations between ungulates and vegetation. Spelled out as some variation of an eruptive sequence, the theory of ungulate-habitat interaction had several implications for natural regulation, including forage deterioration as a natural condition, resulting die-offs as natural, and the idea that predators might affect population fluctuations but were ultimately not necessary. As Caughley had noted, forage deterioration came along with the eruption, specifically in terms of highlining of browse, reduction of browse heights, decrease in productivity, and changes in the composition of species due to preferential grazing. Peek put his finger on the essential issue: "A range ecologist will judge such sites as deteriorated, whether this is natural or not. However, if this occurrence is to be expected in the truly natural situation, then by definition it must be accepted in natural areas, national parks and wilderness as a process that should be allowed to occur."[43] If eruptive sequences did indeed comprise "the natural process," then even "soil erosion and extensive site deterioration" might also be considered natural.[44]

In all the cases involving eruptions of ungulate populations, some sort of human alteration of the landscape had preceded (not necessarily immediately) the noted or hypothesized eruption. As he had suggested to Meagher, Peek was concerned about the absence of wolves in Yellowstone. "Until a truly intact ecosystem with little human influence can be restored for investigation," it was premature to make conclusions about what exactly regulated a native population. Was the goal of reestablishing a total ecosystem "of any practical significance"? Peek answered in the affirmative. He wrote that although management of natural areas was very different from places where wildlife populations were harvested and modifications made to the landscape, "natural evolutionary processes still should be understood and considered when population or habitat manipulation is attempted."[45] Again, the idea of preserving primitive conditions echoed in modern times.

As science redefined human expectations of natural systems during the 1970s and 1980s, park purposes found a complement in ecological understandings of nature. Different standards, said Houston, applied when dealing with natural areas. During the early part of the century many managers viewed winter kill as simply inevitable. As Horace Albright's actions demonstrated, many people believed that winterkill was a loss to be avoided, and so they established feedlots and shot predators. Throughout the era of the Absaroka Conservation Committee, winter loss was interpreted as a symptom of range deterioration. More recently, while hunters and urban visitors to the parks saw starvation, population ecologists saw density dependence at work. Houston pointed out that elk mortality was not a loss, because it provided food for native carnivores.[46] Nothing went to waste in nature—the dead provided new life as grizzlies emerged in the early spring, utilizing winter killed elk for subsistence until other food sources became available. Entomologists know that a host of creeping and crawling life forms assist in cycling nutrients from carcasses back into the soil.

In the 1980s Yellowstone Park applied ideas from a new "nonequilibrium paradigm" in ecology to its assessment of the northern range as well as to its natural fire rationale. This was not a rapid or complete change, nor were the concepts from the equilibrium and nonequilibrium paradigms mutually exclusive. Indeed, during the 1970s Houston and Cole were thinking that a new state of equilibrium (one not requiring hunting in the park or wolves) would become established on the northern range. Although Houston drew from an equilibrium paradigm to explain elements of stability in a dynamic system, in his work we also see the incorporation of concepts from the new nonequilibrium paradigm.

The classic paradigm in ecology centered around equilibrium of ecological systems, and was widely known by its cultural metaphor, the "balance of nature."[47] Scientists tended to see natural systems as closed and inherently self-regulating. According to ecologist Steward T. A. Pickett, cracks in the paradigm started to appear in the mid- to late 1970s. In 1975 Daniel Botkin and M. J. Sobel published an article in the American Naturalist suggesting that instead of climax states, many systems could be characterized as having multiple persistent states. Depending on conditions, more than one level of equilibrium was possible. In the foreword to Douglas Houston's 1982 The Northern Yellowstone Elk, A. R. E. Sinclair suggested that because wolves were missing from Yellowstone, the numbers of elk might equilibrate at a higher number than if wolves were present.[48] Two stable numerical levels of equilibrium, in other words, were possible. Other ideas also served to revise the equilibrium paradigm. In 1979 P. S. White discussed how vegetation systems were subject to disturbance from natural events. Fires, hailstorms, floods, and windstorms all created an impetus for change in a local environment. Finally, the traditional equilibrium paradigm was challenged by ecologists' work on larger scales. Clements, for example, had focused at a coarse scale, and many disturbances were simply invisible at that level. A new paradigm in ecology, labeled the "nonequilibrium paradigm" by Steward T. A. Pickett, Thomas Parker, and Peggy Fiedler, thought of natural systems as open and profoundly influenced by their surroundings. The nonequilibrium paradigm emphasized "process rather than end point." Scientific metaphors for the nonequilibrium paradigm could be found in Pickett's and J. N. Thompson's 1978 discussion of "patch dynamics" and in a "shifting mosaic" considered by F. H. Bormann and G. E. Likens in 1979. A popular metaphor for the idea might be expressed as the "flux of nature."[49]

These concepts of patches, shifts in mosaic patterns, disturbance, and flux were incorporated by biologists thinking about the northern range. Doug Houston used the concept of disturbance in his 1982 analysis of the range. Past manipulations of the herd by direct reduction, he suggested, could be used as experiments. How had the range-herbivore system responded to those disturbances? Present management action also could be viewed as an experiment, with the results carefully monitored. Park biologists used the idea of natural flux in 1986 when they published *Wildlife in Transition*, which presented a rationale for Yellowstone's wildlife management policies. The authors proposed that the northern range was "not in a constant state to begin with." Managers sought "to permit the wild setting to act as it would under primitive conditions," and to preserve "the *process* of all the parts interacting."[50] As ecology emphasized the idea of change, park scientists adopted those notions to the longstanding park goal of preserving natural conditions.

During the 1980s the park's patience with waiting and observing the effects of natural regulation drove park critics and some biologists to exasperation. In 1987 critic Alston Chase called natural regulation "nothing more than the policy of waiting for bad weather."[51] Critics such as Montana Fish and Game biologist Glenn L. Erickson, John Craighead, and Les Pengelly raised enough questions to spur Congress in 1986 to mandate and fund new studies of the northern range. In the late 1980s and early 1990s an increasing amount of research was carried out on the northern range, some funded by the Park Service, the majority performed by biologists associated with institutions outside the NPS. In 1988 Yellowstone held the first annual Meeting of Research and Monitoring on Yellowstone's Northern Range, where scientists, including Cliff Montagne, Charles E. Kay, Michael Coughenour, Mark Boyce, Douglas Frank, Francis J. Singer, James M. Peek, David Mattson, and Montana Fish and Game biologists Kurt Alt and Dan Tyers, presented research and discussed how to proceed with further work. The meeting harkened back to the Absaroka Conservation Committee's discussions about the need for research to determine the trend of the range. The individuals present in 1988 comprised a spectrum of expertise, representing the major viewpoints in the continuing scientific conversation. The group called for coordination and communication in carrying out their research—a good idea because the number of projects was unprecedented. Second, several members of the group suggested they direct the field biologist's endless quest for research money toward federal programs such as Long Term Ecological Research and NSF Ecosystems Program grants.[52] Beginning with the International Biological Program in the 1960s, national priorities and funding for research recognized long-term ecological monitoring and analysis as valuable.

At the first meeting of the northern range research project, the group suggested that "overgrazing" be defined in a more rigorous manner. More than a semantic quibble, the concept of overgrazing was central to continuing critiques of Yellowstone's range management. Michael Coughenour, an ecologist at Colorado State University, and Francis Singer, a Park Service biologist, examined overgrazing, comparing models used by an idealized range manager, a wildlife manager, the Caughley model, the Yellowstone natural-regulation hypothesis, and, finally, a persistence model, which emphasized population persistence even given natural instability. Possible observed effects such as reduction of vegetation biomass, reduced plant productivity, plant mortality due to browsing, an irreversible trend toward denudation, or herbivore population eruption would support or discount the validity of each model. If long-term fire cycles, climate shifts, or "nonequilibrial dynamics" changed natural conditions, wrote Coughenour and Singer, "then it may prove impossible to conclude that elk are either a natural or an unnatural part of the system" based on historical evidence of abundance just before ranchers settled the Yellowstone Valley. "If climate, fire, herbivores, and large predators, or interactions among them, are changing," then perhaps it remained impossible to construct an experiment of natural or artificial regulation.[53] A clear rejection or acceptance of hypotheses relating to the range might not be forthcoming; perhaps strong inference was the best biologists could expect. The authors suggested that the assumptions Cole and Houston had about natural conditions required reexamination, the question of carnivore regulation of populations needed to be reconsidered, the notion of the winter range as self-contained was questionable, and the density-dependent and density-independent factors needed clarification. What is important here is the emphasis on the dynamic conditions ecologists saw in nature: "The possibility that natural systems are not precisely regulated through homeostasis and therefore do not attain static equilibrium should be considered. Although the existence of an equilibrium would make it far easier to specify a management goal, this may be unrealistic."[54] In discussing perceptions of the range in terms of dynamic processes, this interpretation incorporated ecological concepts of recent origin.

The research carried on during the late 1980s did not end debate about the northern range. Charles Kay's 1990 dissertation examined the evidence for and against the natural regulation hypothesis.[55] Using re-photography, Kay showed a decline of willows in riparian communities at several locations. Measuring vegetation inside and outside exclosures, within and outside the park, and examining aspen and willows and other deciduous shrubs, Kay concluded that this vegetation had been reduced due to browsing pressure by elk. He also suggested that the ecosystem had not been in equilibrium since the park's establishment; for these reasons, Kay concluded that the natural regulation hypothesis should be rejected. Kay's alternative hypothesis was that native carnivores and native peoples during prehistoric times acted as very efficient limiting factors on the ungulate population. Since those controls were removed in the park, the elk had overbrowsed the range and riparian communities, effecting very substantial changes in the landscape. Climate and the lack of fire were lesser factors in creating vegetative alterations than were the elk. Natural controls had not successfully limited the number and impact of ungulates on the range.

National Park Service biologists, including Yellowstone Research Division Director John Varley and research biologist Francis Singer, have countered that the preponderance of evidence demonstrated that national regulation was working. That body of scientific research included the work of Douglas Frank, whose dissertation studied the interactions between plants, large mammals, and drought. In a situation similar to the grazing and browsing animals on the African Serengeti, suggested Frank, ungulates actually stimulated underground plant growth by promoting the availability of light, nutrients, and water. Second, elk literally followed increased plant productivity across the landscape, after spring "green up." This positive feedback, "and a possible interaction of climate and ungulate numbers on winter range forage quantity," complicated the calculation of carrying capacity. During severe drought, Frank noted, the climate exerted the primary influence, and the ungulates exerted a secondary influence on plant community species composition.[56] In 1991 Linda Wallace found that grazing increased plant species diversity, and argued that climate had more influence than grazing on system structure. In 1991 Coughenour, Singer, and James Reardon sampled the Parker Transects, established in 1958, finding grasses had maintained or increased in abundance, and forbs first decreased then increased after 1986 in response to drought. They concluded grazing had not degraded the winter range. Yellowstone's Research Division said that grassland studies "in which the range was evaluated not for its similarity to a commercial livestock range but for its ecological well-being as a wild herbivore-rangelands system, show that the Northern Range is in no danger."[57] Willows, suggested park researchers, had declined until about 1959 but had not changed much since that time. Houston maintained that climate and fire suppression were responsible for the decline, and recent work by Singer, Despain, R. G. Cates, and L. Mack suggested willows might have chemical responses to browsing pressure, making them less palatable to browsing animals.[58] Regarding aspen, paleoecological studies of pond sediments showed that in comparison to the previous 14,000 years, vegetation had changed very little during the last 150 years. Analysis of pollen deposited over hundreds of years showed that aspen had always been a relatively rare species in the area.[59] Some botanists agree with the Park Service's assurances that the range is not "declining" or in any danger. These botanists say that while the northern range is grazed hard, they have seen worse on commercial or production-oriented ranges.

The debate over natural regulation shows no signs of running out of steam. Nor should continued controversy come as a surprise—the notion of natural regulation does pose a challenge to some fundamental concepts espoused by professional wildlife managers convinced of the need to intervene in nature, and to the traditions of range managers.[60] In 1995 an ad hoc committee of the Wildlife Society suggested that the experiment with natural regulation was not working out as planned. Citing some of the same studies that Park Service biologists referred to, Frederick Wagner and colleagues argued that herbaceous vegetation composition showed grazing effects. Exotic grasses such as *Phleum* (timothy) had invaded large areas on the northern range. The paleoecological studies of pond sediment had methodological difficulties in that the method was not sensitive enough to answer some of the questions asked of it. An archaeological dig at Lamar Cave revealed few elk bones, thus large elk populations must be a very recent phenomenon. Richard Keigley's work suggested that heavy browsing pressure in Yellowstone caused a decline in cottonwoods along riparian areas. An ornithological study revealed that bird densities and diversity of bird species were lower in heavily browsed riparian vegetation than in lightly browsed places. Wagner and six other experts argued that "the balance of evidence indicates that a large wintering elk herd during park history has profoundly altered the northern-range ecosystem, broadly reducing species, habitat, and landscape diversity."[61]

Wagner and associates also addressed the issue of population regulation. The ungulate herds, they suggested, would not self-regulate below the density at which they had "significant impacts on other components of the ecosystem." Before modern civilization settled the region, "diverse predator communities, aboriginal hunting, and free dispersal all acted with inclement weather, interspecific competition, and density-dependent intraspecific competition for food to impose a heavy limiting weight on ungulate populations."[62] Without those limits populations increased and eventually impacted the ecosystem. The authors argued that "intrinsically driven, Lotka-Volterra-type, herbivore-vegetation limit cycles" had little theoretical basis or supporting empirical evidence.[63] Many wildlife management professionals see the Yellowstone elk population in a similar light, emphatically arguing that ungulate populations can and will eat themselves out of house and home.

Although this continuing discussion over the northern herd includes legitimate issues in community ecology, population ecology, and related fields, this dispute is just the surface manifestation of a more fundamental disagreement over the need for human intervention.[64] In 1995 Wagner and colleagues advocated that the NPS adopt "active management . . . openly, confidently, and unapologetically as the System norm . . . to achieve clearly articulated park goals."[65] The park goal, these writers suggest, should be the maintenance of a "healthy or intact" or a "diverse, intact ecosystem."[66] This goal might also be characterized as "the long-term stability of an ecosystem."[67] Though the park had employed the terms "natural area management" and "natural-process management," University of Wyoming ecologist Mark Boyce in 1991 suggested using "ecological-process management" as a way to get past the ambiguities associated with the word "natural."[68]

But process-management, said Wagner and colleagues, could not be formulated as clear management goals. The parks should set clear objectives and work toward them. Trying to achieve naturalness, or the state of nature that existed before European man exerted influence in the region, was a goal "both unknowable and unattainable."[69] The parks "should abandon narrow, doctrinaire commitments to ideologies like 'natural'; assume a more flexible, ecologically enlightened posture; and embrace whatever active management is needed to reach its goals."[70] This view implies that active management is necessary, and seems to suggest that the authors' goals for the national parks (an "intact ecosystem") are more clear and therefore better than goals that use terms such as naturalness and ecological process. Wagner and associates began with the assumption that park goals are established to fulfill social values. But whose values will the parks seek to fulfill—

the hunter, the tourist in a hurry, the concessionaire, the photographer, the primary school educator, the nature enthusiast, the range manager, or the ecologist?

Boyce suggested that ecological process management did not "imply hands-off management, but rather carefully reasoned intervention with a directed goal. Restoring wolves, perpetuating grizzly bears, replacing exotic fisheries with native aquatic communities, and minimizing human impacts (for example, from recreational use) will require active management."[71] The Yellowstone Research Division's interpretation of the evidence from the northern range emphasized the philosophical differences between the park and some of its critics on issues such as carrying capacity. Economic carrying capacity and ecological carrying capacity comprised quite different notions. The variability created by year-to-year climate changes produced great differences on the range. Range managers realized this and could adjust stocking rates. But while range managers worked toward a goal of stability in grazing systems, the wildlife manager expected variability: "While such variations are the last thing that a commercial range manager may want, they are the very soul of a wild system, and their functionings are one of the things that keep the Yellowstone ecosystem vital and dynamic."[72] A changing ecosystem, in other words, was to be expected.

The fact that NPS land management practices were different did not make them wrong, suggested park biologists. Land managers had the opportunity in Yellowstone to ask questions about the "inherent tendencies of a landscape," knowledge that might be applied to other land management situations. Ecological studies in the park suggested "that the park, with its representative native fauna and vegetation still largely intact, could serve as a baseline, a valuable measuring stick by which others can assess the changes that have occurred on more intensively managed lands."[73] Although Boyce sounded a lot like the Wildlife Division scientists of the 1930s, the Research Division also echoed the hopes of Charles C. Adams and other scientists of the 1920s, in assigning Yellowstone a unique role in ecological research.

In 1997 the managers and biologists of Yellowstone Park issued a concise report, *Yellowstone's Northern Range: Complexity and Change in a Wildland Ecosystem*, summarizing research begun in 1986 when Congress directed the NPS to look into the northern range issue.[74] The studies carried out over ten years largely supported the park's contention that the northern range was not in a significant sense overgrazed, as well as the notion that the ecosystem was far from any danger of collapse as some critics suggested. Yellowstone National Park issued this information in three formats—a large technical report containing the several studies, a glossy executive summary, and an insert distributed in regional newspapers several times during the summer of 1997.[75] The executive summary might be seen as a succinct digest designed to bring interested parties, including senators and congressional representatives, up to speed on difficult and complex issues. *Yellowstone's Northern Range* comprises a clearly stated and quite convincing defense of natural regulation. The U.S. Senate Subcommittee on National Parks held hearings on Yellowstone's management of bison and elk herds in July 1997, during which Charles Kay and Richard Keigley gave testimony criticizing natural regulation.[76]

The ambiguity involved in these issues is symbolized by the fact that when Wagner and the other authors of *Wildlife Policies in the U.S. National Parks* prepared to publish their work, the governing board of the Wildlife Society and the members of the Ad Hoc Committee on National Park Policies and Strategies could not agree on the "content and general message" of their report. Therefore, members of the committee published it under their own names, rather than as an official report of the Wildlife Society.[77] If professional wildlife biologists cannot come to a clear consensus, how shall the rest of us make sense of all this? It is difficult for people not versed in science to grasp the nuances of the scientific issues and debates. Talking with knowledgeable people does not conclusively settle the questions or alleviate the ambiguity.

The historian or the armchair biologist can leave the pleasant library at Mammoth Hot Springs and after a short drive make his or her own inspection of the Lamar Valley. Walking over the range, closely inspecting the willows and aspens in the stream bottoms near Crystal Creek, one can see how elk have acted like a gardener trimming a hedge. Clipping off the new sprouts at the end of each stem, browsing on most plants forces new buds of growth to appear lower on each stem. This browsing keeps most species short and bushy rather than allowing plants to become tall. Stands of aspen send up plenty of new growth outside an exclosure plot, and although this historian found tender aspen shoots insufferably bitter, the elk find it very palatable and hence the young growth never rises to the height of a tree. Looking across the grassland to the pocketed ravines and wooded slopes on the north side of the Yellowstone, one wonders along with the biologists what forces released the aspens eighty years ago to grow into the trees that now turn old. Indeed, the elk have a good deal of influence in creating the living landscape. Yet conditions supposedly unique to the park can be observed elsewhere; outside the park on the Shoshone National Forest, aspen clipped short by browsers can be found on land visited every fall by hunters. In other words, one can find the effects of hard browsing outside the park as well as inside. Supposedly, regulation by hunting keeps a proper balance between the vegetative and browsing components of the system. It is also obvious that variations in climate affect the range conditions.

Daniel Tyers wrote one of the more thoughtful analyses of these conflicting views in his master's thesis. Tyers suggested that although the range was not overgrazed in the sense that traditional range management defined it, neither was the range the same country that trapper Osborne Russell saw in 1835. Several influences had altered the ecology of the northern range, including fire suppression, grazing pressure, human-originated disturbances, and drought. These factors had operated together to shape the northern range, and trying to parse out the degree of responsibility for any one force was fruitless. The important point, wrote Tyers, was that the range absorbed all these disruptions and continued to function. A new equilibrium would be established, thought Tyers, although it might not include the white-tailed deer, the bank beaver, or the same extent of willow thickets and aspen stands, and exotic grasses and forbs would occupy places where once only native species grew. Tyers noted that the loss of plant and animal species, especially the loss of aspen stands, meant "a lowering of the diversity of the environment."[78] Yet preserving the range environment exactly as it stands in any point in time involved a price "too high to pay. It would require intensive manipulation of the resources, a course of action that would more than likely be self-defeating in the amount of additional trauma inflicted on the resource."[79] Tyers believed it may have been better to allow natural processes to decide which elements of the system would persevere.

Ultimately, questions of management technique beg larger ones about the role of humans in nature. Ecologist Daniel Botkin used the 1970 episode at Tsavo National Park to illustrate different views of the proper role of humans in nature. Established in 1948, Tsavo is one of Kenya's largest national parks, encompassing five thousand square miles. In 1969 and 1970 a severe drought parched the landscape. Six thousand elephants decimated the park's vegetation before it became insufficient to sustain them. Ten years later the denuded landscape presented a stark contrast to land just beyond the park border. David Sheldrick, Tsavo's first warden, believed that humans should not intervene in nature, and that eventually the wildlife in the park would achieve a "natural ecological climax."[80] This view assumed that human actions needlessly upset a natural system that would find a new equilibrium on its own. A second interpretation of the events at Tsavo was that because nature varies, human intervention was necessary to protect the vegetative environment by reestablishing a general equilibrium. A third possible interpretation was that Tsavo was too small to sustain the elephants in a natural manner. Although the elephants and their environment had evolved together in the past, the park's wildlife now lived in a restricted habitat, and nature could not establish a new balance.

All three of these viewpoints have been advocated at some point during discussions of Yellowstone's northern range. Direct comparisons between Tsavo and Yellowstone are fraught with difficulty, however, because the parks are significantly different. The grazing animals affect the vegetation in different ways, for example, and the climate history differs. Yet noting similarities in how people perceive parks, wildlife, and the necessity of intervention is striking. During the 1910s, as well as very recently, conservationists argued that Yellowstone Park's artificial boundary shut the elk off from their winter range (the third interpretation). This understanding continues—from 1989 to 1993 a partnership among the Rocky Mountain Elk Foundation, NPS, USFS, and Montana Department of Fish, Wildlife and Parks invested over ten million dollars in twelve separate land acquisitions, securing more than eighty-seven hundred acres of elk winter range north of Yellowstone Park, including the historic OTO ranch.[81] Beginning with the Wildlife Division in the 1930s, many biologists and managers urged intervention to restore natural conditions (the second interpretation). When Wagner and associates called for preserving biodiversity in the park, they echoed the Wildlife Division's appeal for preserving species in danger of extirpation. Ultimately, they argued for the necessity of management, for some kind of action to put things aright in Yellowstone.

The interpretation that nature is quite capable of tending its own affairs goes back to Charles C. Adams and his associates, who looked to natural conditions in Yellowstone as the baseline against which human management of other landscapes might be measured. When Wildlife Division biologists formulated the 1930s policy that "every species shall be left to carry on its struggle for existence unaided," and suggested the "restoration of the primitive faunal condition," they echoed the notion that nature could take care of its own.[82] R. Gerald Wright notes that the "basic premise of natural regulation has been a part of NPS management philosophy" from the inception of the National Park Service.[83] The advocates of natural regulation policy claim a growing body of data demonstrating that Yellowstone's northern range has not been adversely affected. Thus twin traditions concerning the proper role for park managers have coexisted throughout the twentieth century, one emphasizing the necessity of intervention, the other suggesting that nature will establish its own balance. Over the years park biologists and administrators have chosen from them as seemed appropriate to a particular situation.

Are the changes on the northern range natural? Is it wise to allow the biological diversity of the area to shift? Which course should managers take: watching as nature unfolds, or intervening to preserve what someone defines as desirable or natural? Who should define the natural, and what standards should inform that definition? Those sorts of questions return us to the purpose of the parks. Managers chose strategies employing various degrees of intervention to fulfill their interpretation of the park's purpose. The goal of preserving natural conditions, although somewhat subjective, has proved to be a remarkably constant objective despite significant changes in science and management tactics. It remains one of the most vital guidelines of intention the National Park Service could hope to aspire to. Until the 1995 wolf reintroduction in Yellowstone, it appeared that the system would remain without one of its keystone species. Although there were important ecological justifications for placing wolves back in the park, a vision of natural conditions for Yellowstone inspired action and public support.

A rock-solid definition of what is natural will elude us, because that question is wrapped up in our cultural attitudes about our place in nature. In an age when science recognizes the role of change and disturbance in the landscape, discussion will shift from "how do we restore nature's balance?" to consideration of how much change we are willing to allow in the parks. If natural habitats were unlimited, Americans might not mind watching the beaver disappear in Yellowstone. Given the shrinking size of naturally forested areas and continually growing human disturbances in the region, however, landscape changes may bump into other conservation goals, namely the preservation of threatened species.

Perhaps the greatest opportunity for the dissemination of ecological views to the public appeared with the large-scale fires that swept through Yellowstone during the summer of 1988. Two images—destruction, or fire as a natural process, were available to the inquiring mind. Televised and print media chose to emphasize the dramatic theme of destruction and danger, while the opinions of ecologists were lost in the smoke. Although the NPS was caught at a temporary disadvantage in terms of interpreting the fires to the public, in the long run the millions of tourists who visited Yellowstone in the years following the fire have learned a great deal about the cycles of nature and about the rejuvenating aspects of fire in creating a new landscape. Most importantly, the 1988 fires mark a transition toward new views of the park as a changing mosaic, a landscape affected by disturbance and not tending toward some balance of nature, vegetative climax, or equilibrium state.

During the early days of the park, managers had suppressed all wildfires immediately, just as their colleagues in the Forest Service did in the lands surrounding Yellowstone. In 1930 the NPS organized a Field Division of Education and Forestry under Ansel F. Hall, which was reorganized as the Branch of Forestry in 1934, forming the predecessor for all later resource management.[84] This branch of the NPS vigorously suppressed wild fires in Yellowstone for many years. By the 1960s the work of fire ecologists was creating both the rationale and methodologies for controlled burns as forest management techniques, and wilderness managers in both the USFS and NPS began to incorporate those ideas.[85] In 1970 official NPS administrative policy for natural areas recognized the role of natural fire in perpetuating the native flora and fauna of habitats, allowing naturally ignited fires to run their course when a fire would help achieve management objectives.[86] Not everyone agreed with the natural fire policies, however. In 1974 Adolph Murie felt uncomfortable about the "new proposed policy of 'gardening' our park forests, resulting in a patchwork of small burns."[87] No one knew if fire suppression had altered the course of events, he thought, and perhaps human-caused fires had more than made up for controlling the lightning-initiated fires.

In 1972 Houston reported to the Yellowstone superintendent on his research in fire ecology on the northern winter range. Compiled information on fire-scarred trees revealed that fires (dating back to the year 1525) had swept the area every twenty-five to thirty-five years. Perhaps eight to ten very large fires had occurred in the past. The northern part of the park should have burned over at least once and as many as four times since the park had been established. Ninety-nine lightning fires had been suppressed since 1931, and so "having departures from natural conditions in plant succession on the range as a result of fire suppression" was probable. Houston recommended establishing on the northern range "a zone in which natural fires are again permitted to burn."[88] He also suggested trying an experimental program of prescribed burning to rid the park of the crested wheatgrass and smooth brome near Stevens and Rose Creeks, exotics planted as hayfields in earlier days. Houston published his work in *Ecology*, suggesting that changes in vegetation on the northern range were due primarily to a reduced fire frequency, which acted with climatic changes and herbivore foraging to influence vegetation. Reduction of fires resulted in "greater expressions of 'climatic climax' vegetation" than would naturally occur.[89] The lack of wildfires contributed to an increase of conifers (by invasion) and an increase in sagebrush (*Artemisia tridentata*). Houston suggested "the hypothesis that reduction in aspen has been primarily a function of reduced fire frequency, rather than of foraging by ungulates, particularly elk."[90] Finally, Houston argued that interpretations of overgrazing could not be held valid in a natural area until the role of wildfire had been assessed.

Research Biologist Don Despain, a plant ecologist who wrote his dissertation on vegetation in Wyoming's Big Horn Mountains, joined Yellowstone's research team in 1971. Despain wrote that the "extent to which fires are controlled determines the degree of departure from natural conditions."[91] By 1972 land management agencies and Yellowstone in particular had devised a clear rationale for wildfires in wilderness areas. Also that same year Despain and other Yellowstone staff, including Robert E. Sellers, a fire management specialist, devised a wildfire plan for the park, which they described to other land managers at the 1976 Tall Timbers Fire Ecology Conference. Park staff selected wilderness areas on Mirror Plateau and Two Ocean Plateau totaling 340,000 acres for allowing wildfires to run their course. Historically, most fires in the park traveled northeast, so these chosen areas were located to the east and north of the major human visitor concentrations in the park. Lands under the jurisdiction of other federal agencies, that is to say the USFS, were to be protected from fires. Analyzing the fire history on the plateaus for the previous twenty years, Despain and Sellers estimated that if seventeen suppressed fires on the two areas had been allowed to burn until wet weather put them out, those fires might have burned something between a minimum 800 acres and a maximum 6,000 acres. They thought that naturally caused fires, "at least in these areas of Yellowstone National Park, would have plenty of room to run their course even during periods of extreme burning conditions" during July and August. Nature obliged the planners the first year with several small fires. During the next three fire seasons the park monitored natural fires on the plateaus and suppressed fires outside those zones. The 1974 season was hot and dry, suggesting the fire policy was being put to a true test. Ten fires of consequence were allowed to burn from 1972 to 1974, the largest burning 580 acres of lodgepole forest with spruce-fir understory, the smallest burning two-tenths of an acre of whitebark pine habitat, affecting a total of 831 acres. The researchers thought that fires extending more than 1,000 acres were infrequent during the past, and fires of more than 50,000 acres were historically rare.[92]

By 1976 natural fire zones included about 688,000 hectares out of the park's total of 891,000. A fire management plan called for suppression of fires that imperiled human safety, threatened or endangered species, or jeopardized the historic buildings in the park. During the first sixteen years of the natural fire management plan, 235 fires burned a total of 13,851 hectares, averaging just over sixty hectares, the largest burning 2,997 hectares. Only fifteen of those fires burned an area larger than 41 hectares, and most of the thousands of lightning strikes did not ignite or started small fires that went out quickly.[93] By most standards, the policy was a success, restoring fire as an ecological process yet not endangering property or harming the park's wildlife. Although "the fire management plan was without question solid and professionally researched," sixteen years of research could not prepare managers for events that only occurred once in centuries.[94]

Managers and research biologists in Yellowstone were hardly alone as they considered fire's role in a natural or wilderness ecosystem. As previously discussed, fire ecology came into its own during the 1960s, and during the 1970s and 1980s the field of landscape ecology also contributed to thinking about how landscapes such as Yellowstone evolved over time. Landscape ecology looked at ecological change over very large spatial and temporal scales, developed concepts such as mosaics and patches of habitat, and emphasized the role of natural disturbance in changing ecological conditions. Disturbance was not a new concept. In 1913 Charles C. Adams wrote that "disturbances in the natural order may be looked upon as so many huge experiments or trial activities in this process of adjustment."[95] In 1974 H. E. Wright Jr. developed the concept further, and by the time S. T. A. Pickett and P. S. White edited *The Ecology of Natural Disturbance and Patch Dynamics* in 1985, the analysis of large-scale perturbations in a landscape was well developed. Ecologists thinking in terms of landscape scales described vegetation patterns in Yellowstone in terms of a "spatial mosaic" created by past disturbances.[96]

In 1982 botanist William H. Romme published his work on the role of fire in creating landscape diversity in Yellowstone forests. Using fire scars in a subalpine forest, Romme deduced a history of large-scale fires every three hundred to four hundred years, with fuel buildups during the interim time. Romme reconstructed a two-hundred-year sequence of vegetation mosaics that sought to describe landscape diversity in terms of richness, evenness, and patchiness. He found landscape diversity highest following the large fires in the 1700s, and lowest in the late 1800s and early 1900s when even-aged stands of forests predominated. From the early 1930s through the late 1970s, landscape diversity had increased in the study area due to two small fires and growth in the mountain pine beetle population. Romme's landscape reconstructions suggested that subalpine forests in Yellowstone were a "nonsteady-state system characterized by long-term, cyclic changes in landscape composition and diversity."[97] Thinking at the landscape level, in other words, revealed a Yellowstone that did not remain at rest but rather changed continually. Beginning in the early 1970s a new nonequilibrium paradigm emerged, along with ideas of patch dynamics, shifting mosaics, and processes that never aimed at any equilibria or a climax stage.

In 1986 David Parsons, David Graber, James Agee, and Jan Van Wagtendonk sought to resolve some of the ambiguity of NPS fire management policy. These experts from Sequoia and Yosemite National Parks and the Cooperative Park Studies Unit at the University of Washington proposed "that the *principal aim of National Park Service resource management in natural areas is the unimpeded interaction of native ecosystem processes and structural elements.*"[98] In their view, park management over the years had manipulated system processes to provide selected structural elements such as scenery or wildlife. The "changing role of national parks and more sophisticated ecological understanding," however, reduced the need to intervene to only a few situations.[99] They differed with the Leopold Report and with T. M. Bonnicksen and E. C. Stone, arguing that trying to achieve some desired state of vegetation was not an appropriate goal. A static scene should not be the object, but rather management should aim for a dynamic "process." Computer modeling techniques for predicting what the landscape might look like without the interference of modern culture were questionable, and it seemed more economical and instructive to allow natural processes to sort themselves out after one or two controlled burns. Above all, noted the authors, the "biggest flaw in managing for a particular ecosystem is that it seriously compromises the value of park natural areas as living laboratories of natural ecological processes."[100] Parsons and company had inherited Adams's vision for the parks, a place where scientists could watch nature at work.

The summer of 1988 was the driest since 1886, the first year weather statistics were recorded. Precipitation during June, July, and August was below normal, and moisture content of dead fuels was very low as well. William Romme and Don Despain later suggested that "it may have been nearly 300 years since the Yellowstone landscape had been composed of such a flammable mix of forest stands."[101] The intensity and extent of the 1988 fires took the NPS by surprise, spreading rapidly as brisk winds fanned the flames. Ignited by both humans and by lightning, fires starting within the park spread to Forest Service lands, and fires ignited outside the park expanded across the border. U.S. Forest Service crews moved quickly to extinguish fires that threatened lands designated for timber production, and after the fires reached a predetermined threshold size in the park, the NPS actively sought to suppress them. By the time the Park Service decided to take action, however, wind conditions had created fires of monumental extent.

Television crews caught the drama of the event yet did little to explain the rationale of natural-fire policy in wilderness areas. Some of the more striking footage depicted fire crews spraying fire retardant onto the historic Old Faithful Inn as tall flames swept closer through the surrounding lodgepole pine forest. Ohio State University journalism professor Conrad Smith later reflected on the media's role in reporting the fires. When Smith first heard about the fires, he phoned the natural resources department on his campus, asked who was doing research on wildfire, and five minutes later was talking to Steve Arno at the Intermountain Fire Sciences Lab in Missoula. Reporters who were "interested in getting some context could do that from a working pay telephone at Old Faithful."[102] Most reporters did not have a scientific background, and unless they did some homework before they jumped on the next plane to Wyoming, or unless they had reporters back at the office supporting them by seeking out scientific information, the ecological issues related to the fires went unreported. The hurdle of translating science into layman's terms for a story due within hours meant short shrift for explaining ecology. The human drama of the fire crews captivated the audiences of nightly newscasts.

Finally, on September 11 a quarter inch of rain and snowfall common to mountainous environments quelled the fires. Aerial mapping originally suggested over 400,000 hectares burned in the park, a figure later revised to 322,000 hectares, about half in the dramatic canopy burns resulting in blackened and bare trees.[103] In the aftermath the NPS suspended Yellowstone's policy of allowing most natural fires to burn.

A great deal of assessment and evaluation followed. The Greater Yellowstone Coordinating Committee, representing USFS and NPS officials, commissioned a Greater Yellowstone Ecological Assessment Panel to look into the ecological aspects of the great fires. The panel represented some well-known names in ecology, including among others Duke professor of botany Norman L. Christensen, professors of forest resources James K. Agee and James M. Peek, conservation biologist Peter F. Brussard, USFS researcher Jack Ward Thomas, and historian Stephen J. Pyne. The panel asked if the large scale of the fires could be considered natural.[104] Romme and Despain calculated the historical extent of fires in the park, suggesting that the 1988 event was more extensive than fires in any ten-year period dating back to the early eighteenth century, the last time a comparably large area had burned. Romme and Despain suggested that fires had burned smaller areas during the intervening 250 years, because "the forest mosaic was composed largely of early to middle successional stages, so it had relatively low flammability."[105] Others thought that the history of fire suppression during the twentieth century had created a large buildup of fuels. The assessment panel suggested that drought and windy weather had more to do with the scale of the fires than did the type of fuels, pointing out that almost every type of forest age class and category had burned. Clearly, this was very rare. Regardless of whether the scale of the event was natural, human actions may have altered events by igniting fires accounting for over half the burned acreage. Lightning strikes were recorded within the areas of fires ignited by humans, and so even if the scale of fires were unaffected the patterns may have been changed.

The panel suggested that wondering about whether the fires were natural might not be useful: "Avoiding the influence of people may no longer be a realistic or desirable wilderness management goal."[106] The consequences of the fires, and not the causes, comprised the most important question. The panel examined the effects of the fires on hydrology, soils, aquatic ecosystems, patterns of plant succession, and biodiversity. The scientists on the panel saw not destruction, but disturbance, mosaics created by the pattern and intensity of fires, and possibilities for research at landscape scales. Probable effects of the fires included more areas of meadows and young forests in the park, a reduction of sagebrush, an increase in herbaceous vegetation, as well as enriched species diversity, especially wildlife species utilizing edges and more than one habitat type. Although some might suggest that Yellowstone had been restored to a preexisting condition, the panel warned that data would not support the notion. Yellowstone landscapes had changed in the past and would continue to change "if for no other reason than climatic changes and the continued evolution, immigration, emigration, and even possible extinction of plant and animal species. . . . Indeed, such change is the *sine qua non* of wilderness." Some people had proposed that feeding animals, soil stabilization, and reforestation activities should be pursued after the fires, and the panel urged a "light hand" in dealing with the results of the fire. Feeding programs spread disease among the animals and took into account only a single species. Wilderness preserves could not be managed like zoos but sought to preserve the "complexity of dynamic interactions among the various ecosystem components that are essential to its functioning." Likewise, soil erosion was a natural part of the fire's disturbance of the forest, and the panel reminded readers that the species of trees and other vegetation in Yellowstone were adapted to fire, many depending on fire for their perpetuation. Because fire was an "integral process of natural ecosystems," people "must also accept the natural processes of postfire ecosystem change as an integral part of wilderness landscapes."[107] Thus by 1989 scientists outside the Park Service clearly advocated a new view of unpredictable change driven by ecosystem processes. Ecology had "learned enough to know that wilderness landscapes are not predestined to achieve some particular structure or configuration if we simply remove human influences." Rather than aiming for any particular landscape, managers and scientists needed to "articulate clearly the range of landscape configurations that is acceptable" given the overall goals of wilderness preserves.[108]

The panel carefully considered the implications for management. Since the days of the Leopold Report, "the philosophical issues have blurred and the operational problems have multiplied," leading the panel to argue against a laissez-faire management strategy, suggesting it was "not enough to withdraw aggressive suppression from wild areas. Rather, fire management must blend various forms of suppression with various forms of prescribed fire."[109] When disturbance had affected such a great area, commitment to any one management strategy would be unwise. To inform management, scientists once again called for research, yet the panel's idea of proper research fit the times; the panel advocated each research project utilize an ecosystem approach so that many projects might be coordinated, a landscape context for the various projects, and finally long-term studies and monitoring.

With the fires of 1988 the field of landscape ecology became a little better known to a general reading audience. After the fires botanists Dennis H. Knight and Linda L. Wallace pointed out that although the importance of disturbance in landscapes was well known to ecologists, both scientists and politicians were not ready for the scale of fires that occurred once every two centuries. Asking questions about the landscape-scale fires in Yellowstone meant opportunities "to better understand the effects of disturbances on interactions within and between the patches of specific community types that comprise the landscape mosaic and how changes in the mosaic affect animal populations, aquatic ecosystems, and the spread of future disturbances."[110] The lasting legacy of fire ecology, landscape ecology, and the 1988 fires has been a view of Yellowstone as an ever-evolving place, a landscape with no particular destination.

The issue of grizzly bear preservation, the dramatic fires that crossed park boundaries, as well as the NPCA, Conservation Foundation, and NPS reports on external threats in 1979 and 1980 led to new efforts toward interagency cooperation. External threats to Yellowstone did not subside during the 1990s. In December 1995 the World Heritage Committee declared Yellowstone National Park a "World Heritage Site in Danger."[111] The committee named the New World Mine, a proposed development on the site of previous mining activity just to the north of Yellowstone, as the primary threat, along with logging in grizzly habitat and increased tourism. In the 1980s the expansive Forbes ranch just north of the park became available, but the Reagan administration refused to spend appropriated funds to acquire the property. A new-age church from California purchased the land, and emphasizing its private property rights during the late 1980s and early 1990s it sought to drill into the geothermal aquifer (close enough to threaten the park's thermal features), built underground bunkers, and bought firearms in preparation for the end of civilization. Most recently, a real-estate boom created by the new-age church, movie star ranchette development, and other people wanting the country life meant that landowners began to subdivide large ranches at breakneck pace. By 1994 over two million acres of land previously visited only by a few cows, elk, and coyote had been subdivided into plots two hundred acres or smaller in the twenty counties of the ecosystem.

As ranchettes, roads, and cabins both large and small began to crawl across the landscape, rural charm and wilderness qualities began to fade. Indeed, the greatest irony of a popular movement of nature appreciation is that the admirers of nature can love it to death.[112]

The most dramatic danger posed by these external causes is the extinction threat to the grizzly bear. In 1995 bear mortality reached the highest level since 1972.[113] The Greater Yellowstone Coalition, the Wilderness Society, the Great Bear Foundation, and seventeen other environmental groups opposed agency proposals to remove the grizzly bear from protection under the Endangered Species Act ("de-listing"), and in September 1995 U.S. District Judge Paul Friedman ruled that the U.S. Fish and Wildlife recovery plan did not establish clear recovery parameters.[114] Concerned agencies and nonprofit groups agreed on neither the scientific questions nor the proper methods for preserving the species.

Although scientists, conservationists, and some managers saw the park as part of a larger ecosystem during the 1970s and 1980s, creating mechanisms for interaction between five national forests, three state wildlife agencies, the NPS, and the USFWS proved problematic. Interagency planning or cooperation was not new. From the 1910s when the Bureau of Biological Survey sent agents to Yellowstone, or the days of the Absaroka Conservation Committee, interagency cooperation and communication existed. George Hartzog notes that in the 1960s the NPS began to try "cooperative regional planning with the forest service to protect the greater Yellowstone area." They did not experience much success, because "the resource missions" of the USFS and the NPS were "for the most part, incompatible and adversarial."[115] During the 1970s and 1980s, moreover, administration at the top levels of the federal government was in turmoil, which created problems in cooperation between federal agencies.

Chaotic revisions of Park Service policies added to the difficulties of establishing cooperative relationships on a regional level in the Yellowstone country. George Hartzog wrote that in 1977 Carter administration appointees junked the three management categories established by Secretary Udall in 1964, which had designated park units as natural, historical, or recreational, and set out guidelines for the management of each type of park. "Gone were the Leopold policies. Gone was cooperative research and programming with the states for managing excess ungulates. Gone was the programmatic sequence for control of excess ungulates. All were junked."[116] In general, the 1970s proved an unsettled era for the top ranks of the NPS. By

1977 the Nixon and Carter administrations had hired and fired three directors in less than five years.[117] Then came the Reagan administration, when James Watt served as secretary of the interior. The Park Service in the 1980s needed rangers, naturalists, and historians. But according to George Hartzog, during Secretary Watt's administration it got "high-salaried professional planners and administrators assigned to Washington and regional offices."[118] When Secretary Watt demoted the NPS Alaska regional director in 1983, career employees ducked their heads, and a fortress mentality set in. In the mid-1980s political interference in regional and park-level management continued and was exemplified by William Horn, the assistant secretary for Fish, Wildlife and Parks. Hartzog claims that "political bureaucrats in the office of the assistant secretary for Fish, Wildlife and Parks" gave orders to regional directors and park superintendents.[119] On one occasion a resource management ranger proposed a modest change in fishing regulations for his park, whereupon he was called to task at Horn's desk. Before this time, such a decision would be settled by a regional director or perhaps the director. Hartzog noted that the situation was much as Mather and Albright had found it in 1916—political appointees were doing a poor job of caring for the nation's parks. The legacy of Mather and Albright, says Hartzog, was that "they took the politics out of the parks and put it into the director's job."[120] The Reagan administration did not advance professional management of the national park system.

Increasingly during the 1980s public land management issues in the West became very hot political issues. In 1989 legal scholar Robert Keiter suggested that the ecosystem concept was "reshaping the contemporary societal vision of the public lands."[121] Environmental groups, arguing that the federal agencies were not in compliance with the law, used environmental legislation to protect the ecosystem, for example, by stopping specific timber sales in occupied grizzly habitat. Groups such as the Multiple Use Coalition, the Wyoming Heritage Society, and People for the West defended traditional economic activities on public lands, including logging, mining, and grazing. Keiter phrased the essential issue as "whether traditional consumptive-use activities, such as oil and gas drilling, timber harvesting, and road building, are compatible with wilderness values and wildlife conservation goals."[122] Congressional oversight hearings in 1985 criticized the lack of coordination between the land management agencies in the Greater Yellowstone Area (GYA), and discussed the lack of data on resources and activities, the effects of road building, the possibility of adjusting administrative boundaries, and noted difficulties in grizzly bear management.[123] Bruce Goldstein suggested that the federal agencies and environmental groups sought a way out of the impasse by exploring a new strategy for management of public lands in the GYE, an approach referred to as ecosystem management.[124]

Intellectual seeds for ecosystem management had been sown long before among resource management professionals. During the early 1960s, for example, Berkeley professor of forestry Arnold M. Schultz spoke before a faculty seminar on using the ecosystem as a conceptual tool for management. He proposed that concepts from ecology, such as trophic levels, energy and entropy, mineral cycling, the steady state, the relationship between stability and diversity, carrying capacity, and homeostasis be incorporated into management rationales. Schultz suggested that this sort of approach fit parks better than measuring economic benefits or recreation values. The Leopold Report suggested re-creating a primitive condition, which to Schultz implied "preserving or re-creating maximum stability and diversity."[125] Scientists in the mid-1980s defined three basic goals for ecosystem approaches to management, including maintenance and restoration of native plant and animal species, monitoring ecological processes, and integrating sustainable human economies.[126] By the late 1980s resource management professionals were talking about applying theory to everyday management.

Ecosystem management meant federal and state agencies needed to coordinate their activities. Indeed, although conservation organizations could be thorns in the side of an agency, those groups comprised a growing constituency expressing support for interagency cooperation. Nongovernmental organizations, such as the Greater Yellowstone Coalition and the Wilderness Society, publicly advocated agency adoption of ecosystem management. Current laws regulating public land use, wrote Robert Keiter, obligated land managers "to view their responsibilities regionally, taking account of trans-boundary environmental impacts."[127] Specifically, the Endangered Species Act, the National Environmental Policy Act, and the Federal Land Policy and Management Act assigned obligations such as writing environmental impact statements, and the 1982 National Forest Management Act imposed "a clear legal obligation on the Forest Service to coordinate its land use planning process with its neighbors."[128]

At the park level in Yellowstone the NPS had cooperated over the years with the Forest Service on the matter of the elk herd and during the 1940s and 1950s had built consensus through the Absaroka Conservation Committee. In the early 1960s officials of the USFS and the NPS created the

Greater Yellowstone Coordinating Committee (GYCC) as a way to discuss wildlife management, fire policies, and outfitter policies.[129] This committee issued several documents, including an "aggregation report" in 1987, which gathered together the management plans for the national forests and the NPS, described the status and current uses of resources, and projected the state of resources fifteen years into the future.[130] Quietly coordinating some activities between Yellowstone Park and the neighboring national forests, the GYCC carried out its business largely unnoticed until 1990, when the USFS and the NPS wrote a statement of intent, a written declaration of management philosophy and practice for the Yellowstone ecosystem, or as the agencies demurely referred to it, the Greater Yellowstone Area. Few words are more difficult to pin down and define than phrases such as "sustainable development" or "ecosystem management." Yet this is what the agencies were in effect trying to do when they wrote *Vision for the Future*. The draft document, released in July 1990, called for changes in management to enhance coordination between the agencies, and suggested (as environmental groups had pointed out) that the regional economy was changing toward a tourism and service-based economy. The *Vision* document devised a purpose for the future management of the area: "The overarching goal is to conserve the sense of naturalness and maintain ecosystem integrity in the GYA through respect for ecological and geological processes and features that cross administrative boundaries."[131] The *Vision* set no firm administrative guidelines for management, and hence committed itself to neither extreme of absolute preservation nor uncontrolled resource extraction. The *Vision* did not define resource protection and resource use as being mutually exclusive. The principles and processes introduced in the *Vision* would ensure that no matter what the resource use, whether recreation, "protection of biological diversity for the greater good of human society, or timber harvest for national and international markets—ecosystem values are considered first in how the resource is used."[132] Only through research, education, and cooperation could ecosystem values be accomplished, stated the summary. Although the major shift was toward "ecosystem management," the agencies would "not abandon their separate and often quite distinct mandates."[133] Environmental groups noted that no changes in managerial discretion were planned; for the most part they dismissed the document as business as usual and did not actively support the agency effort.[134]

Despite the fact that the *Vision* contained explicit language about providing opportunities for the timber industry, public response on the part of user groups was vociferous. Wearing yellow ribbons around their arms, people from outside and inside the GYA disembarked from buses to throng one of the public hearing sites in Bozeman. A representative of Montana Senator Conrad Burns began the session by effectively lambasting the agencies and the document to the cheers of the folks with yellow armbands. Testimony was emotional—one woman castigated the *Vision*, then waved a small flag and recited the Pledge of Allegiance. A few quiet "environmentalists" and scholars stood up to defend the document as a reasonable exercise in cooperation, or to praise the naturalness of the GYE.[135] Clearly, the politics were so highly charged that ideas about ecosystems or coordination of the simplest plans got lost in the dust.

Local congressional delegations and state legislatures put pressure on the agencies. Two years later a House Civil Service Subcommittee investigated allegations that former National Park Service Regional Director Lorraine Mintzmyer and former Forest Service Regional Director John Mumma had been subjected to political coercion to deviate from environmental law and agency guidelines, then pressured to transfer or quit. The committee concluded that "the Department of Interior engaged in a politically motivated, underhanded operation to destroy the Draft Vision document because it was unacceptable to powerful and moneyed commodity and special interest groups."[136] The subcommittee also confirmed that Mintzmyer had been transferred, and then forced out of the agency, because she supported the Vision process. When the final draft of the *Vision for the Future* was printed in September 1991, it had been reduced to a mere ten pages of pablum.

The GYCC continued work on common management issues, improved data management, defined management area categories, drafted a set of uniform management prescriptions, began to systematize oil and gas leasing on three forests, worked to eliminate black bear baiting, organized changes in guidelines for grizzly bear management, and coordinated policies on outfitters and guides, noxious weeds, and fire management. Coordination between agencies, in other words, continued in the ordinary kinds of ways. Yellowstone staff considered what had gone wrong with the process, noting that "going public with a formal plan to do what you're already doing . . . may generate opposition forces that did not exist before."[137] Indeed, before the *Vision* process, people barely noticed the coordination of routine activities such as outfitter policy, and cooperation on grizzly management did not raise such trouble. The discussion of ecosystem management and long-term planning, however amorphous that was in practice, gained Yellowstone an international audience of professional land managers who were curious to see how Yellowstone would incorporate ecosystem concepts. Yet the fanfare associated with the *Vision* stirred the wrath of user groups who suddenly saw coordination as a conspiracy. Second, "bureaucracies [did] not reward adventurism."[138] Even though Congress had criticized the lack of coordination in 1985, when the NPS and the USFS responded with the *Vision*, political backlash caused heads to roll. Finally, some park staff thought the process had failed to attract a national audience sympathetic to the ecosystem management concept, and so regional user groups dominated the discussion. Those points are revealing. The rejection of the *Vision* document also demonstrates how ideas borrowed from ecology ran into roadblocks when applied to the practical world of management. Once again, the central obstacle to ecological visions of the Yellowstone landscape were political in nature, deriving from a fundamental tension between use and preservation. Finding, or even thinking about achieving a new balance point was decidedly tricky business.

The reintroduction of the wolf in Yellowstone presents in stark terms an old struggle between nature and culture, and it reveals the political basis of the natural world we allow in our national parks. Park guardians and managers had shot and trapped native predators from the early days of civilian and army administrations. Horace Albright had continued the practice, reluctantly proclaiming protection for all predators during the early 1930s, although rangers continued to kill coyotes for several years. Since the 1920s, however, biologists had urged the preservation of natural conditions in Yellowstone. To re-create the native biota disturbed by human hand, the Wildlife Division urged the reintroduction of extirpated species. The Wildlife Division also proposed that predators had a role in controlling ungulate numbers. The range problem was in part caused, they thought, by a release from predators when the wolves, mountain lions, bobcats, and coyotes were exterminated near the park. George Wright, Ben Thompson, and Joseph Dixon suggested that "if suitable range and protection could be procured for all native animals of the park, the wolf might then have a place."[139] In their more general statements about wildlife in the parks, they clearly advocated the protection of native predators and their reintroduction where possible. The absence of the wolf as well as the rare presence of the mountain lion remained an obvious departure from the natural world of Yellowstone as F. V. Hayden had seen it in 1872. To scientists and conservationists interested in wilderness preservation during the 1960s, reintroduction of the wolf was part of the long-standing effort to preserve natural conditions. The case for reintroduction of wolves was bolstered by the idea that these predators would exert some limiting effect on ungulate populations. In 1944 Aldo Leopold found a new book about wolves published by the American Wildlife Institute "intensely disappointing," because it did not mention "the modern curse of excess deer and elk," nor did it provide suggestions on how wolves might "continue their existence with little molestation" in sections of the West.[140] Wolf reintroduction became culturally acceptable only with considerable hesitation seventy years after the last wolf packs were killed off in Yellowstone.

At the 1963 "Conference of Challenges" at Yosemite, Starker Leopold questioned Lon Garrison regarding the possibility of reintroducing the wolf in Yellowstone. Garrison had been making some careful local inquiries and reported the reaction from cattle country had been very negative, "to put it mildly."[141] In the early 1960s Adolph Murie considered wolf reintroductions in national parks desirable, but simply out of the question in Yellowstone. Reintroducing the wolf to Yellowstone was also advocated by two wolf biologists, in 1967 by Canadian Douglas Pimlott and in 1970 by David Mech.[142] Assistant Secretary of the Interior for National Parks and Wildlife Nathaniel H. Reed called a meeting in Yellowstone during the early 1970s to discuss the possibilities. Questionable sightings of wolves in Yellowstone were frequent enough and just believable enough to prompt the NPS to sponsor biologist John Weaver's investigation into the matter. After extensive searches on the ground and from the air, Weaver concluded in 1978 that resident wolves had been extirpated by the 1940s, and recommended transplanting wolves from Canada or Minnesota to restore a population of the native predator.[143] During the 1980s notable support for reintroduction came from Yellowstone's chief of research John Varley, who convincingly made the case for reintroduction to Yellowstone Superintendent Bob Barbee.[144] In The Northern Yellowstone Elk, Douglas Houston called for the return of the gray wolf, commenting that the absence of a viable population of wolves represented "perhaps the single greatest departure from the objective of maintaining natural ecosystems." Yellowstone's objectives and the available prey made the park an ideal spot for reintroduction. In addition, a wolf reintroduction could provide an empirical test of the wolf's effects on a prey base composed of different species.[145] Several factors operating together made wolf reintroduction possible, including legislation on endangered species, the persistent efforts of environmental organizations, solid information on wolf ecology, and a changing national constituency for the parks that increasingly understood Yellowstone in terms of its ecosystem functions.

Environmental legislation formed the first overt driving force in the reintroduction of the wolf in Yellowstone. According to the terms of the 1973 Endangered Species Act, the secretary of the interior listed the Northern Rocky Mountain Wolf (*Canis lupus irremotus*) as endangered, followed in 1978 by the entire species *Canis lupus*, except in Minnesota, where it was declared threatened. The Department of the Interior then established a recovery team that developed a plan for the Northern Rocky Mountain Wolf, completed in 1980 and updated in 1987. The 1987 plan suggested that population recovery required three hundred wolves, or ten breeding pairs for three years in each of three recovery areas in northwestern Montana, central Idaho, and Yellowstone National Park. Natural recolonization was recommended by dispersing wolves for Idaho and northwest Montana, and for Yellowstone the plan suggested a nonessential experimental population whereby wolves attacking livestock could be killed.[146]

The heirs of the Absaroka Conservation Committee launched the major opposition to wolf reintroduction. Two citizen groups known as the No-Wolf Option Committee and the Abundant Wildlife Society of North America waged a publicity campaign that raised issues of concern to stockmen and hunters. Arlene Hanson, chairperson of the No-Wolf Committee, argued that the gray wolf was not endangered, recovery would be expensive, wolves would compete with hunters for game, areas of public lands would be closed to hunting and hiking, agencies would favor the wolf in any conflict with stock animals or other land uses, and that reintroducing the wolf ran the risk of decimating the game populations.[147]

Designating the reintroduced Yellowstone wolf population as nonessential and experimental, made possible by revisions to the Endangered Species Act in 1987, was necessary to address opponents' concerns. The law granted the USFWS and state wildlife officials considerable latitude in dealing with wolves caught in the act of killing domestic cattle or sheep. Agents of Montana Fish and Game, for example, were the most visible government functionaries out on the ground day after day, dealing with hunters and stockmen in the area. State wildlife officers as well as wildlife biologists believed that the only way to actually make reintroduction work was to give the state agencies the ability to respond quickly to ranchers' genuine problems.[148]

One unpleasant alternative would be a continually suspicious group of people who might (as locals said) "shoot, shovel, and shut up," whether or not a particular wolf was caught in the act of attacking stock. Clearly, if the legitimate complaints of ranchers could be dealt with in an efficient manner, reintroduction might have more chances for long-term success. Moreover, overcoming the political resistance to reintroduction meant that stock growers must be convinced that there would be some form of wolf control on public and especially on private lands surrounding Yellowstone.[149]

The rules for management of the nonessential experimental population presented the specific mechanisms to control wolf depredations on cattle and sheep on lands near the park. For those who favored wolves, the rules meant a timely reintroduction. For those with concerns about the effect of wolves on hunting, recreational and commercial uses of public lands, and private property rights, the rules allowed "for any conflicts to be resolved in favor of traditional western lifestyles."[150] In brief, the regulations provided that on private land wolves biting, wounding, or killing domestic stock could be taken, and on leased public lands livestock owners could obtain a forty-five day permit for taking a wolf in the act of attacking livestock. Stockmen were encouraged to notify game officials whenever they had problems in order to document depredations in case the owner of stock did shoot a wolf at some point.[151] Defenders of Wildlife, a nongovernmental organization actively pushing the wolf reintroduction, attempted to assuage the concerns of stock owners in 1990 when the group raised a fund of one hundred thousand dollars for paying ranchers who suffered depredations.[152]

Ecological information about wolves supplied by biologists also proved essential in addressing the concerns of wolf opponents as well as in convincing legislators and winning court decisions. In 1988 the Senate-House Interior Appropriations Conference Committee provided two hundred thousand dollars to the National Park Service to answer questions raised by the 1987 USFWS wolf recovery plan. The committee specifically requested information about how wolves would be controlled both inside and outside the park, how wolves would affect prey species in the park and big-game hunting outside the park, how wolves would affect the grizzly bear population, and how recovery zones would be arranged. The NPS submitted the first two volumes of *Wolves for Yellowstone* to Congress in May 1990, followed by the third and fourth volumes in July 1992. Totaling over 1,350 pages, the report covered a mountain of information about the historical evidence of wolves in Yellowstone, sociological and economic perspectives on reintroduction, the ungulate prey base for wolves, and information on how wolves might interact with other components of the ecosystem, including cattle and bears. *Wolves for Yellowstone* summarized a great deal of available scientific information and provided educated guesses on the probable impacts of Yellowstone wolves based on experiences at other parks and computer modeling of population dynamics.

David Mech, a USFWS wildlife biologist known for his work *The Wolves of Isle Royale*, provided much of the information seeking to answer opponents' concerns.[153] Would wolves destroy the big game herds, or severely limit hunting opportunity? Mech compared the situation in Yellowstone with the known entity of Denali National Park, using the experience gained from 1986 through 1991 as researchers located collared wolves 3,648 times. Research did not indicate that wolves were limiting prey populations at Denali; in fact, caribou numbers were increasing even as wolf numbers increased. The issue of limitation had been the subject of research on Isle Royale for many years. Durwood Allen and then Mech himself had gathered data on the subject, finding prey and predator numbers to vary in ways that defied easy explanation. One important conclusion was that the wolves did not extirpate prey species. R. O. Peterson's more recent work documented a tripling of the moose population while the wolves were protected.[154] In Denali the biologists noted that grizzlies usually drove wolves from carcasses, hence the worry that wolves might severely impact grizzly populations seemed questionable. People had expressed concern that large areas in and around Yellowstone might have to be closed to hiking to protect wolf denning sites. The Denali experience showed that protection of wolf dens need not be overly restrictive to human use; Mech and other biologists at Denali recommended for Yellowstone areas about one mile radius around dens from March 15 to June 15, or one month before and two months after denning. This time span was before the main tourist season. Rather than a menace to humans, the biologists argued, "the wolf should be regarded as a major tourist attraction."[155] At Denali tourists thronged to join the evening howling trips and fully subscribed commercial air safaris. Fifteen percent of the tourists visiting the park observed wolves, and, furthermore, visitors considered the wolves a major attraction of the park. An economic analysis of tourism in *Wolves for Yellowstone* predicted that tourism expenditures in the three states surrounding the park would increase by nineteen million dollars annually as tourists flocked to see wolves in the wild, supporting Mech's observation.

Hunters worried that the reintroduction of the wolf would mean a dramatic reduction in big game numbers and hence in hunting opportunities.[156] Indeed, the NPS report suggested that some reduction in harvest might be required to maintain wolf populations. On the northern border area of the park annual harvests from 1980 to 1989 had averaged 1,512 elk, 532 mule deer, and 31 moose. Biologists used computer population models to compute different possible outcomes for game populations, given different factors such as number of wolves, different rates of predation, and levels of hunter harvest. Models showed that hunting had a greater effect on the population than wolves. Therefore, after wolf recovery bull elk harvests could continue at about 423 per year, but antlerless harvests averaging 916 cows might have to be reduced by 27 percent "if the desired goal is to stabilize the elk population at levels lower than those of the late 1980s."[157] Francis Singer's analysis of the prey base for wolves revealed that the substantial number of ungulates in and near Yellowstone Park could support a recovered population of 100 wolves. From 1980 to 1988 almost 23,000 ungulates wintered in the park, and during summers populations may have exceeded 37,000. If 100 wolves occupied Yellowstone, the ratio would approach 1 wolf per 225 ungulates during winter and 1 wolf for every 378 ungulates during summer. Ratios in other North American wolf habitats ranged between 1 to 96 up to 1 wolf per 328 ungulates. Given the experience of other parks and ranges, it seemed the wolves had substantial resources available in Yellowstone without necessarily needing to feed on domestic stock. The ratios, however, did not explain everything one might want to know about how predation works between predator and prey populations. When ungulate populations are near their ecological carrying capacity, wolf predation "tends to be compensatory with starvation."[158] In other words, when the elk population increased and hard winters took their toll, wolf predation would take many of the elk normally lost to winter kill. But when elk populations were below ecological carrying capacity, wolf predation would be additive to other causes of mortality. Many factors, such as wolves switching their choice of prey, time lags in population response to resources, and variable rates of using nonungulate prey, made confident use of simple ratios problematic.

Yellowstone biologists and managers gathered evidence from other parks and places where wolves and domestic stock lived in close proximity. In Alberta 235,000 to 300,000 cattle grazed on ranges within the home territory of wolves. Although predation was not a major problem for the livestock in-

dustry as a whole, individual ranchers along the Peace River experienced local problems and the government accepted the necessity of meeting their
concerns. The Alberta provincial government reimbursed agriculturists anywhere from 30 to 80 percent of commercial value of livestock lost to predation, depending on available evidence. Coyote predation actually took a
greater toll than bear or wolf predation.[159] Wildlife biologist Douglas Chadwick pointed to the example of Riding Mountain National Park, located in
southwestern Manitoba, as an example of a park where wolves lived close to
domestic stock. During the 1950s wolves had naturally repopulated Riding
Mountain and grew in numbers along with the elk and moose. Researcher
Paul Paquet noted that wolves culled the weakest individuals (both young
and old) from the herd, thus having relatively small effect on the breeding
age population. The most complaints about wildlife from farmers and
ranchers on the surrounding land concerned nuisance beavers, followed by
coyotes, black bears, and finally wolves. Chadwick wrote that reasons for
low conflict included the small size of ranches, as well as the diverse prey
base within the park. The real lesson from Riding Mountain was that "bitter
conflicts with wolves are not inevitable."[160]

In 1991 Congress directed the USFWS to prepare a draft environmental
impact statement, and in 1992 it requested a Final Environmental Impact
Statement (FEIS) to be completed by January 1994. The FEIS predicted a 5 to
20 percent reduction in elk, and reductions of bison and mule deer numbers
of about 10 percent. The effect would be no reduction in antlered harvest,
but probably an 8 percent reduction of antlerless harvest. The report predicted an annual average rate of 19 cattle and 68 sheep lost to depredations
annually, a small number compared to the current 8,340 cattle and 12,993
estimated livestock mortality in the area due to all causes. Land use restrictions were thought probable on sixteen square miles until six wolf packs
were established. The FEIS analyzed five alternatives regarding wolves in
Yellowstone, including an option preventing wolf recovery. Of particular interest is that the most fundamental reason for reintroducing the wolves, the
fact that wolves were the one major part missing from the ecosystem, was
but one of eighteen issues addressed in working up the five management alternatives. Those other issues included control strategies, compensation,
need for education, viable populations, and the cost of the program. Other
major issues, such as hunting harvest, depredations, land use restrictions,
visitor use, and local economies, required not only ecological information
but modern statistical modeling techniques as well to devise useful an-

swers. The FEIS did not address fifteen other issues, such as the question of whether wolves were native to the park, or the taxonomy of wolves, because they were not immediately significant; many of those questions had been answered in *Wolves for Yellowstone*. Clearly, human concerns predominated in the long discussion about wolf reintroduction. After absorbing all the public comment and the biological information, the USFWS recommended the nonessential experimental population.[161]

Changing public attitudes toward wild animals ultimately made reintroduction of the wolf possible. Historian Samuel P. Hays points out how public environmental concerns grew in the postwar United States as people focused more on quality of life issues; appreciation of nature and of wildlife was part of these swelling concerns. For many years hunting comprised the widest wildlife concern, but observation of wildlife was rapidly growing in popularity during the 1960s and 1970s. By 1964, fifty million Americans claimed a keen interest in wildlife observation, and by 1975, fifteen million wildlife photographers pursued their avocation as seventeen million hunters carried on their venerable tradition.[162] By the early 1990s Wyoming enjoyed a $245 million industry in nonconsumptive wildlife uses.[163]

Stephen Kellert's studies in the late 1970s differentiated between utilitarian or dominating values, which many hunters shared, and values associated with nature appreciation, which Hays sees not as naive nature worship but as "a facet of leisure that people desired to complement their lives in the built-up city."[164] In 1985 David McNaught's survey of Yellowstone Park visitors revealed that 74 percent thought the park experience would be improved by the presence of wolves, and 60 percent thought that if wolves did not naturally come back to Yellowstone they should be reintroduced. A survey in 1989 showed that over 74 percent supported the reintroduction of the wolf.[165] Granted, those interested enough in nature to visit the parks in the first place represent a somewhat biased audience, yet favorable attitudes among a national public toward wolf reintroduction were growing. The Science Museum of Minnesota created a world-class natural history exhibit titled *Wolves and Humans*, which traveled to Yellowstone National Park in the summer of 1985, attracting over 215,000 visitors.[166] The exhibit was "studiously objective" and "ahead of its time in recognizing that people could go overboard both in loving and in hating wolves."[167] By 1991, thanks in part to a long informational campaign on the part of Defenders of Wildlife, a national constituency exerted pressure on Congress to reintroduce the wolf. Doug Crowe, special assistant to USFWS Director John Turner, suggested that Congress was running out of patience with the delaying tactics of wolf opponents. While locals in the three states surrounding Yellowstone stalled recovery, the "scope of conflict" expanded, bringing in wolf proponents from across the country.[168] Establishing natural conditions in Yellowstone involved much more than biological rationales, however compelling they seemed to conservationists and ecologists.

In November 1994 the Wyoming Farm Bureau, supported by the legal staff of the Mountain States Legal Foundation and the American Farm Bureau Federation, sued the secretary of the Department of Interior, seeking an injunction against the impending reintroduction. The suit argued that the federal government lacked the authority to capture, transport, and release Canadian wolves in the United States. The suit additionally argued that reintroduction violated the Endangered Species Act, because the experimental populations would not be geographically separated from already-present members of the same species, the Canadian wolves were not the same *Canis lupus irremotus* that once inhabited Yellowstone, and the defendants did not consult with private landowners as they developed the final experimental rules. Finally, the suit noted that as the reports and rules admitted, there would be some losses to livestock. The lawyers from the Mountain States Legal Foundation categorized the predicted losses of 19 cattle and 68 sheep annually due to wolf predation "severe economic injury," arguing that "the viability of their livestock operations will be put at substantial risk."[169] Their opposition, on the other hand, had pointed to the fact that stock growers in the area already lost 8,340 cattle and 12,993 sheep yearly to other sources of mortality. The plaintiffs worried that ranchers would actually have to catch wolves in the act to take action, and thus the protections written into the rules were "not sufficient to prevent livestock losses from the introduced Canadian wolves." The stock growers wanted nothing less than zero losses from wolves. Furthermore, lawyers argued that insufficient protections meant that "Plaintiffs' members cannot adequately protect their livestock from the introduced Canadian wolves." The fact was that sheep might be protected by sheepherders and their dogs, but ranchers driven by the market claimed hiring that labor was too expensive. Because they could not protect their livestock, Farm Bureau members would "suffer irreparable injury" unless the court issued an injunction.[170] The fund established to reimburse ranchers' losses did not impress the lawyers from Denver and Illinois. The suit argued that land use restrictions would disrupt the livestock operations, perhaps causing severe economic injury. Finally, lawyers argued that "all

Americans have an interest in ensuring that the *status quo* is preserved" until the court could consider the case, suggested that "all Americans will suffer" if the wolves were reintroduced, and maintained that once Canadian wolves were reintroduced there would be "no way to return those areas to their original conditions."[171]

On January 3, 1995, U.S. District Judge William Downes denied the appellants' motion for the preliminary injunction; particularly striking about the decision was the persuasiveness of the scientific testimony in the case. The request for an injunction argued that Canadian wolves were different from the wolves that had been, or were currently, in Yellowstone. David Mech had addressed the question of wolf species back in 1991, pointing out that wolf taxonomy was indeed confusing, but New World taxonomists who assigned the subspecies had been too liberal. Only eight subspecies of wolf had been assigned for all of Asia and Europe, but systematists had designated twenty-four subspecies in North America; "most of the twenty-four so-called subspecies are so similar that they cannot be distinguished from one another without measuring great numbers of skulls."[172] Recent analysis showed those might be better lumped into five subspecies, in which case the southwestern Canadian wolves would be the same as the former Yellowstone wolves. Attorneys for the plaintiffs were using a rather obscure scientific discussion about hundreds of skulls scattered in museums across North America. The court turned to the issue of immediate and irreparable injury. First, the restrictions on the use of public lands at denning season were reasonable in that they only would cover one mile, be in force for a limited period, and at any rate only applied to human access and not to grazing animals. Such restrictions would not cause immediate and irreparable injury. Regarding the danger of depredations, the plaintiffs' "reliance upon anecdotal evidence from the turn of the century is insufficient when confronted with the Defendants' persuasive scientific testimony" that ecological conditions had changed since 1900.[173] Ed Bangs, hired in 1988 as the USFWS leader of the wolf recovery effort in Montana, and David Mech explained that wolves had preyed on livestock at the turn of the century because the wildlife had been decimated, and that Yellowstone now contained substantial numbers of wild prey. As a wolf biologist with thirty years experience, Mech cited his study of wolves in Minnesota in testifying that wolves preferred wild prey over domestic animals. Based on his studies elsewhere, Mech testified that wolf populations might cause a decrease in coyote populations that preyed on domestic stock. Thus the issues that the NPS report *Wolves for*

Yellowstone and the FEIS had sought to address ended up in court, with scientists called as expert witnesses. Just as environmentalists sought to use the environmental legislation of the 1970s to prevent timber sales and thus protect bears and de facto wilderness, so the opponents of wolf reintroduction used the law to try to maintain the status quo. Wolf opponents and proponents also used science to advance their claims, but the opponents' emphasis on taxonomy failed to merit attention, and biologists' experience with wolves in other locations carried more weight than "expressions of fear and trepidation, however genuine."[174] On March 21, 1995, Yellowstone and USFWS biologists began releasing the wolves from their holding pens. The ecological vision of Charles C. Adams and of the Wildlife Division finally overcame the long-standing limitations imposed by the regional economy and cultural attitudes. Scientists developed theories of natural conditions and ecosystems over a span of sixty years, ideas that found their maturity in a wider public understanding of Yellowstone as an ecological system.

The controversy over wolf reintroduction has not died down. In December of 1997 Judge William Downes issued his reluctant decision that nearly two hundred reintroduced wolves in Idaho and the Yellowstone region would have to be removed. There are several ironies here, including the fact that this was the judge that ordered the wolf reintroduction to proceed. The second irony was that the Earth Justice Legal Defense Fund, trying to protect wolves in Idaho that had recolonized a few places on their own, found its suit combined with the Farm Bureau's, making for very strange bed partners and some very angry friends of the wolf. The judge's decision centered around the issue of whether wolves had begun to reestablish populations on their own, a problem that seemed settled back in 1995.[175]

From 1975 through the early 1990s ecological ideas began to strongly influence how tourists thought about nature when they visited the park, and how agencies thought about managing Yellowstone. The ecosystem concept took root, even if knowing exactly *how* to manage an ecosystem, establishing interagency mechanisms for cooperation, and then agreeing on a course of action remained a very problematic affair. Yet managers as well as scientists came to see all the elements of the landscape—bears, elk, vegetation, climate, fire, and predators—as interactive. This fell far short of any sort of mystical or holistic philosophy. Rather, scientists viewed the connections between biotic and abiotic elements on the landscape as subtle yet pervasive, and living organisms as interacting in intricate ways. To the extent that the

NPS and other agencies incorporated natural fire regimes, ideas from land-scape ecology, conservation biology, and the ecosystem concept in management policy, the 1980s spelled the demise of single-species thinking in terms of managing Yellowstone's wilderness.

Despite widely accepted views of Yellowstone as the heart of a larger eco-system, agreement on management philosophy proved elusive. Disagreement continued over scientific issues relating to the northern elk herd. The great fires of 1988 raised concerns about natural area management. Proposed wolf reintroduction encountered vociferous resistance based as much on emotion as on information. At the heart of some of these discussions lay persistent questions concerning the twin traditions of intervention in nature and preserving natural conditions. Yellowstone Park managers moved toward an ecologically justified rationale of judicious and cautious management, neither "heavy-handed" nor entirely "hands off."

EPILOGUE

> Letting nature take its course is, and always will be, an ideal.
> Freeman Tilden, *The National Parks*, 1951

The continuous interplay between two competing conceptions of managing the park's biota forms an enduring theme in the history of Yellowstone. Active intervention is as old as the park itself. Early park administrations manipulated wildlife conditions, shooting predators and feeding elk during cold winters to protect and enhance wildlife populations that park visitors wanted to see. Yellowstone rangers actually herded elk back into the protective enclave of the park. Fisheries experts and park authorities encouraged the type of fish anglers preferred, going so far as to destroy pelican eggs on Molly Island. Though some sources discuss this period as merely protection of big game, portraying management as passive, we can see that protection involved vigorous action on the part of managers.

During the 1930s the Wildlife Division brought an ecological awareness to the park. Because division personnel had been students of Joseph Grinnell, their university training prepared them not only for work in systematics but also to see the park wildlife in ecological terms, rather than in terms of protective custody. They set up guiding principles for wildlife management that have remained largely intact, including protection for all native species. At the same time that they brought their ecological vision of wildlife relationships, the Wildlife Division also continued an active management approach in Yellowstone, but in this version of intervention they intended managers to limit actions to reestablishing original ecological conditions altered by human hand. The Wildlife Division was willing to shoot crows, trap small predators, or alter lake levels if it meant the endangered trumpeter swan would survive. They also believed it necessary to limit the number of elk on the northern range. Scientists and managers continued that active management stance throughout the 1940s and 1950s, most conspicuously by controlling the number of elk within the park border, and in less dramatic fashion by suppressing wildfires. Today, the most obvious forms of active management include efforts to sustain native fisheries against exotic invaders. The reintroduction of the wolf, moreover, is clearly an active and interventionist strategy. While justified and rationalized in very modern ways, wolves howling once again in Yellowstone also recall to mind Charles C. Adams's appeal for preserving the primitive conditions found in the national parks.

Alongside the active management tradition existed a very different view and tradition emphasizing the preservation of natural conditions without human intrusions. This perspective promoted baseline research in unmodified landscapes, creating a scientific purpose for the parks. During the 1910s and 1920s ecologists' call for the preservation of natural conditions in Yellowstone initiated this view of the parks as places where scientists might examine nature in localities where original biological conditions remained unmodified. Charles C. Adams, Victor Shelford, Barrington Moore, Joseph Grinnell, Tracey Storer, and others urged the preservation of "natural conditions" as a proper function of national parks. They envisioned the parks, in a way similar to Horace Albright, as a last refuge of nature against a spreading, destructive mechanical civilization. While Albright worried about protecting big game, scientists were concerned about a place remote enough to insulate living ecosystems (in their words, "natural" or "primitive conditions") from alteration. For the Wildlife Division of the early 1930s, the entire goal of management was the restoration of the "primitive balance of nature."[1] In the 1940s and 1950s Adolph and Olaus Murie adapted the idea to include their own view that "wilderness" in parks advanced not only science but nurtured the spirit of people in an overly materialistic age. Olaus Murie's ecological vision of Yellowstone questioned managers' ability to control nature without unexpected and undesirable results. The Muries successfully argued that bringing the Absaroka National Forest's heavy-handed management of wildlife into Yellowstone would subvert the principles of the parks. When park fire experts of the 1980s evoked the image of natural areas as "living laboratories," they hearkened back to an era when scientists advocated research preserves in the parks.[2]

Do we have to choose between the heavy hand of intervention and holding ourselves back from nature in the interests of preserving our natural park landscapes? Intensive land management has met with many failures and undesirable results, exemplified by the extirpation of wildlife species, such as the grizzly bear, from vast areas of our national forests, or the extirpation of elk from the entire midcontinent. Similarly, our hubris in thinking we can control nature sometimes results in frustration. Attempts to control the Mississippi River at its terminus, for example, have meant raising the dikes several times at great expense.[3] Allowing nature to carry out its work, on the other hand, has yielded unexpected results from time to time. The size of the northern herd today is larger than anyone had anticipated. We fear the possible undesirable consequences of watching nature take care of itself, a decision we castigate as neglect. If managers did not closely monitor and take action to protect the Yellowstone grizzly population, and it was extirpated, would the public forgive the federal agencies this lapse of judgment?

The twin traditions of intervention and watching nature at work are both legitimate ways to deal with management of our public lands, each appropriate in certain places and times. The national park manager's dilemma may be not so much a choice between the two, but a judicious selection from the two traditions as ecological conditions over time, scientific knowledge, and political reality allow. Ironies are involved as managers take active steps aimed at preserving or re-creating natural conditions. But ambiguity and difficult choices are not reasons to permanently toss aside a concept that has enabled us to learn a great deal about natural processes.[4]

Both those who seek more active intervention and those who support natural regulation call on science to bolster their case. Yet difficulties remain in looking to science for resolution of management dilemmas. Definitions of central concepts, such as carrying capacity and overgrazing, are disputed. Moreover, seeking out the natural condition of the Yellowstone landscape has led scientists into a dense and tangled thicket. Because natural systems are in flux, how will management choose a point in time or any particular condition that can be called natural? Conceptual difficulties in defining a community or an ecosystem further complicate efforts to decipher the natural.[5] Similarly, looking to science for some sort of litmus test of management policy is a problematic endeavor. Wildlife biologists who advocate reduction of deer in the eastern U.S. parks suggest that science provides good guidance only when management "objectives are highly specific and involve relatively simple ecological relationships."[6] Managing a park bigger than the state of Rhode Island poses much larger and more complicated problems than science alone can resolve. As William F. Porter has argued, "attempts to resolve these issues in science have not been successful. . . . Intervention may be warranted but, at present, the basis of such a decision must be largely political."[7] Yet political answers to management questions in the past favored the useful species over the less useful, the beautiful over the bothersome. Conflicts over Park Service goals have become more contentious, and there is a danger in politicians shaping agency behavior toward serving "their short-term, electoral needs."[8] During the ongoing controversy over wolf reintroductions in Yellowstone, for example, politicians seeking votes from agricultural districts of northwestern states have played hardball, attempting to derail the efforts of the U.S. Fish and Wildlife Service and the National Park Service.

Although science is a powerful tool for understanding the particulars of nature, scientists cannot tell us what the national parks are about, and ecologists cannot tell us to what ends the Park Service should manage Yellowstone. The outcomes we desire in national parks are to a significant degree culturally determined. Though scientific thinking is part and parcel of our culture, answers derived from science do not always seem to satisfy us on issues that concern wildlife. The parks are as much about watching nature as about dissecting it. The nature we expect to find there is one of crystalline waters, exhilarating mountain air, extensive green forests, and abundant wildlife.

Gardening columnist Michael Pollen has suggested that it is not to the wilderness that we should look for the proper relationship between humans and nature, but rather to the garden. More recently, historian William Cronon has suggested there is something troubling about the term "wilderness." As he puts it, our concept of wilderness is based on a "premise that nature, to be natural, must also be pristine—remote from humanity and untouched by our common past." Cronon suggests that this separation of humans from nature, of natural from artificial, is a false dichotomy. Cronon seems to prefer the garden as a metaphor for human relationships with nature, suggesting that we should bring the positive values associated with wilderness along with us into the places where we actually live. Along with others, he argues that wilderness is a cultural construction and that the wild nature people perceive in the national parks is more a product of wishful thinking than a physical reality.[9]

Although scholars debate the meaning of nature and wilderness in carefully hedged essays, a larger popular audience reads books such as Steven Budiansky's *Nature's Keepers*.[10] This sort of popular critique glosses the fine gradations of academic dispute and oversimplifies complicated issues. The popular critique of today's federal management of wilderness, efforts to protect endangered species, and environmentalism in general begins by emphasizing the idea that humans have always had a significant impact on the landscape. Environmental historians, as well as recent histories of Native Americans, have demonstrated that aboriginal populations had a much greater effect on the landscape than previously thought.[11] The next step of the argument is that because human interaction shaped the land, our thinking of the landscape as somehow pristine before European contact is deeply misleading. Additionally, the argument suggests that Native American use of fire to shape ecological conditions in large parts of the continent amounted to purposeful management of natural resources. This line of thinking then suggests that because prehistorical management of the land was the norm, humans today should not abandon their role in shaping nature. This rationale ultimately argues or implies that people *must* manage the landscape. Budiansky equates the necessity for management with a mature outlook on life, suggesting that "we'd better start behaving toward [nature] like grown-ups before we lose her forever."[12]

Authors Alston Chase, Stephen Budiansky, and others attempt to enlist ecology on their side, implying that current ecological views of nature as chaotic and shaped by random events mean that looking to nature for insights into management direction is sheer folly. Chase claims that terms such as "ecosystem" have no basis in reality, and therefore management based on these concepts is hopelessly wrongheaded.[13] These accounts fail to address what science is all about. The public needs to become aware that internal debates are a normal and significant part of gaining and refining scientific knowledge. Defining the limits and meanings of terminology does not mean that scientists have dismissed a concept such as the ecosystem out of hand. The ongoing scientific discussion of difficult ecological issues does not mean that ecology cannot offer important insights. The sense that ultimately there are limits to our abilities to manage nature may be one of the most important lessons ecology offers. Claims to possession of the right sort of ecology fall flat when one looks at scientific journals and finds not the correct answer but rather a spirited conversation that continually refines our knowledge of nature. Critics of natural regulation who imply that their brand of ecology and their use of science is entirely value-free and objective are telling only part of the story.

Chase proposes that government managers have selected the wrong parts of ecology and adopted a philosophy of nonintervention born in the "redwood think tanks of California."[14] Legitimate questions about scientific knowledge and management policy should be aired, yet it is unfortunate when intelligent debate degenerates into an empty and angry antigovernment and antienvironmental discourse. Chase's work appears in *Range Magazine*, accusing the Park Service of deception and practicing misinformed science.[15] These sorts of arguments also are used by people with economic and political agendas. It is no coincidence that the Political Economy Research Center (PERC), which advocates free-market solutions to environmental dilemmas, has taken up and published a special report featuring Charles Kay's "Ecological Malpractice," which emphasizes two species (willow and aspen) in assessing the effect of natural regulation. For PERC, preserving the national parks means fixing "the incentives," in other words, telling the Park Service how it should run the park.[16] Popular critiques of environmentalism, inspired partly by the myth of a nature lover's ideal, have entered the nation's political discourse—in 1995 Representative Helen Chenoweth of Idaho made political hay when she argued that the Clinton administration was promoting and enforcing "a cloudy mixture of New Age mysticism, Native American folklore, and primitive Earth worship."[17] At a time when wolf reintroduction to Yellowstone is still bitterly contested, and after considering the actions of the ACC during the 1950s, one questions the wisdom of allowing our dominant political economy to drive decisions regarding wildlife conservation on our public lands.

Most visitors to the parks are unaware of scholarly debates over definitions of what is natural. Perhaps to most people the debate is purely academic. In the real world, "natural" is simply a matter of degree. We *know* nature when we see it. We also know what an intensely managed landscape looks like—some variant of farmland, factory, highway, logged-off hillside, cows on a pasture, a city or suburban area located a day's drive from Yellowstone. By comparing these known human landscapes against the scene out their window, national park visitors know they are witnessing something "natural," a landscape largely unaffected by human hand. Americans and visitors from around the world come to Yellowstone not to view a garden more exotic than the ones they know at home but to experience a natural landscape that has avoided somehow the extensive manipulation humans have carried out everywhere else. It is thus partly a matter of degree. The tourist who has done a little homework will realize that Yellowstone's grizzly bears exist partly because of allowances people have made outside the park. In other words, the grizzly's continued existence is a bit "unnatural," in the sense that we have to go out of our way to ensure the survival of this species. Yet all tourists recognize the vast difference between the relatively pristine landscape of national park natural areas and the profoundly altered human habitat they call home. We expect a place where creatures are able to roam wild and free. This is why the American public rejected mass reductions of the northern Yellowstone elk herd in the 1960s, and today they are no more ready to accept the slaughter of the bison in Yellowstone.

The purpose of our national parks remains one of the most important cultural considerations regarding the management of our public lands. What do the parks symbolize for us today?[18] The parks represent islands of natural processes in a larger landscape that has been substantially transformed as a result of human intervention. U.S. Forest Service and Bureau of Land Management lands are oriented toward multiple use, emphasizing intensive management and the production of resource commodities. The extractive uses allowed by this approach have forever changed the parameters for the other multiple uses traditionally assigned to the national forests. Logging on a massive scale or establishing mines and oil wells in the national forests surrounding Yellowstone certainly presents wildlife with an altered physical environment. The steady subdivision of private lands near the park with accompanying construction of homes and vacation cabins also represents a significant threat to the wildlife values of the region. For Charles C. Adams and his colleagues, the parks provided naturally functioning areas against which land management practices elsewhere might be compared. For many park managers and biologists who followed, this scientific purpose for the parks formed a lens through which they examined nature in Yellowstone. In a larger sense, preserving natural conditions meant withholding the manipulative hand to provide a landscape where people might watch and wonder at nature, a place to gain a different perspective, and perhaps begin asking questions about the relationship between humans and nature.

Not only scientists but tourists and philosophers still look to the parks as places where nature proceeds according to its own rhythms. The Yellowstone ecosystem, despite the limits our culture and our past place on it, remains "one of the largest, essentially intact, wild ecosystems remaining in the earth's temperate zone."[19] As Charles C. Adams and his colleagues had hoped, it remains one of the last places where biologists can watch functioning natural systems with most of their original complement of animals and plants, largely unimpeded by human intrusion. The reintroduction of the wolf represents a major step in re-creating the natural conditions Adams wanted to preserve. We sometimes think of nature preservation in the parks as the direct descendent of aesthetic preservation. In fact, a complex inter-action among cultural movements, ideal notions about how nature works, changing conservation strategies, scientific information, institutional struc-tures, and a good dose of politics has informed and shaped park policies. The scientists' proposal during the early twentieth century that Yellowstone serve as an ecological control has endured as one of the most significant purposes for the national parks, underlying both management and public understandings of nature in Yellowstone.

NOTES

Introduction

1. Alston Chase, *Playing God in Yellowstone* (San Diego: Harcourt Brace Jovanovich, 1987); Karl Hess Jr., *Rocky Times in Rocky Mountain National Park: An Unnatural History* (Niwot: University Press of Colorado, 1993); Frederic H. Wagner, Ronald Foresta, R. Bruce Gill, et al., *Wildlife Policies in the U.S. National Parks* (Washington DC: Island Press, 1995); Stephen Budiansky, "Yellowstone's Unraveling: The Ecosystem Is in Grave Peril and the Most Damage Is Caused by Elk," *U.S. News and World Report* (September 16, 1996): 80–83.

2. Chase, *Playing God*; of thirteen reviews of *Playing God*, all but one registered objections or uneasiness with the book's treatment of fact, science, or interpretation and analysis of park philosophy; a thoughtful review was written by Holmes Rolston III, "Biology and Philosophy in Yellowstone," *Biology and Philosophy* 5 (1990): 241–58.

3. Stephen R. Kellert and Tim W. Clark, "The Theory and Application of a Wildlife Policy Framework," in William R. Mangun, ed., *Public Policy Issues in Wildlife Management* (New York: Greenwood Press, 1991), 17–36, esp. 20–21.

4. Lee Whittlesey, "Cows All Over the Place! The Historic Setting for the Transmission of Brucellosis to Yellowstone Bison by Domestic Cattle," *Wyoming Annals* 66 (Winter 1994-95): 42–57.

5. Greater Yellowstone Coalition, "Help America's Buffalo Roam Free," 4 p. brochure, in *Greater Yellowstone Report* 13, 4 (Fall 1996); Gene Brodeur, "Winter Kills," *Tributary Magazine* (Bozeman MT: Carter G. Walker) (June 1997): 8–9; David Simpson, "Hunt Offered as Brucellosis Control Plan," *Jackson Hole Guide*, June 25, 1997, 1; Angus M. Thuermer Jr., "Park Says 2,500 Bison Is the Limit," *Jackson Hole News*, June 25, 1997, 1; Doug Peacock, "The Yellowstone Massacre," *Audubon* 99 (May-June 1997): 40–49, 102–3, 106–10.

6. Judith L. Meyer, *The Spirit of Yellowstone: The Cultural Evolution of a National Park* (Lanham MD: Rowman & Littlefield, 1996), 6.

7. Meyer, *Spirit of Yellowstone*, 6, 8, 10.

1. A good review of recent scholarly work on Native American presence in the region is Paul Schullery, *Searching for Yellowstone: Ecology and Wonder in the Last Wilderness* (Boston: Houghton Mifflin, 1997), 21–30; and Mark Spence, "First Wilderness: Indian Removal from Yellowstone National Park" (paper delivered at the Fourth Biennial Scientific Conference on the Greater Yellowstone Ecosystem, October 12–15, 1997, Mammoth WY). See also M. Kat Anderson, "Tending the Wilderness," *Restoration and Management Notes* 14 (Winter 1996): 154–66; Steward T. A. Pickett and Mark J. McDonnell, "Humans as Components of Ecosystems: A Synthesis," in Mark J. McDonnell and Steward T. A. Pickett, eds., *Humans as Components of Ecosystems* (New York: Springer-Verlag, 1993), 310–16; Alan A. Beetle and Alvin Young, "American Prehistory and Range Management," *University of Wyoming Publications* 28 (July 15, 1963): 1–16.

2. David A. Clary, *"The Place Where Hell Bubbled Up": A History of the First National Park* (Washington DC: National Park Service, 1972), 10.

3. Mike Foster, *Strange Genius: The Life of Ferdinand Vandiveer Hayden* (Niwot CO: Roberts Rinehart, 1994), 202.

4. Richard A. Bartlett, *Great Surveys of the American West* (Norman: University of Oklahoma Press, 1962; reprint, 1989), 3–73.

5. On questioning the myth, see Richard West Sellars, "Tracks in the Wilderness: Did Railroad Barons Put Yellowstone Park on America's Map?" *Washington Post*, February 23, 1992, C5; Alfred Runte, *National Parks: The American Experience*, 2nd ed. (Lincoln: University of Nebraska Press, 1987), 41–44. Paul Schullery and Lee Whittlesey, "The Madison Campfire Story: Yellowstone's Creation Myth and Its Legacy" (paper delivered at the Fourth Biennial Conference on the Greater Yellowstone Ecosystem, Mammoth WY, October 12–15, 1997). On Catlin, see Runte, *National Parks*, 26; on Hedges, see Aubrey Haines, *The Yellowstone Story: A History of Our First National Park*, vol. 1 (Yellowstone National Park: Yellowstone Library and Museum Association, 1977), 173.

6. Haines, *Yellowstone Story*, vol. 1, 164; Runte, *National Parks*, 14, 32, and 41.

7. U.S. Geological Survey, *Frederick Vandiveer Hayden and the Founding of the Yellowstone National Park* (Washington DC: GPO, 1973), 18.

8. Sellars, "Tracks in the Wilderness," C5.

9. Joseph L. Sax, *Mountains Without Handrails: Reflections on the National Parks* (Ann Arbor: University of Michigan Press, 1980), 10.

10. U.S.C., title 16, sec. 22; 17 Stat. 32; See Hillory A. Tolson, *Laws Relating to the National Park Service, the National Parks and Monuments* (Dept. of the Interior: GPO, 1933), 26–27.

11. Mary Shivers Culpin, *The History of the Construction of the Road System in Yellowstone* (Denver: National Park Service, 1994); Haines, *Yellowstone Story*, vol. 1, 173; Eric Sandeen, "A History of Yellowstone's Roads" (Review essay), *Yellowstone Science* 4 (Spring 1996): 10–14.

12. Haines, *Yellowstone Story*, vol. 2, 209–55.

13. Quoted in Haines, *Yellowstone Story*, vol. 2, 255.

14. Anne Farrar Hyde, *An American Vision: Far Western Landscape and National Culture, 1820–1920* (New York: New York University Press, 1990), 248–68; Haines, *Yellowstone Story*, vol. 2, 119–31.

15. Paul Schullery, "Yellowstone's Ecological Holocaust," *Montana* 47 (Autumn 1997): 16–33, esp. 21–23. See also Haines, *Yellowstone Story*, vol. 1, 252.

16. Haines, *Yellowstone Story*, vol. 1, 252.

17. Shullery, "Yellowstone's Ecological Holocaust," 24.

18. Shullery, "Yellowstone's Ecological Holocaust," 24.

19. Haines, *Yellowstone Story*, vol. 1, 252; H. Duane Hampton, *How the U.S. Cavalry Saved Our National Parks* (Bloomington: Indiana University Press, 1971).

20. On the Hough expedition, see Haines, *Yellowstone Story*, vol. 2, 58–64. The Yellowstone Park Protection Act can be found at 28 Stat. 73; Theodore Whaley Cart, "The Lacey Act: America's First Nationwide Wildlife Statute," *Forest History* (October 1973): 4–13; see also Jenks Cameron, *The Bureau of Biological Survey: Its History, Activities and Organization* (Baltimore: Johns Hopkins University Press, 1929), 65–83.

21. Wording of the Yellowstone Park Protection Act (28 Stat. 73) is taken from Tolson, *Laws Relating to the N.P.S.*, 30–31; Michael J. Bean, *The Evolution of National Wildlife Law* (Washington DC: Council on Environmental Quality, 1977), 111–20. On wildlife management during military administration of Yellowstone, see also Jerome Kasten, "Early Wildlife Policy of Yellowstone National Park, 1872–1918," master's thesis, East Texas State University, 1966.

22. George M. Wright and Ben H. Thompson, *Wildlife Management in the National Parks*, Fauna of the National Parks Series, no. 2 (Washington DC: GPO, 1934), 59.

23. Haines, *Yellowstone Story*, vol. 2, 68–77.

24. Haines, *Yellowstone Story*, vol. 2, 64; Curt D. Meine, "The Oldest Task in Human History," in Richard L. Knight and Sarah F. Bates, eds., *A New Century for Natural Resources Management* (Washington DC: Island Press, 1995), 7–36; Dian Olson Belanger, *Managing American Wildlife: A History of the International Association of Fish and Wildlife Agencies* (Amherst: University of Massachusetts Press, 1988), 10–19; James B. Trefethen, *An American Crusade for Wildlife* (New York: Winchester Press, 1975), 157–60; Neal Blair, *The History of Wildlife Management in Wyoming* (Casper: Wyoming Game and Fish Department, 1987), 36–43.

25. Belanger, *Managing American Wildlife*, 10–19.

26. Altherr and Reiger contend that Hornaday never gave up hunting; see Thomas L. Altherr and John F. Reiger, "Academic Historians and Hunting: A Call for More and Better Scholarship," *Environmental History Review* 19 (Fall 1995): 39–56.

27. William T. Hornaday, *Our Vanishing Wildlife: Its Extermination and Preservation* (New York: New York Zoological Society, 1913), 387, 392.

28. Fairfield Osborn, "William Temple Hornaday," *Dictionary of American Biography*, vol. 21, 316–17; see also Stephen Fox, *John Muir and His Legacy: The American Conservation Movement* (Boston: Little, Brown and Company, 1981), 148–51; Trefethen, *An American Crusade*, 177–81.

29. William T. Hornaday, "The Wyoming Legislature at the Bar of Public Opinion," broadside, February 23, 1917, file "Elk Winter 1917–20," box N–23, National Archives, Yellowstone National Park Branch, Mammoth WY (hereafter cited as NAYNP); see also Fox, *John Muir and His Legacy*, 148–51.

30. Horace M. Albright, "Game Conservation in Parks," n.d. [c. 1925], vertical files, Yellowstone National Park Library (hereafter cited as YNPL); on Brett and the elk, see file "Wild Animals/Protection and Feeding," box 259, entry 6, RG 79, National Archives, College Park MD (hereafter cited as NACP).

31. John Killorn to secretary of the interior, November 14, 1911, file "Wild Animals," box 259, entry 6, RG 79, NACP.

32. Chief U.S. Biological Survey to R. H. Rutledge, December 26, 1911, file 1, box 230, entry 162, RG 22, NACP; quote in Chief U.S. Biological Survey to H. S. Graves, December 26, 1911, file 1, box 230, entry 162, RG 22, NACP.

33. Yellowstone National Park, 1912 Annual Report, YNPL.

34. Chief Clerk, Dept. Interior to Senator Hoke Smith, February 27, 1913, file "Wild Animals," box 253, entry 6, RG 79, NACP; see also file "Wild Animals," box 254, entry 6, RG 79, NACP; the authority to ship animals from Yellowstone was formalized by Congress on March 4, 1911 (936 Stat 1258) and a clause in the Appropriations Act of August 10, 1912 (37 Stat 292).

35. George B. Grinnell, "Elk Study," n.d. [c. 1913], file "Yellowstone," box 229, entry 162, RG 22, NACP.

36. G. B. Grinnell to Nelson, December 1, 1913, file "Yellowstone," box 229, entry 162, RG 22, NACP.

37. Jenks Cameron, *The Bureau of Biological Survey: Its History, Activities and Organization* (Baltimore: Johns Hopkins University Press, 1929), 12–42, quote on 25.

38. Keir B. Sterling, "Builders of the U.S. Biological Survey, 1885–1930," *Journal of Forest History* (October 1989): 180–87; Cameron, *Bureau of Biological Survey*, 45–46; Belanger, *Managing American Wildlife*, 170.

39. Nelson to G. B. Grinnell, November 22, 1913, file "Yellowstone," box 229, entry 162, RG 22, NACP.

40. E. W. Nelson to Charles Sheldon, March 6, 1917, file "Yellowstone," box 229, entry 162, RG 22, NACP.

41. Vernon Bailey to Mr. Ernest W. Shaw [Forest Supervisor, Livingston MT], October 28, 1915, file "Yellowstone," box 229, entry 162, RG 22, NACP; biographical material on Bailey from Thomas R. Dunlap, *Saving America's Wildlife* (Princeton: Princeton University Press, 1988), 40.

42. E. W. Nelson to Emerson Hough, March 13, 1917, file "Yellowstone," box 229, entry 162, RG 22, NACP.

43. J. W. Nelson, "Working Plan for the Northern Yellowstone Elk Herd," November 9, 1917, file "Yellowstone," box 229, entry 162, RG 22, NACP.

44. S. W. McClure to James Wilson, May 10, 1912, file "Yellowstone," box 229, entry 162, RG 22, NACP.

45. Graves to Henshaw, September 1, 1914, file "Yellowstone," box 229, entry 162, RG 22, NACP.

46. Hough to E. W. Nelson, March 9, 1917, file "Yellowstone," box 229, entry 162, RG 22, NACP.

47. Mary E. Elliott to secretary of the interior, January 14, 1914, file "Yellowstone," box 229, entry 162, RG 22, NACP.

48. Rumsey to Redmund Cross, Esq., April 5, 1916, file "Yellowstone," box 229, entry 162, RG 22, NACP.

49. E. W. Nelson to Stephen T. Mather, February 14, 1916, file "Yellowstone," box 229, entry 162, RG 22, NACP.

50. William T. Hornaday, "Wyoming Legislature," file "Elk Winter 1917–20," box N–23, NAYNP.

51. Richard A. Bartlett, *Yellowstone: A Wilderness Besieged* (Tucson: University of Arizona Press, 1985), 336–37.

52. U.S. Forest Service, "Hundreds of Elk Slaughtered for Teeth," n.d. [c. 1916], file "Yellowstone," box 229, entry 162, RG 22, NACP.

53. Chief Biological Survey to Emerson Hough, January 13, 1917, file "Yellowstone," box 229, entry 162, RG 22, NACP.

54. Nelson to G. B. Grinnell, November 22, 1913, file "Yellowstone," box 229, entry 162, RG 22, NACP.

55. J. W. Nelson, "Working Plan," November 9, 1917, file "Yellowstone," box 229, entry 162, RG 22, NACP.

CHAPTER 2 · Conservation Thought and Yellowstone

1. Roderick Nash, *Wilderness and the American Mind*, 3rd ed. (New Haven: Yale University Press, 1982), 180.

2. Haines, *Yellowstone Story*, vol. 2, 284–85.

3. On the NPS organic act, 39 Stat. 535, see Tolson, *Laws Relating to the N.P.S.*, 41; Fox, *John Muir and His Legacy*, 146.

4. Robert Shankland, *Steve Mather of the National Parks* (New York: Alfred A. Knopf, 1970), 101.

5. T. H. Watkins, "National Parks, National Paradox," *Audubon* 99 (July-August 1997): 40–43.

6. Horace M. Albright, "Game Conservation in Parks," n.d. [c. 1925], vertical files, YNPL.

7. Richard West Sellars, *Preserving Nature in the National Parks: A History* (New Haven: Yale University Press, 1997), 29; Robin W. Winks, "The National Park Service Act of 1916: 'A Contradictory Mandate'?" *Denver University Law Review* 74 (1997): 575–623.

8. Roderick Nash, *Wilderness and the American Mind*, 3rd ed. (New Haven: Yale University Press, 1982), 141–60; Terence Young, "Social Reform Through the Parks: The American Civic Association's Program for a Better America," *Journal of Historical Geography* 22 (1996): 460–72.

9. Joseph Grinnell and Tracy I. Storer, "Animal Life as an Asset of National Parks," *Science* n.s., 44, no. 1133, September 15, 1916, 375–80.

10. Memo G. W. Field [illeg.] to Chief [Nelson] January 25, 1919, file "Yellowstone," box 229, entry 162, RG 22, NACP.

11. J. W. Nelson, "The Preservation of Our American Elk" (paper presented to Grand Lodge of Elks, Atlantic City, July 7–12, 1919), file "Yellowstone," box 229, entry 162, RG 22, NACP.

12. M. R. Wilson to H. L. Myers, February 17, 1919, file "Yellowstone," box 229, entry 162, RG 22, NACP.

13. Draft letter Dept. of Interior to Mr. Esp, December 17, 1919, file "Yellowstone," box 229, entry 162, RG 22, NACP.

14. Donald C. Swain, *Wilderness Defender: Horace Albright* (Chicago: University of Chicago Press, 1970), 121.

15. Nelson to Burnham, December 30, 1919, file "Yellowstone," box 229, entry 162, RG 22, NACP.

16. Nelson to J. A. McGuire, December 27, 1919, file "Yellowstone," box 229, entry 162, RG 22, NACP.

17. W. L. McAtee, Notes on BBS personnel, box 73, McAtee Papers, Library of Congress, Washington DC (hereafter cited as LOC).

18. Chief Biological Survey to Emerson Hough, Esq., January 13, 1917, file "Yellowstone," box 229, entry 162, RG 22, NACP.

19. [illeg.] Office of the secretary of agriculture to secretary of the interior, February 23, 1917, file "Yellowstone," box 229, entry 162, RG 22, NACP.

20. Graves to Nelson, October 29, 1918, file "Yellowstone," box 229, entry 162, RG 22, NACP.

21. Biographical information in Henry Clepper, *Leaders of American Conservation* (New York: Ronald Press, 1971), 140–41; Richard H. Stroud, ed., *National Leaders of American Conservation* (Washington DC: Smithsonian Institution Press, 1985), 176.

22. Biographical information in *The National Cyclopaedia of American Biography*, vol. 26, 434–35; *Dictionary of American Biography*, vol. 21, Supplement One, 571–72.

23. Albright to Charles Sheldon, April 11, 1918, file "Yellowstone," box 229, entry

162, RG 22, NACP.

24. Nash, *Wilderness*, 152.

25. Henry S. Graves and E. W. Nelson, "Our National Elk Herds," December 23, 1918, file "Yellowstone," box 229, entry 162, RG 22, NACP.

26. Henry S. Graves, "The Yellowstone Elk: A Program," file "Yellowstone," box 229, entry 162, RG 22, NACP.

27. Graves and Nelson, "Our National Elk Herds," file "Yellowstone," box 229, entry 162, RG 22, NACP.

28. William Rush, "Northern Yellowstone Elk Study" (Helena: Montana Fish and Game Commission, April 1932), 5. Executive Order No. 3053, February 23, 1917, withdrew lands from settlement. Thirteen thousand acres of that area was revoked from withdrawal by E. O. 10355 of May 26, 1952. May 26, 1926, additions to the national forests can be found at 44 Stat. 655. Lee Whittlesey, "Report on the Origins and Legislative History of Gallatin National Forest," April 1, 1997, YNPL.

29. John Weaver, "The Wolves of Yellowstone," in Paul Schullery, ed., *The Yellowstone Wolf: A Guide and Sourcebook* (Worland WY: High Plains Publishing Company, 1996), 3–33. Schullery and Lee Whittlesey, "Documentary Record of Wolves and Related Wildlife Species in the Yellowstone National Park Area Prior to 1882," in *Wolves for Yellowstone?: A Report to the United States Congress* vol. 4 (Yellowstone National Park: YNP Research Division, July 1992), 1-1 to 1-173.

30. Vernon Bailey to Elmer Lindsley, October 8, 1915, file "Yellowstone," box 229, entry 162, RG 22, NACP.

31. Weaver, "The Wolves of Yellowstone," 12–13.

32. Graves to Dr. H. W. Henshaw, March 8, 1916, file "Yellowstone," box 229, entry 162, RG 22, NACP.

33. Chief Biological Survey to Emerson Hough, Esq., January 13, 1917, file "Yellowstone," box 229, entry 162, RG 22, NACP.

34. Bartlett, *Yellowstone: A Wilderness Besieged*, 336–37; Haines, *Yellowstone Story*, vol. 2, 459. Horace M. Albright to Charles C. Adams, December 6, 1919, file "Elk Winter 1917–20" box N-23, YNP Archives.

35. Horace M. Albright to Charles C. Adams, December 6, 1919, file "Elk Winter 1917–20," box N-23, NAYNP; see also Albright, "Game Conservation in Parks," n.d. [c. 1925], vertical files, YNPL.

36. Yellowstone National Park, Annual Superintendent's Report, 1920, YNP Archives.

37. R. S. Yard, "The Disaster to the Yellowstone Elk Herd," National Parks Association, December 30, 1919, file "Yellowstone," box 229, entry 162, RG 22, NACP.

38. Albright, "Game Conservation in Parks" n.d. [c. 1925], vertical files, YNPL.

39. Ernest Thompson Seton, *Wild Animals I Have Known* (New York: Charles Scribner's Sons, 1942); Ralph H. Lutts, *The Nature Fakers: Wildlife, Science & Sentiment* (Golden CO: Fulcrum, 1990).

40. See also Thomas Dunlap, *Saving America's Wildlife* (Princeton: Princeton University Press, 1988), 27.

41. U.S. Stat., vol. 28, p. 73, chap. 72, sec. 4; Tolson, *Laws Relating to the N.P.S.*, 30–31; see also John Ise, *Our National Park Policy: A Critical History* (Baltimore: Johns Hopkins University Press, 1961), 45–48.

42. Weaver, "The Wolves of Yellowstone," 26–27.

43. Albright, "Game Conservation in Parks," n.d. [c. 1925], vertical files, YNPL.

44. Robert P. McIntosh, "Ecology Since 1900," in Frank N. Egerton, ed., *History of American Ecology* (New York: Arno Press, 1977), 356; *The National Cyclopaedia of American Biography*, vol. 46, 258–59; Robert A. Croker, *Pioneer Ecologist: The Life and Work of Victor Ernest Shelford, 1877–1968* (Washington DC: Smithsonian Institution Press, 1991), 121; Gregg Mitman, *The State of Nature: Ecology, Community, and American Social Thought, 1900–1950* (Chicago: University of Chicago Press, 1992), 36; biographical information on Adams can be found in Ralph S. Palmer, "Resolution of Respect, Dr. Charles C. Adams (1873–1955)," *Bulletin of the Ecological Society of America* 37 (1956): 103–5; Paul B. Sears, "Charles C. Adams, Ecologist," *Science* 123 (1956): 974; Philip P. Calvert, "Dr. Charles Christopher Adams," *Entomological News* 67 (July 1956): 169–71; Hugh M. Raup, "Charles C. Adams, 1873–1955," *Annals of the Association of American Geographers* 49 (1959): 164–67.

45. Mitman, *State of Nature*, 44.

46. Adams, *Guide to the Study*, 3.

47. Mitman, *State of Nature*, 46.

48. Adams, *Guide to the Study*, 6, 7.

49. Adams, *Guide to the Study*, 41.

50. Adams, *Guide to the Study*, 36, 37, 40.

51. Adams, *Guide to the Study*, 24–26. See Nash, *Wilderness*, 198.

52. Nelson to R. S. Yard, December 30, 1916, file "Yellowstone," box 229, entry 162, RG 22, NACP. See Nash, *Wilderness*, 141–60 for a discussion of these ideas that he associates with the wilderness movement.

53. Thomas R. Dunlap, *Saving America's Wildlife* (Princeton: Princeton University Press, 1988), 49–50.

54. Dunlap, *Saving America's Wildlife*, 53–54, quote on 53; Alden H. Miller, "Joseph Grinnell," *Systematic Zoology* 13 (1964): 235–42, esp. 236; and Elizabeth Noble Shor, "Joseph Grinnell," *Dictionary of Scientific Biography*, 545.

55. Wayne Hanley, *Natural History in America: From Mark Catesby to Rachel Carson* (New York: Quadrangle, 1977).

56. Frank N. Egerton, "Changing Concepts of the Balance of Nature," *Quarterly Review of Biology* 48 (1973): 322–50, esp. 324, 335, 341.

57. Grinnell and Storer, "Animal Life as an Asset," *Science* n.s., 44, no. 1133, September 15, 1916, 375–80.

58. Grinnell and Storer, "Animal Life as an Asset," 378.

59. Grinnell and Storer, "Animal Life as an Asset," 378.

60. Grinnell and Storer, "Animal Life as an Asset," 379.

61. Vernon Bailey to Robert S. Yard, September 27, 1917, file "Yellowstone," box 229, entry 162, RG 22, NACP.

62. Ecological Society of America, Committee on the Preservation of Natural Conditions, *Preservation of Natural Conditions* (Springfield IL: Schnepp & Barnes, 1922); Croker, *Pioneer Ecologist*, 123–24; Robert L. Burgess, "The Ecological Society of America," in Egerton, ed., *History of American Ecology*, 1–23; Charles C. Adams, "Ecological Conditions in National Forests and in National Parks," *Scientific Monthly* 20 (June 1925): 561–93.

63. Barrington Moore, "Importance of Natural Conditions in National Parks," in George Bird Grinnell and Charles Sheldon, eds., *Hunting and Conservation* (New Haven: Yale University Press, 1925), 340–55, quote on 353.

64. Charles C. Adams, "Roosevelt Wild Life State Memorial," *Roosevelt Wild Life Bulletin* 1 (December 1921): 11–17.

65. Jane Maienschein, *100 Years Exploring Life, 1888–1988: The Marine Biological Laboratory at Woods Hole* (Boston: Jones and Bartlett Publishers, 1989), 23.

66. See Charles C. Adams, "Suggestions for Research on North American Big Game and Fur-bearing Animals," *Roosevelt Wild Life Bulletin* 1 (December 1921): 34–41.

67. Haines, *Yellowstone Story*, vol. 2, 274, 366.

68. Elizabeth Noble Shor, "Joseph Grinnell," *Dictionary of Scientific Biography*, vol. 12, 545; on Heller, see Dunlap, *Saving America's Wildlife*, 54.

69. See staff lists in *Roosevelt Wild Life Bulletin* vol. 1, August 1922, and vol. 2, February 1924.

70. Milton P. Skinner, "The Birds of the Yellowstone National Park," *Roosevelt Wild Life Bulletin* 3 (February 1925): 7–189; and Skinner, "The Predatory and Fur-Bearing Animals of the Yellowstone National Park," *Roosevelt Wild Life Bulletin* 4 (June 1927): 163–281.

71. Milton P. Skinner, *The Bears of Yellowstone* (Chicago: A. C. McClurg, 1925), 35, 44.

72. Skinner, *Bears of Yellowstone*, 57, 45.

73. Moore, "Importance of Natural Conditions," 340, 344.

74. Moore, "Importance of Natural Conditions," 347.

75. Moore, "Importance of Natural Conditions," 344.

76. "Hough Puts the Blame upon the Forest Service," *New York Evening Post*, February 5, 1921, 11, file "Yellowstone," box 229, entry 162, RG 22, NACP.

77. James McBride, Chief Ranger's Report. December 1920, file "Part 9," box 243, entry central files, RG 79, NACP.

78. C. Frank Brockman, "Park Naturalists and the Evolution of National Park Service

Interpretation through World War II," *Journal of Forest History* 21 (January 1978): 24–43, esp. 30; Denise S. Vick, "Yellowstone National Park and the Education of Adults," Ph.D. diss., University of Wyoming, 1986. See also Lee Whittlesey, *Yellowstone's Horse-and-Buggy Tour Guides: Interpreting the Grand Old Park, 1872–1920*, unpublished ms., YNPL.

79. Chester Lindsley, Monthly Report, December 1920, box 243, central files, RG 79, NACP.

80. Brockman, "Park Naturalists," 24–43, esp. 31.

81. George C. Ruhle, "Importance of Scientific Research in the National Parks," in *Proceedings of the First Park Naturalists' Training Conference*, November 1–30, 1929, YNPL, 151.

82. Dorr G. Yeager, "Making an Inventory of Our Scientific Assets," in *Proceedings of the First Park Naturalists' Training Conference*, November 1–30, 1929, YNPL.

83. C. Frank Brockman, "The Place of the Park Naturalist in the Research Program," in *Proceedings of the First Park Naturalists' Training Conference*, November 1–30, 1929, YNPL, 158.

84. Dorr G. Yeager, "Recorded Scientific Information and Its Bearing on the General Park Administrative Program," in *Proceedings of the First Park Naturalists' Training Conference*, November 1–30, 1929, YNPL, 164.

85. Alfred Runte, *Yosemite: The Embattled Wilderness* (Lincoln: University of Nebraska Press, 1990), 135.

86. R. Gerald Wright, *Wildlife Research and Management in the National Parks* (Chicago: University of Illinois Press, 1991), 13.

87. Robert Sterling Yard, "The People and the National Parks," *The Survey* 48, 13 (August 1, 1922): 550.

88. Horace M. Albright, Superintendent's Monthly Report, April 1921, file "Part 9," box 243, entry central files, RG 79, NACP.

89. Cammerer to Albright, September 30, 1926, file "Yellowstone," box 484, entry 7, RG 79, NACP.

90. Sam T. Woodring, "Predatory Animals," *Ranger Naturalists Manual of Yellowstone National Park*, June 1, 1929, YNPL.

91. Brockman, "Park Naturalists," 43.

92. Runte, *National Parks*, 134.

93. Marguerite S. Shaffer, "'See America First': Re-Envisioning Nation and Region through Western Tourism," *Pacific Historical Review* 45 (November 1996): 559–81; and Marguerite Sands Shaffer, "See America First: Tourism and National Identity, 1905–30," Ph.D. diss., Harvard University, 1994.

94. Haines, *Yellowstone Story*, vol. 2, 134–40, 267–75.

95. See Paul S. Sutter, "Driven Wild: The Intellectual and Cultural Origins of Wilderness Advocacy during the Interwar Years," Ph.D. diss., University of Kansas, 1997; see also Stephen Fox, "We Want No Straddlers," *Wilderness* 48 (Winter 1984): 5–19.

96. Shankland, *Steve Mather*, 255; Linda Flint McClelland, *Presenting Nature: The Historic Landscape Design of the National Park Service, 1916 to 1942* (Washington DC: National Park Service, 1993), 6; Ethan Carr, *Wilderness by Design: Landscape Architecture and the National Park Service* (Lincoln: University of Nebraska Press, 1998), 81–92.

97. Sellars, *Preserving Nature*, 88–90.

98. See Keith R. Benson, "From Museum Research to Laboratory Research: The Transformation of Natural History into Academic Biology," 49–86, in Ronald Rainger, Keith R. Benson, and Jane Maienschein, eds., *The American Development of Biology* (Philadelphia: University of Pennsylvania Press, 1988).

99. Bo Sweeney [assistant secretary, Dept. Interior] to Barton W. Evermann, March 29, 1915, file "Wild Animals/Elk/Part 1–4," box 254, entry 6, RG 79, NACP.

100. Barton W. Evermann, to Mark R. Daniels, March 11, 1915, file "Wild Animals," box 254, entry 6, RG 79, NACP.

101. Barton W. Evermann to Stephen T. Mather, December 1, 1919, file "Wild Animals," box 254, entry 6, RG 79, NACP.

102. G. O. Shields to Dr. Palmer, February 11, 1910, file 1, entry 162, box 230, RG 22, NACP.

103. Lee H. Whittlesey, *Yellowstone Place Names* (Helena: Montana Historical Society Press, 1988), 59.

104. "Bow and Arrow Men Find Bruin Needs Some Brake," *Livingston Enterprise*, n.d. [c. June 1–14, 1920], file "Wild Animals," box 254, entry 6, RG 79, NACP.

105. Saxton Pope to Mather, August 28, 1920, file "Wild Animals," box 254, entry 6, RG 79, NACP.

106. Horace Albright to director NPS July 5, 1920, file "Wild Animals," box 254, entry 6, RG 79, NACP.

107. Pope to Mather, August 28, 1920, file "Wild Animals," box 254, entry 6, RG 79, NACP.

108. Albright to Evermann, July 5, 1920, file "Wild Animals/Elk Part 1," box 254, entry 6, RG 79 NACP.

109. Albright to director NPS, June 21, 1920, file "Wild Animals," box 254, entry 6, RG 79, NACP.

110. Pope to Albright, July 12, 1920, file "Wild Animals," box 254, entry 6, RG 79, NACP.

111. Saxton Pope to Charles Adams, November 9, 1920, box 52, Charles C. Adams Papers, Western Michigan University Archives, Kalamazoo MI (hereafter cited as WMUA).

112. Albright to director NPS, June 21, 1920, file "Wild Animals," box 254, entry 6, RG 79, NACP.

113. Pope to Mather, August 28, 1920, file "Wild Animals," box 254, entry 6, RG 79, NACP.

114. Saxton Pope, "Hunting Grizzly with the Bow: That the Age-old Implement of the Chase Still Holds Its Place among Modern Weapons Is Conclusively Proved by Two California Sportsmen," *Forest and Stream/Rod and Gun* 40 (October 1920): 533–36, 565–68.

115. Harry S. New to Mather, August 23, 1920, file "Wild Animals," box 254, entry 6, RG 79, NACP.

116. Albright to Stanley A. Easton, April 15, 1924, file "Wild Animals," box 254, entry 6, RG 79, NACP.

117. Fox, *John Muir and His Legacy*, 162.

118. Arthur C. Ringland, "Our National Parks and National Forests," [with comment by Robert Sterling Yard], c. 1926, box 187, J. C. Merriam Collection, LOC.

119. National Parks Association, "National Park Standards," file NPA, box 16, entry 19, RG 79, NACP.

120. See *Roosevelt Wild Life Bulletin* 1 (August 1922): 104–5.

121. Robert H. Rose, "Hermon Carey Bumpus," August 3, 1971, file B-B88-hc, American Heritage Center, University of Wyoming (hereafter cited as AHC); Hermon Carey Bumpus Jr., *Hermon Carey Bumpus: Yankee Naturalist* (Minneapolis: University of Minnesota Press, 1947).

122. Bumpus's proposal can be found in box 187, J. C. Merriam papers, LOC.

123. Letter R. S. Yard to John C. Merriam, May 18, 1928, box 187, J. C. Merriam papers, LOC.

124. John C. Merriam, "Inspiration and Education in National Parks," Typescript, n.d. [c. 1927], 3, box 187, J. C. Merriam Papers, LOC.

125. Merriam, "Inspiration and Education," 3.

126. Minutes, Annual Meeting, Trustees of the National Parks Association, May 19, 1927, p. 7, box 187, J. C. Merriam Papers, LOC.

127. Letter John C. Merriam to Committee on Study of Educational Problems in National Parks, December 26, 1929, box 132, J. C. Merriam Papers, LOC.

128. H. M. Albright to Wyoming Fish and Game Commission, June 22, 1926, box N-90, NAYNP.

129. Swain, *Wilderness Defender*, ix. On the greater Yellowstone movement, see Haines, *Yellowstone Story*, vol. 2, 319–36.

130. Haines, *Yellowstone Story*, vol. 2, 332.

131. H. M. Albright to Wyoming Fish and Game Commission, June 22, 1926, box N-90, NAYNP.

132. This definition of the northern range is from William Rush, "Northern Yellowstone Elk Study," Montana Fish and Game Commission, April 1932, 71.

133. Rush, "Northern Yellowstone Elk Study," 35.

134. Memo Arthur Ringland to Dr. Bell, September 16, 1929, file "Yellowstone," box 480, entry 7, RG 79, NACP.

135. Yellowstone National Park Boundary Commission, *Final Report* (Washington: GPO, January 5, 1931), 71.

136. Yellowstone National Park Boundary Commission, *Final Report*, 32.

CHAPTER 3 · **Wild Life Division and Ecology of Intervention**

1. Meine, "The Oldest Task in Human History," 7–36.

2. This organization was initially named the "Wild Life Survey," and stayed so until the NPS funded the work in 1932, when the unit was renamed the "Wild Life Division." It kept that name through the spring of 1934, and after that took the name "Wildlife Division." To minimize confusion, the latter name and spelling will be used throughout the narrative.

3. S. T. A. Pickett and Richard S. Ostfeld, "The Shifting Paradigm in Ecology," in Richard L. Knight and Sarah F. Bates, eds., *A New Century for Natural Resources Management* (Washington DC: Island Press, 1995), 261–78.

4. Thomas R. Dunlap, *Saving America's Wildlife* (Princeton: Princeton University Press, 1988), 50–61, 70–79.

5. Richard West Sellars, "The Rise and Decline of Ecological Attitudes in National Park Management, 1929–1940," part 1, *George Wright Forum* 10(1) (1993): 55–78; part 2, "Natural Resource Management under Directors Albright and Cammerer," *George Wright Forum* 10(2) (1993): 79–109; part 3, "Growth and Diversification of the National Park Service," *George Wright Forum* 10(3) (1993): 38–54.

6. Belanger, *Managing American Wildlife*, 10–19.

7. Meine, "The Oldest Task in Human History," 7–36; on taking surplus, see Belanger, *Managing American Wildlife*, 31.

8. Gary G. Gray, *Wildlife and People: The Human Dimensions of Wildlife Ecology* (Urbana: University of Illinois Press, 1993), 164–65; Frederick F. Gilbert and Donald G. Dodds, *The Philosophy and Practice of Wildlife Management*, 2nd ed. (Malabar FL: Krieger, 1992), 6–11.

9. Chase, *Playing God*, 41.

10. Haines, *Yellowstone Story*, vol. 2, 89–93; see also John D. Varley, "A History of Fish Stocking Activities in Yellowstone National Park Between 1881 and 1980," Information Paper no. 35, January 1, 1981, YNPL; John D. Varley and Paul Schullery, *Freshwater Wilderness: Yellowstone Fishes & Their World* (Yellowstone National Park: Yellowstone Library and Museum Association, 1983); Mary Ann Franke, "A Grand Experiment: 100 Years of Fisheries Management in Yellowstone, part 1," *Yellowstone Science* 4 (Fall 1996): 2–7.

11. Varley and Schullery, *Freshwater Wilderness*, 102.

12. Quoted in George W. Miller, "American White Pelican/Pelecanus erythroprhynchos," Yellowstone Park WY, March 31, 1932, box 480, entry 7, RG 79, NACP, 12.

13. George W. Bennett, "Henry Baldwin Ward," in Henry Clepper, ed., *Leaders of American Conservation* (New York: Ronald Press, 1971).

14. Henry B. Ward, "The Pelicans of Yellowstone Lake," 2, box 480, entry 7, RG 79, NACP.

15. Ward, "The Pelicans of Yellowstone Lake," 20, 21.

16. Donald Worster, *Nature's Economy: A History of Ecological Ideas* (Cambridge: Cambridge University Press, 1985), 292–315. See also Matthew D. Evenden, "The Laborers of Nature: Economic Ornithology and the Role of Birds as Agents of Biological Pest Control in North American Agriculture, ca. 1880–1930," *Forest and Conservation History* 39 (1995): 172–83.

17. Harry J. Liek to George W. Miller, January 22, 1932, file "Pelicans/Material," vertical files, YNPL.

18. C. F. Culler to Guy D. Edwards [acting superintendent YNP], November 27, 1931, file "Pelicans/Material," vertical files, YNPL.

19. C. F. Culler to Guy D. Edwards, 385. Charles C. Adams, "The Relation of Wild Life to the Public in National and State Parks," *Roosevelt Wildlife Bulletin* 2, 4 (February 1925), quotes from 383, 384, 385; George W. Miller used long excerpts from Adams in his report, "American White Pelican," 12–14.

20. Foster quoted in letter Toll to Dixon, October 29, 1929, box N-48, NAYNP.

21. Maurice C. Hall, "Investigations at Yellowstone Lake, 1930," August 3, 1930, file "Pelican," vertical files, YNPL.

22. Hall, "Investigations."

23. J. C. Merriam to Albright, March 16, 1929, box 3, John Campbell Merriam Papers, LOC.

24. R. Gerald Wright, *Wildlife Research and Management in the National Parks* (Urbana: University of Illinois Press, 1992), 14.

25. George M. Wright, Joseph S. Dixon, and Ben H. Thompson, *A Preliminary Survey of Faunal Relations in National Parks* (Fauna Series no. 1), May 1932 (Washington DC: National Park Service, GPO, 1933), iv; Ben H. Thompson, "George Melendez Wright: A Biographical Sketch," *George Wright Forum* 7, 2 (1990): 2–8; Harold C. Bryant, "George Melendez Wright-Roger Wolcott Toll" [Obituary], *Journal of Mammalogy* 17 (1936): 191–92; Richard West Sellars, *Preserving Nature*, 95.

26. Letter Dixon to Bryant, July 18, 1930, box 480, entry 7, RG 79, NACP.

27. "Park Service Dooms Killers of Trumpeter Swans," *Washington Star*, September 29, 1931, file "Trumpeter Swan," box 480, entry 7, RG 79, NACP.

28. Letter Wright to director NPS, August 25, 1931, file "Trumpeter Swan," box 480, entry 7, RG-79, NACP.

29. Letter Dixon to Bryant, July 18, 1930, box 480, entry 7, RG 79, NACP.

30. See Jane Maienschein, *Transforming Traditions in American Biology, 1880–1915* (Baltimore: Johns Hopkins University Press, 1991).

31. Ben H. Thompson, "American White Pelican," February 12, 1932, 5, 10. file "Pelicans/Material," vertical files, YNPL.

32. Thompson, "American White Pelican," 7.

33. Thompson, "American White Pelican," 10.

34. Letter Ben H. Thompson to Toll, February 12, 1932, file "Pelicans/Material," vertical files, YNPL.

35. Miller, "American White Pelican," 32.

36. Memo Baggley to Toll, April 5, 1932, file "Pelicans," vertical files, YNPL.

37. Memo Toll to Baggley, April 21, 1932, file "Pelicans/Material," vertical files, YNPL.

38. George B. Hartzog Jr., *Battling for the National Parks* (Mt. Kisco NY: Moyer Bell, 1988), 107.

39. Felton Gibbons and Deborah Strom, *Neighbors to the Birds: A History of Birdwatching in America* (New York: W. W. Norton, 1988), 143–46.

40. Emergency Conservation Committee, "The Last of the White Pelican," Pamphlet, June 1931, file "Pelicans," vertical files, YNPL.

41. Dunlap, *Saving America's Wildlife*, 56, 78.

42. W. L. McAtee. "A Little Essay on Vermin," *Bird Lore* 33 (November–December 1931): 381–84, quote on 383.

43. Letter Guy D. Edwards to Captain F. C. Culler, November 11, 1931, file "Pelicans," vertical files, YNPL.

44. Letter Foster to Guy D. Edwards, June 15, 1932, file "Birds," box 1, entry 35, RG 79, NACP.

45. David Madsen, Typescript, 5 p., May 10, 1932, box 4, entry 35, RG 79, NACP.

46. Letter Guy D. Edwards to the director, May 21, 1932, file "Pelicans," vertical files, YNPL.

47. Letter Cammerer to Toll, May 28, 1932, file "Pelicans," vertical files, YNPL.

48. Letter Guy D. Edwards to Frank R. Oastler, October 19, 1932, file "Birds/Pelicans," box 480, entry 7, RG 79, NACP.

49. Letter Guy D. Edwards to Frank R. Oastler, October 19, 1932.

50. Emergency Conservation Committee, "The Slaughter of the Yellowstone Park Pelicans," Pamphlet, September 1932, file "Birds/Pelicans," box 480, entry 7, RG 79, NACP.

51. Memo Albright to H. C. Bryant [with Bryant's annotation], November 28, 1932, file "Birds/Pelicans," box 480, entry 7, RG 79, NACP.

52. Letter Harry McGuire to Albright, December 27, 1932, file "Birds/Pelicans," box 480, entry 7, RG 79, NACP.

53. This three-page lampoon can be found in box 480, entry 7, RG 79, NACP.

54. Robin Doughty, *Feather Fashions and Bird Preservation: A Study in Nature Protection* (Berkeley: University of California Press, 1975); Mark V. Barrow Jr., "Birds and Boundaries: Community, Practice, and Conservation in North American Ornithology, 1865–1935," Ph.D. diss., Harvard University, 1992; Oliver H. Orr Jr., *Saving American Birds: T. Gilbert Pearson and the Founding of the Audubon Movement* (Gainesville: University Press of Florida, 1992).

55. Letter Frank Oastler to Gilbert Pearson, October 13, 1932, file "Birds/Pelicans," box 480, entry 7, RG 79, NACP.

56. Letter Frank F. Gander to secretary of the interior, November 28, 1932, file "Birds/Pelicans," box 480, entry 7, RG 79, NACP.

57. Letter Walter B. Sheppard to Albright, December 17, 1932, file "Birds/Pelicans," box 480, entry 7, RG 79, NACP.

58. Letter Albright to Pearson, October 17, 1932, file "Birds/Pelicans," box 480, entry 7, RG 79, NACP.

59. Letter John B. May to Albright, November 4, 1932, file "Birds/Pelicans," box 480, entry 7, RG 79, NACP.

60. Letter Albright to A. B. Howell, November 10, 1932, file "Birds/Pelicans," box 480, entry 7, RG 79, NACP.

61. Dunlap, *Saving America's Wildlife*, 80.

62. Quoted in Letter Albright to superintendent Yellowstone, January 15, 1929, file "Bears," box 481, entry 7, RG 79, NACP.

63. Naomi Crowlin to Department of the Interior, July 16, 1930, file "Bears," box 481, entry 7, RG 79, NACP.

64. E. L. Quinn, September 11, 1929, file "1929–31," box N-48, NAYNP.

65. M. P. Skinner, "June Notes on the Animals," 1921, file "Superintendent's Monthly Reports, Part 9," box 243, RG 79, NACP.

66. Albright to Dixon, November 9, 1931, file "1929–31," box N-48, NAYNP.

67. A. E. Demaray to F. S. Montgomery, September 19, 1936, file unmarked, box N-48, NAYNP.

68. A. E. Demaray to F. S. Montgomery, September 19, 1936, 4.

69. Dixon to Albright, December 15, 1931, file "Bears, Part 2," box 481, RG 79, NACP.

70. Dixon to Albright, December 15, 1931.

71. Dixon to Albright, December 15, 1931, 8.

72. Wright to Toll, August 25, 1931, file "1929–31," box N-48, NAYNP.

73. Memo Rush to Toll, August 10, 1931, box N-52, NAYNP.

74. Memo Rush to Toll, August 10, 1931.

75. Rush to Dixon, September 6, 1931, file "1929–31," box N-48, NAYNP.

76. E. T. Scoyen to Guy D. Edwards, January 18, 1932, box N-52, NAYNP.

77. O. A. Tomlinson to Dixon, January 14, 1932, box N-52, NAYNP.

78. Toll to Wright, September 22, 1932, box N-52, NAYNP.

79. Francis D. LaNoue, "A Suggested Plan for Controlling Destructive Bears," March 4, 1933, file 9, box 2, Olaus Murie Collection, Denver Public Library (hereafter cited as DPL).

80. Wright to Toll, August 25, 1931, file "1929–31," box N-48, NAYNP.

81. David H. Madsen to Toll, August 20, 1931, file "1929–31," box N-48, NAYNP.

82. Wright to Toll, August 25, 1931, file "1929–31," box N-48, NAYNP.

83. Joseph Dixon, "Report on the Bear Situation in Yellowstone," September 1929, file "1929–31," box N-48, NAYNP.

84. Memo Rush to Toll, August 10, 1931, box N-52, NAYNP.

85. Madsen to Dixon, January 13, 1932, file "Bears," box 1, entry 35, RG 79, NACP.

86. Albright to Dixon, November 9, 1931, file "1929–31," box N-48, NAYNP.

87. Albright to Evermann, March 20, 1931, file "1929–31," box N-48, NAYNP.

88. Ann Sutton and Myron Sutton, "Harold Bryant, Pioneer," *Nature Magazine* 48 (January 1955): 38–40; Marcus Kraus, "Science Education in the National Parks of the United States," Ph.D. diss., New York University, 1973, 139.

89. H. C. Bryant to Wright, October 16, 1931, file "1929–31," box N-48, NAYNP.

90. Dixon to Bryant, October 28, 1931, file "1929–31," box N-48, NAYNP.

91. YNP superintendent's office to director NPS, October 1, 1931, box N-52, NAYNP.

92. Dixon to Madsen, January 4, 1932.

93. Albright to Evermann, March 20, 1931, file "1929–31," box N-48, NAYNP.

94. W. M. Rush, "Northern Yellowstone Elk Study," Montana Fish and Game Commission, April 1932, 64.

95. Albright to Dixon, November 9, 1931, file "1929–31," box N-48, NAYNP.

96. Madsen to Dixon, January 13, 1932, file "Bears," box 1, entry 35, RG 79, NACP.

97. C. Max Bauer to Thompson, August 27, 1934, box N-48, NAYNP.

98. Thompson to Bauer, September 3, 1934, box N-48, NAYNP.

99. Memo Rush to Toll, August 10, 1931, box N-52, NAYNP.

100. George F. Baggley, "Outline of Method for Bear Control," May 10, 1932, box N-52, NAYNP.

101. Toll to Wright, September 22, 1932, box N-52, NAYNP.

102. Toll to Wright, September 22, 1932.

103. Toll to Wright, September 22, 1932, box N-52, NAYNP.

104. Madsen to Toll, June 14, 1933, file "Bears," box 1, entry 35, RG 79, NACP.

105. Baggley, "Outline of Method."

106. Albright to Dixon, November 9, 1931, file "1929–31," box N-48, NAYNP.

107. Forage utilization habits of elk can be gleaned from YNP Annual Wildlife Reports, especially 1967–68, and from scientific studies such as Glen F. Cole, "The Elk of Grand Teton and Southern Yellowstone National Parks," Yellowstone National Park: National Park Service, 1969, 1978.

108. Milton P. Skinner, "The Predatory and Fur-Bearing Animals," 163–281; Schullery and Whittlesey, "Documentary Record of Wolves," 1-1 to 1-173.

109. Rush, "Northern Yellowstone Elk Study," 42.

110. Rush, "Northern Yellowstone Elk Study," 64; see also Yellowstone National Park, "Wildlife Management Background Information," December 4, 1964, file "Elk Management Program 1967," box N-70, NAYNP.

111. Rush, "Northern Yellowstone Elk Study," 48.

112. Rush, "Northern Yellowstone Elk Study," 72.

113. Rush, "Northern Yellowstone Elk Study," 73.

114. Rush, "Northern Yellowstone Elk Study," 119.

115. Ronald C. Tobey, Saving the Prairies: The Life Cycle of the Founding School of American Plant Ecology, 1895–1955 (Berkeley: University of California Press, 1981), 68.

116. Rush, "Northern Yellowstone Elk Study," 120.

117. Rush, "Northern Yellowstone Elk Study," 65, 126.

118. Rush, "Northern Yellowstone Elk Study," 65, 66.

119. Biographical material on Olaus Murie can be found in Robert L. Casebeer, "Olaus Johan Murie, 1889–1963," Journal of Wildlife Management 28 (1964): 191–92; Larry Roop, "A Man to Remember: Olaus Murie," Wyoming Wildlife (December 1970): 15–17; Peter Wild, Pioneer Conservationists of Western America (Missoula MT: Mountain Press, 1979), 121. Quote from Yellowstone National Park Boundary Commission, Final Report, Washington DC: GPO, January 5, 1931, 71.

120. Daniel Bruce Tyers, "The Condition of the Northern Winter Range in Yellowstone National Park—A Discussion of the Controversy," master's thesis, Montana State University, 1981, 24.

121. Rush, "Northern Yellowstone Elk Study," 66, 127.

122. Rush, "Northern Yellowstone Elk Study," 81, 127.

123. Rush, "Northern Yellowstone Elk Study," 66, 81, 127.

124. Rush, "Northern Yellowstone Elk Study," 87–88, 124.

125. Rush, "Northern Yellowstone Elk Study," 67.

126. Tobey, Saving the Prairies, 152–53; Jerry L. Holechek, Rex D. Pieper, and Carlton H. Herbel, Range Management: Principles and Practices, 2nd ed. (Englewood Cliffs NJ: Prentice Hall, 1995), 50–53.

127. W. Leslie Pengelly, "Thunder on the Yellowstone," Naturalist 14 (1963): 18–25, 22; Holechek, Pieper, and Herbel, Range Management, 177–78; John Macnab, "Carry-

ing Capacity and Related Slippery Shibboleths," *Wildlife Society Bulletin* 13 (1985): 403–10.

128. C. John Burk, "The Kaibab Deer Incident: A Long–Persisting Myth," *BioScience* 23 (February 1973).

129. Thomas Dunlap, "That Kaibab Myth," *Journal of Forest History* 32 (1988): 60–68, see also 258–90; Dunlap, "Values for Varmits: Predator Control and Environmental Ideas, 1920–1939," *Pacific History Review* 53 (1984): 141–61; Dunlap, *Saving America's Wildlife*, 48–61.

130. Daniel B. Botkin, *Discordant Harmonies: A New Ecology for the Twenty–First Century* (New York: Oxford University Press, 1990), 80–89, 54–56, 32–49; Frank N. Egerton, "Changing Concepts of the Balance of Nature," *Quarterly Review of Biology* 48 (1973): 322–50.

131. Adams, *Guide to the Study of Animal Ecology*, 28.

132. Charles C. Adams, "The Importance of Preserving Wilderness Conditions," New York State Museum Bulletin, 1929, p. 41, file "Parks," box 150, entry 7, NACP.

133. Adams, "The Importance of Preserving Wilderness Conditions," 41, italics in original.

134. Wright and Thompson, *Wildlife Management*, 85.

135. Wright and Thompson, *Wildlife Management*, 86.

136. Roger W. Toll, Superintendent's Report, 1934.

137. See elk reduction files, boxes N-64 to N-67, N-70, NAYNP.

138. See elk reduction files, boxes N-64 to N-67, N-70, NAYNP.

139. Yellowstone National Park, "A Cooperative Management Plan for the Northern Yellowstone Elk Herd and Its Habitat," 1967, file "Elk Management Program 1967," box N-70, NAYNP.

140. The best accounts are Dunlap, "Values for Varmits"; Dunlap, *Saving America's Wildlife*; and Worster, *Nature's Economy*.

141. Wright, Dixon, and Thompson, *A Preliminary Survey*, 35.

142. Richard West Sellars, "Natural Resource Management under Directors Albright and Cammerer," *George Wright Forum* 10, 2 (1993): 79–109, 94.

143. Wright and Thompson, *Wildlife Management*, 71.

144. Alan MacEachern, "Rationality and Rationalization in Canadian National Parks Predator Policy," in Chad Gaffield and Pam Gaffield, eds., *Consuming Canada: Readings in Environmental History* (Toronto: Copp Clark, 1995), 197–212, esp. 199.

145. Wright, Dixon, and Thompson, *A Preliminary Survey*, 147.

146. Biographical material on Adolph Murie can be found in box 2, Adolph Murie Collection, AHC; see Dunlap, *Saving America's Wildlife*, 74–77.

147. Adolph Murie, *Ecology of the Coyote in the Yellowstone*, Fauna Series, no. 4 (Washington DC: GPO, 1940), 122.

148. A. Murie, *Ecology of the Coyote*, 43–45, 118.

149. Olaus Murie to Dr. Harold E. Anthony, December 5, 1945, file "Correspondence 1945," box 1, Olaus J. and Margaret Murie Collection, AHC.

150. Sellars, "The Rise and Decline of Ecological Attitudes," 55–78, quote on 65.

151. Wright, Dixon, and Thompson, *A Preliminary Survey*, 37.

152. Wright and Thompson, *Wildlife Management*, 52.

153. Wright and Thompson, *Wildlife Management*, iv, 25.

154. Wright and Thompson, *Wildlife Management*, 3, 13.

155. Wright, Dixon, and Thompson, *A Preliminary Survey*, 54, 80.

156. Wright and Thompson, *Wildlife Management*, 25.

157. Wright, Dixon, and Thompson, *A Preliminary Survey*, 5.

158. Harold C. Bryant, "George Melendez Wright-Roger Wolcott Toll," [Obituary], *Journal of Mammalogy* 17 (1936): 191–92; R. Gerald Wright, "The Evolution of Science in the National Parks and Its Impact on Wildlife Management," Typescript, Appendix I, YNPL; R. Gerald Wright, *Wildlife Research and Management*, 18.

159. Bryant, "George Melendez Wright-Roger Wolcott Toll," 191–92.

CHAPTER 4 · **Managing the Natural during the Postwar Era**

1. George B. Hartzog Jr., *Battling for the National Parks* (Mt. Kisco NY: Moyer Bell, 1988), 81.

2. Letter Drury to Lawrence C. Merriam, March 28, 1951, file "Merriam," box 12, entry 19, RG 79, NACP.

3. Hartzog, *Battling for the National Parks*, 83; Mark W. T. Harvey, *A Symbol of Wilderness: Echo Park and the American Conservation Movement* (Albuquerque: University of New Mexico Press, 1994), 101–4.

4. R. Gerald Wright, "The Evolution of Science."

5. File "Personnel Information," box 1, Maynard Barrows Collection, AHC.

6. John M. Good [YNP chief naturalist, 1963–68], interview, July 26, 1995.

7. National Park Service, "An Information Manual of Yellowstone National Park," 1945, 103.

8. Memo Rogers to regional director, May 12, 1943, file "Nature Study," box 145, RG 79, National Archives–Central Plains Region, Kansas City (hereafter cited as NACPR).

9. Absaroka Wildlife Conservation Committee, minutes of meeting [hereafter cited as ACC minutes], May 9, 1943, box N-25, NAYNP; unless listed otherwise, all ACC minutes are from box N-25.

10. ACC minutes, May 6–7, 1944, 5.

11. Gilbert and Dodds, *Philosophy and Practice of Wildlife Management*, 80, see also 106, 109.

12. ACC minutes, May 9, 1943, 5.

13. ACC minutes, September 25–26, 1943, 8, 9.

14. A. Murie, *Ecology of the Coyote*, 147, 148.

15. ACC minutes, September 25–26, 1943, 8, 9.

16. ACC minutes, September 23–24, 1950, 6.

17. ACC minutes, September 23–24, 1950, 6, 8.

18. ACC minutes, May 26–27, 1951, 4, 5.

19. Memo Rogers to Region Two director, September 26, 1950, box N-25, NAYNP.

20. ACC minutes, May 26–27, 1951, 5.

21. ACC minutes, May 27–28, 1950, 26.

22. ACC minutes, October 6–7, 1951, 5.

23. Olaus J. Murie, *The Elk of North America* (Harrisburg PA: Stackpole, 1951), 315.

24. ACC minutes, May 6–7, 1944, 7.

25. ACC minutes, September 21–22, 1946, 3, 12.

26. ACC minutes, October 4–5, 1947, 11.

27. ACC minutes, September 21–22, 1946, 10.

28. See R. L. Grimm, "Northern Yellowstone Winter Range Studies," *Journal of Wildlife Management* 3 (1939): 295–306.

29. V. H. Cahalane, "Wildlife Surpluses in the National Parks," *Transactions of the North American Wildlife Conference* 6 (1941): 355–61; Cahalane, "Elk Management and Herd Regulation—Yellowstone National Park," *Transactions of the North American Wildlife Conference* 8 (1943): 95–101.

30. ACC minutes, May 15–16, 1948, 15.

31. Rush, "Northern Yellowstone Elk Study," 77.

32. Rush, "Northern Yellowstone Elk Study," 7, 13.

33. ACC minutes, May 6–7, 1944, 2.

34. O. Murie, *Elk of North America*, 289.

35. ACC minutes, September 18–19, 1948, 19.

36. ACC minutes, September 18–19, 1948, 22.

37. ACC minutes, May 14–15, 1949, 11.

38. ACC minutes, May 14–15, 1949, 12.

39. ACC minutes, May 14–15, 1949, 10.

40. ACC minutes, September 17–18, 1949, 8, 9.

41. Letter Rogers to ACC, August 29, 1949, reprinted in ACC minutes, September 17–18, 1949, 3–4.

42. ACC minutes, May 24–25, 1952, 10.

43. Memo Howard W. Baker to YNP superintendent, November 7, 1952; with ACC minutes, September 1952, box N-25, NAYNP.

44. ACC minutes, May 16–17, 1953, 14, 26.

45. ACC minutes, May 22–23, 1954, 10.

46. ACC minutes, May 22–23, 1954, 13.

47. ACC minutes, May 22–23, 1954, 10, 13, 15.

48. Meine, "The Oldest Task in Human History," 7–36.

49. Olaus Murie to Newton B. Drury, January 11, 1951, file "National Park Service," box 3, Olaus Murie Collection, Western History Collection, DPL.

50. Memo Drury to secretary of the interior, December 14, 1943, box N-52, NAYNP.

51. Wright and Thompson, *Wildlife Management*, 60.

52. Memo Rogers to director, August 26, 1940, file "YNP," box 26, entry 19, RG 79, NACP.

53. Memo superintendent to director, March 20, 1941, file "Buffalo–Vol. 1," box 147, RG 79, NACPR.

54. ACC minutes, May 6–7, 1944, 3.

55. ACC minutes, May 6–7, 1944, 4.

56. Victor H. Cahalane, "Restoration of Wild Bison," April 22, 1944, 6, document no. D-486, NPS Technical Information Center, Denver (hereafter cited as NPS–TIC).

57. Cahalane, "Restoration of Wild Bison," 9.

58. Memo Lawrence C. Merriam to director, April 14, 1948.

59. Drury to Butcher, December 4, 1943, file "National Parks Association," box 16, entry 19, RG 79, NACP.

60. Albright to Drury, October 29, 1943, file "Bison-YNP," box 25, entry 19, RG 79, NACP.

61. Albright to Drury, December 1, 1943, file "Bison-YNP," box 25, entry 19, RG 79, NACP.

62. Drury to Albright, December 8, 1943, file "Bison-YNP," box 25, entry 19, RG 79, NACP.

63. Drury to Albright, January 7, 1944, file "Bison-YNP," box 25, entry 19, RG 79, NACP.

64. Albright to Drury, February 25, 1944, file "Bison-YNP," box 25, entry 19, RG 79, NACP.

65. Drury to Albright, March 11, 1944, file "Bison-YNP," box 25, entry 19, RG 79, NACP.

66. "Comments on Lamar Bison," 20, file "Bison," box 2, Olaus Murie Collection, DPL.

67. Memo Drury to secretary of the interior, December 14, 1943, box N-52, NAYNP.

68. Drury to Albright, December 8, 1943, file "Bison-YNP," box 25, entry 19, RG 79, NACP.

69. Rush, "Northern Yellowstone Elk Study," 108. See also Whittlesey, "Cows All Over the Place!"

70. Memo YNP superintendent to director, November 15, 1941, 2, box N-52, NAYNP.

71. Olaus J. Murie to Drury, March 24, 1944, file "Bear," box 2, Olaus Murie Papers, DPL.

72. Ralph Miller to NPS, August 17, 1938, file unmarked, box N-48, NAYNP.

73. Robert L. Daugherty to Joe [Dixon], July 16, 1940, file unmarked, box N-48, NAYNP.

74. Memo Cahalane to director, October 8, 1937, file unmarked, box N-48, NAYNP.

75. "Report of Personal Injury," June 22, 1958, box 3, RG 79, NACPR.

76. Memo superintendent YNP to director, November 15, 1941, box N-52, NAYNP.

77. Memo Joseph S. Dixon to Victor H. Cahalane, January 3, 1941, file unmarked, box N-48, NAYNP.

78. Edmund B. Rogers to P. C. Gontard, September 10, 1942, box N-52, NAYNP.

79. Memo Drury to secretary of the interior, September 15, 1944, file "Yellowstone," box 26, entry 19, RG 79, NACP.

80. Olaus J. Murie to W. B. Bell, May 21, 1943, file "9–Bears," box 2, Olaus Murie Collection, DPL.

81. Memo Drury to [unnamed; numerous recipients], c. December 10, 1945, vertical files, YNPL.

82. Olaus J. Murie, "Progress Report on the Yellowstone Bear Study," Summer 1943, 2, box 1, Adolph Murie Collection, AHC.

83. Murie, "Progress Report," 11.

84. Letter Rogers to W. D. Trueblood, September 13, 1944, box N-52, NAYNP.

85. Memo L. C. Merriam to the director, April 22, 1943, box N-52, NAYNP.

86. Olaus J. Murie, "Report on Study of Bears in Yellowstone National Park for the Summer of 1944," 4, box 1, Adolph Murie Collection, AHC.

87. Memo L. C. Merriam to director, April 22, 1943, box N-52, NAYNP.

88. Olaus J. Murie, "Report on Study of Bears," 4.

89. Olaus J. Murie to Newton B. Drury, December 27, 1945, file "Bears," box 2, Olaus Murie Collection, DPL.

90. Wright and Thompson, *Wildlife Management*, 70.

91. George F. Baggley, "Status and Distribution of the Grizzly Bear (Ursus horribilis) in the United States," March 9, 1936, file unmarked, box N-48, NAYNP.

92. Yellowstone National Park, "Circular No. 9," June 14, 1946, box N-52, NAYNP.

93. Memo Drury to [unnamed; numerous recipients], c. December 10, 1945, vertical files, YNPL.

94. Memo superintendent YNP to Region Two director, March 5, 1946, box N-52, NAYNP.

95. Albright to Drury, May 6, 1946, file "Yellowstone," box 26, entry 19, RG 79, NACP.

96. Albright to Drury, September 7, 1944, file "Bison-YNP," box 25, entry 19, RG 79, NACP.

97. Albright to Drury, May 6, 1946, file "Yellowstone," box 26, entry 19, RG 79, NACP.

98. Albright to Drury, July 19, 1944, file "Bison-YNP," box 25, entry 19, RG 79, NACP.

99. Memo Drury to regional director, October 4, 1945, file "YNP," box 26, entry 19, RG 79, NACP.

100. "Excerpts of Comments on the Abolition of 'Bear Show' in Yellowstone National Park," January 5, 1946, p. 1, file "Yellowstone," box 26, entry 19, RG 79, NACP.

101. "Excerpts of Comments on the Abolition of 'Bear Show.'"

102. "Excerpts of Comments on the Abolition of 'Bear Show,'" 2.

103. "Excerpts of Comments on the Abolition of 'Bear Show,'" 6.

104. "Excerpts of Comments on the Abolition of 'Bear Show,'" 5; biographical information from Richard H. Stroud, *National Leaders of American Conservation* (Washington DC: Smithsonian Institution Press, 1985), 345–46.

105. "Excerpts of Comments on the Abolition of 'Bear Show,'" 2.

106. "Excerpts of Comments on the Abolition of 'Bear Show,'" 2.

107. Rogers to Edge, September 6, 1949, box N-52, NAYNP.

108. Memo David de L. Condon to superintendent, December 8, 1958, file "Ecology of the Grizzly Bear," box N-91, NAYNP. David deLancey Condon's name shows up in park documents with a wonderful variety of spellings.

109. Drury to Yard, February 15, 1943, file "Wilderness Society," box 25, entry 19, RG 79, NACP.

110. Drury to Yard, January 7, 1943, file "Wilderness Society," box 25, entry 19, RG 79, NACP.

111. Resolution of the ASM, April 20, 1946, quoted in the Wilderness Society, "Memorandum for the Legislative Reference Service," March 1, 1949, 29–30, file "Wilderness Society," box 25, entry 19, RG 79, NACP.

112. Peter Wild, *Pioneer Conservationists of Western America* (Missoula MT: Mountain Press, 1979), 113–30, esp. 121.

113. Olaus Murie to Frederick Law Olmsted, January 16, 1950, file "Policy in Parks," box 3, Adolph Murie Collection, AHC.

114. Olaus Murie to Frederick Law Olmsted, January 16, 1950, 2, 3. See also Sax, *Mountains Without Handrails*, 10–15, 79–90 for a recent interpretation echoing these themes.

115. Olaus Murie to Frederick Law Olmsted, January 16, 1950, 4, 5.

116. Freeman Tilden, *The National Parks: What They Mean to You and Me* (New York: Alfred A. Knopf, 1951), 18–19.

117. Garrison, *Making of a Ranger*, 285.

118. Garrison, *Making of a Ranger*, 287.

119. Samuel P. Hays, *Beauty, Health, and Permanence: Environmental Politics in the United States, 1955–1985* (Cambridge: Cambridge University Press, 1989).

120. National Park Service, "Preservation of Natural and Wilderness Values in the National Parks," March 1957, vertical files, YNPL.

121. National Park Service, "Preservation of Natural and Wilderness Values," 8, 9.

122. Arthur F. McEvoy, *The Fisherman's Problem: Ecology and Law in the California Fisheries 1850–1980* (Cambridge: Cambridge University Press, 1990), 92.

CHAPTER 5 · **Natural Yellowstone**

1. Runte, *National Parks*, 144.

2. Ted Trueblood, "Too Many Elk," *Field and Stream* (July 1963): 36–39.

3. Letter Lon Garrison to John D. Hunter, March 6, 1980, file A-1 "Lon Garrison," NAYNP.

4. Scott Edward Hanley, "Wildlife Management in Yellowstone National Park, 1962–1976," master's thesis, University of Wyoming, 1992, 10–22; Yellowstone National Park, "Record of Elk Reductions," file "Elk Management Program 1967," box N-70, NAYNP.

5. "Group Wants Hunting," *Billings Gazette*, December 10, 1961; "Nutter Seeks Public Hunting," *Billings Gazette*, December 9, 1961; Hanley, "Wildlife Management," 10–22.

6. "Elk Slaughter Protests Rage On," *Billings Gazette*, December 6, 1961, 18.

7. U.S. Congress, Committee on Interior and Insular Affairs, "Elk Reduction Program in Yellowstone National Park," Bozeman MT, December 18, 1962, YNPL.

8. Letter Lon Garrison to John D. Hunter, March 6, 1980, file A-1 "Lon Garrison," NAYNP; Lemuel A. Garrison interview transcript, box 214, NPS oral history transcripts, Western History Collection, DPL.

9. Hanley, "Wildlife Management," 20; see also W. Leslie Pengelly, "Thunder on the Yellowstone," *Naturalist* 14 (1963): 18–25.

10. Arthur H. Carhart, "Shall We Hunt in the National Parks?" *Sports Afield* (December 1961): 36–37, 100–102.

11. Memo Elt Davis to regional director, December 27, 1960, box N-64, NAYNP.

12. Letter F. Howard Brady to Alden J. Erskine, April 26, 1962, file "Overall Animal Census and Inventory 1957–1962," box N-9, NAYNP.

13. Earl R. Nott, "Report of Show–me Trip," file "Wildlife Management (general) 1957–1962," box N-9, NAYNP.

14. Robert C. Sykes, "Plumbers vs. Plungers," file "Overall Animal Census and Inventory 1957–1962," box N-9, NAYNP.

15. Burton W. Marston to Thomas Kimball, Wildlife Advisory Board, June 5, 1962, box 548, Western History Collection, DPL.

16. R. Gerald Wright, *Wildlife Research and Management*, 23.

17. Lowell Sumner, "Ecological Research in the National Parks of the United States," file "NPS/Other Parks," vertical files, NAYNP; Chase, *Playing God*, 241–42.

18. Wright, *Wildlife Research and Management*, 24.

19. Wright, *Wildlife Research and Management*, 25.

20. Wright, *Wildlife Research and Management*, 25, 26.

21. Wright, *Wildlife Research and Management*, 26; Hanley, "Wildlife Management," 22, 28.

22. Carol Henrietta Leigh Rydell, "Aldo Starker Leopold: Wildlife Biologist and Public Policy Maker," master's thesis, Montana State University, 1993, 65.

23. Aldo Starker Leopold, S. A. Cain, C. M. Cottam, et al., "Wildlife Management in the National Parks" (Washington DC: Advisory Board on Wildlife Management, 1963), 10; the Leopold Report was reprinted in several places, including *Transactions of the North American Wildlife and Natural Resources Conference* 28 (1963): 28–45.

24. Leopold et al., "Wildlife Management," 10.

25. Hanley, "Wildlife Management," 27; William E. Towell to A. Starker Leopold, June 7, 1962, box 548, Western History Collection, DPL. See other correspondence in Envelope 2, box 548, Advisory Board, Western History Collection, DPL.

26. Hanley, "Wildlife Management," 30–31; see also correspondence in Envelope 2, box 548, Advisory Board, Western History Collection, DPL.

27. Allan Lovaas, "People and the Gallatin Elk Herd," Helena MT, Montana Fish and Game Department, 1970, 26–32, 39, 4; see also file "Laws & Legal Matters 1964," box N-77, NAYNP.

28. George Sprugel, Howard Stagner, and Robert M Linn, "National Parks as Natural Science Research Areas," *Trends in Parks & Recreation* 1 (1964); Ronald A. Foresta, *America's National Parks and Their Keepers* (Washington DC: Resources for the Future, 1984), 98.

29. A. Starker Leopold, "Wildlife Management in the Future," presented at Conference of Challenges, Yosemite National Park, c. Fall 1963, 12, file "Wildlife Advisory Board," box 5, Adolph Murie Collection, AHC.

30. Hartzog, *Battling for the National Parks*, 103.

31. Leopold et al., "Wildlife Management," 3.

32. Wright, Dixon, and Thompson, *A Preliminary Survey*, 2.

33. Leopold et al., "Wildlife Management," 12.

34. Leopold et al., "Wildlife Management," 4.

35. Leopold et al., "Wildlife Management," 9, 10.

36. Leopold et al., "Wildlife Management," 10, 11.

37. Adolph Murie, "Comments on Udall's Advisory Board on Wildlife in the National Parks," 1963, file "Leopold Report Murie Comment," box 4, Adolph Murie Collection, AHC.

38. A. Murie, "Comments," 6.

39. Adolph Murie, "A Plea for Idealism in National Parks," c. January 1964, 9, box 1, Adolph Murie Collection, AHC.

40. Memo Adolph Murie to Richard Prasil [Western Region Biologist], January 14, 1964; box 1, Adolph Murie Collection, AHC.

41. A. Murie, "Comments," 9.

42. A. Murie, "Comments," 6, 7.

43. A. Murie, "A Plea for Idealism," 5.

44. A. Murie, "A Plea for Idealism," 7.

45. National Academy of Sciences, "A Report by the Advisory Committee to the National Park Service on Research," Washington DC, 1963, 6, National Park Service Library, Denver (hereafter cited as NPSLD).

46. R. Gerald Wright, *Wildlife Research and Management*, 23–24.

47. National Academy of Sciences, "A Report by the Advisory Committee," xi–xii.

48. National Academy of Sciences, "A Report by the Advisory Committee," x–xi; Wright, *Wildlife Research and Management*, 26.

49. Wright, *Wildlife Research and Management*, 26–27, 32.

50. National Academy of Sciences, "A Report by the Advisory Committee," 22.

51. National Academy of Sciences, "A Report by the Advisory Committee," 18.

52. Michael G. Barbour, "Ecological Fragmentation in the Fifties," in William Cronon, ed., *Uncommon Ground: Toward Reinventing Nature* (New York: W. W. Norton & Company, 1995), 233–55.

53. National Academy of Sciences, "A Report by the Advisory Committee," 21.

54. Wright, *Wildlife Research and Management*, 42.

55. Michael Frome, *Regreening the National Parks* (Tucson: University of Arizona Press, 1992), 140–57.

56. B. Riley McClelland, "The Ecosystem—A Unifying Concept for the Management of Natural Areas in the National Park System," master's thesis, Colorado State University, 1968, 114.

57. F. Fraser Darling and Noel D. Eichhorn, *Man and Nature in the National Parks* (Washington DC: Conservation Foundation, 1967); Noel D. Eichhorn, "The Special Role of National Parks," in F. Fraser Darling and John P. Milton, eds., *Future Environments of North America* (Garden City NY: Natural History Press, 1966), 335–41; Robert Cahn, "Will Success Spoil the National Parks?" *Christian Science Monitor* 1968, vertical

files, NAYNP. On the dilemma of use and preservation, see William C. Everhart, *The National Park Service* (New York: Praeger, 1972), 80–98.

58. Robert D. Barbee, "A Discussion of Ecological Management in the National Park System," master's thesis, Colorado State University, August 1968, 35.

59. Barbee, "A Discussion of Ecological Management," 51.

60. Thomas McNamee, *The Return of the Wolf to Yellowstone* (New York: Henry Holt and Company, 1997), 106; Haines places the basis of natural regulation with the work of Adolph Murie; see Haines, *Yellowstone Story*, vol. 2, 381–82.

61. Lemuel A. Garrison, Foreword to "Meeting at Canyon Village," May 25, 1962, file "Northern Yellowstone Elk Herd 1962," box N–78, NAYNP.

62. Newspaper articles on the 1967 reduction can be found in file "1967 Elk Reduction, YNP/Newspaper Articles," box N-70, NAYNP.

63. U.S. Senate Committee on Appropriations, "Control of Elk Population, Yellowstone National Park," Casper WY, March 11, 1967 [hereafter cited as Casper hearings], 1.

64. Letter Earl M. Thomas to Fred Hafner, January 25, 1966, file "Management Plans, Wildlife and Range," box N-75, NAYNP.

65. Casper hearings, 77.

66. Casper hearings, 70.

67. Thanks to the Park County Historical Society (Wyoming) for helping to sort out the identities of Ned and Nedward Frost. Ned Frost (1881–1957) guided many parties into Yellowstone and opened Cody's first curio shop in 1919. See obituary, *Cody Enterprise*, November 21, 1957; Fred and Dora Burris, "It Began with Grizzlies!" *Cody Enterprise*, May 2, 1984, B-1, 6; Eileen F. Starr, "Ned Frost: The Heart and Soul of Wyoming's Preservation Movement," *Preservation Wyoming* (State Historic Preservation Office newsletter), January 1995, 1, 27. See also Lee Whittlesey, *Yellowstone Place Names* (Helena: Montana Historical Society, 1988), 59.

68. Casper hearings, 71.

69. Hartzog, *Battling for the National Parks*, 104–5.

70. Hartzog, *Battling for the National Parks*, 252–53.

71. Robert Howe, 1963 Annual Wildlife Report; William J. Barmore, 1967 Annual Wildlife Report; file N26 "Annual Wildlife Report 1962–1978," box N-75, NAYNP.

72. Casper hearings, 69.

73. John Wilbrecht and Russell Robbins, "History of the National Elk Refuge," in Mark S. Boyce and Larry D. Hayden-Wing, eds., *North American Elk: Ecology, Behavior and Management* (Laramie: University of Wyoming, 1979), 248–54.

74. Glen F. Cole, "Elk Ecology and Management Investigations," NPS Report, March 1965, 53. vertical files, NAYNP.

75. Cole, "Elk Ecology."

76. Memo Cole to YNP superintendent, October 11, 1967, file "Management Plans, Wildlife & Range," box N-75, NAYNP.

77. Memo Cole to YNP superintendent, January 29, 1968, file "Management Plans, Wildlife & Range," box N-75; YNP Annual Wildlife Report, 1967–68, file "Annual Wildlife Reports 1962–1978," box N-75, NAYNP.

78. Minutes of Northern Yellowstone Elk Herd Management Meeting, Mammoth, Yellowstone National Park, September 27, 1968, file "1966–72/Elk" box N-69, NAYNP.

79. YNP Annual Wildlife Report, 1968–69, file "Annual Wildlife Reports 1962–1978," box N-75, NAYNP.

80. Glen F. Cole, "Elk and the Yellowstone Ecosystem," Office of Natural Science Studies, NPS, February 1969, vertical files, NAYNP.

81. Memo Cole to YNP superintendent, January 29, 1968, file "Management Plans, Wildlife & Range," box N-75, NAYNP.

82. U.S. Fish and Wildlife Service, "50 Years of Achievement: The Cooperative Research Unit Program in Fisheries and Wildlife 1935–1985" (Washington DC: U.S. Department of the Interior, 1984), unpaginated.

83. Craighead to Superintendent Anderson, June 25, 1969, file "1966–72/Elk" box N-69, NAYNP.

84. Memo Barmore to Cole, March 13, 1968, box N-69, NAYNP; Chase, Playing God, 52.

85. William J. Barmore, "Conflicts in Recreation—Elk versus Aspen in Yellowstone National Park" (paper presented at the twentieth annual meeting of the American Society of Range Management, Seattle, February 13–17, 1967), 17 p. typescript, vertical files, YNPL.

86. William J. Barmore, interview with author, July 28, 1992, Wilson WY.

87. Anderson to Craighead, July 2, 1969, file "1966–72/Elk" box N-69, NAYNP.

88. Glen F. Cole, "The Elk of Grand Teton and Southern Yellowstone National Parks," Research Report GRTE–N-1, 1969, reissue by Office of Natural Science Studies, National Park Service, 1978, vertical files, NAYNP; see also Glen F. Cole, "An Ecological Rationale for the Natural or Artificial Regulation of Native Ungulates in Parks," Transactions of the North American Wildlife and Natural Resources Conference 36 (1971): 417–25.

89. Robert Leo Smith, Elements of Ecology, 3rd ed. (New York: HarperCollins, 1992), 190–95.

90. Sharon Kingsland, Modeling Nature: Episodes in the History of Population Ecology (Chicago: University of Chicago Press, 1985), 154–58; see also Daniel B. Botkin, Discordant Harmonies: A New Ecology for the Twenty–First Century (New York: Oxford University Press, 1990), 37–42.

91. Kingsland, Modeling Nature, 171; Botkin, Discordant Harmonies, 47–48.

92. Thomas G. Scott, "Paul L. Errington, 1902–1962," *Journal of Wildlife Management* 27 (1963): 321–24.

93. William R. Clark and Darryl W. Kroeker, "Population Dynamics of Muskrats in Experimental Marshes at Delta, Manitoba," *Canadian Journal of Zoology* 71 (1993): 1620–28, quote on 1620.

94. Kingsland, *Modeling Nature*, 173–74. Other notable published works on population dynamics at that time included Lawrence B. Slobodkin, *Growth and Regulation of Animal Populations* (New York: Holt, Rinehart and Winston, 1961). A few years later a collection of essays on the subject was published: Ian A. McLaren, ed., *Natural Regulation of Animal Populations* (New York: Atherton Press, 1971).

95. Cole, "A Naturally Regulated Elk Population," 70. See also M. E. Solomon, "Meaning of Density-Dependence and Related Terms in Population Dynamics," in Ian A. McLaren, ed., *Natural Regulation of Animal Populations* (New York: Atherton Press, 1971), 22–29.

96. William R. Clark, personal communication, December 1997.

97. Robert Leo Smith, *Elements of Ecology*, 3rd ed. (New York: HarperCollins, 1992), 190–95. Doug Johnson, "Population Analysis," in T. A. Bookhout, ed., *Research and Management Techniques for Wildlife and Habitats* (Bethesda MD: Wildlife Society, 1994), 419–44, esp. 421–24.

98. John M. Good, interview with author, July 26, 1995, Mammoth WY.

99. Letter Glen Cole to superintendent GTNP, August 31, 1965, file "Park Policy Insect Control," box 3, Adolph Murie Collection, AHC.

100. Mary Meagher, interview with author, Yellowstone National Park, September 1995.

101. Douglas Houston, personal communication, January 9, 1997; Graeme Caughley, "Eruption of Ungulate Populations, with Emphasis on Himalayan Thar in New Zealand," *Ecology* 51 (Winter 1970): 53–72.

102. Caughley, "Eruption of Ungulate Populations," 54.

103. Caughley, "Eruption of Ungulate Populations," 70.

104. Caughley, "Eruption of Ungulate Populations," 67, 69, 70.

105. Cole, "Elk and the Yellowstone Ecosystem"; Cole, "Mission-Oriented Research in Natural Areas of the National Park Service," May 1969, Wildlife/Briefing Book, YNPL.

106. Douglas B. Houston, "The Northern Yellowstone Elk/Parts I and II/History and Demography," April 1974. vertical files, YNPL.

107. Houston, "History and Demography," 78.

108. See Cole, "Elk and the Yellowstone Ecosystem"; Cole, "Mission-Oriented Research in Natural Areas of the National Park Service"; for a critique of Cole and Houston during the early 1970s see Alan A. Beetle, "The Zootic Disclimax Concept," *Journal of Range Management* 27 (1974): 30–32.

109. Houston, "History and Demography," 81.

110. Houston, *Northern Yellowstone Elk,* 111–13.

111. Cole, "Mission-Oriented Research."

112. Houston, "History and Demography," 77.

113. YNP Annual Wildlife Report, 1971–72, file "Annual Wildlife Reports 1962–1978," box N-75, NAYNP.

114. John J. Craighead, project proposal, "A Study of the Ecology of the Grizzly Bear," n.d., box N-91, NAYNP.

115. Memo Charles H. McCurdy to West District interpreters, July 15, 1963, box N-52, NAYNP.

116. Memo Robert E. Howe to chief park ranger, May 11, 1964, file "West District Ranger," box N-52, NAYNP.

117. John Craighead to John McLaughlin, June 28, 1965, file "Craighead," box N-91, NAYNP; there are several accounts of the controversy between the NPS and the Craighead brothers: Thomas McNamee, *The Grizzly Bear,* 2nd ed. (New York: Penguin, 1990), 105–22; Paul Schullery, *The Bears of Yellowstone* (Boulder CO: Roberts Rinehart, 1986), 114–48; Frank Craighead, *Track of the Grizzly* (San Francisco: Sierra Club Books, 1979), 191–230; R. Gerald Wright, *Wildlife Research and Management,* 112–17.

118. John Craighead to John McLaughlin, June 28, 1965, file "Craighead," box N-91, NAYNP.

119. McNamee, *Grizzly Bear,* 103.

120. John Craighead to John McLaughlin, June 28, 1965, box N-91, NAYNP.

121. Letter Harry V. Reynolds Jr. to Ian [McTaggert] Cowan, January 19, 1974, in U.S. Congress, Senate, *Proposed Critical Habitat Area for Grizzly Bears,* Committee on Appropriations, 94th Congress, 2nd session, 1976, 146–52, 151, 149.

122. John M. Good, interview with author, July 26, 1995.

123. John Craighead to John McLaughlin, June 28, 1965, box N-91, NAYNP.

124. Anderson to John J. Craighead, April 7, 1969. Unaccessioned material ["Tim's box"], NAYNP.

125. Adolph Murie to regional chief of interpretation, March 5, 1962. box 4, Adolph Murie Collection, AHC.

126. Quoted in Schullery, *Bears of Yellowstone,* 118; John J. Craighead and Frank C. Craighead, "Management of Bears in Yellowstone National Park," July 1967, box N-36, NAYNP.

127. Schullery, *Bears of Yellowstone,* 117–22.

128. Memo Robert M. Linn to Joseph P. Linduska [associate director Bureau of Sport Fisheries and Wildlife], May 21, 1968, box N-36, NAYNP.

129. Memo Robert M. Linn to Joseph P. Linduska.

130. Memo John M. Good to superintendent, July 6, 1967, box N-91, NAYNP.

131. Letter John S. Gottschalk to John J. Craighead, August 8, 1969, box N-36, NAYNP.

132. Letter John S. Gottschalk to John J. Craighead.

133. Letter John S. Gottschalk to John J. Craighead.

134. Schullery, *Bears of Yellowstone*, 127–28; McNamee, *Grizzly Bear*, 113.

135. Mary Meagher, personal communication, December 1997.

136. McNamee, *Grizzly Bear*, 114–15.

137. R. Gerald Wright, *Wildlife Research and Management*, 115.

138. Wright, *Wildlife Research and Management*, 115.

139. Wright, *Wildlife Research and Management*, 116; Schullery, *Bears of Yellowstone*, 143–45.

140. McNamee, *Grizzly Bear*, 116.

141. McNamee, *Grizzly Bear*, 116, 120.

142. Wright, *Wildlife Research and Management*, 116.

143. Glen Cole, Doug Houston, and Mary Meagher, "Jack Kenneth Anderson, 1917–1985," file "Biography," vertical files, YNPL.

144. Kingsland, *Modeling Nature*, 206.

145. McNamee, *Grizzly Bear*, 109.

146. Hartzog, *Battling for the National Parks*, 91.

147. Chase, *Playing God*, 373. See also Karl Hess Jr., *Rocky Times in Rocky Mountain National Park: An Unnatural History* (Niwot CO: University Press of Colorado, 1993).

148. Chase, *Playing God*, 319, 47.

CHAPTER 6 · **Greater Yellowstone**

1. McNamee, *Grizzly Bear*, 118.

2. McNamee, *Grizzly Bear*, 157–58; Schullery, *Bears of Yellowstone*, 69–70.

3. Michael J. Bean, "Fortify the Act," *National Parks* (May-June 1993): 22–23; Fraser Shilling, "Do Habitat Conservation Plans Protect Endangered Species?" *Science* 276 (1997): 1662–63; David S. Wilcove, Margaret McMillan, and Keith C. Winston, "What Exactly Is an Endangered Species? An Analysis of the U.S. Endangered Species List: 1985–1991," *Conservation Biology* 7 (1993): 87–93; Andrea Easter-Pilcher, "Implementing the Endangered Species Act," *BioScience* 46 (1996): 355–63; Daniel J. Rohlf, "Six Biological Reasons Why the Endangered Species Act Doesn't Work—And What to Do about It," *Conservation Biology* 5 (1991): 273–82.

4. McNamee, *Grizzly Bear*, 200.

5. McNamee, *Grizzly Bear*, 169; see also, "Proposed Critical Habitat Area for Grizzly Bears," Senate Committee on Appropriations Hearings, 94th Congress, Cody WY, November 4, 1976.

6. McNamee, *Grizzly Bear*, 190.

7. McNamee, *Grizzly Bear*, 183–84.

8. McNamee, *Grizzly Bear*, 121.

9. McNamee, *Grizzly Bear*, 121, 137.

10. McNamee, *Grizzly Bear*, 194; Schullery, *Bears of Yellowstone*, 155.

11. William D. Newmark, "Legal and Biotic Boundaries of Western North American National Parks: A Problem of Congruence," *Biological Conservation* 33 (1985): 197–208, esp. 201. See also William D. Newmark, "Extinction of Mammal Populations in Western North American National Parks," *Conservation Biology* 9 (1995): 512–26.

12. David Quammen, *Song of the Dodo: Island Biogeography in an Age of Extinctions* (New York: Scribner, 1996), 390.

13. Quammen, *Song of the Dodo*, 487–93; Quammen, "The Newmark Warning: Why Our National Parks Are Resembling Desert Isles," *Outside* (May 1988): 31–33.

14. Robert B. Keiter, "On Protecting the National Parks from the External Threats Dilemma," *Land and Water Law Review* 20 (1985): 355–420, quote on 359; John C. Freemuth, *Islands Under Siege: National Parks and the Politics of External Threats* (Lawrence: University Press of Kansas, 1991): 18–19.

15. Keiter, "On Protecting the National Parks," 361; Freemuth, *Islands Under Siege*, 21; Runte, *National Parks*, 262–63.

16. Greater Yellowstone Coalition, *Greater Yellowstone Report* 7 (Fall 1990): 2.

17. Frederic H. Wagner, "American Wildlife Management at the Crossroads," *Wildlife Society Bulletin* 17 (1989): 354–60, quotes on 354, 358. See other essays in vol. 17 of the *Wildlife Society Bulletin* discussing the relationship between the two fields, as well as Fred L. Bunnell and Linda A. Dupuis, "*Conservation Biology*'s Literature Revisited: Wine or Vinaigrette?" *Wildlife Society Bulletin* (1995): 56–62.

18. Louisa Willcox, "No Freeboard for Yellowstone's Grizzlies," *Greater Yellowstone Report* 4 (Fall 1987): 1, 8–10, quote on 9.

19. Keiter, "Law and Ecology in Yellowstone," 967; see also Robert B. Keiter, "Observations on the Future Debate over 'Delisting' the Grizzly Bear in the Greater Yellowstone Ecosystem," *Environmental Professional* 13 (1991): 248–53.

20. Rick Reese, *Greater Yellowstone: The National Park and Adjacent Wild Lands* (Helena: Montana Magazine, 1994).

21. Garrison, *Making of a Ranger*, 279.

22. Chase, *Playing God*, 204–17.

23. McNamee, *Grizzly Bear*, 174–76; Chase, *Playing God*, 204–17.

24. Richard Schneebeck, "State Participation in Federal Policy Making for the Yellowstone Ecosystem: A Meaningful Solution or Business as Usual?" *Land and Water Law Review* 21 (1986): 397–416, esp. 415.

25. Chase, *Playing God*, 220–27, quote on 227.

26. Schullery, *Bears of Yellowstone*, 154.

27. Laura Soullière Harrison, *Architecture in the Parks: National Historic Landmark Theme Study* (Washington DC: NPS, November 1986), 311–23.

28. Chase, *Playing God*, 228.

29. Schneebeck, "State Participation in Federal Policy Making," 397–416, esp. 415; Schullery, *Bears of Yellowstone*, 152, 154.

30. Schneebeck, "State Participation in Federal Policy Making," 411, 415.

31. William R. Lowry, *The Capacity for Wonder: Preserving National Parks* (Washington DC: Brookings Institution, 1994), 156–60.

32. Francis J. Singer, "The Ungulate Prey Base for Wolves in Yellowstone National Park," in Robert B. Keiter and Mark S. Boyce, eds., *The Greater Yellowstone Ecosystem: Redefining America's Wilderness Heritage* (New Haven: Yale University Press, 1991), 323–48, esp. 334, 338.

33. Houston, *Northern Yellowstone Elk*, 248–352, quote on 93. See also Douglas Houston and Mary Meagher, *Yellowstone and the Biology of Time* (in press).

34. Houston, *Northern Yellowstone Elk*, 98.

35. Houston, *Northern Yellowstone Elk*, 101, 134.

36. Houston, *Northern Yellowstone Elk*, 135.

37. John Macnab, "Carrying Capacity and Related Slippery Shibboleths," *Wildlife Society Bulletin* 13 (1985): 403–10, quote on 403.

38. Graeme Caughley, "Wildlife Management and the Dynamics of Ungulate Populations," in T. H. Coaker, ed., *Applied Biology*, vol. 1 (New York: Academic Press, 1976), 183–246; Graeme Caughley, "What Is This Thing Called Carrying Capacity?" in Boyce and Hayden-Wing, eds., *North American Elk*, 2–8; S. J. McNaughton, "Grassland Herbivore Dynamics," in A. R. E. Sinclair and M. Norton-Griffiths, eds., *Serengeti—Dynamics of an Ecosystem* (Chicago: University of Chicago Press, 1979), 46–81; Sinclair, *The African Buffalo: A Study of Resource Limitation of Populations* (Chicago: University of Chicago Press, 1977).

39. Houston, *Northern Yellowstone Elk*, 68.

40. Houston, *Northern Yellowstone Elk*, 66, 68.

41. Peek to Meagher, n.d. [c. autumn 1979], box N-77, NAYNP.

42. James M. Peek, "Natural Regulation of Ungulates (What Constitutes a Real Wilderness?)," *Wildlife Society Bulletin* 8 (1980): 217–27.

43. Peek, "Natural Regulation of Ungulates," 219. On the judgment of the range ecologist, Peek cites L. Ellison, "Influence of Grazing on Plant Succession of Rangelands," *Botanical Review* 26 (1960): 1–78.

44. Peek, "Natural Regulation of Ungulates," 225.

45. Peek, "Natural Regulation of Ungulates, 225.

46. Houston, *Northern Yellowstone Elk*, 65.

47. Steward T. A. Pickett, V. Thomas Parker, and Peggy L. Fiedler, "The New Paradigm in Ecology: Implications for Conservation Biology above the Species Level," in Peggy L. Fiedler and Subodh K. Jain, eds., *Conservation Biology: The Theory and Practice of Nature Conservation Preservation and Management* (New York: Chapman and Hall, 1992), 66–70.

48. Houston, *Northern Yellowstone Elk*, xvi.

49. Pickett, Parker, and Fiedler, 70–72; see also D. L. DeAngelis and J. C. Waterhouse, "Equilibrium and Nonequilibrium Concepts in Ecological Models," *Ecological Monographs* 57 (1987): 1–21.

50. Don Despain, Douglas Houston, Mary Meagher, and Paul Schullery, *Wildlife in Transition: Man and Nature on Yellowstone's Northern Range* (Boulder CO: Roberts Rinehart, 1986), 8.

51. Chase, *Playing God*, 84.

52. National Park Service, *First Annual Meeting of Research and Monitoring on Yellowstone's Northern Range*, January 28–29, 1988, Mammoth WY, 1988, vertical files, YNPL.

53. Michael B. Coughenour and Francis J. Singer, "The Concept of Overgrazing and Its Application to Yellowstone's Northern Range," in Keiter and Boyce, eds., *Greater Yellowstone Ecosystem*, 209–30, quotes on 224.

54. Coughenour and Singer, "The Concept of Overgrazing," 226.

55. Charles Edward Kay, "Yellowstone's Northern Elk Herd: A Critical Evaluation of the 'Natural Regulation' Paradigm," Ph.D. diss., Utah State University, 1990.

56. Douglas Alan Frank, "Interactive Ecology of Plants, Large Mammalian Herbivores, and Drought in Yellowstone National Park," Ph.D. diss., Syracuse University, December 1990, 125, 108–9.

57. Research Division, Yellowstone National Park, "Interim Report Yellowstone National Park Northern Range Research," April 1992, 13–15, quote on 15.

58. Research Division, Yellowstone National Park, "Interim Report," 16.

59. Cathy Whitlock, Sherilyn C. Fritz, and Daniel R. Engstrom, "A Prehistoric Perspective on the Northern Range," in Keiter and Boyce, eds., *Greater Yellowstone Ecosystem*, 289–305, esp. 296.

60. See Mark S. Boyce, "If I Were Superintendent. . . .," in *Proceedings of the Second Biennial Conference on the Greater Yellowstone Ecosystem: The Ecological Implications of Fire in Greater Yellowstone* (Yellowstone National Park, September 19–21, 1993; Fairfield WA: International Association of Wildland Fire, 1996), 201–8.

61. Wagner, Foresta, Gill et al., *Wildlife Policies*, 51–54, quote on 54.

62. Wagner et al., *Wildlife Policies*, 182.

63. Wagner et al., *Wildlife Policies*, 149.

64. For a recent account of ecologists' critiques of the park, see Greg Hanscom, "Is

Nature Running Too Wild in Yellowstone?" *High Country News* 15 (September 1997): 8–11. See also Ted Williams, "Deregulating the Wild," *Audubon* 99 (July-August 1997): 56–63, 92–94; George Wuerthner, "The Great Elk Controversy," *Wild Forest Review* 1 (February 1994): 57–59.

65. Wagner et al., *Wildlife Policies*, 178

66. Wagner et al., *Wildlife Policies*, 54, 174.

67. William F. Porter, Michael A. Coffey, and John Hadidian, "In Search of a Litmus Test: Wildlife Management in U.S. National Parks," *Wildlife Society Bulletin* 22 (1994): 302–6.

68. Mark S. Boyce, "Natural Regulation or Control?" in Keiter and Boyce, eds., *Greater Yellowstone Ecosystem*, 183–208, quote on 190.

69. Wagner et al., *Wildlife Policies*, 145.

70. Wagner et al., *Wildlife Policies*, 180.

71. Boyce, "Natural Regulation or Control?," 203.

72. YNP Interim Report, 22.

73. YNP Interim Report, 22.

74. National Park Service, "Yellowstone's Northern Range: Complexity & Change in a Wildland Ecosystem" (Yellowstone National Park: National Park Service, 1997).

75. The Technical Report featured twenty-eight reports, many of them republished after their appearance in scientific journals. "Effects of Grazing by Wild Ungulates in Yellowstone National Park," U.S. Department of the Interior, National Park Service, Yellowstone National Park, Technical Report NPS/NRYELL/NRTR/96–01, 1996.

76. U.S. General Accounting Office, "Wildlife Management: Issues Concerning the Mangement of Bison and Elk Herds in Yellowstone National Park," testimony before the Subcommittee on National Parks, U.S. Senate, July 10, 1997, GAO Report no. GAO/T-RCED-97-200.

77. Wagner et al., *Wildlife Policies*, 4–5. See Sam McNaughton's review of *Wildlife Policies in the U.S. National Parks* in *Journal of Wildlife Management* 60 (1996): 685–87.

78. Daniel Bruce Tyers, "The Condition of the Northern Winter Range in Yellowstone National Park—A Discussion of the Controversy," master's thesis, Montana State University, 1981, 157.

79. Tyers, "The Condition of the Northern Winter Range," 158.

80. Botkin, *Discordant Harmonies*, 17; Raymond Bonner, *At the Hand of Man: Peril and Hope for Africa's Wildlife* (New York: Alfred A. Knopf, 1993), 104–8.

81. Joel Berger, "Greater Yellowstone's Native Ungulates: Myths and Realities," *Conservation Biology* 5 (1991): 353–63; "Purchase of Last Piece of Elk Winter Range Ends Project," *Bozeman Daily Chronicle*, July 1, 1993, 18.

82. Wright, Dixon, and Thompson, *A Preliminary Survey*, 147; Wright and Thompson, *Wildlife Management*, 126.

83. R. Gerald Wright, "Wildlife Issues in National Parks," in William J. Chandler, ed., *Audubon Wildlife Report 1988* (New York: Academic Press, 1988), 169–96, 192.

84. R. Gerald Wright, "The Evolution of Science in the National Parks and Its Impact on Wildlife Management," appendix 1, 1. Typescript, YNPL.

85. See the annual proceedings of the Tall Timbers Fire Ecology Conference, Tall Timbers Research Station, Tallahassee FL, beginning in 1962.

86. Robert E. Sellers and Don G. Despain, "Fire Management in Yellowstone National Park," *Proceedings of the Tall Timbers Fire Ecology Conference and Intermountain Fire Research Council Fire and Land Management Symposium* 14 (1976): 99–113, esp. 100.

87. Letter Adolph Murie to Bruce Hamilton, January 22, 1974, file "Research 1973–74," box 1, Adolph Murie Collection, AHC.

88. Memo Douglas B. Houston to superintendent, February 2, 1972, box N-90, NAYNP.

89. Douglas B. Houston, "Wildfires in Northern Yellowstone National Park," *Ecology* 54 (1973): 1111–17, quote on 1115.

90. Houston, "Wildfires in Northern Yellowstone," 1116.

91. Don G. Despain, "Fire as an Ecological Force in Yellowstone Ecosystems," Information Paper no. 16, March 1972, 3, vertical files, YNPL.

92. Sellers and Despain, "Fire Management in Yellowstone National Park," 103.

93. John D. Varley and Paul Schullery, "Reality and Opportunity in the Yellowstone Fires of 1988," in Keiter and Boyce, eds., *Greater Yellowstone Ecosystem*, 109.

94. Varley and Schullery, "Reality and Opportunity in the Yellowstone Fires of 1988," 109.

95. Charles C. Adams, *Guide to the Study of Animal Ecology* (New York: Macmillan, 1913), 33.

96. Dennis H. Knight and Linda L. Wallace, "The Yellowstone Fires: Issues in Landscape Ecology," *BioScience* 39 (1989): 700.

97. William H. Romme, "Fire and Landscape Diversity in Subalpine Forests of Yellowstone National Park," *Ecological Monographs* 52 (1982): 199–221, quote on 199.

98. David J. Parsons, David M. Graber, James K. Agee, et al., "Natural Fire Management in National Parks," *Environmental Management* 10 (1986): 21–24, quote on 21.

99. Parsons et al., "Natural Fire Management," 21.

100. Parsons et al., "Natural Fire Management," 23.

101. William H. Romme and Don G. Despain, "Historical Perspective on the Yellowstone Fires of 1988," *BioScience* 39 (1989): 695–99, quote on 696.

102. "Yellowstone and the News," interview with Conrad Smith, *Yellowstone Science* 2 (Winter 1994): 9–14, quote on 14.

103. Varley and Schullery, "Yellowstone Fires," 113.

104. Norman L. Christensen, James K. Agee, Peter F. Brussard, et al., "Interpreting the Yellowstone Fires of 1988," *BioScience* 39 (1989): 678–85, esp. 679.

105. Christensen et al., "Interpreting the Yellowstone Fires of 1988," 697.

106. Christensen et al., "Interpreting the Yellowstone Fires of 1988," 680.

107. Christensen et al., "Interpreting the Yellowstone Fires of 1988," 683.

108. Christensen et al., "Interpreting the Yellowstone Fires of 1988," 680, 683, 685.

109. Christensen et al., "Interpreting the Yellowstone Fires of 1988," 684.

110. Knight and Wallace, "Yellowstone Fires," quote on 705.

111. Brian Kuehl, "World Heritage Committee Designates Yellowstone 'In Danger,'" *Greater Yellowstone Report* 13 (Winter 1996): 11.

112. William K. Stevens, "Latest Threat to Yellowstone: Admirers Are Loving It to Death," *New York Times*, September 13, 1994, B5, B8; Nash, *Wilderness and the American Mind*, 316–41.

113. Tim Stevens, "Grizzly Mortality Rate in Greater Yellowstone Highest Since 1972," *Greater Yellowstone Report* 13 (Winter 1996): 19.

114. Tim Stevens, "Lawsuit Settlement Helps Set Stage for True Grizzly Recovery in Lower 48," *Greater Yellowstone Report* 13, 4 (Fall 1996): 10–11.

115. Hartzog, *Battling for the National Parks*, 258.

116. Hartzog, *Battling for the National Parks*, 254.

117. Hartzog, *Battling for the National Parks*, 265.

118. Hartzog, *Battling for the National Parks*, 267.

119. Hartzog, *Battling for the National Parks*, 269.

120. Hartzog, *Battling for the National Parks*, 254, 265, 267, 269, 273; see also Lowry, *Capacity for Wonder*, 2, 13–18, 32–33.

121. Robert B. Keiter, "Taking Account of the Ecosystem on the Public Domain: Law and Ecology in the Greater Yellowstone Region," *University of Colorado Law Review* 60 (1989): 923–1007, 933.

122. Keiter, "Law and Ecology in Yellowstone," 927.

123. Greater Yellowstone Coordinating Committee, *A Framework for Coordination in the Greater Yellowstone Area*, September 1991, 2, YNP vertical files; see also Bruce Goldstein, "The Struggle over Ecosystem Management at Yellowstone," *BioScience* 42 (1992): 184.

124. Goldstein, "Struggle over Ecosystem Management," esp. 184.

125. Arnold M. Schultz, "The Ecosystem as a Conceptual Tool in the Management of Natural Resources," in S. V. Ciriacy-Wantrup and James J. Parsons, eds., *Natural Resources: Quality and Quantity* (Berkeley: University of California Press, 1967), 139–61, quote on 158.

126. T. W. Clark and D. Zaunbrecher, "The Greater Yellowstone Ecosystem: The Eco-

system Concept in Natural Resource Policy and Management," *Renewable Resources Journal* 5, 2 (1987): 8–19.

127. Keiter, "Law and Ecology in Yellowstone," 928.

128. Keiter, "Law and Ecology in Yellowstone," 928, 988.

129. Keiter, "Law and Ecology in Yellowstone," 985.

130. Greater Yellowstone Coordinating Committee, "Coordinated Management in the Greater Yellowstone Area: A Summary of National Park and National Forest Cooperative Activities, 1992," 1992, 3.

131. Quoted in "Agencies Embrace Ecosystem Model," Greater Yellowstone Report 7 (Fall 1990): 3.

132. Greater Yellowstone Coordinating Committee, *Vision for the Future: A Framework for Coordination in the Greater Yellowstone Area*, draft, August 1990, YNP vertical files, p. 4-1.

133. Greater Yellowstone Coordinating Committee, *Vision for the Future.*

134. Goldstein, "Struggle over Ecosystem Management," 186; see also Robert D. Barbee, Paul Schullery, and John D. Varley, "The Yellowstone Vision: An Experiment That Failed or a Vote for Posterity?" Conference proceedings, "Partnerships in Parks and Preservation," Albany NY, September 9–12, 1991; John Freemuth, "Ecosystem Management and Its Place in the National Park Service," *Denver University Law Review* 74 (1997): 697–727, esp. 711–20.

135. Personal observation.

136. Ed Lewis, "Conspiracy Destroyed Greater Yellowstone Vision," *Greater Yellowstone Report* 10 (Winter 1993): 3.

137. Barbee, Schullery, and Varley, "Yellowstone Vision," 85.

138. Barbee, Schullery, and Varley, "Yellowstone Vision," 85.

139. Wright, Dixon, and Thompson, *A Preliminary Survey*, 116.

140. Aldo Leopold, review of Stanley P. Young and Edward H. Goldman, "The Wolves of North America," *Journal of Forestry* 42 (1944): 928–29.

141. A. Starker Leopold, "Wildlife Management in the Future," 9.

142. L. David Mech, "Returning the Wolf to Yellowstone," in Keiter and Boyce, eds., *Greater Yellowstone Ecosystem*, 309–22.

143. Mech, "Returning the Wolf," 311; Hank Fischer, *Wolf Wars: The Remarkable Inside Story of the Restoration of Wolves to Yellowstone* (Helena MT: Falcon Press, 1995), 42–43.

144. Fischer, *Wolf Wars*, 68–69.

145. Houston, *Northern Yellowstone Elk*, 201.

146. U.S. District Court, Wyoming, Wyoming Farm Bureau Federation vs. Bruce Babbitt et al., Civil no. 94-CV-286-D, "Order Denying Plaintiffs' Motion for Preliminary Injunction," January 3, 1995. Yellowstone Center for Resources.

147. "No-Wolf Keeps up Information Blitz," *Cody Enterprise*, April 1, 1992. See also

Larry Bourret, "Wolves for Wyoming?: View of the Wyoming Farm Bureau," *Wyoming Wildlife* 56 (January 1992): 10–13.

148. Kurt Alt [Montana Department of Fish Wildlife and Parks], interview with author, July 15, 1994.

149. Letter L. David Mech to Ed Bangs, October 12, 1993; YNP Center for Resources; John Talbott, "Wolves for Wyoming?: View of the Wyoming Game and Fish Department," *Wyoming Wildlife* 56 (January 1992): 18–23.

150. USDI Fish and Wildlife Service, "14 Commonly Asked Questions about the Experimental Rules for Wolves," c. November 1994.

151. USDI Fish and Wildlife Service, "14 Commonly Asked Questions," USDI Fish and Wildlife Service, "Establishment of a Nonessential Experimental Population of Gray Wolves in Yellowstone National Park in Wyoming, Idaho, Montana, Central Idaho and Southwestern Montana; Final Rules," *Federal Register* 59, 224 (1994): 60252-81.

152. "$100,000 for Wolf Depredation Raised," *Bozeman Daily Chronicle*, November 4, 1990.

153. L. David Mech, *The Wolves of Isle Royale*, Fauna of the National Parks Series, no. 7 (Washington DC: GPO, 1966).

154. L. David Mech, Thomas J. Meier, and John W. Burch, "Denali Park Wolf Studies: Implications for Yellowstone," *Transactions of the North American Wildlife and Natural Resources Conference* 56 (1991): 86–90, esp. 87–88.

155. Mech, Meier, and Burch, "Denali Park Wolf Studies," 89.

156. Larry Bourret, "Wolves for Wyoming?: View of the Wyoming Farm Bureau," *Wyoming Wildlife* 56 (January 1992): 10–13.

157. Norman A. Bishop, "Yellowstone Wolf Answers—A Second Digest," 10, YNP Center for Resources, Yellowstone National Park.

158. Francis J. Singer, "The Ungulate Prey Base for Wolves in Yellowstone National Park," in Keiter and Boyce, eds., *Greater Yellowstone Ecosystem*, 323–48, quote on 342.

159. Letter Michael J. Dorrance to Norman Bishop, June 13, 1991. YNP Center for Resources.

160. Douglas H. Chadwick, "Manitoba's Wolves: A Model for Yellowstone?" *Defenders* 62 (March/April 1987): 30–36.

161. USDI Fish and Wildlife Service, "The Reintroduction of Gray Wolves to Yellowstone National Park and Central Idaho: Summary of Final Environmental Impact Statement," May 1994, Washington DC: GPO.

162. Samuel P. Hays, *Beauty, Health, and Permanence: Environmental Politics in the United States, 1955–1985* (Cambridge: Cambridge University Press, 1989), 2–3, 111–17.

163. Rene Askins, "Wolves for Wyoming?: View of the Wolf Fund," *Wyoming Wildlife* 56 (January 1992): 14–17.

164. Hays, *Beauty, Health, and Permanence*, 115.

165. Fischer, *Wolf Wars*, 69–70; Bishop, "Yellowstone Wolf Answers," 4–5.

166. Fischer, *Wolf Wars*, 70.

167. Fischer, *Wolf Wars*, 71.

168. Michael Milstein, "Compromise Urged in Wolf Debate," *Billings Gazette*, December 6, 1991.

169. *Wyoming Farm Bureau Federation et al., v. Bruce Babbitt*, sec. Dept. of Interior et al., Civil No. 94-CV-286-D, U.S. District Court, District of Wyoming, November 25, 1994, Yellowstone Center for Resources, 26; see also Bourret, "Wolves for Wyoming?" 10–13.

170. *Wyoming Farm Bureau Federation et al., v. Bruce Babbitt*, sec. Dept. of Interior et al., 27.

171. *Wyoming Farm Bureau Federation et al., v. Bruce Babbitt*, sec. Dept. of Interior et al., 30–31.

172. Mech, "Returning the Wolf," 315.

173. "Order Denying Plaintiffs' Motion for Preliminary Injunction," *Wyoming Farm Bureau Federation et al., v. Bruce Babbitt*, sec. Dept. of Interior et al., Civil No. 94-CV-286-D, U.S. District Court, District of Wyoming, 9.

174. "Order Denying Plaintiffs' Motion," *Wyoming Farm Bureau Federation et al., v. Bruce Babbitt*, sec. Dept. of Interior et al., 10.

175. *High Country News*, January 19, 1998, 4; see also *High Country News*, December 22, 1997.

Epilogue

1. Wright and Thompson, *Wildlife Management*, 126.

2. David J. Parsons, David M. Graber, James K. Agee et al., "Natural Fire Management in National Parks," *Environmental Management* 10 (1986): 21–24, quote on 23.

3. John A. McPhee, *The Control of Nature* (New York: Farrar, Straus & Giroux, 1989).

4. Mark Boyce thoughtfully discusses the middle ground between the extremes in "If I Were Superintendent. . . .," *Proceedings of the Second Biennial Conference on the Greater Yellowstone Ecosystem: The Ecological Implications of Fire in Greater Yellowstone* (September 19–21, 1993, Yellowstone National Park; Fairfield WA: International Association of Wildland Fire, 1996), 201–8; see also Robert B. Keiter, "Preserving Nature in the National Parks: Law, Policy, and Science in a Dynamic Environment," *Denver University Law Review* 74 (1997): 649–95.

5. Kristin S. Shrader-Frechette and Earl D. McCoy, "Natural Landscapes, Natural Communities, and Natural Ecosystems," *Forest and Conservation History* 39 (July 1995): 138–42.

6. William F. Porter, Michael A. Coffey, and John Hadidian, "In Search of a Litmus Test: Wildlife Management in U.S. National Parks," *Wildlife Society Bulletin* 22 (1994): 302–6.

7. William F. Porter, "Burgeoning Ungulate Populations in National Parks: Is Inter-

vention Warranted?" in Dale R. McCullough and Reginald H. Barrett, eds., *Wildlife 2001: Populations* (London: Elsevier Applied Science, 1992). See also Frederic Wagner, "Principles for the Conservation of Wild Living Resources: Another Perspective," *Ecological Applications* 6 (1996): 365–67.

8. Lowry, *Capacity for Wonder*, 2.

9. Michael Pollan, *Second Nature: A Gardener's Education* (New York: Delta, 1991), 58–59, 134–35; William Cronon, "The Trouble with Wilderness, or, Getting Back to the Wrong Nature," *Environmental History* 1 (1996): 7–28; William Cronon, ed., *Uncommon Ground: Toward Reinventing Nature* (New York: W. W. Norton & Co., 1995). Two valuable responses are David M. Graber, "Resolute Biocentrism: The Dilemma of Wilderness in National Parks," in Michael E. Soule and Gary Lease, eds., *Reinventing Nature?: Responses to Postmodern Deconstruction* (Washington DC: Island Press, 1995), 123–35; and Donald Worster, "The Wilderness of History," *Wild Earth* 7 (Fall 1997): 9–13.

10. Stephen Budiansky, *Nature's Keepers: The New Science of Nature Management* (New York: Free Press, 1995); see also Stuart L. Pimm "Nature Lovers and Other Villains," *Nature* 378 (1995): 104–5.

11. M. Kat Anderson, "Tending the Wilderness," *Restoration and Management Notes* 14 (winter 1996): 154–66; Steward T. A. Pickett and Mark J. McDonnell, "Humans as Components of Ecosystems: A Synthesis," in Mark J. McDonnell and Steward T. A. Pickett, eds., *Humans as Components of Ecosystems: The Ecology of Subtle Human Effects and Populated Areas* (New York: Springer-Verlag, 1993); Arturo Gomez-Pompa and Andrea Kaus, "Taming the Wilderness Myth," *BioScience* 42 (1992): 271–79.

12. Budiansky, *Nature's Keepers*, 26.

13. See Alston Chase, *In a Dark Wood: The Fight over Forests and the Rising Tyranny of Ecology* (Boston: Houghton Mifflin, 1995), 7–10, 416–18.

14. Chase, *Playing God*, 373.

15. Alston Chase, "The Dark Side: A Corrupt System of Preservation Science Muzzles the Government's Own Honest Scholars," *Range Magazine* 5 (Summer 1997): 4–8, 62. National Park Service critic Karl Hess Jr. (*Rocky Times in Rocky Mountain National Park*) similarly expresses an antigovernment rhetorical stance in a recent essay, "John Wesley Powell and the Unmaking of the West," *Environmental History* 2 (January 1997): 7–28; see Donald Worster's reply in *Environmental History* 2 (April 1997): 216–19.

16. Charles E. Kay, "Yellowstone: Ecological Malpractice," PERC *Reports* 15, 2 (June 1997): 5–39, quote on 4.

17. Quoted in McNamee, *Return of the Wolf*, 101.

18. See Joseph L. Sax, *Mountains without Handrails: Reflections on the National Parks* (Ann Arbor: University of Michigan Press, 1980), 12–15.

19. John D. Varley, "Managing Yellowstone National Park into the Twenty-first Century: The Park as an Aquarium," in James K. Agee and Darryll R. Johnson, eds., *Ecosystem Management for Parks and Wilderness* (Seattle: University of Washington Press, 1988), 216–25, quote on 218.

SOURCES

Manuscript Collections, Resources for Documents and Reports, and Photograph Sources

American Heritage Center, Laramie WY (AHC)

  Craighead Family Collection
  Adolph Murie Collection
  Olaus Murie Collection
  Maynard Barrows Collection

Denver Public Library, Conservation Manuscripts Collection (DPL)

  Rosalie Edge Papers
  Olaus Murie Papers

Library of Congress Manuscript Division, Washington DC (LOC)

  John C. Merriam Collection
  W. L. McAttee Collection

National Archives, Central Plains Region, Kansas City MO (NACPR)

  RG 79 Records of the National Park Service

National Archives, College Park MD (NACP)

  RG 22 Records of Fish and Wildlife Service
  RG 79 Records of the National Park Service
  RG 35 Records of David Madsen

National Park Service, Harpers Ferry Center, Harpers Ferry WV
supplied several photographs from its extensive collection.

National Park Service Library, Denver (NPSLD)

National Park Service Technical Information Center, Denver (NPS-TIC)

Western Michigan University, Kalamazoo MI

  Regional History Collections
  Charles C. Adams Papers

Yellowstone Center for Resources, Mammoth WY

Yellowstone National Park Archives (NAYNP)

All photographs credited to Yellowstone Photo Archives are from Record Group 79, National Archives and Records Administration, Yellowstone National Park. RG 79 Records of the National Park Service

Yellowstone National Park Library (YNPL)

Essential Sources

Information about the history of wildlife in America and shifting attitudes about wildlife can be found in Thomas R. Dunlap, *Saving America's Wildlife* (Princeton: Princeton University Press, 1988); Lisa Mighetto, *Wild Animals and American Environmental Ethics* (Tucson: University of Arizona Press, 1991); James B. Trefethen, *An American Crusade for Wildlife* (New York: Winchester Press, 1975); and Tom McNamee, *The Grizzly Bear*, 2nd ed. (New York: Penguin, 1990). "People and the Gallatin Elk Herd," by Allan Lovaas (Helena: Montana Fish and Game Department, 1970) yielded useful information germane to this study, and Gary G. Gray's *Wildlife and People: The Human Dimensions of Wildlife Ecology* (Urbana: University of Illinois Press, 1993) provides perspective on human valuation of wildlife. On the history of wildlife management, see Dian Olson Belanger, *Managing American Wildlife: A History of the International Association of Fish and Wildlife Agencies* (Amherst: University of Massachusetts Press, 1988).

Sources in the history of ecology useful for this study included Sharon Kingsland, *Modeling Nature: Episodes in the History of Population Ecology* (Chicago: University of Chicago Press, 1985); Daniel B. Botkin, *Discordant Harmonies: A New Ecology for the Twenty-First Century* (New York: Oxford University Press, 1990); Frank Benjamin Golley, *A History of the Ecosystem Concept in Ecology: More than the Sum of the Parts* (New Haven: Yale University Press, 1993); Robert A. Croker, *Pioneer Ecologist: The Life and Work of Victor Ernest Shelford, 1877–1968* (Washington DC: Smithsonian Institution Press, 1991); Robert P. McIntosh, *The Background of Ecology: Concept and Theory* (Cambridge: Cambridge University Press, 1985); Frank N. Egerton, "Changing Concepts of the Balance of Nature," *Quarterly Revue of Biology* 48 (1973): 322–50; Egerton's "The History and Present Entanglements of Some General Ecological Perspectives," in *Humans as Components of Ecosystems*, eds. Mark J. McDonnell and Steward T. A. Pickett (New York: Springer-Verlag, 1993); Ronald C. Tobey's *Saving the Prairies: The Life Cycle of the Founding School of American Plant Ecology, 1895–1955* (Berkeley: University of California Press, 1981); and last but not least Donald Worster's *Nature's Economy: A History of Ecological Ideas*, 2nd ed. (Cambridge: Cambridge University Press, 1994). Holmes Rolston presents a thoughtful analysis of central issues in "Biology and Philosophy in Yellowstone," *Biology and Philosophy* 5 (1990): 241–58. Two articles seem particularly important in thinking about what ecology tells us about nature and our parks: Kristin S. Shrader-Frechette and Earl D. McCoy's "Natural Landscapes, Natural Communities, and Natural Ecosystems," *Forest and Conservation History* 39 (July 1995):

138–42; and Steward T. A. Pickett and Richard S. Ostfeld, "The Shifting Paradigm in Ecology," in *A New Century for Natural Resources Management*, eds. Richard L. Knight and Sarah F. Bates (Washington DC: Island Press, 1995), 261–78.

Those interested in the history of Yellowstone National Park will find two recent books of considerable interest: Paul Schullery's *Searching for Yellowstone: Ecology and Wonder in the Last Wilderness* (Boston: Houghton Mifflin, 1997), and Judith L. Meyer's *The Spirit of Yellowstone: The Cultural Evolution of a National Park* (Lanham MD: Rowman & Littlefield Publishers, 1996). Readers also will want to consult, sooner or later, the bible of the literature on Yellowstone, Aubrey Haines's *The Yellowstone Story*, 2 vols. (Yellowstone National Park: Yellowstone Library and Museum Association, 1977). Other useful sources include Richard A. Bartlett, *Yellowstone: A Wilderness Besieged* (Tucson: University of Arizona Press, 1985); Bartlett's *Nature's Yellowstone* (Tucson: University of Arizona Press, 1974); as well as Robert W. Righter's *Crucible for Conservation: The Creation of Grand Teton National Park* (Boulder: Colorado Associated University Press, 1982).

Books essential to the study of the national parks include Alfred Runte's *National Parks: The American Experience* (Lincoln: University of Nebraska Press, 1987), and his more recent *Yosemite: The Embattled Wilderness* (Lincoln: University of Nebraska Press, 1990). An excellent historical account of resource management in the National Park Service may be found in Richard West Sellars, *Preserving Nature in the National Parks: A History* (New Haven: Yale University Press, 1997). A second essential resource geared more specifically to the history of wildlife management in the parks is R. Gerald Wright's *Wildlife Research and Management in the National Parks* (Urbana: University of Illinois Press, 1991). A thoughtful recent interpretation of park policies in Alaska is Theodore Catton's *Inhabited Wilderness: Indians, Eskimos, and National Parks in Alaska* (Albuquerque: University of New Mexico Press, 1997). External threats to the parks are examined in John C. Freemuth, *Islands Under Siege: National Parks and the Politics of External Threats* (Lawrence: University Press of Kansas, 1991). Other good beginning places include Michael Frome, *Regreening the National Parks* (Tucson: University of Arizona Press, 1992); Ronald A. Foresta, *America's National Parks and Their Keepers* (Washington DC: Resources for the Future, 1984); William C. Everhart, *The National Park Service* (Boulder: Westview Press, 1983); F. Fraser Darling and Noel D. Eichhorn, *Man and Nature in the National Parks* (Washington DC: Conservation Foundation, 1967); and John Ise, *Our National Park Policy: A Critical History* (Baltimore: Johns Hopkins University Press, 1961). Readers pondering what the national parks are about will find Joseph L. Sax's *Mountains Without Handrails: Reflections on the National Parks* (Ann Arbor: University of Michigan Press, 1980) an immensely helpful work. An insightful comparison between U.S. and Canadian parks is found in William R. Lowry, *The Capacity for Wonder: Preserving National Parks* (Washington DC: Brookings Institution, 1994). Ethan Carr discusses the role of landscape architects in park development in *Wilderness by Design: Landscape Architecture and the National Park Service* (Lincoln: University of Nebraska Press, 1998); as does Linda Flint McClelland in *Building the National*

Parks: Historic Landscape Design and Construction (Baltimore: Johns Hopkins University Press, 1998).

Sources specific to the history of wildlife and wildlife management in Yellowstone include Don Despain, Douglas Houston, Mary Meagher, and Paul Schullery, *Wildlife in Transition: Man and Nature on Yellowstone's Northern Range* (Boulder CO: Roberts Rinehart, 1986); Douglas B. Houston, *The Northern Yellowstone Elk: Ecology and Management* (New York: Macmillan, 1982); Daniel B. Tyers, "The Condition of the Northern Winter Range in Yellowstone National Park—A Discussion of the Controversy" (master's thesis, Montana State University, 1981); and Scott Edward Hanley, "Wildlife Management in Yellowstone National Park, 1962–1976" (master's thesis, University of Wyoming, 1992). John J. Craighead, Jay S. Sumner, and John A. Mitchell's *The Grizzly Bears of Yellowstone: Their Ecology in the Yellowstone Ecosystem, 1959–1992* (Washington DC: Island Press, 1995) contains information on the history of bear management, as does Paul Schullery's *The Bears of Yellowstone* (rev. ed., Boulder CO: Roberts Rinehart, 1986). Hank Fischer's *Wolf Wars: The Remarkable Inside Story of the Restoration of Wolves to Yellowstone* (Helena MT: Falcon Press, 1995) discusses the wolf reintroduction. To understand wildlife management in the West, one must grasp the role of the state agencies. A useful source in this context is Neal Blair, *The History of Wildlife Management in Wyoming* (Casper: Wyoming Game and Fish Department, 1987).

A scientific critique of NPS wildlife management policy is found in Frederic H. Wagner, Ronald Foresta, R. Bruce Gill, Dale R. McCullough, Michael R. Pelton, William F. Porter, and Hal Salwasser's *Wildlife Policies in the U.S. National Parks* (Washington DC: Island Press, 1995). Charles E. Kay has emphasized the condition of willows and aspen as a measure of the range in "Yellowstone's Northern Elk Herd: A Critical Evaluation of the 'Natural Regulation' Paradigm" (Ph.D. diss., Utah State University, 1990). Other critiques include Karl Hess Jr., *Rocky Times in Rocky Mountain National Park: An Unnatural History* (Niwot: University Press of Colorado, 1993). The popular critique can be found in Alston Chase, *Playing God in Yellowstone* (San Diego: Harcourt Brace Jovanovich, 1987).

INDEX

Absaroka Conservation Committee (ACC),
147, 226, 272, 297; as consensus
builder, 150–52, 290; and coyotes, 155–
62; and ecological view, 174; and elk
management plan, 170, 163–64; and
managerial ethos, 154; opposes elk reductions, 153, 221–22; and park purposes, 174; as pressure group, 152, 159–
60; and special season, 163–64; and
sportsmen's influence, 153–55, 171–73;
and stockmen's influence, 154–55, 158–
60. See also Kern, George
Absaroka Mountains, 74
Absaroka National Forest, 72, 154–55, 262
ACC. See Absaroka Conservation Committee
Adams, Charles C., 33, 280; on balance of
nature, 134–35; on bear management,
192; biography of, 37–38; on disturbance, 284; and early YNP research,
44–45; on ecology, 38; at National Conference on Outdoor Recreation, 66; and
park purposes, 149, 250, 305; and pelicans, 80, 83–84, 91, 96; and Pope expedition, 62–63; and preservation of natural conditions, 37, 39–40, 43, 45–46,
135, 313–14; and scientific purpose for
YNP, xiv, 39, 308. See also ecology; natural conditions; science
Albright, Horace M.: and bears, 109, 125,
191–92; and bison, 179–81; and game
protection, 27, 33, 65, 74; and naturalists, 49, and other agencies, 70–71; and
park purposes, 181, 308; and pelican

controversy, 83, 93–94, 96–97; and Pope
expedition, 59–65; and predators, 36,
138, 141; and preservation, 64, 77, 104,
117; and research, 217, 224; and tourism,
45– 46, 57, 86, 106, 180, 191; and Wildlife Division, 79, 87. See also National
Park Service; Yellowstone National Park
American Civic Association, 59, 179
American Game Protective Association, 29,
65, 77
American Society of Mammalogists, 105,
194
Anderson, Jack K., 224, 227, 241–42, 248
Animal and Plant Health Inspection Service, xvii

Baggley, George F., 91–92, 95, 97; and
bears, 108, 122, 125, 190
Bailey, Vernon, 18–21, 31, 42
balance of nature: and ACC, 162–63; and
bears, 125; as classical paradigm, 271;
and fluctuation, 134–35; Joseph Grinnell on, 41–42; history of, 41, 134; management to restore, 86, 161, 163; Barrington Moore on, 46; and Wildlife
Division, 75–76. See also equilibrium;
science
Barbee, Robert D., 219, 296
Barmore, William J., 216, 269; and aspen
studies, 236; and end of elk reductions,
223–24, 227–28
Bauer, C. Max, 121, 151; defends coyotes,
155–58

bears, general: aversive conditioning of, 186, 189; and bear shows, 109–10, 112, 120–21; and bear show closure, 186–87, 192–93; control of, 109, 114–15, 122–23; 185, 246, 253; damages and injuries from, 106–12, 184–85; and dump closures, 243–46; early research on, 45; feeding prohibited, 185–86; and fences, 188; and garbage problem, 109–10, 116–17, 122, 124, 187–88, 238–39; and managerial ethos, 122; and natural conditions, 184, 186, 192–93, 245; and park purposes, 114, 189–90, 193; population estimates of, 112, 115–16, 120, 124, 246–47; as surplus, 114–17, 120, 123; tagging of, suspended, 241–42; tourists feeding the, 106, 111–12, 114; translocation of, 108, 122. See also Albright, Horace M.; bears, grizzly; wildlife; wildlife policies

bears, grizzly: as ecosystem bears, 243, 248, 253–56; and Endangered Species Act, 253–54; extinction concerns about, 65, 190, 193, 237, 290; and Grant Village site, 263–64; and Pope expedition, 59–65, 222; population estimates of, 246–47; recovery plan for, 254–55; research on, 237–48, 252–53; threats to, 254–55, 257–58, 260. See also bears, general; Craighead, John and Frank; Interagency Grizzly Bear Study Team; wildlife; wildlife policies

Benevolent and Protective Order of Elks, 15, 21, 27

biodiversity, 259, 280, 287

biologists and national park purposes, 204. See also ecology; natural history tradition; naturalists; science; Wildlife Division; wildlife management

bison: and brucellosis, xvii, 183–84; and the buffalo ranch, 148; history of YNP herd, xv–xviii; and management for a natural herd, 178, 181–82; propagated in YNP, 11–12; reductions of, 175–80, 182. See also wildlife management; wildlife policies

Boone and Crockett Club, 29, 46, 72

Botkin, Daniel B., 271, 279

Boyce, Mark, 272

Bryant, Arthur C., 78

Bryant, Harold C.: biography of, 50, 118; and Education Division, 52, and Adolph Murie, 141; and park purposes, 118–19; and pelicans, 78, 100–102; on George M. Wright, 145–46

Bucknall, Edmund J., 237

Bumpus, Hermon C., 264

Bureau of Biological Survey: and the Absaroka Conservation Committee, 152; cooperation with USFS, 28–29, 290; and early wildlife management, 16–20; and economic ornithology, 82; and game wardens, 12; and interagency rivalries, 28; and W. L. McAtee, 93; and predators, 36, 56, 138, 141; and the Wildlife Division, 146. See also U.S. Fish and Wildlife Service

Bureau of Fisheries, 83–84, 94–95, 104, 106. See also Bureau of Sport Fisheries; U.S. Fish Commission

Bureau of Sport Fisheries, 209, 244; and NPS Wildlife branch, 150. See also U.S. Fish and Wildlife Service

Butcher, Devereux, 179, 192

Cahalane, Victor, 141, 146, 148, 150, 166; and bears, 185–86; and bison, 178; and elk control, 165

Cain, Stanley, 245

California Academy of Sciences, 59–60, 62, 117

Cammerer, Arno B., 97, 103, 141

Camp Fire Club, 29, 65; and bison, 179–80

Carhart, Arthur H., 204

carrying capacity, 133, 135, 152, 165, 167, 267–69

Caughley, Graeme, 232–34, 268–69

Chapman, Frank M., 66

Chapman, Oscar, 149, 198

Chase, Alston, 249, 272, 311–12

Child, Frank, 238

Chittenden, Hiram M., 6

Clements, Frederic, 128, 218. See also ecology; equilibrium; science; succession

Cole, Glen F., 224–25, 227–28; and Craig-

preservation (cont.)
conditions; natural resource management; wildlife management
Presnall, Clifford C., 141
primitive conditions. See natural conditions

Quammen, David, 256–57

ranchers. See Absaroka Conservation Committee; stockmen
range management: assumptions of, questioned, 168–69, 237, 267–69; compared to natural areas, 277; concepts of, 133; emergence of, 133; and overgrazing concept, 235–36; as a perspective, 164–65, 228, 275; and study methods, 127–30, 165, 170, 266. See also carrying capacity; elk; natural resource management; science; succession
rangers, 150; and NPS Ranger Division, 48–49, 52–57; and park purposes, 204; shifts in attitude of, 91–92
Replogle, Wayne, 197
Reynolds, Harry V., 241
Ringland, Arthur, 72
roads, 5–8
Robbins, William J., 215
Robbins Report, 215–18, 250; on natural conditions, 217–18
Rocky Mountain Elk Foundation, 280
Rocky Mountain National Park, 150
Rogers, Edmund B.: and bears, 185, 190–91, 193; and bison, 148, 176–77; endorses coyote control, 160–61
Roosevelt Wild Life Experiment Station, 44–46, 83. See also Adams, Charles C.
Runte, Alfred, 4
Rush, William: and bears, 113–14, 116–17, 121, 185; and bison, 183; and elk, 125–37, 165, 209, 235
Russell, Carl P., 87, 141, 150

science (biological): advocated for NPS, 211, 216–17; and agency interests, 81; and ambiguity, 309; competing ideas of, xix, 311–12; conflicting with preservation, 59; and conservation biology, 259;

and island biogeography, 256–58; and landscape ecology, 285, 289; and museum collecting, 59–65, 117; NPS organization of, 146, 148–50; in NPS priorities, 147, 206–7; NPS program of, critiqued, 247; and park purposes, 217–18; population biology/ecology, 117, 153, 229–34; and problem-oriented research, 224, 237; and roots of NPS research, 52; social context of, 245, 248; used by conservationists, 258–60, 305; used by NPS critics, 305, 311–12; and the Wildlife Division, 75–76, 90, 145; and wildlife research, 49–52. See also carrying capacity; density dependence; equilibrium; natural history tradition; range management; succession; wildlife
Sears, Paul B., 192
Sellars, Richard West, 72, 138, 142
Shelford, Victor E., 43, 308
Sheppard, Walter B., 102
Shields, G. O., 29, 65, 77
Sierra Club, 263
Sinclair, A. R. E., 231, 268
Singer, Francis J., 272–74
Skinner, Curtis K., 138, 150
Skinner, Milton P.: and bears, 108; biography of, 45, 49; and elk, 126, 235; and pelicans, 81, 91
Society for Conservation Biology, 259–60
Society for Range Management, 133
Sprugel, George, 211
Stagner, Howard, 206–7
state game agencies. See Montana Fish and Game Department; Wyoming Fish and Game Department
stockmen, 27, 141–42, 155, 297–98, 303–5. See Absaroka Conservation Committee
Storer, Tracy I., 117, 133; on natural conditions, 41–43, 192, 308; on park recreation, 26
succession, 128, 215, 218; retrogressive, 129, 267. See also Clements, Frederic; ecology; science
Sumner, Lowell, 206
swans, trumpeter, 75, 88–91